JUMP*CUT*

D0901573

"The cinema for a free people isn't a carnival sideshow. The screen is for singing the sufferings of the past, the struggles of yesterday, and the hopes of today."
—filmmaker Joris Ivens

*JUMP*CUT

HOLLYWOOD, POLITICS AND COUNTER CINEMA

Edited by
PETER STEVEN

Published by
Between The Lines,
229 College St.,
Toronto, Ont. M5T 1R4

Typeset by
Dumont Press Graphix
97 Victoria St. N.,
Kitchener, Ont.

Cover design by
Arthur Steven

Printed and bound in Canada by
Hignell Printing Ltd.

Between The Lines is a joint project of Dumont Press Graphix, Kitchener, and the Development Education Centre, Toronto. It receives financial assistance from the Canada Council and the Ontario Arts Council.

THE WORKERS UNION OF

Canadian Cataloguing in Publication Data
Main entry under title:
Jump cut: Hollywood, politics and counter-cinema
Articles previously published in Jump cut magazine, Chicago.
Includes index.
Bibliography: p. 390.
ISBN 0-919946-54-2 (bound)   0-919946-55-0 (pbk.)
.1. Moving-pictures — Political aspects — Addresses, essays, lectures. 2. Social problems in motion pictures — Addresses, essays, lectures. 3. Subculture — Addresses, essays, lectures.
I. Steven, Peter, 1950-   . II. Jump cut.
PN1995.J85 1985   791.43'01   C85-098422-X

JUMP CUT
Definitions

*I (a) an abrupt transition between shots, sometimes
deliberate, that jars the viewer's sense of the continuity
of time and space.*

*(b) for example, a person in a film is shown starting to
cross a room and then in a second shot, without a
change in camera angle, suddenly appears at the other
side as if magically or involuntarily jumping there.*

II "In Breathless *Jean-Luc Godard violates canons of
spatial, temporal, and graphic continuity by his
systematic use of the* jump cut. . . . *These cuts, far from
flowing smoothly, function to disorient the spectator."*
(David Bordwell and Kristin Thompson, Film Art)

*III a film magazine founded in Chicago and Berkeley, Spring
1974.*

Lillian Gish in Broken Blossoms

CONTENTS

PART THREE

PART FOUR

PART FIVE

PREFACE

Since 1974 *Jump Cut* magazine has been producing some of the most provocative and challenging film criticism in the English-speaking world. Editorials and articles have taken on not only Hollywood and academic film study but also many types of left cultural writing, arguing for an independent socialist and feminist analysis of the cinema. This book brings together some of the key articles from *Jump Cut* over the first ten years of its life.

The book also provides an introduction to Hollywood and four other key movements within cinema today, and outlines several approaches towards political film criticism. The authors explore a broad range of films — from Hollywood's *Star Wars* to the new documentaries on El Salvador and Nicaragua — and discuss a wide variety of issues concerning film and society. The articles can best be described as broadly socialist and feminist in orientation. But against this general backdrop, the authors represent a fascinating diversity of interests and backgrounds. Some are film scholars; others work as teachers, critics, producers and film users. Because of this diversity *Jump Cut* has a reputation for serious criticism and analysis that is neither stuffily academic nor pop-culture fluff. That approach is evident in all the articles here. The ideas are demanding yet the writing should be accessible to general readers familiar with contemporary film and political struggles.

As the editor of this volume it seems appropriate to say where I'm coming from and what sparked me to choose these particular articles. My day-to-day work is in film distribution — as a member of DEC Films, a self-managed collective that represents independent political filmmakers. Our primary goal is political education and the building of a critical audience for left and feminist media. Consequently, my selection of articles derives more from the realities of activism than academia, so this book should be of special use to those interested in film criticism as a tool or background for political work. I also write — and behave, I suppose — as a Canadian, bringing with me decidedly mixed feelings about U.S. popular culture: a mix of infatuation and repulsion shared by many outside the United States. I lived in Chicago for four years in the 1970s and have continued to work on *Jump Cut* since then, so I write about the magazine as an insider, but my view of U.S. popular culture and politics stems from my position on the periphery. It is a periphery most often ignored or taken for granted in ''American'' studies. My perspective may not personally give me any special insights, but as an activist I'm confident that the history and experience of the Canadian left provide me with a distinctive critical orientation.

I have three aims for this book. The first is to introduce to a wider public the kind of film criticism published in *Jump Cut*. Although the magazine has a small print run of about 6,000 and is virtually impossible to find in some cities, I'm convinced that a much larger audience exists for political criticism of the cinema. I hope therefore that these articles will lead readers to follow the ongoing debates in the magazine itself.

Second, I hope throughout the five sections of the book to direct readers toward several models for doing political analysis of the cinema. For example, while each of the essays on Hollywood in Part One stands on its own, it is also possible to develop a fuller understanding of the institution of dominant cinema by considering the articles as a group, by comparing the approaches and concerns of the different authors. Similarly, each section of the book, when taken as a whole, brings into focus an outline for a radical film criticism that moves beyond the essays as taken alone. This kind of collective outline, mapping similarities of approach and analysis, should not suggest that *Jump Cut* has developed a comprehensive theory of cinema — much less a party line. This is simply not the case. What makes *Jump Cut* special and somewhat unique is the conscious way that it evolves. And this makes it easier to step back and summarize *Jump Cut*'s history and approach over the past ten years. I hope readers will be encouraged by this anthology to make those kinds of connections and evaluations, and be therefore better able to discern models and tools for practising radical cultural work.

Finally, I want this book to spur readers to look at specific films and film movements more closely. Those of us on the left working for social and political change — particularly those who seldom consider cultural issues — need to understand the crucial role played by films of the dominant cinema in advanced capitalism. Hollywood remains a significant purveyor of racist, sexist and homophobic ideas in North America, and a key instrument of U.S. imperialism in the Third World. At the same time it is a major site of ideological struggle for all those who understand the role that entertainment plays among movie audiences. We also need to think much more clearly about those films that seek to challenge dominant cinema and the dominant society. Serious critical practice for independent left, feminist, gay-lesbian and radical Third World films has scarcely begun. The work here represents first steps in that direction. These essays stem from concrete political experiences and grow from a desire to intervene in immediate as well as long-term struggles. They emphasize the political nature of filmmaking and film viewing.

I am painfully aware of whole areas treated by *Jump Cut* but neglected by this collection, and terrific articles not included. In particular, the theoretical work on European films, the wide-ranging analyses of the Brazilian cinema, and the extensive studies of German women directors have unfortunately been left aside and will have to be taken up in a second volume.

Some readers may question the omission of certain articles but I doubt that anyone can challenge the value of the writing that is included here. I encourage people who read some of these essays when they first appeared to reread them now as part of a series and a larger whole. In my case juxtaposition and comparison have greatly increased my understanding of political cinema and strengthened my commitment to *Jump Cut*'s continuing project.

SPECIAL THANKS

I would like to thank the many people who generously gave support, advice and suggestions for this project. The text of the introduction was greatly improved by the criticism and suggestions of Ian Anderson, Ferne Cristall, Jane Gaines, Todd Milton, Geri Sadoway, and Ellen Seiter.

Elizabeth Stevens and Victoria Schultz graciously allowed me to use stills from *In the Best Interests of the Children* and *Women in Arms* on the cover. Thanks also to Christine Choy for allowing me use of her photos.

I am particularly grateful to my father, Art, for his cover and design, and to the alert and sensitive editing of Robert Clarke at Between The Lines. Of course a project such as this could not have come about without the original work and co-operation of the many contributing writers. I hope they will be pleased with the context given their ideas and the structure of the whole.

And finally, I thank those who first made this book possible, the editors of *Jump Cut*: John Hess, Chuck Kleinhans, and Julia Lesage.

P.S., Toronto, February 1985

ACKNOWLEDGMENTS

Except where noted otherwise, all the articles in this book first appeared in *Jump Cut* (JC). Others, as indicated, have also appeared elsewhere, and the editor gratefully acknowledges permission to reprint them.

Charles Eckert's "Shirley Temple and the House of Rockefeller," JC 2: 1974. The editor gratefully acknowleges the estate of Charles Eckert for permission to reprint.

Jane Feuer's "Hollywood Musicals," JC 23: 1980, was published in a slightly different form in Jane Feuer, *The Hollywood Musical* (British Film Institute, 1982). Reprinted here by permission of the BFI.

Chuck Kleinhans's "Working-Class Film Heroes," JC 2: 1974.

Dan Rubey's "Star Wars," JC 18: 1978.

Claire Whitaker's "Hollywood Transformed," JC 24/25: 1981.

Russell Campbell's "Radical Cinema in the 1930s," JC 14: 1977, was reprinted as a chapter in *Cinema Strikes Back* (Ann Arbor: UMI Press, 1983). Reprinted by permission of the author.

John Hess's "Notes on U.S. Radical Film, 1967-80," JC 21: 1979, also appeared as two articles in the French journal *CinemAction:* Part One, "Apprendre des Femmes," trans. Michel Euvrara, No. 9, Fall 1979; and Part Two, "Un Courant Issu de la Nouvelle Gauche," trans. Marie-Pierre Hennebelle, No. 10-11, Spring 1980. Reprinted by permission of the author.

Linda Gordon's "Union Maids," JC 14: 1977.

Sherry Millner's "Third World Newsreel," JC 27: 1982.

Clyde Taylor's "Decolonizing the Image," JC 28: 1984.

Peter Steven's "Interview with the Filmmakers," (*A Wives' Tale*), JC 26: 1981.

Sara Halprin's "In Review," (*A Wives' Tale*), JC 26: 1981.

Linda Artel and Susan Wengraf's "Positive Images," JC 18: 1978. Their book *Positive Images* was published by Bootlegger Press, San Francisco, 1976. Sections from the introduction reprinted by permission of the authors.

Diane Waldman's "There's More to a Positive Image Than Meets the Eye," JC 18: 1978.

B. Ruby Rich's "In the Name of Feminist Film Criticism," JC 9: 1978, also appeared in a slightly different form in *Heresies* 19. Reprinted by permission of the author.

Serafina K. Bathrick's "A Beauty and a Buddy," JC 21: 1979.

Patricia Erens's "In Defense of Stars," JC 21: 1979.

Julia Lesage's "Artful Racism, Artful Rape," JC 26: 1981.

Michelle Citron and Ellen Seiter's "Perils of Feminist Film Teaching," JC 26: 1981.

Tom Waugh and Chuck Kleinhans's "Gays, Straights, Film, and the Left," JC 16: 1977.

Richard Dyer's "Rejecting Straight Ideals," JC 18: 1978, originally appeared as "Gays in Film" in *Gay Left* 2. Reprinted by permission of the author.

Edith Becker, Michelle Citron et al., "Lesbians and Film," JC 24/25: 1981.

Michelle Citron's "Comic Critique," JC 24/25: 1981.

Clyde Taylor's "Third World Cinema," JC 23: 1980, first appeared in African Film Society Update 4: September 1979. Reprinted by permission of the author.

Teshome Gabriel's "Xala," JC 27: 1981, first appeared in *Presence Africaine* 116, in French.

Julianne Burton's "Film and Revolution in Cuba," JC 19: 1978, was excerpted from a longer piece that appeared in Guy Hennebelle and Alfonso Gumcio Dagron, *Les Cinemas de l'Amerique Latine* (Paris: 1981). Reprinted by permission of the author.

Tom Waugh's "In Solidarity," JC 22: 1980.

Julia Lesage's "For Our Urgent Use," JC 27: 1982.

Thanks to Val Almenderez at the Academy of Motion Picture Arts and Sciences and Mary Corliss at the Museum of Modern Art for help in locating photographs.

Credit is due to MGM/UA for *Barkleys of Broadway* still, Twentieth Century Fox for Shirley Temple still, Dorothy Arzner for Dorothy Arzner still, and Universal for Shirley MacLaine still.

JUMP CUT

INTRODUCTION

Hollywood and Counter-Cinema: The Roots of Jump Cut

PETER STEVEN

JESUS Elegant $71,000
Seattle Oct. 3, 1979.
The rains have arrived, sparking first run grosses. Also providing a lift
this week are some snappy newcomers. JESUS, Warner's religioso
release, is pacing the B.O. race with a great $56,000 at four Seattle
hardtops.

Variety

Variety magazine and its rave reports of "box office magic" represent
the voice of dominant cinema. It's a voice magnified many times over:
Hollywood, Wall Street, *People* and the vast machinery of other mainstream U.S. media have the money and the clout to cast it into every
nook and cranny of North America and around most of the planet.

But at the same time there are other, different voices — different
languages — calling for radically new *types* of films, and for a new
approach to cinema. These voices don't have the backing of Wall Street
and Madison Avenue but they are present nevertheless and very active
in parallel nooks and crannies in North America and beyond, and especially in the Third World. Some of those voices can be found in this
book.

Hollywood talks about product. The writers here talk about specific
audiences and how certain films produce a particular blend of art and
ideology. They call for a political criticism of the cinema.

Of course, this analysis doesn't come out of thin air. It represents
the logical parallel and catalyst for a number of cinema movements that
have emerged worldwide to challenge Hollywood and the dominant
media. Over the last 15 years radical Third World filmmakers, the

women's movement, gays and lesbians, and the independent left in North America have produced four strong alternatives to the mainstream cinema. In fact, these four movements of film activity stand for more than an alternative. Because all four embody political movements that challenge the dominant society, and because many of the key films consciously challenge conventions of style and approach in dominant cinema, they are often referred to as counter-cinema.

Political films are most often associated with the great European directors such as Jean-Luc Godard, Bernardo Bertolucci, Andrzej Wajda and Margarethe von Trotta. I have no wish to dispute this orientation. Works as diverse as Gillo Pontecorvo's *The Battle of Algiers* (1966) and Godard's *Tout Va Bien* (1971) will continue to influence the European political scene and world cinema. But we need to extend the political-film category and recognize that movements of radical filmmaking are flourishing in other parts of the world. This book concentrates on three areas — North America, Africa and Latin America.

Independent political filmmakers in North America are less well known and generally work on a much more modest scale than their European counterparts. Sometimes they have been completely ignored or misrepresented by the critical establishment. But I would insist that their work is no less important. Stylistically it is inventive; politically it is rooted in the major conflicts of our era; and above all it has found devoted and growing audiences. In scale of operation Third World cinema lies somewhere between North America and Europe. The new African and Cuban cinemas especially have found large audiences in their home countries and some of the filmmakers work with substantial budgets. They are as a result often better known than most North American independents, yet they receive little of the critical or industry support accorded the Europeans.

A few major films from these counter-cinemas are widely known: for example, the documentaries of U.S. filmmaker Emile de Antonio, such as *In the Year of the Pig* on Vietnam (1968) and *Millhouse* (1971) on Richard Nixon; Barbara Kopple's *Harlan County, U.S.A.* (1975); the feature films of Senegal's Ousmane Sembène; or Diego de la Texera's *El Salvador: The People Will Win* (1981). But these works also form part of much broader movements of filmmakers and audiences. The films coming out of these movements tend to lack funding, adequate distribution, and a mass audience (in Hollywood terms). But the connections of this counter-cinema to a social and political base plus the conviction and inventiveness of many of the filmmakers guarantee a continued growth in the years ahead.

There is a wealth of such films and filmmakers: from the innovative Film and Photo League in the United States of the depression era; to the feminist cinema of Chantal Akerman and Michelle Citron in the 1980s;

the comic avant garde of Jan Oxenberg; or the documentary work of Joris Ivens in revolutionary Cuba and the grassroots video in the new Nicaragua. This body of filmmaking and the political movements represented have provided a subversive counterpoint to the work and experience of the dominant cinema.

The magazine *Jump Cut* not only emerged as part of the course of these counter-cinemas, but also helped to shape their direction and analysis. At the same time it offered an important new political and social critique of the dominant cinema, a critique that benefited greatly from its juxtaposition — or integration — with the traditions and practices of radical filmmaking and politics. *Jump Cut*'s style and approach found their source and inspiration in both the political activity of the New Left of the 1960s and selected older views on film and culture developed by the Old Left of the 1930s and 1940s. At the same time — and just as importantly — these political roots were supplemented by the specific evolving practice of filmmakers aligned with those move- · ments. That practice, in conjunction with the politics, led to the left counter-cinema that continues to thrive today.

THE ROOTS OF JUMP CUT: THE NEW LEFT

Jump Cut's low-budget appearance, tabloid format and plain graphic style exemplify its New Left origins. Cartoon and irreverent humor, usually directed towards more solemn film publications, maintain the counter-cultural style and feel associated with the underground press of the 1960s. But the magazine's New Left roots run deeper than that.

Jump Cut prides itself on being absolutely independent of political parties and institutions. The magazine receives only minimal advertising revenue. But its financial independence does not imply a purely subjective agenda lacking connections to other movements and groups in society. Rather, *Jump Cut* sees itself as accountable to a whole range of independent left and women's groups and activities. Unlike the 1930s, when most progressive politics in the United States centered on the Communist Party, the industrial unions, and the New Deal, political debate and activity since the 1960s have revolved around specific coalitions: a diverse set of complexities and contradictions often referred to as The Movement. The contrasting political notions of independence and accountability established within this movement have set up a dynamic tension for *Jump Cut*'s politics and aesthetics. This tension provides a unifying force for the magazine's editorials, and a context — though often unrecognized — for much of the critical writing.

As an offshoot of the U.S. New Left, *Jump Cut* remains strongly critical of academia. During a period filled with campus revolts over the Vietnam war, the New Left directed a vigorous attack against the entire educational system, especially the lack of contact between university learning and the serious issues facing U.S. society. Students and radical academics began to question the traditional division of disciplines, and the disregard for women's and Third World history, for Afro-American, Latino, Native and Asian-American cultures. In addition to this, film and media studies in general presented new problems that did not fit tidily within the conventional boundaries of academia.

Therefore, *Jump Cut* continually attempts to widen the kinds of discourse appropriate to serious film criticism. The articles in this book on film-use for political activists (Julia Lesage on Central American films), on the experience of various audiences (Claire Whitaker on lesbian viewers), and on film teaching (Michelle Citron and Ellen Seiter) all attest to this goal of pushing film study into a broader context than usual for academics.

There is a difference, however, between anti-academic and anti-intellectual. An anti-intellectual stance often rejects attempts to theorize from everyday or popular experience. The ideology of populism supports that stance and considers popular culture naively, as a true reflection of popular tastes and ideals. In *Jump Cut* a healthy disdain for populism runs through most of the writing, a disdain directed especially at the "popular cultism" so readily available in film magazines. It is a form of populism found not just in the "fanzines."

In the early issues *Jump Cut* made a point of taking Hollywood seriously, including a limited acceptance of genre studies and auteur theory (see in particular John Hess's two-part critique of French auteurism in Nos. 1 and 2, 1974). A number of articles dissected the cycle of Youth Culture Films fashionable at the end of the 1960s. This made sense to the editors and followed from their background in the New Left and its interest in popular culture. The editorial in *Jump Cut* No. 2 outlined the editors' basic approach to Hollywood:

A true radical criticism must understand the role of entertainment in society and recognize uncomplicated amusement as a worthy human activity.

We are especially wary of two fallacies frequently held by radical intellectuals interested in film. The first is to see Hollywood films as the most direct type of indoctrination: a kind of propaganda for the status quo which is mindlessly swallowed by the mass audience. This is not only wrong, it is elitist, for it implies that the critic by virtue of his or her radical and/or intellectual nature is insulated from the effects of commercial films, while common people are totally naive in their viewing. The second fallacy — an inverse of the first — assumes that films are unimportant because "politics" is more important than "culture" (as if the two could be readily separated in practice), or because films are just distractions. But clearly Hollywood films are a significant part of bourgeois ideological hegemony. And as such they influence the consciousness with which objective conditions are perceived.

It seems appropriate then to begin this book with a study of Hollywood, because *Jump Cut*'s first two years were characterized by attempts to grapple with that bastion of culture and ideology: the dominant cinema.

From the first issue *Jump Cut* also took up feminism, the politics of racism, and the role of liberation movements in the Third World. This clearly represented a shift away from the Old Left's hopes for revolution based largely on the working class. *Jump Cut*'s more broadly defined sense of politics has, if anything, become more pronounced in subsequent issues. The exchange between Chuck Kleinhans and Tom Waugh on gay male politics in Part Four shows this development and provides an example of self-criticism and the conscious evolution of the magazine. Where the Old Left's cultural criticism might have subsumed most political issues into class dynamics, *Jump Cut* argues for healthy diversity within the left.

As part of the New Left, *Jump Cut* has criticized the Communist Party U.S.A., not so much for its position on the Soviet Union, but rather for the narrowness of its cultural theory and the secretive tactics of the party in the Popular Front Days. Thus many articles and editorial comments stress the need for a more open politics. For example, the essay by Linda Gordon on *Union Maids* in Part Two criticizes the film for accepting the timidity of the Old Left and suppressing the CP background of the three women organizers who star in the film. In addition, the editorial in *Jump Cut* No. 2, quoted above, makes it clear that one of the magazine's main aims has been to argue for the political nature of culture. The Chinese Cultural Revolution exerted a strong influence here, and on the rejection by most *Jump Cut* writers of the orthodox base-superstructure model of Marxism as rigidly applied in most Soviet aesthetics.

Yet *Jump Cut* as a New Left project was certainly not cut off from the political and cultural debates of the 1930s and 1940s. There are deep roots here as well. As editor John Hess puts it, "The search for a bridge was very conscious. We felt that the dismissal and ignorance of the Old Left by the New Left was a mistake."

THE ROOTS OF JUMP CUT: THE OLD LEFT

Jump Cut retains many elements of the Old Left's cultural criticism. Nearly all its writers adhere to a class analysis of U.S. society, despite differences in emphasis about class boundaries and the potential of various class fractions. Of course, the concept of social class means different things to different writers. The leap from simply recognizing class to analyzing cultural institutions and the role of artists in class terms involves a more precise theoretical and empirical understanding. Nevertheless, for nearly all the essays in this book, the basis for studying texts and audiences rests on categories of social class.

An important distinction can be made here between social-democratic and socialist analysis. Social democrats often recognize the existence of class divisions in society; socialists take this one step further and argue that class divisions also inevitably produce class conflict and struggle. The distinction between these two kinds of analysis seldom appears explicitly in the articles in this book, but the tension between the positions of class-in-itself and class conflict often arises as the authors wrestle with questions of ideology, the role of progressive artists in Hollywood, and the tensions between nationalism and socialism in Third World cinema.

A specifically socialist approach to class and culture also emerges. The use of class analysis by the writers in this book often leads to a series of related questions. For instance, does the class outlook of artists visibly affect their work? How does the class nature of the film industry affect the content and style of particular films? Can contradictions in works of art be related to class contradictions? Do class differences among audiences affect the character and very existence of film genres? How do class differences among audiences determine the meanings of specific films, or the ways a film functions in society? The essay on working-class heroes by Chuck Kleinhans, in Part One, lays out an approach to many of these questions of social class and begins to weave a thread that runs throughout the rest of the book.

It is difficult to generalize about the traditions of Marxist aesthetics, but three groups of writers stand out. Clearly, Brecht, Lukács and Sartre tower above all others as major artists and theorists for the twentieth century. They make up one group that also includes many important iconoclasts, humanists, and utopians, who have all found in Marxism a vital source for their creative and critical work. A second body of more orthodox writing, deriving from Soviet models, is elaborated in the film criticism of Harry Alan Potamkin, John Howard Lawson and Irwin Silber. These critics' analyses of popular cinema pay considerable attention to the specifics of the medium, and many of the questions they addressed remain important in the 1980s. Lawson in particular was astute in relating thematic trends in Hollywood to concurrent issues in the society at large. A third group, usually only party hacks, has had little interest in the specific qualities and emotions of art production. They merely apply generalized Marxist concepts onto the cinema with little regard for specific films and real audiences. To my mind *Jump Cut* writers have inherited both the legacy of the iconoclasts and some of the baggage of the orthodox.

Many writers within the Marxist tradition have emphasized the need to study particular works, usually making an attempt to trace connections and parallels between art production and society at large. Here there are essentially two areas of concentration: studies of great bourgeois artists (Marx on Balzac, Lenin on Tolstoy, Lukács on Scott); and studies of work in popular genres and traditions, such as folk music, the music hall and the early cinema (Brecht and Benjamin on working-class entertainments, Eisenstein on Chaplin and Griffith).

By and large *Jump Cut* writers have eschewed the high-art, great-artist orientation, in fact going some distance to debunk cherished icons — especially the ''fathers'' of the world cinema. Julia Lesage's essays on Jean Renoir's *La Regle de Jeu* and D.W. Griffith's *Broken Blossoms* (the latter included here) provide models for the reworking of great-artist studies within the sphere of Marxist-feminist criticism.

The traditional Marxist interest in popular working-class entertainments becomes greatly extended within *Jump Cut*, as part of a general post-war trend towards more comprehensive definitions of art itself. Many *Jump Cut* writers refer back to earlier questions posed by Marxists concerning popular art, and extend that analysis onto a broader terrain. John Howard Lawson would never have written about Shirley Temple, and so Charles Eckert's essay ''Shirley Temple and the House of Rockefeller'' reveals a clear break with the past. Yet Eckert develops a number of issues well known to earlier radical critics. For example, he aims to trace connections (however complex) between Shirley's capacity for love and the ideological needs of the U.S. ruling class in the 1930s. In another vein, writers tracing the growths of Third World cinema point to ways in which filmmakers have used popular and traditional forms to create new works of decolonized art. The essays by Clyde Taylor and Julianne Burton emphasize the overwhelming power of cultural imperialism yet they also stress the forms of resistance embedded in much Third World popular culture.

The realism-naturalism debate — a series of questions that stretches back to the writings of Marx and Engels — remains alive in many of the essays in this volume. These debates over realism grapple with creative representations of the world, both in description and in tendentiousness: the class viewpoint. Classic Marxist aesthetics draws a distinction between two types of description. There is naturalism, a form of empiricism in art, which is satisfied to record, describe, or document observable phenomena; and there is realism, an approach that attempts to document structures and patterns not necessarily immediate or observable. Much of the film criticism in *Jump Cut* rests on this kind of distinction. For example, in her criticism of ''Positive Images'' in Part Three, Diane Waldman places that distinction between naturalism and realism at the heart of her argument.

However, for many of the writers here, a work of realism also goes beyond documentation to provide analysis from a clear social point of view. For some Marxists in the past, art with a social point of view led straight into the den of Socialist Realism; for others, then and now, realism need not correspond with any one set of formal approaches. Radical filmmakers themselves confounded easy definitions of realism, of what revealed and raised consciousness, of what worked and what didn't. So, one further set of roots should be examined in order to know the context in which *Jump Cut* originally appeared. It is a context that continues to nourish the magazine.

THE ROOTS OF JUMP CUT: A DOCUMENTARY AND EXPERIMENTAL RENAISSANCE

In the 1960s lightweight 16mm cameras and tape recorders became widely available, quickly followed by Super 8 in 1965 and portable video in 1968. These developments coincided with and stimulated the renewed interest in documentary films of all kinds, an interest that had been underway since the advent of cinéma vérité and direct cinema in the late 1950s. The combination of technological developments and the documentary renaissance crystallized in at least three movements of radical film practice in the early 1970s, which in turn formed the basis for the more fully developed counter-cinema later in the decade.

One movement emerged from the growing opposition to the Vietnam war and was fed by a critique of the way the dominant media handled not only the war but also the opposition itself. Thus the attempt to document and explain the anti-war movement was the immediate aim of the Newsreel documentary group formed just after the 1967 March on the Pentagon. As John Hess argues in his essay on U.S. radical film in Part Two, Newsreel was a catalyst for a rebirth in left filmmaking, which had been dormant since the 1940s. Many of the people involved in the late 1960s remain active today, building a counter-cinema that can trace a direct lineage to the early Newsreel group.

Second, the women's movement quickly grasped the value of documentary filmmaking — especially the observational style. In the late 1960s and early 1970s many feminist documentaries were produced — a form that especially encouraged the technique of drawing on the speech of women in the ''real world.'' Of course, women took up narrative and experimental work as well, as Ruby Rich points out in her article ''In the Name of Feminist Film Criticism.'' But these early documentaries were especially important, states Rich, because of the "validative" role they played in emphasizing the faces, relations, and speech of women previously ignored by Hollywood and the male avant-garde. By 1974, the year *Jump Cut* started, a solid base for left and feminist film and distribution had been established.

Finally, the 1960s saw a tremendous upsurge in documentary filmmaking in the Third World. In addition to the great anticolonial movements in Africa, Asia and Latin America, the introduction in the Third World of the new lightweight equipment encouraged filmmakers to document the cultures around them, celebrate their rich history, and communicate with others. These new forms of film practice have been a direct stimulus to the criticism and theory produced by *Jump Cut* writers.

In addition to documentary production, another very different connection was created from the incredible energy of experimental and avant-garde filmmakers. They stirred up new interest in questions of film aesthetics, radical form and content, sexuality, and visual literacy, questions that many *Jump Cut* writers have found provocative for political filmmaking and criticism. The relationship between the demands of political criticism and experimental work have often been tense, but the influence of experimental cinema has perhaps played more of a role in the magazine than has been acknowledged. It's a subject for further discussion.

COUNTER-CINEMA OF THE INDEPENDENT LEFT

In the 1980s, *Jump Cut*'s areas of concern are somewhat broader than those associated with its origins and antecedents. Many issues of film theory, such as the meaning and applicability of semiology and psychoanalysis, are a source of continuing debate within the magazine, and at the same time the magazine has continued to explore the new openings in the political environment and radical film movements: the counter-cinemas.

Since the mid-1970s it has been possible to talk of a left counter-cinema: a cinema practice that looks to and identifies with political movements in society and has developed a conscious critique of the dominant media. Above all, the counter-cinema has produced a tremendous range of films. The essays in Part Two illustrate these achievements.

The film *Union Maids* (1977) provides the best known example of the entire movement. *Union Maids* is certainly not a radical film in form, but in it Julia Reichert and Jim Klein created a structure and tone of oral history that proved to be an immensely fruitful model for many filmmakers. Also, the film continues to be widely distributed and often used explicitly as a work that challenges the dominant media through its socialist-feminist point of view and its emphasis on oral history rather than Voice of God narration.

Third World Newsreel stands as an equally important achievement. In an interview with Sherry Millner, Newsreel member Christine Choy, a major figure in left film since the early 1970s, raises many of the vital issues of left counter-cinema. She speaks, for example, of funding problems, of the pressures for a slicker style, of racism in the media and on the left.

There has also been a feeling of renaissance in black cinema in the United States, yet the wide range of work being produced by Afro-American filmmakers has not yet gained the critical attention it deserves. This is partly due to neglect and partly because the black cinema is generally not oriented to the same cultural sources as the white left. As Clyde Taylor argues, many filmmakers of color have preferred to work with fictional or mixed documentary forms, to a greater degree than white independent filmmakers. Because of these differences it remains difficult to generalize about left counter-cinema across the board — no one style dominates.

Part Two concludes with two pieces on the Quebec film *A Wives' Tale* (1980), certainly one of the strongest and most complex works of political cinema made in North America in the 1970s. Both the essay and the interview with the filmmakers stress the relationship that was built up between the filmmakers and the working-class women who were the subject of the film. The political background of the women's movement and close relations with the women in the film encouraged the filmmakers to examine the complexities of the union, the families, and the women's group with a sophistication that is rare in documentary filmmaking.

Yet despite the strength of these films and their widespread use in political and community organizing there has been little critical attention paid to their specific strategies as films. In contrast to the theory and criticism devoted to narrative fiction and experimental work, documentary criticism is underdeveloped. Also neglected is the whole question of film-use by various audiences: how political documentaries succeed or fail in arguing their case and engaging spectators.

The articles here point the way forward to this kind of critical work and suggest strategies for the future.

WOMEN'S COUNTER-CINEMA

An emphasis on *Jump Cut*'s left-wing character does not, however, do justice to the magazine's feminism. At the time of its formation *Jump Cut* was strongly influenced by the magazine *Women and Film*, produced in California. That publication was a source of ideas as well as a compatible project, and in fact some of the same people were involved in both journals. The demise of *Women and Film* in 1975 probably went unnoticed by most *Jump Cut* readers, but certainly galvanized *Jump Cut*'s editors to pay more systematic attention to feminist criticism. Since then there has been a steady advance in feminist cinema debate: from women's responses to male-dominated film production to a film criticism based firmly on women's concerns.

The debate in feminist film has grown in scope as well, developing feminist theory around woman as spectator. Of course these developments aren't unique to *Jump Cut*. They've taken place against a background of the growing power of the women's movement. What is impressive, as the essays in this book show, is the *range* of serious work, including criticism arising from the experience and political struggles of lesbian artists and audiences. I think it is important to stress this range; discussion on a number of fronts has always been a goal for the women writing in *Jump Cut*. For example, in an article not published here, Sara Halprin argues strongly for such a range of interests in her critique of a "dominant discourse" of feminist criticism. Halprin disputes histories of feminist criticism that set up an absolute progression from "sociological" approaches to "structural, semiotic, psychoanalytic theory." (See "Writing in the Margins," *Jump Cut* No. 29, 1984.) In this volume, Ruby Rich's groundbreaking essay provides a model of openness to many different types of feminist cinema. It is a model of advocacy as well, urging feminists to study and to "name" women's films in all their variety lest they be lost in the margins.

The essays in Part Three argue on a number of levels for the need to develop theory based both on women's personal experience and on a wide political agenda. All the writers reject a simplistic sociology and emphasize the specificity of cinema as a practice and an institution. Yet they retain a commitment to take social contexts seriously, and this results in a continual widening of the areas of discourse appropriate to feminist criticism.

Many *Jump Cut* editorials have pushed to establish socialist-feminist criteria for all cinema practice — from North American avant-garde to Third World documentaries, from filmmaking to film viewing. In addition, the editors have sought the writing of women from different fields, not only those who have specialized in the film-theory jungle of academia. The writing in this book reflects those aims. The women's movement and feminist theory have influenced the essays in all five parts.

GAY AND LESBIAN COUNTER-CINEMA

A new era of openly gay and lesbian politics and film began after New York's Stonewall riots of 1969. By the mid-1970s many films from the perspective of the gay and lesbian liberation movements had been produced. In criticism too, an exciting process of rediscovery and re-evaluation of homosexual artists in Hollywood and the avant-garde was well under way.

Jump Cut No. 16, published in 1977, featured a Special Section on gay men and film. The collectively written editorial, which was the first treatment of gay cinema in the magazine, argued for the need to take up gay and lesbian criticism within the left: "Active support for lesbian and gay male liberation emerges as a logical concomitant of the feminist struggle against patriarchy."

But this process of the magazine "coming out" had not been without difficulties. In the introduction to the Special Section, editor Chuck Kleinhans summarized the history:

> While *Jump Cut* has already published the work of lesbian critics, submissions have been fairly rare — not surprisingly given the seemingly straight identification of the publication and given the left-wing political orientation of *Jump Cut* which doubtless further restricts possible contributions. . . .
>
> Few radical lesbians see writing film criticism for a magazine whose readers are mostly straights as a priority issue. . . .
>
> But, if it is difficult for straights of both sexes and particularly men to publicly take a position on sexual politics today, it is also essential that one try to do so.

Two main themes emerge from these statements:
- The lesbian and gay movements of the 1970s, including the issues connected to film and critical practice, stem from and remain closely connected to the women's movement.
- The issues of lesbian and gay cinema must involve more than support for the civil rights of minorities. Filmmakers and critics must address the whole question of the *patriarchy* — an ideology and set of institutions that affect all sexual relations.

The cinema plays a crucial role in constantly recreating a sexist and anti-gay social fabric. In particular, two areas of daily life — sex-role stereotypes and a narrowly defined family ideology — are often learned and reinforced primarily through films and television. For these reasons, criticism of Hollywood and the construction of lesbian and gay counter-cinemas are of crucial importance to the entire left.

The authors of "Lesbians and Film," in Part Four, give specific reasons for their work.

Creation of a lesbian film criticism is particularly urgent, given the intensified use of the lesbian as a negative sign in Hollywood movies and the continuing space assigned to lesbians as gratification of male fantasy in pornography and a distressing number of male avant-garde films. . . .
    There is the lesbian as villainess . . . the lesbian as vampire, both metaphorically . . . and quite literally. . . in the genre of lesbian vampire movies. There is the brutal bull dyke.

The article goes on to treat the major issues facing lesbian criticism and the goals of a counter-cinema, including the desire for, and problems with, positive images; the open representation of sexuality; the role of lesbian filmmakers within the avant-garde; the use of traditional versus experimental cinematic forms.

THIRD WORLD COUNTER-CINEMA

The articles collected here on Third World cinema represent another driving force behind *Jump Cut*'s project as a whole, particularly in the 1980s. Since the 1979 Bard College Conference on U.S. Alternative Cinema, Afro-American, Latino and Asian-American filmmakers have become a stronger presence within the left media. Consequently, there is a growing knowledge of radical Third World filmmaking — films made in the Third World and those made by people of color in North America. Clyde Taylor, in his essay which opens Part Five, argues for the need to study Third World filmmaking for its own sake and also for what we in North America can learn from it.

    Following Taylor's argument I have highlighted articles on the African and Cuban cinema. These chapters show the need to do more than simply appreciate the vitality of radical Third World filmmaking. They outline how Third World films often establish models for forms, content, relations with audiences, the nature of popular culture, and the political role of cinema. A film such as Sarah Gómez's *One Way Or Another,* discussed by Julianne Burton, is more than a fascinating vignette of Cuban life. It provides a model for political filmmaking that engages its audience and could prove to be fruitful to filmmakers and critics here in North America. The Cuban cinema is also important since it goes right back to the early 1960s, and its dynamism and militancy have strongly influenced radicals in both Latin and North America.

    Much of the new African cinema is at once political and formally innovative. This is quite clear in the incredibly rich films of Ousmane Sembène. In his article about Sembène's film *Xala,* Teshome Gabriel explains:

> If we accept the notion that artistic choice also connotes ideological choice, we must begin to investigate the ideological weight carried by a film's formal elements. Spectator involvement in *Xala* does not come, I would contend, from the plot and story structure alone but also from the

execution of some basic cinematic elements such as editing, composition, camera positioning and movement.

The use of films in Europe and North America for Third World solidarity work dates from the 1930s with films such as Joris Ivens's *The Spanish Earth,* and reappears in the 1960s linked with the worldwide Vietnam solidarity. Tom Waugh's essay on Ivens shows the kind of cinema that can be achieved by progressive filmmakers working in co-operation with local people in the Third World. Ivens's representations of the underdeveloped and socialist countries are especially revealing when contrasted with those regularly presented by the dominant media.

This contrast is further developed by Julia Lesage in "For Our Urgent Use." She not only compares radical and mainstream films but also stresses differences between radical North American films and latino films from Central America. She argues, "For example, what a North American film audience may interpret as an image connoting 'poverty' may signify 'a farm family's daily life' in its country of origin."

Afro-American and Asian-American filmmakers find a natural solidarity with artists in Africa and Asia, and look to the Third World for political and cinematic models. Yet Third World cinema continues to be avoided in the generally racist atmosphere of academic film studies. The growing strength of counter-cinemas made by people of color in North America should spur the left to study and support Third World cinema here and abroad. I expect that writing on Third World film will play a greater role in *Jump Cut* in the years to come.

WHY DON'T THEY LIKE ANYTHING?

Some *Jump Cut* readers have complained that the magazine tends continually to present a negative response to films. This feeling on the part of readers may stem partly from the fact that *Jump Cut* sets itself up stylistically and semantically as non-elitist, youthful, non-academic, and in format like a tabloid. Many of the covers use familiar Hollywood faces. Readers assume that a tabloid format makes for light reading, preferably in bed. Thus some of them are surprised and disappointed when the articles turn out to be more demanding, politically and theoretically, than they expect.

In fact, *Jump Cut*'s seemingly "hard line" towards Hollywood is usually balanced by a range of enthusiasms for independent North American and Third World cinemas. This is a tendency illustrated by Michelle Citron's appreciation for the work of Jan Oxenberg and Clyde Taylor's call to study Third World cinema in order to "rehumanize international film craft." As for Hollywood itself, on closer inspection even the hard line taken in some essays contains complexities of enjoyment, response, and identification. Julia Lesage's fascinating essay on *Broken Blossoms* and the vigorous debate about Shirley MacLaine, both included in Part Three, make explicit the many levels of critical response possible in approaching Hollywood fiction.

But there is also a legitimate criticism here that *Jump Cut* editors and writers need to recognize and address. In the past too many of the articles on Hollywood seemed like sour grapes. Too often the result was a grim trashing of genuinely popular films, while the explicit political criticism only served to disparage the enjoyment (innocent or not) that audiences found in the film. That sort of criticism makes readers feel ignorant or foolish, and in the end fails to provide the tools necessary for understanding texts and contexts.

At the same time *Jump Cut* demands a lot from its readers, and questions easy assumptions about what constitutes a "popular" film. The magazine does not cater solely to the tastes of cinephiles or film buffs: the kind of people who know everything about Westerns but nothing about Native Indians. There is another type of filmgoer: the people who may attend movies regularly but are continually frustrated, shocked, or bored by what they see. *Jump Cut* is more inclined to consider this other rather alienated audience than most film publications. This springs from a belief that there is a large potential audience that wants to look at film from a more critical, broad perspective, not simply that of the dominant cinema. This is not to say that all those who do attend Hollywood films have bought all the ideological goods. Because of these complexities, it remains for students of Hollywood to be precise with terms such as "mass audience" and "popular cinema."

From the beginning *Jump Cut* has been critical of the left's treatment of dominant cinema. In the early issues that criticism remained somewhat subdued. Ten years later (*Jump Cut* No. 28) editors Kleinhans and Hess delivered an explicit attack on left film orthodoxy, showing the similarities of left and bourgeois reviews of Warren Beatty's *Reds* (1981). For Hess and Kleinhans both kinds of reviewing offer only a personal response and fixed position on the film; neither kind of review offers the reader tools for understanding, nor do the reviews accept the possible diversity of response.

Obviously, criticism that offers tools for understanding remains an ideal, certainly not always achieved in *Jump Cut* or elsewhere. To my mind the articles in this book all stretch beyond personal response and fixed positions and help us understand Hollywood as a whole — preparing us for the next hot subgenre and wave of special effects just around the corner. The articles also highlight the radical alternatives of counter-cinema, now developing on many fronts.

JUMP CUT

PART ONE

HOLLYWOOD: THE DOMINANT CINEMA

Shirley Temple

INTRODUCTION

> To acknowledge Hollywood is to acknowledge reality. No consideration
> of film can get very far without facing the inescapable fact of Hollywood.
> *Jump Cut* Editorial No. 2, 1974.

Readers will most likely be familiar with two kinds of writing about
Hollywood. One kind accepts the institutional status quo of the film
industry and concentrates on the minute details of individual movies and
their stars, directors, and grosses. You see this kind of writing in the
glossy magazines that surround the supermarket check-out counters, as
well as in newspaper reviews and respected film journals. It is certainly
the more common approach, appearing daily in the media and strongly
encouraged in most film schools.

The second approach condemns Hollywood as a major source of
"mass culture," seeing its products as indistinguishable from each
other. This second kind of writing is most often associated with views
from the left, though many quite conservative authors wield this
approach as well.

The writers in Part One of this book suggest a third way of looking
at Hollywood. They attempt to widen the boundaries of discussion
while holding to an understanding of the specifics of cinema. They
examine texts, contexts, production, and audiences, and don't collapse
one into the others in the way common to standard approaches. For this
reason these essays provide a model for a new political analysis of
Hollywood films.

Charles Eckert's discussion of charity, song, and dance in the amaz-
ingly popular Shirley Temple films of the 1930s introduces the key
concepts of ideology and social class. These concepts provide a theoretical framework that helps to make political sense of dominant cinema.
Eckert wrote a number of distinctive essays about Hollywood in the
1930s and each was marked by original research into the film industry
and his broad knowledge of U.S. society. As a model of lively political
criticism, derived from French theories of structuralism and semiology,
it is hard to better Eckert's juggling of detail with theoretical synthesis.

Dan Rubey on *Star Wars* and Jane Feuer on movie musicals concentrate on the complexities of typical Hollywood genres. Both authors
trace earlier traditions, artistic and ideological, and suggest how these
films work on us while giving pleasure. Chuck Kleinhans treats another

popular cycle in "Working-Class Film Heroes." The films he discusses, *The Last American Hero* and *Evel Knievel,* marked a renewal of Hollywood's interest in working-class characters and settings, an interest later seen in films such as *Rocky, Saturday Night Fever, Flashdance* and *Country.* Kleinhans's essay, which appeared in 1974, set the tone for many subsequent *Jump Cut* articles through his balancing act between serious criticism and the obvious attractions of the films for working-class audiences.

Claire Whitaker takes that discussion of pleasure one step further, arguing that the pleasure derived from films is often intertwined with many dangerous and unhealthy ideologies circulating through our society. The lesbian viewers she interviews speak of their attempts to salvage role models and aesthetic enjoyment from conventional Hollywood fare.

These approaches don't cover every facet of Hollywood, but taken together they do provide models for a more sophisticated critical practice: one that concentrates on the political and ideological context of Hollywood films, but at the same time recognizes the compelling social impact — the entertainment value — of those films. The essays suggest that radical counter-cinemas face a powerful, changing, and often subtle opponent that can't easily be dismissed.

CHAPTER 1.

Shirley Temple
and the House of Rockefeller

CHARLES ECKERT

Through the mid-depression years of 1934 to 1938 Shirley Temple was a phenomenon of the first magnitude: she led in box-office grosses, single-handedly revived Fox and influenced its merger with 20th Century, had more products named after her than any other star, and became as intimately experienced at home and abroad as President Franklin Roosevelt. Her significance was then, and has been ever since, accounted for by an appeal to universals: to her cuteness, her precocious talents, her appeal to parental love, and so forth. But one can no more imagine her having precisely the same effect upon audiences of any other decade of this century than one can imagine Clint Eastwood and William S. Hart exchanging personas.

One would not feel impelled to state so tawdry a truism if it were not for the anticipated resistance to a serious study of Shirley Temple, and especially to a study that regards her, in part, as a kind of artifact thrown up by a unique concatenation of social and economic forces. One anticipates resistance because Shirley was, first of all, a child (and therefore uncomplex, innocent of history) and, secondly, because the sense of the numinous that surrounds her is unlike that which surrounds culture heroes or political leaders, in that it is deeply sentimental and somehow purified. But this very numinosity, this sense of transcendental and irrational significance, if we measure it only by its degree, should alert us to the fact that we are dealing with a highly over-determined object (in the Freudian sense of an object affected by more than one determinant).

A search for external determinants, however, initially faces a difficult paradox: there is no evidence in any of Shirley's films or in anything contemporaneously written about her that she was touched by the realities of the depression. For instance, in the mid-1930s, when 20 million people were on relief, Shirley awoke in the morning singing a song entitled "Early Bird"; in the brutally demanding business of filmmaking, she thought everyone was playing games; and as for economics, Shirley thought a nickel was worth more than a dollar.

All of this would be intimidating if it were not that external determinants often cannot be perceived in a finished object, whether that determinant be the repression that produces a pun or the sweated labor that produces a shirt. And Shirley in film and story was as highly finished an object as a Christmas tree ornament. Some contemporary libels against her that depicted her as a 30-year-old dwarf or as bald-headed, and the irreverencies of critics who called her the moppet with the "slightly sinister repertoire of tricks" show that the surface was often too perfect to be accepted and that deceit was suspected. But libels are not theories, and everything written about Shirley was ultimately unable to explain her — or to exorcise her.

We might begin to chip at her surface (analytically, not iconoclastically) by noting that the industry she worked in was possibly more exposed to influences emanating from society, and in particular from its economic base, than any other. To the disruption of production, distribution and consumption shared by all industries one must add the intense economically-determined ideological pressures that bore upon an industry whose commodities were emotions and ideas. Politicians directly charged Hollywood with the task of "cheering Americans up"; and such studio ideologues as Jack Warner and Louis B. Mayer gloried in their new roles as shapers of public attitudes.

But far more significant pressures arose out of the grim economic histories of the major studios. By 1936 all of them had come under the financial control of either Morgan or Rockefeller financial interests (see F.D. Klingender and S. Legge, *Money Behind the Screen,* 1937). In addition to rendering films more formulaic and innocuous, this domination drew Hollywood into a relationship of pandering to the most conservative canons of capitalist ideology.

It is not my intention to recount this history, but rather to assess its effects upon the content of Shirley's films and her public persona. To do this systematically I must first survey a portion of the economic history for the period 1930-34 and describe the ideology it gave rise to. At this point my study will move synchronically, from the economic base through the ideology to Shirley Temple (her first feature films were made in 1934). I will then hedge on the synchrony by including films from 1935 and 1936 (on the pretext that Shirley's films conservatively repeated situations and themes).

ECONOMICS AND IDEOLOGY

The most persistent spectre that the depression offered to those who had come through the crash with some or most of their fortunes intact was, as it turned out, not that of Lenin or Mussolini, although articles on communism and fascism filled the magazines, but that of a small child dressed in welfare clothing, looking, as he was usually depicted, like a gaunt Jackie Coogan, but unsmiling, unresponsive, pausing to stare through the windows of cafeterias or grocery stores, his legs noticeably thin and his stomach slightly swollen. This spectre had thousands of incarnations.

''We were practising for a chorus and a little boy about 12 years old was in the front line. He was clean in his overalls, but didn't have very much on under them. He was standing in the line when all at once he pitched forward in a dead faint. This was two o'clock in the afternoon. . . . He had not had anything to eat since the day before.''

''Mrs. Schmidt took her son Albert, five years old, into the kitchen and turned on the gas. . . . 'I don't know what I am going to give the children to eat,' said a note she had written for her husband. 'They are already half-starved. I think it best to go into eternity and take little Albert along.' ''

''Five hundred school children, most with haggard faces and in tattered clothes, paraded through Chicago's downtown section . . . to demand that the school system provide them with food.''

''I love children and have often wanted to have children of my own. But to have one now, as I am going to, is almost more than I can stand. . . . I have four step-children, so there are six in my family. I have suffered so much in the past few years, and have seen my family suffer for even enough food. . . . I need fruit and vegetables. I need rest. I need yards of material for shirts and gowns. I have no blankets. I need baby clothes. . . . I hate charity . . . but my condition now forces me not only to take charity but even to ask for it.''

These children are, of course, symbolic, both in the context of the depression and of this article. What they symbolized was the flashpoint of the millions on relief who showed themselves, early on in the depression, largely immune to acts of revolt and willing to tough out the hard times if their children's minimal needs for food and clothing could be met. In November 1930 Hoover was forced to reply to the observation by the White House Conference on Child Health and Protection that six million American children were chronically undernourished.

''But that we not be discouraged,'' Hoover said, ''let us bear in mind that there are thirty-five million reasonably normal, cheerful human electrons, radiating joy and mischief and hope and faith. Their faces are turned toward the light — theirs is the life of great adventure.

These are the vivid, romping everyday children, our own and our neighbors.''

This may have washed with some at this early stage of the depression, but later on the tactics had to be more frontal. ''No One Is Starving,'' the *New York Times* and *Herald Tribune* announced in front-page headlines on March 17, 1932. This was the substance of telegrams from 39 governors. The issue of starvation was debated, and many cases of death by starvation were adduced by newspapers; but the statement, which begged the issues of chronic malnutrition and near-starvation, was essentially true. And it was vitally important for those in positions of wealth and power that it remain essentially true.

To this end, the most minimal subsistence needs had to be provided. And as the estimate of those needing help rose, reaching about 20 million on the eve of the election in 1932, it became increasingly likely that a federal relief program would have to be inaugurated. But to the captains of industry and the traditionally wealthy who made up Hoover's official and private entourages, the prospect of massive federal relief was dismaying. All of the initial reactions of Hoover and the class he so steadfastly represented had been self-serving. Tariffs were placed upon foreign imports, absurdly low income taxes upon the wealthy were reduced even further and federal reserves were hoarded in a miserly fashion or loaned at reduced rates to select banks and industries. The remedy for the depression, the country was told, lay in the protection, and where possible the augmentation, of the capital resources of the wealthy, for these resources were the key to renewed economic growth and revived employment.

Such naked opportunism at so desperate an hour had to be dressed in emperor's clothes of the first order. And Hoover and his supporters spent most of their time spinning and sewing. What they fashioned was a formidable ideological garment. The economy of the country was fueled, not by labor, but by money. Those who possessed money would bring the country out of the depression as their confidence was restored by a protective and solicitous government. If the needy millions were served instead, a double blow would be struck at the nation's strength. First of all, the capital resources of the government and of the wealthy (who would have to be taxed) would be depleted. And, secondly, the moral fibre of those who received relief would be weakened — perhaps beyond repair.

The latter argument, less amenable to mystification because it was not couched in financial terms, needed more than assertion to give it weight. Recourse was therefore made to the deities who dwelled in the deepest recesses of the capitalist ethos. Initiative, Work and Thrift were summoned forth, blinking at the light. An accusing finger was pointed at England where the dole had robbed thousands of any interest in self-help. Hoover's attacks upon the evils of relief were echoed at state and local levels; and it became common to insist that those who received relief, even a single meal, do some work, such as sweeping streets in compensation. This demeaning, utterly alienating "work" became one of the most common experiences of the depression, and one of its scandals.

Early in the depression William Green, President of the American Federation of Labor, led organized labor in denouncing the dole and unemployment insurance as "paternalistic, demoralizing and destructive." Governor Roosevelt of New York, thinking of the votes he would need to get into the White House, asked in fall of 1931 for an increase in state taxes to give "necessary food, clothing and shelter" but noted that "under no circumstances shall any actual money be paid in the form of a dole."

"What an incredible absurdity," observed a writer in *The Nation*. "What is there about cold cash that makes a man like Governor Roosevelt think that giving dollar bills to a starving man or woman is worse for his character than presenting him with a suit of clothes which he might buy for himself?" Indeed, the only ones who seemed to be taken in by the argument that relief destroyed character were reactionary governors and grim county relief agents.

Clearly some other ideological weapon was needed, one which could effect material changes in conditions rather than merely mask the hardened indifference of the Hoover administration. And one was found, calculatedly developed, and financed with some of the cold cash that was anathema to the poor. Declaring that "no one with a spark of sympathy can contemplate unmoved the possibilities of suffering," Hoover, late in 1931, appointed Walter S. Gifford Director of the President's Organization on Unemployment Relief and Owen D. Young, Chairman of the Committee on Mobilization of Relief Resources. In their official capacities they took out a series of full-page advertisements in major magazines.

Tonight, Say This to Your Wife,
Then Look Into Her Eyes!

"I gave a lot more than we had planned. Are you angry?"

If you should tell her that you merely "contributed" — that you gave no more than you really felt obligated to — her eyes will tell you nothing. But deep down in her woman's heart she will feel just a little disappointed — a tiny bit ashamed.

But tonight — *confess* to her that you have dug into the very bottom of your pocket — that you gave perhaps a little *more* than you could afford — that you opened not just your purse, but your heart as well.

In her eyes you'll see neither reproach nor anger. *Trust* her to understand. . . .

It is true — the world *respects* the man who lives within his income. But the world *adores* the man who *gives* BEYOND his income.

No — when you tell her that you have given somewhat *more* than you had planned, you will see no censure in her eyes. But *love!*

The President's Organization on Unemployment Relief
Walter S. Gifford, Director
Committee on Mobilization of Relief Resources
Owen D. Young, Chairman

The vulgarity of this charade can more fully be appreciated if we know that Gifford was President of AT&T, and Young Chairman of the Board of Directors of General Electric. This attempt to shift the burden of charitable work to the middle class and the poor was, ironically, unnecessary. As a reporter observed at a later date, ''In Philadelphia, as in most other cities, the poor are taking care of the poor.'' But face-saving was the order of the day, and to the advertisements and the repeated appeals to local charities by Hoover one must add the many charity balls, at one of which debutantes got dressed up in hobo clothes and dined at red and white checked tables on cornbread and hotdogs.

Then there were, of course, the publicized, and the modestly unpublicized, donations of the wealthy to charity. In March of 1933 when the income tax statistics for 1931 were finally published a *Nation* reporter noted ''The results are startling, even to those who never had much faith in the philanthropy of the wealthy.'' The figures ''destroy completely the myth of the generosity of America's millionaires.'' What they specifically showed was that contributions were usually of an order that reduced net taxable income to a favorable level — and no more.

But the endorsement of charity by those in power made the attacks upon the concept of welfare more consistent. Early in 1932 the Costigan-LaFollette Bill was voted down by both parties. It would have allocated $350 million for aid to local welfare agencies. A critic noted, ''The Democrats want to win the next election. . . . They are constantly currying favor with big business and entrenched wealth. They will do nothing to offend Wall Street. . . . In the words of the Washington correspondent of the Federated Press, the Democrats are 'buying the next election with the lives of the children of the unemployed.' ''

If the Democrats hoped to buy it by actively demonstrating their conservatism, Hoover made his bid by requesting and getting federal relief grants of $300 million just before the 1932 election. Since the number of needy was about 20 million, the grant provided $15 per person per year, or about four cents per day. But it was doubtful that many were listening to Hoover, because shortly before he made the request Roosevelt had accepted the nomination for President with the words:

40

What do the people of America want more than anything else? In my mind, two things: Work: work, with all the moral and spiritual values that go with work. And with work, a reasonable measure of security. . . . I say that the whole primary responsibility for relief rests with localities now, as ever, yet the Federal Government has always had and still has a continuing responsibility for the broader public welfare. It will soon fulfill that responsibility.

The ominous sound of the whole passage seemed to be drowned out in the resonant final line, "It will soon fulfill that responsibility."

Roosevelt did, of course, act on the issue of unemployment. The National Recovery Administration Works Progress Administration and Conference of Catholic Charities produced jobs — at rather pathetic wages — for some. But a distinction must be made between the creation of a few hundred thousand jobs and the vast needs of 20 million destitute. When Roosevelt addressed the first CCC men by radio in July 1933, he said, "You are evidence that we are seeking to get away, as fast as we possibly can, from the dole, from soup kitchens and from free lodging. . . ." And when, a few months later, he signed the Federal Emergency Relief Act which allocated a token $500 million for grants to states, he implored citizens to "voluntarily contribute to the pressing needs of welfare services." A sense of foreboding gripped at least one reporter: "Just why this note should have been sounded when it was hoped the federal government was about to initiate a bold, vigorous and constructive policy in relief . . . is not easy to understand."

But it soon became easier. In October 1933 Roosevelt addressed the Conference of Catholic Charities: "It is for us to redouble our efforts to care for those who must still depend upon relief. . . . Many times I have insisted that every community and every state must first do their share." In January 1934 he addressed Congress on the budget: "The cornerstone of the foundation is the good credit of the government. If we maintain the course I have outlined we can look forward to . . . increased volume of business, more general profit, greater employment, a diminution of relief expenditures . . . and greater human happiness." And, finally, in an address to NRA authorities in March 1934: "The aim of this whole effort is to restore our rich domestic market by raising its vast consuming capacity." By degrees, in a purely rhetorical process, relief was demoted in importance, then mentioned in passing, then forgotten.

But Roosevelt was not only more politically expedient than Hoover, he was more culpable. Hoover was insulated from and insensitive to mass thought and feeling. He could call children "cheerful human electrons" and think he would be understood. Roosevelt was a common sentimentalist. At Warm Springs in Georgia he helped maintain a hospital for crippled children (he had suffered from polio himself) and he

41

loved to visit it. He also liked to lecture the children, on one occasion anticipating the thesis of this article with a bed-time exploration of the relation of economics to society. "We hear much these days of two adjectives — social and economic. . . . Here at Warm Springs we have proved that they go hand in hand." The proof, to summarize Roosevelt's prolix demonstration, lay in the fact that almost every crippled child required the care of an adult; rehabilitation made the child a "useful member of society" and released the adult "to be an economically useful unit in the community."

In another address on the occasion of his birthday and the holding of over 6,000 birthday balls to raise funds for Warm Springs, Roosevelt said, "Let us well remember that every child and indeed every person who is restored to useful citizenship is an asset to the country and is enabled to 'pull his own weight in the boat.' In the long run, by helping this work we are not contributing to charity, but we are contributing to the building of a sound nation." The image of crippled children compelled to heave at the oars would be monstrous if it were not so ingenuously political.

One final anecdote. Roosevelt, a former boy scout, was asked to address the scouts upon the occasion of their twenty-fifth birthday in February 1934. He asked Harry Hopkins, his relief administrator, for ideas. Hopkins suggested that the scouts be asked to collect furnishings, bedding and clothes for those on relief. Roosevelt liked the idea and announced it, adding "Already I have received offers of co-operation from Governors of States, from Mayors and other community leaders. . . . I ask you to join with me and the Eagle Scouts and our President and Chief Scout Executive who are here with me in the White House in giving again the Scout oath. All stand! Give the Scout sign! Repeat with me the Scout oath! 'On my honor . . .' " and so forth.

As the second year of Roosevelt's administration drew to a close in the winter of 1934, sufficient federal relief was no longer a serious possibility. Commentators noted that the impression that the Democrats would act had utterly demoralized charity efforts. And yet in New York alone there were 354,000 on relief, 77,000 more than a year before. Relief applications were coming in at the rate of 1,500 a day. One reporter passing through Ohio discovered families receiving one and a half cents per person. *The Nation* noted, "Within the greatest anthill of the Western Hemisphere the machinery has slowed down. One out of six New Yorkers depends on the dole. One out of three of the city's working population is out of work."

As the days grew shorter and grayer it became obvious that for millions the hardest times were still ahead. Those already mentally and physically stunted by years of malnutrition would know many more years of diminished existence before the economic boom of World War

II would turn the depression around. And a few parents, broken under the responsibility of caring for hungry, ill and constantly irritable children, would kill one or more of them — and sometimes themselves. But then, on the other hand, there was Shirley Temple.

SHIRLEY, AND LOVE

Since birth, Shirley had never awakened at night. She had never been ill, although her mother seemed to remember "a little cold once." She refused to take a bottle and had to be fed with a spoon at three months. She spoke at six months and walked at thirteen. She arose every morning either singing or reciting the lines she had memorized for her day's work. She was a genius with an IQ of 155. She did not mark her books, scrawl on wallpaper or break her toys. Doctors and dentists wrote her mother asking for the secrets of her diet and hygiene: her mother responded that there weren't any. Her relations with her parents were totally loving and natural. She had no concern for, or sense of, herself, and was consequently unspoilable.

If her mother were not so straightforward a woman, and if there were not independent corroborators for some of these facts, one would have to presume that Shirley was not real — that she was a rosy image of childhood projected like a dialectical adumbration from the pallid bodies and distressed psyches of millions of depression children. But she was real.

Her biographies are not, as with most Hollywood stars, cosmeticized myths, but something on the order of fundamentalist "witnessings."

> The cameraman tells me that she went through this emotional scene in such a miraculous way that the crew was spellbound, and when she finished they just stared fascinated. "I wanted to reach out and touch her as she went by," said Tony Ugrin who makes all her still pictures. "I could hardly believe she was real." Or, Adolfe Menjou speaking: "That Temple kid. She scares me. She's . . . She's. . . ." He finally settled for "She's an Ethel Barrymore at four."

Shirley's relation to the depression history I have outlined goes far beyond this dialectical play between her biographies and the real childhoods of many depression children, however. And it is at once easy and difficult to conceptualize. There is a felt resonance between the persona she assumed in her films and the ideology of charity that no one can miss. But to state *why* it exists demands a theory for her studio's conscious or unconscious ideological bias, and the making of distinctions between unintended ideology (propaganda of the Gifford-Young sort), opportunistic seizing upon current ideas and issues (the "topical" film syndrome), and a more diffuse attunement to the movie audience's moods and concerns. When one takes into account Fox's financial difficulties in 1934, its resurgence with Shirley Temple, and its merger with 20th Century under the guidance of Rockefeller banking interests, one feels that the *least* that should be anticipated is a lackeying to the same interests that dominated Hoover and Roosevelt.

But such lackeying need not appear as a message or the espousal of a class view; it can as well operate (and more freely) as a principle of suppression and obfuscation. Shirley's films and her biographies do contain messages of the Gifford-Young sort — one should care for the unfortunate, work is a happy activity — but they seem more remarkable for what they do not contain, or contain only in the form of displaced and distorted contents.

I will assume that this contention is a viable one and rest the case for it upon the analysis which follows. But before beginning, a few biographical facts are needed to place Shirley relative to the history already outlined.

Shirley was born April 23, 1928, six months before the crash. She was discovered at a dance studio in 1933, given bit parts in shorts, then graduated to a musical number in Fox's *Stand Up and Cheer* early in 1934. During the number she pauses for a moment, puckers, leans forward and blows a little marshmallow kiss past the camera. Audiences emerged from the experience disoriented and possessive. After another minor role in *Change of Heart* Shirley was moved up to feature roles in *Little Miss Marker* (Paramount), *Baby, Take A Bow* (Fox), *Now and Forever* (Paramount), and *Bright Eyes* (Fox), all produced in 1934. The box-office grosses made both studios incredulous. No star of the 1930s had affected audiences so. Fox tied up its property with major contracts and produced nine more films in the next two years, the period of our concern.

Shirley's most intimate connections with depression history are those found in her films. I will deal opportunistically with the details of these films: what I shall principally omit are Shirley's functions as an entertainer — her many dances, songs, exchanges with other cute children, and so forth. In any given film the sheer quantity of sequences in which Shirley entertains may make her other functions seem peripheral. But in the 11 films made between 1934 and 1936 the sequences devoted to plot and the development of a persona predominate.

In these films Shirley is often an orphan or motherless (*Little Miss Marker, Bright Eyes, Curly Top, Dimples, Captain January*) or unwanted (*Our Little Girl*). She is usually identified with a non-working proletariat made up of the dispossessed and the outcast (clearly in *Baby, Take A Bow, Little Miss Marker* and *Dimples;* more covertly in *Our Little Girl, Now and Forever,* and *The Poor Little Rich Girl*).

And when she is of well-to-do origins (*The Little Colonel, Poor Little Rich Girl* and *The Littlest Rebel*) she shows affinities for servants, blacks and itinerants.

Her principal functions in virtually all of these films are to soften hard hearts (especially of the wealthy), to intercede on behalf of others, to effect liaisons between members of opposed social classes and occasionally to regenerate.

We can detect some very obvious forms of repression, displacement and condensation at work within this complex. Although proletarian in association, Shirley is seldom the daughter of a worker, much less an unemployed one. In the two films in which her parents are workers (*Little Miss Marker, Bright Eyes*), they are killed before the film begins or during it. Therefore the fact that the proletariat *works* is generally suppressed in the films. What proletarians do to get money is con people, beg or steal. This libelous class portrait is softened by comedy and irony, which function, as they usually do, as displaced attitudes of superiority and prejudice. A comical proletariat is also a lovable one, opening the way to identification, and even to charitable feeling.

Shirley's acts of softening, interceding and the rest are spontaneous ones, originating in her love of others. Not only do they function as condensations of all of the mid-depression schemes for the care of the needy, but they repress the concepts of *duty* to give or of a responsibility to *share* (income tax, federal spending). The solution Shirley offers is natural: one opens one's heart, *à la* Gifford and Young, and the most implacable realities alter or disperse. We should also note that Shirley's love is of a special order. It is not, like God's, a universal *mana* flowing through all things, but a love that is elicited by *need*. Shirley turns like a lodestone towards the flintiest characters in her films: the wizened wealthy, the defensive unloved, figures of cold authority like Army officers, and tough criminals. She assaults, penetrates and opens them, making it possible for them to *give* of themselves. All of this returns upon her at times, forcing her into situations where she must decide who *needs* her most. It is her agony, her calvary, and it brings her to her most despairing moments. This confluence of needing, giving, of deciding whose need is greatest also obviously suggests the relief experience.

So strongly overdetermined is Shirley's capacity for love that she virtually exists within it. In Freudian terms she has no id, ego or superego. She is an unstructured reification of the libido, much as Einstein in popular myth reified the capacity for thought. Einstein's brain bulged his forehead, dwarfed his body and stood his hair on end. Shirley's capacity for love drew her into a small, warm ball, curled her hair, dimpled her cheeks and knees, and set her in perpetual motion — dancing, strutting, beaming, wheedling, chiding, radiating, kissing. And since her love was indiscriminate, extending to pinched misers or to common hobos, it was a social, even a political, force on a par with the idea of democracy or the Constitution.

That all of this has great ideological potential scarcely needs arguing; but it would be naive to trace Shirley's film persona exclusively to an origin in the policies of the Hoover and Roosevelt administrations. One senses, rather, that Shirley is a locus at which this and other forces intersect, including those of the mitigation of reality through fantasy, the exacerbated emotions relating to insufficiently cared for children, the commonly stated philosophy of pulling together to whip the depression, and others. Yet it would seem equally naive to discount the fact that Shirley and her burden of love appeared at a moment when the official ideology of charity had reached a final and unyielding form and when the public sources of charitable support were drying up.

SHIRLEY: HER WORK, HER MONEY

But depression attitudes towards charity, as we saw earlier, rested on forces emanating from the economic base; and I have so far said nothing of Shirley's relation to economics. Here we must move between her films and her biographies. For our purposes all of this material has the same status: it simply tells us all that people knew about Shirley. We have already noted that one of her functions was to pass between needy people — to be orphaned, exchanged, adopted. She always wound up in the possession of the person who needed her most. And he who possessed her owned the unique philosopher's stone of a depressed economy, the stone whose touch transmuted poverty to abundance, harsh reality to effulgent fantasy, sadness to vertiginous joy. All of this works as a displacement of the social uses and the efficacy of money.

If the argument needs strengthening, we do not have to seek far. Shirley's absolute value was a constant subject of speculation. The usual figure quoted was $10 million — in depression dollars an almost inconceivable sum. As a writer in the *Ladies Home Journal* put it in a symptomatic passage, ''When she was born the doctor had no way of knowing that the celestial script called for him to say, not 'It's a girl' but 'It's a gold mine.' '' Her father was a bank clerk at the time of her discovery (1932) but through his fame (which could attract deposits) he soon became manager of a posh branch of the California Bank. This conjunction of a banker and an inestimably valuable property is in itself suggestive, especially for an era when bankers such as J.P. Morgan symbolized the capitalist system.

It would take too much space to repeat even a sampling of the stories that concern other white, middle-class parents' hopes that their child might prove to be a financial bonanza like Shirley Temple. The following passage from the *Saturday Evening Post* will have to epitomize them:

> The other studios would like a Shirley too. Her name would be Millicent, for all they care. They test her. They test little Gertie, too, and Annabelle. Hundreds of them, thousands of them. No fields are drilled for oil, no hills are mined for gold with more desperation, more persistence, more prayers, more hopes. So far, no dice. Maybe you have a little Shirley in your home. Maybe you don't suspect it. Mr. and Mrs. George Temple didn't.

If we add to all of this Shirley's function as an asset to the Fox studios, her golden locks and the value of her name to the producers of Shirley Temple dolls and other products, the imagery closes in. She is subsumed to that class of objects which symbolize capitalism's false democracy: the Comstock Lode, the Irish Sweepstakes, the legacy from a distant relative. And if we join her inestimable value with her inability to be shared we discover a deep resonance with the depression-era notion of what capital was: a vital force whose efficacy would be destroyed if it was shared.

Even Shirley's capacity for love is rendered economic by our awareness that Fox duplicated the Hoover-Roosevelt tactic of espousing compassion for anterior economic motives (specifically, by making a profit from the spectacle of compassion). And because of the unique nature of the star-centered movie industry of the 1930s, Shirley was a power for monopoly control of film distribution.

This intricate nexus of functions and meanings contains enough material for a major study of how capitalism simultaneously asserts and denies its fetishistic attachment to money and embeds these attitudes in the metaphoric surfaces of the commodities it creates. Shirley, orphaned, often in poor clothes, with nothing to give but her love, was paradoxically specular with the idea of money. And the paradox could as easily be perceived as an oxymoron in which the terms need/abundance were indissolubly fused.

Of course, paradoxes and oxymorons are classical devices for the creation of numinous effects of the sort I referred to earlier. By the time she had made her first 11 films Shirley's name alone gave off little intaglios of energy, like a saint's head in a religious woodcut. A blind man came to the studio and asked to run his hands over her face. A woman wrote her father asking him to conceive a second Shirley upon her — or perhaps she upon him. Some 11 industries paid Shirley to produce commodities bearing her name, and several of them grew rich. And Shirley's mother drew $1,000 a week just to keep her daughter healthy and functioning and primed for work.

And it is Shirley's relation to her work that we must next, and finally, consider, both because it received constant attention in her biographies and because it may lead us to fresh insights into her relations to love and money. The commonplace that most work under capitalism is alienated seems never more valid than during those crisis moments known as depressions. Work during such periods is not only more affected by feelings of personal insecurity, but by a very real harshening of work conditions.

For instance, millions of workers during the early 1930s suffered from one or more of the following conditions: speed-up, reduced work hours, reduced salaries; the firing of high salaried employees and the employing of those willing to work for much less; exposure to deteriorated and dangerous machinery and a general reduction of safety standards; thought and speech control so intense in some plants that workers never spoke except to ask or give instructions; inability to question deductions from paychecks; beatings by strike-breaking Pinkertons and thugs; and compelled acquiescence to the searches of their homes by company men looking for stolen articles.

And there were the ultimate forms of alienated work: street-cleaning, mopping a floor, painting a wall in exchange for a meal, often a bowl of soup and a piece of baker's stale bread. This was the work that saved one from the loss of initiative and character. One cannot read far in the records of any class of workers during the depression without discovering how abrasive and anxiety-ridden most working experiences were.

None of the biographical articles on Shirley failed to describe her attitudes toward her work. I will give just two examples. First, from *Time:*

> Her work entails no effort. She plays at acting as other small girls play at dolls. Her training began so long ago that she now absorbs instruction almost subconsciously. While her director explains how he wants a scene played, Shirley looks at her feet, apparently thinking of more important matters. When the take starts, she not only knows her own function but frequently that of the other actors. . . . She is not sensitive when criticized. . . . In one morning, Shirley Temple's crony and hero, Tap Dancer Bill Robinson . . . taught her a soft-shoe number, a waltz clog and three tap routines. She learned them without looking at him, by listening to his feet.

Second, from an article written by her mother:

> I never urged Shirley to go to the studio with me. She wanted to go then, as she wants to go now. Motion-picture acting is simply part of her play life. It is untinged with worry about tomorrow or fear of failure. A few times when we have left the studio together, she has looked up at me and said, "Mommy, did I do all right?" Since there is no right or wrong about it, but only Shirley playing, I have replied, noncommittally, "All right." That was the end of it. . . . I do not know whether Shirley under-

stands the plays in which she appears. We do not discuss plots or characters, or, indeed, any phase of her motion-picture work. Her playing is really play. She learns her lines rapidly, just as any child learns nursery rhymes or stories. . . . We usually go over the script the first time with enthusiasm. Sometimes, when it is issued, Shirley cannot wait until we get home to hear her lines read. "Turn on the dashboard lights," she said one night, "and read my lines while you drive."

And for this work, accomplished with joy and ease, Shirley received $10,000 per week and over 3,500 letters thanking her for the pleasure she gave. The disparity between Shirley's work and the reality of most depression working experiences was ludicrous; and the frequency and consistency of descriptions of the sort just quoted indicates that the disparity was also mesmerizing, much like the disclosure in 1932 that J.P. Morgan paid no income taxes.

Shirley's relation to work adds a further counter to the set already made up of her relations to love and to money; but does it also establish interrelationships with them? One is reminded of Marx's acute observation that money, considered in its relation to the work that produces it, has a repressive and censoring role. It shares this role with most commodities, which are designed and finished so as to conceal traces of the labor that has gone into them. To clarify the point by example, the lace produced by child labor in Nottingham in the 1860s was finished under very exacting standards of quality and cleanliness, effectively effacing evidence of the hand-labor that produced it. The well-to-do who bought it could in no palpable way be reminded of work, or of workers, or the exploitative class structure of their society, much less be led to inquire into the circumstances that saw up to 20 children crowded into an airless, fetid, 12-foot-square room, working under the whip of a mistress for from 12 to 16 hours a day, with their shoes removed, even in winter, so the lace would not be soiled.

One might say, then, that Shirley stands in the same relation to work as does a piece of Nottingham lace or a dollar bill: she censors or conceals work. The relation is not exact, for millions knew that she was awakened every morning by a mother who got her to start reciting her lines and kept her at it all the way to the studio. It was just that Shirley's work was self-obliterating — a whole deck of cards vanished in the air, or rather magically transmuted into $10,000 a week worth of prepubescent games.

But there is an exact correspondence to Marx's insight, in the relation between Shirley's films and work. One probably could not find a depression commodity more like a piece of Nottingham lace than a Shirley Temple film. Her directors, writers, cameramen, composers and the rest were never written about, never mentioned, except as witnesses to something Shirley said or did. And the films they produced obliterate all traces of their craft. They are consummate examples of minimal direction, invisible editing, unobtrusive camera-work and musical scoring, and characterless dialogue. Every burr or edge was honed away, and the whole buffed to a high finish.

THE MAGICAL POWERS OF SHIRLEY

There are other relations between love, money and work that I do not have space to develop, and in some instances am not certain that I have grasped. Let me, however, attempt to give some rigor to the analysis made so far.

I have argued that the ideology of charity was the creation of a class intent upon motivating others to absorb the economic burdens imposed by the depression. This privileged class regarded itself as possessed of initiative, as self-made through hard work; and it saw in all governmental plans for aid a potential subversion of the doctrine of initiative.

Charity, then, came to be characterized as the bulwark of initiative. Money was a censored topic (for obvious reasons — Nelson Rockefeller today will not allow reporters to question him about his wealth); but there were clear implications that money as a charitable gift was benevolent, whereas money in the form of a dole was destructive. Money, then, was ambivalent and repressed, whereas charity and initiative were univalent and foregrounded.

In Shirley Temple's films and biographies, through a slight but very important displacement, charity appears as love and initiative as work. Both love and work are abstracted from all social and psychological realities. They have no causes; they are unmotivated. They appear in Shirley merely as prodigious innate capcities, something like Merlin's wisdom or Lancelot's strength; and they are magical in their powers — they can transform reality and spontaneously create well-being and happiness.

Money, in keeping with its ambivalent nature, is subjected to two opposing operations. In Shirley's films and the depictions of real life attitudes toward money, it is censored out of existence. It is less than destructive. It is nothing. But in an opposing movement, found largely in Shirley's biographies, money breaks free and induces an inebriated fantasy that a Caliban would embrace, a vision of gold descending from the heavens, a treasure produced from a little girl's joy and curls and laughter. This fantasy is removed from all thought of effort or anxiety; people can simply sit back in their chairs and, like a Lotus-eater, let the drugged vision possess them.

But any attempt to further clarify these relations would probably be wrong-headed since it would argue for coherence where there is often only a muddled interplay of the forces of censorship and obfuscation. It seems more appropriate to let the whole discourse dissolve back into the existential mass of depression history and Shirley and her films.

I will start it on its way by attacking the last point I made. I said that Shirley's films have no creators. This is untrue. The advertising copy for her films tells us that Shirley Temple made them — sometimes, we must presume, between playing with her pet rabbits and eating her favourite dish, canned peaches and ice cream. I also implied that many workers and their children suffered in material ways during the depression. But President Hoover wisely observed that the depression was "only a state of mind," and Shirley's life and work provide exemplary proof that Hoover was right. And I hinted that cold cash might have been more desirable to a starving man than a child's warm touch. There is a perverse logic to this; but the thought is materialistic and, above all, dehumanizing. Shirley's films never get into such Jesuitical quandaries; they keep the only authentic solution constantly before our eyes: the transforming power of love.

And with those props knocked from beneath the specious edifice of my argument, it shatters, expires and sinks beneath the dark tarn of history from which it was fallaciously raised. But at the point where the last bubbles appear, something bobs to the surface. It begins to rise in the air and to glow, assuming the shape of a luminous being. And now, having attained full power, it begins to flash off and on like a theatre marquee, and its feet begin to do little tap dance routines. It is Shirley Temple! Reborn. Released from the rational spell cast upon her by those sorcerers, Freud and Marx. And now we hear her voice announcing that the depression is over, that it never existed, that it is ending endlessly in each and every of her films, that these films are playing at our neighbourhood theatres and that we should come and see them, and that we must learn to love children and to weep for them and open our hearts to them, that we mustn't hate rich people because most of them are old and unhappy and unloved, that we should learn to sing at our work and dance away our weariness, that anyone can be an old sourpuss about rickets and protein-deficiency but only Shirley Temple fans can laugh their pathology away.

And now that we have immersed ourselves in these egregious irrationalities and utterly clogged the process of thought we once again should be in the proper state of mind to see Shirley's films, and perhaps to accept her as simply and naively as she accepted her labors in Hollywood's expedient vineyards.

CHAPTER 2.

Hollywood Musicals:
Mass Art as Folk Art

JANE FEUER

In their discussion of the evolution of the British music hall, Stuart Hall and Paddy Whannel suggest that the emergence of individual performers or "stars" performing on stage marked the transition from "folk" art to "popular" art. Folk art, they say, was an integral part of a communal way of life, very close to everyday living: "ritual celebrations of folk or community."[1] Indeed, often the art as "craft" was simply a traditional form of work. According to Hall and Whannel, "The threshold of participation was high, the material familiar, since it had been repeated or handed down, with slight variation, from one generation to the next." But in the shift to the music hall form, the result was, "The community had become an 'audience': the art had been individualized."

As Hall and Whannel describe it, popular art may have many things in common with folk art — in particular a direct contact between audience and performer — but it differs from folk art in that "the audience-as-community has come to depend on the performer's skills, and on the force of a personal style, to articulate its common values and interpret its experience."[2]

The Hollywood musical is one degree further removed from "folk" art in that it involves mechanical reproduction and mass distribution. As such, alienation between performer and audience is far greater than in a live entertainment format, whether folk or popular. On the phenomenological level, alienation means that the performer's "aura" is absent.[3] On the economic level, relations of production are alienated from those of consumption: the performers do not consume the product and the consumers do not produce the product.

The musical as a genre perceives the gap between producer and consumer, the breakdown of community designated by the very distinction between "performer" and "audience," as a breach which it must heal. The musical seeks to bridge the gap through a valorization of "community" as an ideal concept. With this value system based on community, the producing and consuming functions severed by the passage of musical entertainment from folk to popular to mass status are rejoined in the aesthetic work of the texts. In this way, the material forces of history which produced Entertainment come to exist in a perpetual past which is also a perpetual present.

As a result, musicals provide a particularly clear example of naturalization, in which ideology acts to make the cultural seem natural. This is because Hollywood musicals are not only entertainment in themselves, but also are frequently *about* the production of entertainment. The musical is thus "self-reflexive," as well as being generally reflexive regarding Hollywood and mass entertainment as a whole.

Musicals make mass entertainment (a product of capitalism) appear as folk entertainment (a product of pre-industrial society) through a process I call "creation and erasure." In this process one effect or practice in a film is cancelled out through the operation of another effect or practice. It is a process that operates in musicals at many levels, encompassing both form and expression.[4] At a certain "micro" level, an effect may be created in order that we view the very process of cancellation of that effect by another. This is the erasure, an example being the way "rehearsals" in musicals often appear as polished, finished products. However, creation and erasure appear to operate at a "macro" level as well, in the naturalization of mass entertainment practices in general.

At every level the human values and relations associated with folk art are substituted for the economic values and relations associated with mass-produced art. Through this system of exchange, the economic relations are erased as the human relations are created. The result is that the mode of production of the Hollywood musical itself is suppressed in and through the genre's structuring discourse. The Hollywood musical becomes a mass art which aspires to the condition of a folk art: produced and consumed by the same integrated community.

BRICOLAGE VS. ENGINEERING

In the song "Moses Supposes" from *Singin' in the Rain* (1952), Gene Kelly and Donald O'Connor make use of the room furnishings and tools of the elocution teacher to create a dance. This is typical of an entire category of numbers in which performers make use of props-at-hand, things perhaps intended for other ends, to create the imaginary world of the musical number. In "Moses," the room furnishings and tools were seemingly not put there for Kelly and O'Connor to dance with (though of course we know they were), yet they form the finite material stratum out of which the number may be created. If no props are at hand, the performer will simulate props using his/her body as a tool; whence the inclusion of mime in such dances. The body-as-prop notion defines the naturalized narrative dancing favored at MGM.

The impression of spontaneity in these numbers stems from an effect of *bricolage* or tinkering. French anthropologist Claude Lévi-Strauss has used the term bricolage to describe the cognitive processes of "folk" cultures, cultures which are pre-scientific. For Lévi-Strauss, primitive thought is a kind of intellectual bricolage. In creating cultural and intellectual artifacts, primitive people make use of materials-at-hand that may not bear any relationship to the intended project but which appear to be all they have to work with.

Lévi-Strauss contrasts the *bricoleur* of folk cultures to the engineer of modern scientific thought whose tasks are subordinated to "the availability of raw material and tools conceived and procured for the purposes of the project."[5] In applying this distinction to the discourse of the musical, one might say that the Kelly and O'Connor number is carefully engineered to give an effect of bricolage. Engineering is a prerequisite for the creation of effects of "tinkering," of utter spontaneity in the Hollywood musical. The bricolage number represents an attempt to erase engineering (a characteristic of mass life) by substituting bricolage (a characteristic of folk life).

The hallmark of the prop dance for both Astaire and Kelly is that props must not appear as "props." Rather, they must give the impression of being actual objects in the environment. Indeed, Kelly has referred to an environmental conception for choreography as his "hobby horse." Environmental choreography abounds in the collaborations of Kelly and director Stanley Donen. "Prehistoric Man" in *On the Town* (1949) uses an anthropological museum. Most of the numbers in *Singin' in the Rain* use props-at-hand. In *It's Always Fair Weather* (1955), garbage-can lids become part of a dance in the streets. Of all Kelly's environmental conceptions, the one that gives the greatest impression of spontaneity makes use of a newspaper and squeaky floorboard (*Summer Stock,* 1950). However, it is a number whose ostensible function is to satirize the Kelly prop number which, ironically, makes the most elaborate use of props-at-hand.

In "Someone at Last" (*A Star Is Born,* Warner Brothers, 1954), Judy Garland (Vicki Lester) recreates at home a production number from a Hollywood musical in which she is starring. Garland uses only the props available in her living room to simulate the elaborate number:

she turns on the lamp ("lights"), positions a table ("camera") and begins the "action." She uses the elastic backs of a chair for a harp, a pillow for an accordion, a lampshade for a coolie's hat, a leopardskin rug for an African costume. Her surprise at discovering each object at exactly the needed time makes us forget that these objects were carefully positioned there for her use. Thus she is constantly erasing the work of production through a pretense of spontaneity.

Perhaps more than in any other number of this type, the audience receives the impression that the number is actually being developed on the spot, that Judy Garland is rebuilding the phony, calculated studio production number around her own intimate environment. And yet this number is actually the most calculated of all. The more it appears as bricolage, the more it erases its own creation through engineering.

Although they may appear as polar opposites, the bricolage and the engineered number are actually closely related. We frequently see both practices within the scope of a single number. In "Shoes With Wings On," Fred Astaire's animated number in *The Barkleys of Broadway* (1949), elaborate process photography is needed to create the effect of spontaneous dancing with the shoes: objects in the immediate environment of the shoemaker he portrays. Even Kelly's apparently simple and spontaneous dance with the newspaper and floor board could not have been achieved on a stage.

What would seem to be antithetical practices become instead twin images of a paradox. That paradox consists in the need for the most calculated engineering to produce effects of spontaneous evolution, and, as a corollary, the need to foreground not the technology but rather the dance itself in all its seeming transparency. An economic contradiction — between industrially produced and hand-crafted "products" — underlies the aesthetic paradox. The musical's solution to both the paradox and the contradiction is provided by a discourse appropriated from folk relations. Bricolage and engineering stand in a relationship of creation and erasure to each other. Engineering, as the mode of production of the Hollywood musical, is replaced by a discourse that foregrounds bricolage. In this substitution, the calculation behind the numbers is erased and their spontaneous quality is recuperated. The spontaneous creation of musical numbers *in* the films masks the calculated creation *of* the films.

THE MASKING OF CHOREOGRAPHY AND REHEARSALS

In discussing the work of the bricolage number I referred to choreographic conception without analyzing the choreography itself. In fact, dance style is an integral part of the effect of such numbers. In "prop" numbers and elsewhere, Hollywood musicals employ choreography that could only by a great stretch of the imagination be referred to as "dancing." Such "non-choreography" implies that choreography is erased, precisely the effect this dance style gives.

By erasing choreography as a calculated dance strategy, non-choreography implies that dancing is utterly natural and easy. Both the group folk dance and the bricolage number reflect this view. Michael Wood remarks of Astaire and Kelly that "walking could become dancing at any minute," and indeed such a continuity is always stressed.[6] Dances that employ completely ordinary movements rather than "steps" (for example, Bobby Van's jumping number in *That's Entertainment,* 1974) aim for an effect of natural body movements within a choreographed narrative framework.

Perhaps the best example of non-choreography as the *erasure* of choreography is a dance performed by Michael Kidd, Dan Dailey and Gene Kelly on the streets of New York early in *It's Always Fair Weather*. Given three professional dancers to work with (unlike *On The Town,* in that the choreography had to be adjusted to non-dancers), Kelly and Donen's choreography is nevertheless resolutely amateurish. It is ultra-spontaneous, bordering on ordinary horsing around. One segment consists of the everyday movement of running down streets; another segment features *clumsiness*, the very opposite of that quality most closely associated with choreographed ballet and with Astaire: grace. Choreography is erased as the three buddies gracelessly stomp around on garbage can lids. By masking the fact that numbers are choreographed, the Hollywood musical denies that it takes work to produce dance routines. Rather, dance in the musical is seen as having the spontaneous and effortless quality of folk dance.

The nature of the recuperation from folk dance is particularly clear in group dances that are presented as actual folk or community rituals, notably the young people's segment of the Fourth of July sequence in *Summer Holiday* (1946) and "Skip to My Lou" from *Meet Me in St. Louis* (1944), both choreographed by Charles Walters. The pure "folk" performance represents the zero degree of audience manipulation in that performer and audience are one and the same. In a true group folk dance, for example, the choreographer is the community; in the MGM group "folk" dance however, the choreographer is Charles Walters masquerading as the community.

If non-choreography erases the work behind dancing, another common deception of the Hollywood musical — the presentation of finished numbers as rehearsals — masks the fact that, to quote Gene Kelly in *Summer Stock,* "putting on a show is hard work." By passing off a rehearsal as a final show, however, the spontaneity and casualness of the rehearsal environment are retained without having to expose the labor expended in creating the number. Fred Astaire and Ginger

Rogers would perform their most dazzling footwork in the context of rehearsal numbers (for example, "I'll Be Hard to Handle" from *Roberta,* 1934, and "I'm Putting All My Eggs in One Basket" from *Follow the Fleet,* 1936). In these "bogus" rehearsal numbers, there is a work-in-progress effect but no demystification of the rehearsal process. The masking of choreography and the masking of rehearsals are closely related in function. Both serve to erase the work that goes into producing musical entertainment. This in turn erases the work of production of the texts themselves. Valorizing spontaneity ultimately disguises the fact that musical entertainment is an industry, and that putting on a show (or putting on a Hollywood musical) is a matter of a labor force producing a product for consumption.

AMATEURS AND PROFESSIONALS

When Fred Astaire and Ginger Rogers do a number more dependent on virtuosity than romance, it might be presented in the context of an amateur ballroom dancing competition (as in "Let Yourself Go" in *Follow the Fleet*). When Judy Garland stands up to sing in MGM musicals, more likely than not she is performing on an amateur basis at a party or in a barn rather than "playing the Palace." When Gene Kelly is not dancing with Cyd Charisse or Leslie Caron, he is likely to be dancing with children (in *Living in a Big Way,* 1947, *Anchors Away,* 1945, and *An American in Paris,* 1951).

For a genre which not only represents professional entertainment but also is frequently *about* professional entertainment, there is a remarkable emphasis on the joys of being an amateur.

To understand this incongruity, it is instructive to recall the etymology of the word "amateur," from the Latin *amator,* lover. It is precisely the distinction between singing and dancing in a formalized arena for economic profit, and singing and dancing for the love of it, that distinguishes the professional from the amateur entertainer. All folk art is amateur entertainment in this sense. One of the reasons Hollywood needs to redefine popular entertainment as folk art is to soften the association with professionalism.

The two factors separating professional entertainers from their audience are profit motive and "talent," their stardom. Both are aspects of professionalism. Stardom is a product of the emergence of popular and mass entertainment out of communal folk art. The profit motive is a product of the same historical process at the economic rather than the human level. The valorization of the amateur through the erasure of professionalism solves both dilemmas at once.

In the backstage musical, professionalism is alienating at two levels: between text and spectator and within the texts themselves. Many musicals solve this problem by eliminating the backstage context entirely. In this way singing and dancing may emerge from the joys of ordinary life. An entire subgenre of Hollywood musicals taking place in small towns, the west or other "folk" community settings permits the natural emergence of amateur forms of entertainment employing folk motifs.[7] Even so professional a singer as Judy Garland frequently portrayed an amateur entertainer in her early films with Mickey Rooney and in her late "folk" musicals such as *The Harvey Girls* (1946) and *In the Good Old Summertime* (1949). The cakewalk number with Margaret O'Brien and Judy Garland in *Meet Me in St. Louis* is perhaps the best example of the ideological gains of such amateurization. No matter how many times one sees the film, this performance comes across as absolutely natural and spontaneous. It might be said that Gene Kelly built a career around such non-professional roles.

Yet even casting professional entertainers as amateurs does not give spectators a sense of participation in the creation of their own entertainment. In order to do this, the Hollywood musical's alienated production and consumption must be erased through a valorization of community.

THE BACKSTAGE COMMUNITY

The title number in both stage and screen versions (1943 and 1955) of *Oklahoma!* celebrates simultaneously the union of the couple and the incipient statehood of the territory in which they reside. Thus in many folk musicals, the creation of the narrative through the couple parallels the creation of a stable community. The folk subgenre as a whole represents the most obvious means by which the Hollywood musical seeks to recapture a utopian sense of communality even as the musical itself exemplifies the new, alienated mass art.

In addition to the folk dance, the folk musical commonly employs two musical techniques for linking community to entertainment: the sing-along and the passed-along (my term) song. The sing-along, as an entertainment format in which the audience is both producer and consumer, has long been an authentic folk form in ordinary life, linking the concepts of community and entertainment. The passed-along song, a device whereby a diegetically* performed song is started by one person and then taken up and "passed along" by others in the family or

---

Diegesis derives from the Greek word for narrative. When the term is used by theorists and students of film, it allows them "to designate the imaginary world of the fiction without building in a bias toward realism or even illusionism, as the word *mimesis* does." (Bill Nichols, *Ideology and the Image: Social Representation in the Cinema and Other Media* [Bloomington: Indiana University Press, 1982], pp. 317-318.)

community, appears to be a specifically cinematic form. Two well-known examples of passed-along songs are the title number performed at the beginning of *Meet Me in St. Louis* and "Isn't It Romantic?" from *Love Me Tonight* (1932). Such numbers almost always employ film techniques such as travelling shots and montage sequences to illustrate the spread of music *by* the folk *through* the folk.

In *Lady Be Good* (1942), we are shown the familiar Gershwin tune, presumably just composed by the diegetic husband and wife songwriting team, spreading in a montage sequence through various ethnic groups, languages and nationalities. Not only is "Lady Be Good" a contagious "folk" phenomenon, but it is also international in scope, making of the entire world a community through song — not unlike the Coke commercial of the 1970s: "I'd like to teach the world to sing. . . ." The fact that *Lady Be Good* is also the title of the film helps to make the analogy between the montage sequence within the film and the hoped-for effect of the film itself. In this example, entertainment products are "magically" communally produced and consumed yet diffused through "mass" media. The means of production of the Hollywood musical are erased as the means of diffusion of the Hollywood musical are re-created in symbolic fashion through the montage sequence.

In the backstage musical not only is community created between

Mass art as folk art: A system of exchange

Characteristics of folk art created	Technique for erasing	Characteristics of mass art erased
Uses materials at hand	*"Bricolage"*	Engineering
Spontaneous and effortless	1. "Non"-choreography	1. Preparation, calculation and *work* of producing entertainment
	2. Passing off finished numbers as rehearsals	2. Entertainment industry as *labor* producing a product
Done for love or ritual value	Valorization of the amateur	Profit motive through professionalism
Communally produced and consumed	The Backstage Community	Film as industry; alienated production and consumption
HUMAN RELATIONS	Binding	ECONOMIC RELATIONS

Note: Erasing mass art equals replacing economic relations with human relations.

performer and audience but it is also created within the realm of the theatre, the world of the stage. The inscription of community into theatre is accomplished in two major ways. Within the narratives, community is created through the co-operative effort of putting on the show, an effort achieved by substituting co-operation for competition at the human level. Within the numbers, community is asserted through the insertion of "folk" numbers and folk motifs into the diegetic show.

Warner Brothers' musicals of the early 1930s place a premium on co-operation and group participation in the success of the final show. Collective endeavor is celebrated in the anonymous spectacle of the Busby Berkeley production number. The plots of these films stress the need for theatrical community in two directions. Within the community of the show, obstacles to the show's success stem from an internal struggle in which personal greed (usually embodied in a temperamental star) leads to undervaluation of the virtues of co-operative effort. Meanwhile, forces may be working from outside the show to undermine the collective endeavor. In *Footlight Parade* (1933), a rival producer is stealing James Cagney's ideas; in *Dames* (1933), a falsely prudish moral society wants to censor the show; in *Gold Diggers of 1933*, lack of funding cripples the production. In the ultimately successful effort to put on the final show, the theatrical community overcomes both the internal and external, the human and economic, obstacles.

Paralleling the development of the folk musical proper in the 1940s and 1950s was a related practice of inserting folk motifs into proscenium numbers in backstage musicals. Frequently such numbers feature country motifs in both costume and dance formations, as in "Hoe Down" in *Babes on Broadway* (1941) or "Louisiana Hayride" in *The Band Wagon* (1953). Or they may feature low-life motifs in the form of tramps ("A Couple of Swells" in *Easter Parade*, 1948) or gangster and moll (in *Words and Music*, 1948 and *Royal Wedding*, 1951).

A third alternative is seen in numbers whose content refers to country life, as does Judy Garland's opening number ("I Wish I Was Back in Michigan, Down on the Farm") in *Easter Parade* (1948). Proscenium numbers with folk motifs are related to an extremely common plot paradigm in the Hollywood musical: plots in which a country or small town girl comes to New York to try for her big break on Broadway. Both "Broadway Ballet" in *Singin' in the Rain* and "Born in a Trunk" in *A Star Is Born* make fun of this conventional plot, as does the stage spoof of the backstage musical, *Dames At Sea*. The girl in the backstage musical need not come from Iowa, but she must be shown as having her roots in the provinces, thus retaining an association with community. If, in *Broadway Melody of 1936*, Eleanor Powell comes from Albany, then Albany comes to represent the small rural town, "back home." The entire rhetoric of *On The Town* is expended upon transforming New York City into Meadowville, Indiana. The relevance to community of this pervasive plot in the backstage musical is evident: even after the girl becomes a star (a professional entertainer) on Broadway, she retains an identity with a hypothetical "folk": that of rural Americana.This identity may be recuperated by the entertainment world, an exchange insisted upon in *Easter Parade,* where the success of the show comes to depend upon it.

The same exchange may be accomplished by incorporating folk numbers into shows. *Summer Stock* illustrates how a folk number is used in the final "show" of a backstage musical. In a show entitled "Fall in Love" principals (Gene Kelly and Judy Garland) and chorus alike start by informing the diegetic audience that both the show and falling in love are "all for you." The number emphasizes conventions of professional entertainment in that cast and chorus are dressed in formal attire, with Kelly in the (for him) uncharacteristic Astaire uniform of top hat, white tie and tails. But the passed-along format of the number is folk-derived.

After this first number, creation and erasure become even more apparent. Kelly and Garland reprise "You Wonderful You" as a comedy turn in front of the stage curtain, in candy-striped turn-of-the-century garb reminiscent of *Meet Me in St. Louis*. The song has already played a significant role in the film. In its first performance, Kelly introduced Garland to the joys of professional entertainment, thereby valorizing amateur entertainment by asserting that even professionals do it for love. Kelly reprised the song himself, whistling it while he danced with the newspaper and squeaky floorboard. The first reprise valorized spontaneity, erasing the work of producing entertainment. The second reprise — the number in the final show — now associates the number with community, erasing the alienation of producer and consumer.

Such a "folk" motif is carried over into a following hillbilly number reminiscent in style if not in quality of "A Couple of Swells." Professional entertainment is re-created in the penultimate number (Garland's well-known "Get Happy"), only to be erased in the finale, which consists of a diegetic folk number from earlier in the film, reprised by full cast and chorus within the show. In the first performance of the song ("Howdy, Neighbor, Happy Harvest"), Judy Garland had expressed her communal country roots — at that point antithetical to the spirit of entertainment. The number included the neighboring farmers in the celebration of Garland's acquisition of a tractor. In the narrative, the tractor was destroyed and then restored by the entertainers; its restoration represented a significant step in uniting community and entertainment through the union of farmer Garland and performer Kelly. Now, in the final number of the show, community is inscribed into entertainment, erasing professional entertainment but creating folk entertainment. The number is also addressed to the film spectator through the intermediary of the diegetic audience. It ends with the lines,

Remember, neighbors, when you work for Mother
Nature, you get paid by Father Time.

These lines are sung with Kelly and Garland united in front of the chorus with arms lifted up in address. We do not see the diegetic audience; rather, the spectator is included in the address to offscreen space. The spectator is invited to participate in a harvest ritual taking place in the finale of a "Broadway" show. In a sense "Oklahoma!" is inscribed into the final show of a backstage musical. In this way the ritual erasure of performer-audience alienation is accomplished.

At the same time and through the same discourse, the economic relationship between spectator and entertainment institution is erased. Instead of working for MGM and getting paid by the spectator, the song asserts that performer and audience alike are working for "Mother Nature" and getting paid by "Father Time." The economic relations underlying professional entertainment and mass art are erased by the economic relations underlying pre-industrial communities and folk art. The final song of *Summer Stock* says this loud and clear.

READING THE TEXT'S SILENCES

Although the ideology of entertainment is especially clear in a reflexive form such as the Hollywood musical, the operations described here are by no means unique to the musical (as the example of the Coke commercial makes clear). Nostalgia for folk relations permeates our entertainment forms, finding its latest resting place on television. Shows such as *Laverne and Shirley, Little House on the Prairie, Family* and *The Waltons* valorize community in their context. Other shows, for example *Good Morning, America* and *Donahue,* appropriate folk relations in their format: the former with its butcher, its baker, and its Rona Barrett; the latter with its nineteenth-century participatory "town meeting" format.

In one sense, the valorization of community is utopian, playing a significant role in art that is both progressive (*Norma Rae*, 1979) or revolutionary (Miklós Jancsó or the later films of Jean-Luc Godard). Although it is perfectly possible for individual audience members to read the valorization of community as progressive in mass entertainment forms as well, I believe that the evidence renders such a reading unusual and unlikely. For the thrust of the operation of ideology in mass entertainment is regressive rather than progressive; and moreover, regressive in such a way as to naturalize the relationship between mass art and its audience as one of community rather than alienation.

British film theory has followed Louis Althusser in viewing ideology as a practical "lived" world view which is opposed to the theoretical nature of "science." "Structuralist" definitions have in common a notion of bourgeois ideology as naturalizing, as dehistoricizing, and as largely unconscious in its operation.[8] This structuralist view of ideology may provide a way out of the naturalized bind by its refusal to accept anything as natural. Structural analysis teaches us to look not at what media such as television say, nor even how they say it, but rather to look for that which is written in a text's silences. In this way, a radical consciousness may emerge from the reading of what appears to be a text totally transparent in its bourgeois ideology; or a text, like that of the musical, which may seem to say nothing at all. Only by the critical rewriting of that which has been erased will the operation of ideology in Hollywood's entertainment films be rendered explicit.

NOTES

[1] Stuart Hall and Paddy Whannel, *The Popular Arts* (New York: Pantheon Books, 1965), pp. 56-66.

[2] *Ibid.*

[3] See Walter Benjamin, "The Work of Art in the Age of Mechanical Reproduction," reprinted in Gerald Mast and Marshall Cohen, eds., *Film Theory and Criticism: Introductory Readings* (New York: Oxford University Press, 1974), pp. 622-23.

[4] See also my book *The Hollywood Musical* (London: BFI, 1981), for a discussion of "creation and erasure" on a larger scale.

[5] Claude Lévi-Strauss, *The Savage Mind,* trans., George Weidenfeld (Chicago: University of Chicago Press, 1966), p. 17.

[6] Michael Wood, *America in the Movies* (New York: Basic Books, 1975), p. 148.

[7] The "folk" subgenre is the formulation of Charles F. Altman. Its development is traced in his article, "Pour une étude sémentique/Syntaxique du genre hollywoodien: Le musical folklorique", *Ça/Cinéma,* forthcoming. [Also see Altman, *Genre: The Musical* (London, BFI), 1981, ed.]

[8] I am referring to the work of Louis Althusser and Pierre Macherey in France: and to the work of the journal *Screen* and Terry Eagleton in Britain.

CHAPTER 3.

Working-Class Film Heroes: Junior Johnson, Evel Knievel and the Film Audience

CHUCK KLEINHANS

In *The Benny Goodman Story* (1955), the young Benny receives his first musical instrument and training at Chicago's Hull House, a settlement house for immigrants and the poor. Benny is a child of the immigrant slums, but in the movie this fact seems not to really matter: the rest of the film resolutely ignores matters of class. In this the film is a typical Hollywood presentation of the American myth of success. It centers on the hero's trials and triumphs, and considers his class origins only long enough to establish the initial "rags" of the "rags to riches" theme.

In success-myth films, aspiring racial and ethnic minority members of the working class have generally had two career paths open to them: the entertainment business (*The Jazz Singer,* 1927, *Yankee Doodle Dandy,* 1942); and sports (*The Babe Ruth Story,* 1948, *Gentleman Jim,* 1942). Such films treat the hero's class and racial/ethnic background perfunctorily, unless the subject is inescapable, as with *Jim Thorpe — All American* (1951), which gives a liberal nod of recognition to the racism that confronts the Indian athlete; and *Your Cheatin' Heart* (1964), which sentimentally traces Hank Williams's career as a country music singer.

In the early 1970s, however, two Hollywood success-myth films, *Evel Knievel* (1972) and *The Last American Hero* (1973), diverged from the traditional direction by presenting heroes whose working-class origins are central to the narrative. Doubtless, Hollywood's new cultural pluralism — the shift from conceiving of a homogeneous public to making films for well defined audiences such as youths and blacks — was an economically motivated adjustment to market realities. Significantly, both real-life subjects of these two films attained celebrity status among a specific audience: the white working class. Motorcycle daredevil Evel Knievel and champion stock-car racer Junior Johnson remain little known in the U.S. middle class.

These two films depict working-class heroes, both in the sense that their class origins are not ignored or hidden, and that they are heroes to the working class. For their intended audience the films are "closer to real life" than films depicting middle-class protagonists with middle-class problems. Yet both films remain within the limits of bourgeois ideology, particularly in dealing with the success myth, for they affirm that individual success is both possible and worth pursuing.

The very distribution of these films indicates that they were specifically aimed at the white working-class audience. *The Last American Hero* was released by Fox initially in the summer of 1973 on the drive-in circuit, which is itself a class-distinguished phenomenon providing relatively inexpensive admissions and back-of-the-car free child care. After remarkable success, *The Last American Hero* finally opened in New York City houses without ever having had a critics' screening. When it was reviewed, the results were generally favorable. (It was later retitled as *Hard Driver* for television showings.)

Evel Knievel achieved a popular initial success and was a steady second half of double bills at drive-ins for several years. Additionally, it was chosen as a trump card by a major television network to win the prime-time ratings battle in the first week of the 1973-74 season because of its appeal to Middle America — the majority of TV viewers.

But what is perhaps most significant about *Evel Knievel* and *The Last American Hero* is the type of ironic and sometimes ambiguous biographies they present. More specifically, a look at several themes — danger and skill, the relationship of the hero to authority, the role of women, the depiction of class differences, the use of action as a solution to problems — indicates the kind of appeal the films carry for a mass audience.

SUCCESS: MYTH AND REALITY

The media convey information through both form and content. That information and the way it is presented shape audience sensibility: the question, then, is one of ideology.

Modern discussions of ideology begin with Marx's well-known formulation in his *Contribution to the Critique of Political Economy:* "It is not the consciousness of men that determines their existence, but, on the contrary, their social existence determines their consciousness.'' Obviously, Marx's point about the relation between social existence and consciousness cannot be taken in a mechanistic way. In contemporary life, mass culture mediates one's consciousness of social reality, and film is such a mediation.

The typical success image in cinema is presented through characters who succeed or fail through their own individual activity and outlook. Film thus reinforces tendencies favorable to the status quo by implicitly denying even the possibilities of group activity for life's goals, or of measuring success in political terms.

The success myth is so pervasive in U.S. life that it needs little description: America is the land of opportunity, males go from log cabin to White House, the virtues of a Horatio Alger ensure success. The function of the myth in American life is to encourage hope and a belief in individual opportunity. Because of its promise of reward for hard labor, the myth serves to distract people from seeing institutional obstacles to striving, and from considering the small number of wealthy and powerful at the top of the success pyramid in comparison to the massive base of "failures." The myth promises to those who lack money, educational advantages and influence — the vast majority of Americans — that a personality committed to ambition, determination, perseverance, temperance and hard work will earn its appropriate reward.

The reality of success and failure in the U.S., especially for the working class, is at variance with the myth. In one of the best studies of the reality and myth of success among industrial workers, *Automobile Workers and the American Dream,* Ely Chinoy points out that external conditions, not subjective factors, determine success for the working class.[1] Soon after beginning their careers, the blue-collar workers find a ceiling on their upward mobility and level of achievement. Subjectively, when members of the working class find their aspirations impossible to achieve yet still accept the prevailing ideology of individualism, the result is self-blame and an elaborate defensive rationalization of their position.

Evel Knievel and *The Last American Hero* are particularly interesting because they do not simply present the standard success myth. They instead deal with it in an ambiguous way by qualifying wholehearted admiration for their respective heroes. In short, they accommodate the myth in the light of undeniable reality.

The traditional pattern of romance follows a protagonist through early adventures to a crucial test. The test proves that the main character deserves the title of hero, as with Beowulf, Saint George and other basic romance protagonists. Typically, a romance clearly distinguishes the hero and the heroine, who together represent the desirable ideals, from the villains, who embody threats to virtue's triumph. While both *Evel*

Knievel and *The Last American Hero* follow the romance scheme, they also introduce significant irony. The hero and heroine are tarnished, and they do not simply oppose the villains but join them in a symbiotic if distasteful union.

In *The Last American Hero* this issue of compromise forms a central theme. As a beginning driver, Junior (Jeff Bridges) scorns his rivals, who are hired by wealthy patrons. But his pride in his self-made status is shattered in a race when he totals his car, the sum of his assets. Without the cash or credit to buy a new racing machine, he must become an employee in order to drive, and he makes the distasteful decision to work for the owner he most hates, Burton Colt. Colt tightly controls his employees, treating his drivers callously by using a one-way radio to tell them exactly what to do during a race. When Colt's instructions become too obnoxious, Junior responds by tearing the radio apart, a defiance permitted only because he wins the race.

In *Evel Knievel* the theme of compromise is minor, for Evel (George Hamilton) constantly defies restrictions. Though he is forced to obey his doctor when immobilized by injuries, once patched up he escapes to the hospital parking lot where he rides a motorcycle while still in several casts, celebrating his bravado until he comically falls off. Constant reference to his dream of jumping his cycle over the Grand Canyon emphasizes his ambition and his wish to defy the laws of the physical universe.

For the most part, compromise comes about through Evel's extreme ambivalence. For example, he fears and scorns the crowds who find his potential or actual injury or death amusing; yet he performs for them and tells them half-mockingly and half-seriously, "It is truly an honor to risk my life for you." He acts similarly with the press and autograph seekers, first verbally rejecting them and then in fact submitting happily to their attentions.

In the film this somewhat schizophrenic behavior seems to pass beyond the normal neurosis allowed a professional daredevil. While in some cases his nervousness is mildly comic (he fears that fans will crush him, tear his clothes off, injure him, as they did to Elvis Presley), Evel resolves everything through action and never exhibits fear in doing his stunts, at the same time paying the price of never finding repose. When his wife suggests a Mexican vacation to find some quiet, he replies that the water makes you sick.

Evel's retort to his wife indicates another element of ironic romance. In the typical romance the main characters usually find a temporal and/or spatial place outside of the common world, which allows the relaxed practice of life without threats. Both films, however, adopt an ironic stance and say there is no place or time of innocence. Once involved in the quest the hero cannot return to a simpler life or attain it when he accomplishes his goal.

For Junior and Marge in *The Last American Hero* not even a love tryst is safe, for Marge's former lover and Junior's archrival as a driver, Kyle Kingman, enters her apartment with his own key (although he graciously leaves when he finds the couple in bed). Once Junior begins professional driving, he cannot go back to his former life in the Appalachian hollows. His father returns from a prison sentence for moonshining and emphatically tells his sons that there will be no more stills on his property, thereby putting the lid on Junior's other employable skill.

Nor can Junior return to his friends once he has become a winner — a point made visually after he wins the big race. At that time, as he climbs the stairs leading to the press room for his post-victory press conference, Junior looks down on the small figures of his old buddies standing in the dusk. He has just told Colt that they will have to be hired as his pit crew, but the difference between Junior, above, and the friends below on the ground in the growing darkness, with the buddies' physical actions, their characteristic "goofing," shows a quantitative and qualitative chasm between the hero and his old companions. As Junior enters the press room he disappears behind the door, but his shadow is silhouetted on the wall in freeze frame. The film ends not with the man, but with a two-dimensional media image of the winning hero.

Junior cannot go home again, nor can he rest: a season of racing and years of seasons lie ahead. Similarly with Evel Knievel: waiting for the big jump that concludes the film, he paces in a room with wide picture windows looking out onto the race track — a constant reminder that there is always a jump coming up, that there is always a quantitative increase in the number of cars he might jump over. In the typical romance the hero's achievement restores order and virtue. In these films achievement — winning the race or jumping over 19 cars — represents the attainment of hero status, but restores nothing. The film hero's accomplishment proves only bravery and prowess and does not bestow autonomous power, great wealth or physical well-being. This is a reversal of the traditional romance where winning the crucial battle ensures ascension to the throne or at the very least chief-advisor status, along with gifts of wealth, marriage to the heroine, and the establishment of a new social order promising peace, fertility and plenitude.

In his book *Blue-Collar Life,* sociologist Arthur B. Shostak argues that the appeal of the typical romance pattern presenting a moral man pitted against the forces of the "outside" fits the blue-collar male's disposition to posit a general "us/them" dichotomy in life, with "us" usually seen as the extended family, ethnic group or neighborhood (all of which may have considerable overlap).[2] For example, the pattern is common in westerns where the villain enters into conflict with a serene society or is a bad element that must be expunged, or in a variation where the good guy comes up against a corrupt environment. Action films often present the same pattern of a moral man hamstrung by institutions, by "them."[3]

In the case of *Evel Knievel* and *The Last American Hero,* although the pattern is ironic, it remains intact and is not inverted by the end. In the balance, both Evel and Junior remain "moral" though not pure in their encounters. The outside, "them," is still suspect: Evel twice states his exaggerated fears that his wife will be "kidnapped, raped, or something" if she goes outside without him, but his obsessive protectiveness is motivated by virtuous concern. Similarly, Junior's first big race on the professional circuit exhibits not only his backwoods' ignorance of city ways but also his distance from his fellow drivers who "parade around like movie stars," as he tells his family. In both films the hero faces the problem of maintaining his native qualities and virtues in a quest for success that involves facing the "outside" and its inherent corruption. The resultant ambiguities in the characters' biographies are seen in several themes, including that of danger.

DANGER AND SKILL

To find excitement in physical danger is a common enough component of our culture. In *The Last American Hero* and *Evel Knievel* the hero's approach to danger is directly related to his nerve, courage and above all to his skill. Working within the narrow tolerances of daredevil motorcycle jumping or high speed stock car racing, Junior and Evel must have skill to avoid injury or death. The two biographical films have little need to belabor the point, for their audiences already know it. For both characters survival is a genuine accomplishment at the end of the jump or race.

In *Evel Knievel* the point is made principally through the episode of Knievel's jump in Las Vegas, where he crashes on descent. It is a scene vividly shown in slow-motion documentary footage of his body as it agonizingly jolts and twists. *The Last American Hero* depicts danger through shots of high speed accidents during various races.

According to both films, adolescence is the crucial time for teaching oneself the technical skills needed for later survival and success. Junior learns high-speed driving by running moonshine whiskey past federal tax agents on back roads at night, and Evel's daredevil motorcycle skills come from his considerable teenage experience escaping traffic cops. At this formative stage of the hero's development the central villains are the police, portrayed in both films as stupid buffoons. In *Evel Knievel* an early sequence finds Evel in a Butte, Montana, bar where he has a local reputation for creating excitement. Even as a teenager Evel knows how to build crowd expectation, a skill he later uses to good effect in his daredevil performances. After tantalizing his "audience" he proceeds to break into a hardware store across the street. Finding the money locked in a safe, he has the police notified of a burglary in progress. When the cop arrives, Evel volunteers to go in, if given a gun. He re-enters, shoots open the safe, sends the gullible cop off after the "burglar" and, in a Robin Hood gesture, distributes the cash to his audience. In a similar episode, undaunted when he dynamites a wall inside city hall (the wrong wall — he has opened the men's washroom) and fails to find money, Evel goes to pick up more explosives at a mining company warehouse, while the police investigate the damage at city hall and eventually conclude that someone tried to commit suicide in the washroom. Evel returns to finish the job just as the police leave, and then blows open the safe he initially sought.

The first sequence in *The Last American Hero* delivers the same message of police incompetence. Almost trapped by the feds, Junior escapes through a combination of daring and skill by executing a "bootleg turn" — a high-speed 180-degree turn on a one-lane road. Another time Junior is warned of a roadblock ahead on his police-band radio. He sounds a siren and shows a red flasher, which the police take for one of their own. To the embarrassment of the agents, with the roadblock opened, Junior's whiskey-running Mustang roars through. However, his glory is short-lived since the feds proceed to find the family still and smash it and jail Junior's father.

Living with danger through skill and "drive" is important for both heroes because the alternative is deadening work. Earning a living in routine ways is portrayed as mechanical and alienating. Evel promises his future wife adventure and travel — both impossible if they stay in their Montana home town. In *The Last American Hero* Junior maintains his father's prime value — independence. During a crucial home scene, Junior and his brother talk. Wayne says that a neighbor is willing to take Junior on as an apprentice garage mechanic at $2.10 an hour. Junior scorns the idea: apprenticeship is absurd for him, for he has already built his own racer, and besides, he argues, no garage mechanic will ever have his name in the newspaper, except for his obituary.

Following this scene Junior visits his jailed father, who counsels that racing is too dangerous to do merely for the money. The son confesses that it is more than that, and paternal wisdom confirms the young man's decision to race.

Father: Your mother is always after me to get out of the whiskey business. You was too young to remember, but after my first time in the pen, to please her I hired on at the sawmill. [Soundtrack unclear] . . . permission to go to the can. Pretty much like here. It didn't seem to worry most of the boys. They put in their time, lookin' ahead to payday, but not me. That paycheck wasn't money, it was a bill of sale. Three months of that . . . back to whiskey. It's hard on your ma. But damn foolishness to one person is breath of life to another.

The Last American Hero and *Evel Knievel* depict living with danger through skill as an emblem of independence in a society that demands acquiescence to authority and offers alienating and deadening work. This is appealing for the films' audiences because it offers a daydream response to the real problem of the nature of work in advanced industrial capitalism. It is neither a realistic nor a desirable solution to problems in the audience's life but a fantasy displacement. Obviously this produces a strong element of ambiguity within the films. They recognize a genuine working-class problem, but they postulate only a defensive individual escape, rather than a direct social and political solution.

AUTHORITY AND THE SYSTEM

The attitude to authority and the social system in both films follows a similar pattern: acknowledging a genuine problem, but proposing an ambiguous solution. In both films the protagonists grow in knowledge as they learn how to bargain with and outwit authority figures so as to establish themselves in the best possible position within the system. They learn to what degree authority can be challenged.

For Evel Knievel, although the police embody authority and their antagonism to him is a long-established fact, they are basically good-natured stupid buffoons, not truly malicious villains. Similarly, in Evel's successful ''present,'' his doctor also serves as a buffoon villain. Evel sees the M.D.'s insistence that he rest to repair his broken bones as a conspiracy to keep him from jumping.

In *The Last American Hero* we see police idiocy in a farcical episode in which Junior is using a small fuel-oil truck to transport whiskey. Pursued by a trooper, he finally has to slow down and he opens a valve that dumps the load onto the highway. The policeman, a visual stereotype of the fat southern state trooper, demonstrates the alcoholic content of Junior's load by lighting a match to the liquid, which stains a long stretch of highway. Looking back at the burning trail, Junior can smugly point out that the evidence is now destroyed.

More seriously, in *The Last American Hero* Junior learns that he has to fight the system with money when he faces the fact that the criminal justice system is essentially corrupt. After the jailing of his father, Junior brings a lawyer to the jail. The lawyer explains that the sentence will only be six months if the father is contrite and promises to

71

renounce illegal whiskey-making. When the prisoner objects, the following dialogue takes place.

Lawyer: Elroy, Elroy. Now, I drink your whiskey . . . boys in the courthouse drink it. Wouldn't be surprised if His Honor had a jar or two tucked away somewhere. But that has no bearing . . .

Father: The hell it don't! City Hall's so full of crooks they're falling out of the windows! Country club boys with their payoffs and kickbacks. . . . Where do you go to find a little justice?

Lawyer: Depends on what you can afford.

The lawyer explains his fee and "extras" (that is, bribes), which guarantee better prison treatment, and advises Junior, "It's kind of like justice, son. You get what you pay for." The need for ready cash to pay for the "extras" motivates Junior's first attempts at racing.

In addition, Junior and Evel both have crucial formative experiences through confrontations with entrepreneurs. In both cases the lesson learned is never to accept the boss's terms, but bargain for your own. Evel's first jump for pay comes at a small rodeo show run by a red-nosed, bumptious promoter who recounts his distinguished past, which includes running the largest reptile garden in the southwest. Evel's native wit gets him his job — jumping two pickup trucks placed end to end — and he successfully haggles his price from $50 if he's successful and $25 if he's not, to $50 win or lose. Just before Evel's stunt, the promoter's callousness is revealed when a veteran cowboy who befriended Evel is killed in the Brahma bull-riding event. When the promoter covers up the death, Evel completes his jump and leaves in anger, aware that his own potential death or injury would be treated in exactly the same way by the rodeo boss. The rest of the picture implies that Evel operates as a free professional since the financial arrangements and bookings are never mentioned. (In real life Evel Knievel is sponsored by Harley Davidson, the motorcycle company, and Olympia Beer, and is promoted by a sports public relations firm.)

Junior's first encounter with a businessman is similar to Evel's. In the face of Junior's persistence, the owner-operator of a small dirt track relents and allows Junior to enter a demolition derby. After the event, Junior insists on moving up to racing, and is again successful through persistence, but finally his independence gets to be too much for the track operator and Junior is barred from further racing there. The young man's response is to move up to the true professional circuit. Here he is aided by Marge, who gives him a rule book that proves his eligibility and a track pass that lets him see the owner of the large track at Hickory, N.C. Again Junior has to talk his way into starting.

To this point the young racer is shown as an expert self-promoter. But Junior soon comes into a conflict that his cockiness cannot overcome. Junior instinctively dislikes racing-team owner Burton Colt when he sees how Colt constantly harasses his drivers. Forced to drop out of a race because of car trouble, Junior is approached by Colt, who is looking for a new driver. Colt says to Junior, "You got the talent , but I got the bankroll." Junior scorns the offer, saying he will make it on his talent, but Colt is unruffled, "Dream on, boy, dream on."

Junior's dreams are ended when he is finally faced with the economic reality that he can no longer subsidize his racing through whiskey-making. He returns to Colt and strikes a bargain, becoming the "hired jockey" he had previously scorned. Junior's talent gives him his only edge, plus his chance to throw away the one-way radio Colt uses to direct his drivers. It also allows him to bargain with Colt for a bigger share of the winnings and his own pit crew. The film makes clear the tenuousness of the arrangement, its distastefulness to Junior, and the inevitability of having to make a bargain.

In both the cases of Junior and Evel, skill and achievement are portrayed as the only bargaining tool for more money and better working conditions. For employees it is the only source of leverage and freedom. Thus, while the system, the police and entrepreneurs are all pictured as corrupt, foolish or exploitative, the only way out posited is through individual chutzpa and skill.

ROLE OF WOMEN

The Last American Hero and *Evel Knievel* both devote considerable time to the heroes' pursuit of the heroines. But the role of women in both films is much more than a simple "love interest." Evel's courtship of Linda (Sue Lyon) expresses themes of general character development: his persistence, aggressiveness and victory over institutions.

The sequences of their courtship are set in the context of school. Evel motorcycles past Linda on her way to school, makes her drop her books and then dares her to ride with him on the cycle, despite her suspicion of him as a "hood." While with her, Evel's show-off ways quickly lead to a police chase. In the next courtship sequence Evel stands outside a high-school dance looking in. As a dropout he is excluded, and his cycle, like the cowboy's faithful horse, provides his consolation. Later, as Linda is ice-skating with school girlfriends, Evel arrives. Ever showing off, Evel does some fancy skating turns, and then tricks Linda into his car by giving her the keys (so nothing can happen). He then hotwires the car and drives off with her. The sequence ends with a long-shot of the car parked in snowy woods and the implication that they have had intercourse.

Later Linda finds Evel in the high-school gym, practising basketball. Evel carries on with his typical bravado: "I don't need a stinkin' letterman sweater to know I'm a hero." Linda informs him, "I'm going to college. I want an education. I don't want to be a waitress at the Mountain Inn and spend the rest of my life here."

Evel's subsequent abduction of Linda from her college residence is visually one of the film's better moments. Denied entrance by the housemother because it is late, he drives his cycle up the long front steps, knocking down the door, and roars up a spiral staircase to Linda's room.

The film implies that Evel's successful wresting of Linda from education as an institution and into his vagabond life satisfies her urge not to be a waitress in a small Rocky Mountain town. Yet Linda's only role as Mrs. Knievel is to encourage her husband, to worry about his health and safety, reassure him and keep his scrapbook up to date. The message, though certainly stereotyped, fits the frequent pattern of working-class women moving directly from parental family (extended in this case to college as an *in loco parentis* institution) to marriage. Linda realistically assesses her future in Butte, and her uncomplaining acceptance of a traditional marital role is clearly shown as her alternative to waitressing or school.

While Linda is defined throughout the film by her relation to Evel, Marge Denison (Valerie Perrine) in *The Last American Hero* is her own person. When we and Junior first meet her, she is considerably more experienced than the young man. Marge functions in the film as Junior's double. She has gone from rural/small-town southern upbringing to urban life. Along the way she has learned that the price of success is compromise, a lesson she tries to impress on Junior, who of course must learn it himself. Her initial stance towards Junior is to help him in a rather sisterly way: providing the rule book and track pass to help him enter big-time racing. As secretary to the track manager she also gets Junior a special rate at the drivers' motel and informs him of a free "boo-fay" dinner. Junior reciprocates by inviting Marge, but she has a date, so he sends her flowers. When Marge finds she's been stood up she aggressively seeks out Junior and goes to the buffet with him. There Junior finds Marge is both popular and well-known among the drivers. Since she says she has "tons of work to do" he takes her home early, and later phones her . . . but a sleepy Kyle Kingman answers the phone.

The next sequence has Marge talking with Kyle, who has just won a race. However, Kyle's wife unexpectedly arrives. Sending her husband off to get her a drink ("What good's a husband who can't service his wife?"), she puts Marge down as a racing-circuit groupie and gives some gratuitous advice: "Take a tip from me, sugar: if you can't sell it, sit on it."

Junior takes Marge home, they console each other's loss, physically and emotionally, and Marge relates her past. She was a fat teenager and her mother sent her to business school in Atlanta. There she was once invited to a college fraternity party ("Now nobody on the face of God's green earth thinks he's smarter than those fraternity boys"), which turned out to be a "pig party." Her date received a prize for bringing the second ugliest woman. Marge goes on, "Oh, I cried for a couple of weeks and I got comical calls in the middle of the night — there's a lot of jokers in Atlanta — and I left about a month later."

Junior's response is to affirm that Marge is the most beautiful woman he's ever known. But the relationship, though sealed physically, remains undefined. When Junior wins his first big race, Marge is off with another racer, explaining that she has many friends and Junior is still just one of them.

Marge has found the independence within her situation that Junior seeks as well. He attains it through his exceptional driving skill, while she uses her secretarial skills at the tracks on the seasonal circuit and her sexual and personal attractiveness. And from her actions it is clear that the future relation of the two must be based on equality. Both Junior and Marge have made the best of the situation in which they find themselves.

The portraits of these two women have a certain general class accuracy. For both women the emotional quality of the relationship is not the primary factor in their actions. This attitude, formed both from working-class realities and the socialization of adolescent women, differs markedly from the general attitude of middle-class women, who place emotional quality first in priorities.[4]

CLASS PORTRAYAL

Neither Evel Knievel nor Junior move distinctly into the middle class, except as measured by income. Junior maintains his Appalachian roots and is distinguished from other drivers by his more conservative dress and demeanor. Before the big race that concludes the film, Junior joins in a pre-race prayer while other drivers are seen ignoring the spiritual message booming over the track PA system. Junior's authenticity is virtually swallowed up in the racing world, just as during the national anthem the U.S. flag is almost squeezed out by product flags for Champion spark plugs and Coke. Although the final shots of the film indicate that Junior cannot go back home, the film also indicates approvingly that he will not join the fast-living crowd of the other drivers.

In *Evel Knievel* the hero, who attained his position by scorning the institutions of law and education, is glorified as the man who will never rest on his past achievements or play it safe, but who will always continue his allegiance to an inner code of daring and a respect for "his" audiences, who are clearly Middle Americans.

Both pictures, however, distort their real life subjects in significant ways. *The Last American Hero* is loosely based on Tom Wolfe's essay of the same name, reprinted in Wolfe's *The Kandy-Kolored Tangerine-Flake Streamline Baby*. [5] The journalist describes Junior Johnson as a hero to the southern white working class. But Wolfe adds some background that the film's scriptwriters have discarded. Junior Johnson grossed $100,000 in the 1963 racing season and was the owner of his own chicken farm (42,000 birds) and a road-grading enterprise in his home county. Junior had also served time in a federal prison for his whiskey activities. More significantly, Wolfe puts Junior in a more distinct class position by describing how the moonshining of whiskey has an economic basis that goes back to the 1794 Whiskey Rebellion of western Pennsylvania farmers against the encroachment of federal authority representing urban and eastern seaboard interests. Wolfe also clearly outlines the domination of racing by Detroit automakers; the Burton Colts do not even exist in the real world of stock-car racing. Wolfe puts Junior's reputation into a distinct class and regional framework: Junior, man and myth, is rooted in the values of the rural southern white working class. In the film, in contrast to the essay, Junior's appeal is more generalized.

While the real Junior Johnson is actually more generalized in the film as Junior Jackson (film name), the screen Evel Knievel is narrower than the image of the public performer. The live Evel is given to moralistic platitudes that match his patriotic suit and cycle. His official publicity describes him as a high-school sports star, a family man (children are not mentioned in the film), a rugged individual, and downplays his early scrapes with the police. In public Evel sometimes scorns the film (though a 16mm print is usually shown at the motor-sports shows where he performs). And the picture is not entirely complimentary: it indicates he is abnormally neurotic, an egomaniac at least, fearful of his audience, and that his wife was not a virgin on the day of their marriage — none of which, presumably, the real Evel would appreciate being said about him.

Whatever the truth about the real figures, within both films the two antagonists are portrayed as heroic representatives of their class. Junior's personal integrity is unchallenged and in *Evel Knievel* the point is made at the end, following Evel's spectacularly photographed four-and-one-half minute slow-motion jump over 19 cars. In a shot from a plane forward and above we see him riding in open western country and hear a voice-over monologue. Though phrased with some of the consistent self-mocking we have seen throughout, by camera attention on Evel and its placement at the end of the film this monologue has to be seen as a significant statement of the film's theme:

... Celebrities like myself, Elvis, Frank Sinatra, John Wayne ... we have a responsibility. There are many good people who look at our lives and it gives theirs some meaning. They come out from their jobs — most of which are meaningless to them — and they watch me jump 20 cars and maybe get splattered. It means something to them. They jump right alongside of me. They take the handlebars in their hands and for one split second they're all daredevils. I am the last gladiator in the new Rome. I go into the arena and compete against destruction and I win. And next week I go out there and I do it again. And this time, civilization being what it is and all, we have very little choice about our life. The only thing really left us is a choice about our death. And mine will be ... glorious! (Visual: cut to camera over handlebars looking down the road. Cut: camera moving down road, then out over the Grand Canyon. Freeze with credit roll.)

THE ACTION THEME

As in any success-story film, both movies picture the obstacles in the way of success. What is particularly interesting in both *Evel Knievel* and *The Last American Hero* is not the use of barriers to retard the dramatic action but the consistent depiction of direct action as the solution to all problems facing the hero. Evel and Junior constantly maintain their desire to win and express that desire in direct, immediate action. Thus any problem Evel faces — whether he is being chased for a traffic violation or wants to be alone with Linda or must overcome his ambivalence and touchiness about risking his life — he solves through action: he attempts to outrun the police, hotwires the car, makes his jump. In *The Last American Hero* the same pattern is reinforced by shock cuts that answer the problem posed in the preceding sequence. Will Junior get to drive in the demolition derby? There is a shock cut to a sledge hammer going through a car windshield: yes, he is preparing a car for the event.

Basically, the action theme in both films posits the impossible. The underlying assumption is that the hero's impulse is right, that introspection is bad and action is good. However, the depiction of the hero's unhampered drive to the top is at distinct variance with the audience's reality. In fact, simply acting, playing out the "little-engine-that-could" theory of advancement without considering the factors external to one's will, is not a sufficient guide to individual advancement.

The depiction of the action theme and its appeal to a working-class audience must be seen in light of its middle-class inverse. To grossly generalize, we can distinguish two stages of bourgeois ideology dealing with success:

1) The naive success myth in which adherence to certain code virtues such as postponement of gratification, respect for authority, hard

work and ambition is shown to lead invariably to success (money, power, esteem).

2) The sophisticated or ironic success myth in which the price of material success is shown to be spiritual and social emptiness. We could call this the bourgeois failure myth, or the sour-grapes version of the naive success myth.

The second stage or version is dominant at present. In fact, although the ironic version of the success myth was historically the intelligentsia's defense of its marginal position under capitalism, it has been generalized into a tool of ideological repression of the lower middle class and working class. Its dominance in modern U.S. thought is precisely why *Citizen Kane* (1941) and the play *Death of a Salesman* are so quintessentially "American."

This sour-grapes version is basically unsatisfactory for its audience because it can only be pessimistic. Disagreement with this version of the myth is a component of the common person's complaint of too much sex and violence on the screen. An earlier version of this expression of disagreement was the frequent complaint that "serious" films were not "uplifting," that is, optimistic about humans.

Part of the appeal of *The Last American Hero* and *Evel Knievel* lies in the fact that they do indeed react against the failure myth. However, being made within the Hollywood system, they rest on a basic lie — that success is possible for the working class through internal virtue pursued by an individual route. These two films reject the excessive attention to the consequences of action found in the failure myth — an attention that leads to despair, cynicism and inaction. In contrast to the anguished modern anti-hero, these films propose, through their primary focus on *means* rather than *consequences,* heroes who represent a healthy reaction against the interior self-examination recommended by bourgeois ideology. They indicate that the hero's problems are not basically subjective and psychological and they reject circular examination of self. The portrait of Marge, for example, makes a distinct break with the tradition that women must examine and question their motives and the future consequences of their actions, or that they must pay if they resolve their problems through action not preceded by agonizing reflection.

These two films can be seen as more "sophisticated" than one might initially expect. Evel is compulsive in creating his own myth from everything at hand, in proclaiming himself a hero while covering the traces of his self-promotion. This gives the picture a certain ironic tone in which one is never quite sure about what is being presented. Is it a straight story, or a straight story overlaid with the director's eye exposing Evel's own comic and amusing neurosis? Actually, it is even more complicated: a straight story that includes Evel's self-parody as he promotes himself to hero status for his own gain. The film says that if you have to hustle for a living you may as well be egomaniacal and megalomaniacal about it. One could never, within the context of the film, begrudge Evel his attitude and actions. Thus Evel's self-inflated comparison of himself with Elvis Presley and John Wayne is not merely laughable, but wry.

HOLLYWOOD'S AUDIENCES AND CRITICS

At this point in considering these films we can see that they are appealing to a working-class audience in their rejection of the failure myth. But at the same time, along with that rejection, by adhering to the idea that success is possible within the present system and that success is individual, the films remain within the prescribed limits of bourgeois ideology. If one pursues the success myth and then fails, one can only blame oneself. Chinoy comments:

> To the extent that workers focus blame for their failure to rise above the level of wage labor upon themselves rather than upon the institutions that govern the pursuit of wealth or upon the persons who control those institutions, American society escapes the consequences of its own contradictions.

In order to get a better perspective on the relation of the success/failure myth to film, a further consideration of the Hollywood film audience is in order.

While auteur criticism provided a valuable corrective to the previously dominant snobbish dismissal of Hollywood film, auteurism has prompted a confused view of the Hollywood audience. A ready example of this is provided by a film journal's self-promotional statement: "The *Journal of Popular Film* does not ignore the unalterable fact that the box-office, the American public, has determined the developmental thrust of its films." The motivation behind a journal of popular film is a healthy reaction against the elitist high-culture notion that the mass audience has an inherent mediocrity (at best) in its taste and intellectual capacity, and that a film's popularity proves its aesthetic inferiority. Yet the defense of popular culture, as presented above, repeats a basic high-culture assumption: that consumers determine the products and services they consume. (Or, as the highbrow critic puts it: the lowbrow public gets the crap it deserves.)

Of course the idea of consumer determination is widely promoted by merchants of all types of goods and services: celebrating a democracy of taste ("consumers are free to choose"), they justify a low-level product. The only conclusion that can be drawn from following this deteriorated line of reasoning is that the majority of people are childish in their selection of art and entertainment.

It is curious that film criticism persists in following such a weak line of thought in the face of the widely-publicized "consumer revolt" of recent years. At the same time that it has become household wisdom that U.S. consumers do not have safe and environmentally adequate (much less reliable and economical) automobiles, nutritious food, safe and inexpensive pharmaceuticals, and so on, film criticism has taken little notice of the reason for poor-quality consumer goods and services — the capitalist system — nor has it applied a critique based on this understanding to its own object of study: the consumption of film entertainment.

The unexamined "unalterable fact" that "the American public has determined the developmental thrust of its films" turns out to be, on modest consideration , not a fact at all but an opinionated wish and a false one. Run-of-the-mill mainstream U.S. sociology long ago documented the common-sense observation that choice in consumption is determined principally by the external condition of availability and secondarily by the subjective condition of sensibility, which rests on cultural atmosphere and training before the age of consent.[6]

Any statement about U.S. film audiences that assumes a free-market economy and a consumer free will and free choice is as false as a lemonade-stand analogy used to explain contemporary capitalism.

Another frequently unexamined idea about the film-audience relationship is that movies mirror their audience. This is often qualified by the notice that the image is distorted. However, films are not distorting mirrors, for a distorting mirror exaggerates a whole. Rather, they are selective mirrors which do not usually serve as overt indoctrination (as in jingoistic war films). Films also state covertly through selection. Thus we must ask of any film not merely what is presented but also what is left out, particularly in key areas such as class, race and sex. We can say, shifting to André Bazin's metaphor, that films are a window on the world, only if we also say that the film almost always opens on a vista dominated by upper-middle-class white heterosexual males who accept the prevailing orthodoxies even when the film is about how miserable they are in such a situation.

While investigating a working-class community, Herbert J. Gans found that its members tended to select what was self-confirming or culturally self-validating when given images in the mass media.[7] In the context of my argument, it would seem that the working-class attitude to the hero is a combination of romantic acceptance *and* a pre-set cynicism that discounts exaggeration. From this point of view, the ironic stance inherent in *Evel Knievel* and *The Last American Hero* would not interrupt audience response but actually mesh with it. Junior and Evel are accepted as heroes, but since their portrayal is qualified through irony, the audience can accept this too, as an internal debunking of sorts.

In a parallel case, Shostak argues that the popularity of exposé journalism among the working class (for example, the old *Confidential* and the current *National Enquirer*) can be attributed in part to a desire to put celebrities in their place. The typical newspaper sports pages exhibit this tendency, for over time they both build the heroism of an athlete and expose an achilles heel of hot temper, egotism or excessive partying in season. Precisely because of their directors' ironic stance to their heroes, neither *Evel Knievel* (dir. Marvin Chomsky) nor *The Last American Hero* (dir. Lamont Johnson) can be interrogated for clear answers to the social problems they raise.

Just as the working-class film audience selects what is self-validating in the media, so too does the middle class. A striking example is provided by Robert Warshow's classic essay, "The Gangster as Tragic Hero," which describes the comforting nature of the failure myth as presented in the gangster film. On a close reading, Warshow's analysis far better describes the appeal of the gangster film to the liberal middle-class intellectual than to anyone else.[8]

Within the Hollywood film, about the only healthy look at the success and failure dynamic in a social perspective including class terms is found in Preston Sturges's comedies of the 1940s, perhaps because Sturges himself had so thoroughly internalized the contradictions of success and failure. What is most revealing about Hollywood success/failure films is what they do not show. First, they ignore the absence of opportunity and its root source in the very nature of capitalist social organization. Even in those rare cases where a film does depict absence of opportunity, as in Raoul Walsh's *The Roaring Twenties* (1939) where returning veterans from World War I face unemployment and therefore turn to crime, the dominating message is Warshow's "comforting failure."

The second omission is the feasibility of group action and the possibility of defining success as not merely rising above one's fellows but rising *with* them. The closest Hollywood generally comes to any depiction of group achievement is always with an *in extremis* situation: the stranded platoon, the sinking ship, the lifeboat. (Such films usually present some variant of the theory of "natural selection" since most of the group dies by the end.) Interestingly enough, such films are also generally the only ones that explicitly deal with class differences as a theme. The exception that proves the rule is the Hollywood films of European directors such as Fritz Lang, Jean Renoir, and Ernst Lubitsch. In this context, *The Last American Hero* offers an interesting comparison with *Red Line — 7000* (1965), a film that critic Andrew Sarris referred to as "quintessentially and self-consciously Hawksian" and which treats stock-car racing with a studied indifference to the drivers' class backgrounds.

When we talk about film audience we always mean an aggregate of various audiences, which can be described by distinguishing their nationality, language, sex, class, race, religion, age, occupation or political views. In other words, there is never a homogeneous audience for a Hollywood film. To say this is not to argue for a nominalism claiming every individual's response is totally unique. Obviously, some degree of generalization is necessary for critical thought. If we recognize that there are many "audiences," it allows us to avoid the error of overgeneralization in using such terms as "the American film-viewing public" or the "universal appeal of director X" or "America's sex symbol" without further specification. When reviewers or critics generalize about "audience" they are actually revealing the most chauvinistic ethnocentricity — elevating their own sex, class, race and other attributes to the level of the universal.

The challenge of changing the cinema demands a deep probing of several areas by film students and filmmakers. A radical cinema must consider exactly who is the audience for a film and face up to variety within that audience. It must also consider the audience's tendency both to accept and reject parts of the film on the basis of what it finds to be self-validating. This means that new ways of overcoming such acceptance and rejection must be found to deliver a radical message. Finally, film alone does not change consciousness. We must directly link the struggle to change consciousness with the struggle to change the external conditions of the audience's life.

NOTES

[1] Ely Chinoy, *Automobile Workers and the American Dream* (New York: Random House, 1955).

[2] Arthur B. Shostak, *Blue-Collar Life* (Englewood Cliffs, New Jersey: Prentice-Hall, 1964).

[3] For an excellent political analysis of *Dirty Harry* along these lines, see Anthony Chase's "The Strange Romance of Dirty Harry..." in *The Velvet Lighttrap,* (January 1972).

[4] See Mirra Komarovsky, *Blue-Collar Marriage* (New York: Random House, 1962); Lee Rainwater, *Workingman's Wife* (New York: Oceana Publications, 1959).

[5] Tom Wolfe, *The Kandy-Kolored Tangerine-Flake Streamline Baby* (New York: Simon and Schuster, 1966).

[6] For a concise essay on the subject, see C. Wright Mills, "The Cultural Apparatus," in his *Power, Politics and People* (New York: Oxford, 1963).

[7] Herbert J. Gans, *The Urban Villagers* (New York: The Free Press, 1962).

[8] Robert Warshow, *The Immediate Experience* (New York: Atheneum, 1975).

CHAPTER 4.

Star Wars: "Not So Long Ago, Not So Far Away"

DAN RUBEY

George Lucas's enormously popular *Star Wars* (1977) plugs into the central nervous system of its audience by mixing a North American love of machinery with the heroic myths and dreams of western European civilization.[1] It is a technological fairy tale that reflects in the symbolic language of its images the desires and ambiguities produced by living inside a machine-oriented society supported by anachronistic ideologies of individual heroism and metaphysical justification.

Star Wars embraces technology in order to enjoy the sensations of power and exhilaration and then falls back on heroic individual action and the metaphysical, non-rational Force to solve the problems of eroded values and depersonalized experiences created by that technology. The film's combination of traditional models of individual combat with the technology of electronic warfare re-romanticizes war, creating a new set of heroic images appropriate to a technological age and the kind of electronic warfare waged in Vietnam. In the end, the meaning of *Star Wars* and much of its appeal depend on the ways in which the striking special effects reinforce the fantasies and mythic echoes of the plot.

THE VISUAL IMAGES

The visual aesthetic of *Star Wars* is a machine aesthetic, one that invests machine surfaces with the life and interest denied human forms. The film uses images of size, speed, sharp contrasts and violent action to create a visual counterpart to the plot structures in which the young rebels are menaced by monstrous and powerful enemies.

The creators of *Star Wars* meant its visual and aural experience to be as overwhelming as possible. The 70mm film and Dolby quadraphonic sound amplify the impact of the images and the volume of the sound, enclosing the viewer in the world of the film. The general visual pattern involves contrasts between overwhelmingly large images and vulnerably small ones.

In the opening shot, for example, a tiny spaceship is pursued by another ship, an enormous one, which slowly enters the screen from the right top corner, moves into the center of the screen, and finally fills it entirely, engulfing the smaller ship. This visual dichotomy of small and large reinforces the dichotomy of good-young-less-powerful versus evil-older-more-powerful. These dichotomies together organize the plot, and help the audience participate emotionally in the vulnerability of Luke and the Princess, hero and heroine.

Most of the film's special effects involve either explosions or simulations of dazzling speed and acceleration, usually in the form of bright light against a black background, as in the explosion of the Death Star or the jump into hyperspace. Stark contrasts of light and dark, black and white, are used to organize shots: the white ships against the black void of space, Darth Vader's black robes and Luke and the Princess's white ones. When the colors are not simply black and white, they are usually restricted to metallic gold and silver, the colors of the world of spaceships and robots. These patterns and the ear-shattering noises create a machine ambience for the film: they create a basically inhuman atmosphere — hard-edged, dry and metallic. In images of the enormous battleship, or the Death Star, or Darth Vader's face-mask, technology initially seems menacing. But every frame of the film celebrates machines and the speed and power they seem to promise, and the special effects create a technological kick for the audience.

The special effects of *Star Wars* derive largely from *2001: a Space Odyssey* (1968), but a second-generation computer technology makes them much more sophisticated.[2] Lucas's effects are classier and he can do more with them, particularly in simulating three-dimensional movement. But *2001* director Stanley Kubrick introduced new kinds of special effects to try to create visual images of a different order of reality and to force his audiences to participate in the disorientation of the characters in the film. Lucas simply uses special effects to heighten the intensity of his combat sequences, to make them super-real, while at the same time keeping us firmly grounded in the familiar world of World War II dogfights and police-movie car chases.

The special effects in *2001* move us out of the technological world portrayed in the film and create feelings of otherness, other spaces, other kinds of experiences. In *Star Wars* the special effects involve us more deeply in the technological, machine-oriented ambience of the film, producing visceral effects that heighten our involvement in the conventional patterns of the fantasy structure.

Compare, for example, the shot in *2001* where the space pod with Bowman in it rushes between the converging horizontal and vertical planes of colored lights in deep space, and the parallel shot in *Star Wars* where Luke and the other pilots attack the Death Star by flying at great speed down a narrow trench in the surface of the space station. In both films the tremendous speed and acceleration produce excitement and a touch of fear in the audience. The film *2001* simply presents the visual effect, with only a vague context for it (''Beyond Infinity''), and this lack of definition increases the audience's sense of disorientation. Bowman's helplessness inside the machine, his inability to control or even understand what is happening to him, gives the scene a powerful sense of ambiguity and anxiety. On the one hand the pod is his only protection in this tremendously threatening environment, the only thing that is keeping him alive and connected to reality. But on the other hand the pod itself seems like a trap, something encapsulating him, keeping him from the world outside. The very word ''pod'' suggests a seed pod, and the whole sequence becomes an experience of birth or rebirth.

In the comparable scene in *Star Wars*, the combat context creates a focus for the feelings of anxiety and excitement generated by the visual effects, and transforms the anxiety into feelings of aggression and violence. Since the feelings of unease are given a specific focus on the plot level — the desire for the destruction of the space station — the explosion of the Death Star serves as catharsis. The sequence generates a desire to use the machine more skillfully, not to escape from it. For Kubrick, the dependence on technology is simply one stage in evolution, and the obelisks represent an extra-human reality; in *Star Wars* the Force is a better bombsight.

In *Star Wars* the special effects — the speed, lasers, explosions, the jump into hyperspace, the noise — excite and satisfy the audience almost apart from any connection to the narrative line. The constant contrasts of large and small call up feelings of vulnerability and powerlessness which in turn reflect the frustrations (general and specific) of the youthful audience the film is aimed at. These frustrations are then satisfied by the feelings of enormous power created by the film's machine aesthetic and the special effects of speed, power and violence. The machine ambience of the film provides an illusion of power and control, the ability to escape the limitations of our bodies. It enables us to take on the nature of our machines and share in their power and relative invulnerability — the bionic fantasy of television shows and comic books. Machines move as fast as we can think, erasing the gap between thought and performance, desire and satisfaction, making us into comic book superheroes.

But this fusion with the machine and machine sensibility has some strongly dehumanizing side-effects, partly as a result of placing the machine between ourselves and what it acts on, and in part traceable to the nature of the film medium itself. As sophisticated viewers of film we have learned to pay attention solely to what is presented to us on the screen and not to speculate about what is not shown. (Less cinematically-sophisticated audiences interrupt the film to ask questions about characters who have disappeared from the screen.[3]) So when ships or planets blow up, we do not think about the people who presumably die in those explosions. The special effects tend to exist for their own sake, regardless of their function in the plot, and we take them in without examining their implications.

As a visual image the destruction of the planet Alderaan looks very much like the explosion of the Death Star, and Obi-Wan Kenobi's brief attack of heartburn does not convince us that something tragic has happened. We do not experience the deaths of the people on the planet, and thus those people do not exist in the film. The explosions are visual experiences to be enjoyed in aesthetic terms. Everything is a visual trip, an aesthetic experience.

This act of turning war into aesthetic experience seems connected to the increased use of airplanes in World War II, and to the images of the air war created in both the news media and in films about the war. World War II films tend to move in one of two directions — towards infantry "war is hell" movies that record the blood and guts suffering of the war on the ground, and occasionally its effect on the civilian population; or towards air-war, fighter-pilot films that romanticize war and combat and take place in the more abstract and generalized realm of the sky. These differences reflect real differences in the two modes of warfare, that of the ground troops who have no escape from the war and its implications, and the pilots who live in protected rear areas and fly to the war as if going to work, experiencing combat as moments of great intensity and exhilaration spaced out by respites in comparatively comfortable surroundings.

The actual physical detachment from the realities of war on the ground lends itself to the aesthetization of war and to a psychic detachment from what is really going on, which is evident in the treatment of the war in the media. In a Movietone News film clip reproduced in Marcel Ophul's film on the Nuremberg trials, *Memory of Justice* (1975), the narrator describes footage of the night fire-bombing of Dresden, perhaps the greatest Allied atrocity of the war, as "magnificent bombing shots." And, in fact, aesthetically the footage is very beautiful. But such a judgment completely leaves out any translation of what those images actually mean — the burning and destruction of the city and the hideous deaths of 35,000 civilians.

These air-war films are the lineal ancestors of the combat sequences in *Star Wars*. Lucas used actual footage of dogfights in those films to construct his own sequences. Lucas explains:

> The dogfight sequence was extremely hard to cut and edit. We had story-boards that we had taken from old movies intercut with pilots talking and stuff, so you could edit the whole sequence in real time.[4]

But despite its roots in World War II films, the sophisticated level of technology in *Star Wars* — the use of computers, missiles and lasers, the flashing space-age control panels, the beeping radar gun-sights — actually reflects the air war in Vietnam, the technological warfare of what pilots called "the Blue Machine," the U.S. Air Force. *Star Wars* is the first war movie of a new age of electronic combat, a prediction of what war will feel like for combatants completely encapsulated in technology, like the soldiers in Robert Heinlein's *Starship Troopers* (written in 1959).

The dogfights and one-man fighters are a romantic attempt to recapture the glamor of WWII films and disassociate ourselves from the destructive role that our bombers and rockets actually played in Vietnam by projecting that aspect of the war onto the Death Star. By associating the bad guys with the heavily armored Death Star, which destroys a helpless planet, and the good guys with the small one-man fighters, *Star Wars* uses an image of ourselves from the past as a defense against our more recent history.

But this separation is not so simple. The technology of the air war in Vietnam was a natural outgrowth of the more primitive machines of World War II, and the attitudes of the pilots about what they were doing in Vietnam was fundamentally the same as the attitude expressed in the Movietone News film of the fire-bombing of Dresden. Totally cut off from the effects of what they were doing by the speed and accuracy of their machines, the pilots viewed their bombing runs as aesthetic experiences, as exciting and exhilarating moments in their lives — the experience that *Star Wars* recreates through its use of special effects. In Peter Davis's *Hearts and Minds* (1974), one of the pilots says that the bombing runs were like "a singer singing an aria." The pilots took pride in their technical expertise; they found the excitement of seeing the bombs explode to be "incredible" or "thrilling, deeply satisfying." But they never saw any people, or any blood. As one flyer says, "You could never see the people. You never saw any blood. You could never hear any screams. It was very clean. I was a technician."

Robert Lifton argues in his study of Vietnam veterans that technological warfare like the American air war in Vietnam has an avoidance of guilt built into it. Lifton says, "Increasing technicizing of the war makes certain that the people we kill are outside of our immediate and imaginative vision."[5] In this kind of war, in which the killers and their victims are separated by such vast distances, the only awareness of the "enemy" comes as electronic feedback in the form of blips on a screen. This technological detachment from the realities of war makes possible what Lifton calls *"numbed warfare:* killing with a near-total separation of act from idea."[6] The sensory equipment of the machines becomes an extension of the pilot's sensory equipment — a substitute for it — and along with it the pilots seem to take on the machine's lack of moral sensibility as well.

Fred Branfman records a statement by a flyer in a *Washington Monthly* article on the era of the Blue Machine in Laos:

> You become a part of the machine as you really do it. Guys who fly keep their professionality. . . . I haven't bombed now for three months and I really feel out of shape. The key is to be able to bomb without really thinking about it, automatically, to take evasive action. . . instinctively — to be able to do this you have to be flying every day.[7]

This statement is a good description of Luke's final attack on the Death Star, the scene in which he switches off his gun-sight and releases the missile instinctively, in a fantasy of bionic fusion with his ship, a fusion made possible by the Force.

Star Wars reproduces the sensory experience and the excitement of technological warfare with its use of special effects, and then uses the plot to provide a romance-fantasy structure that glamorizes and justifies this kind of experience. The film articulates and feeds on its audience's feelings of frustration and desires for escape, mobility and power. It satisfies those frustrations and desires with conventional fantasies about good and evil, the family romance, vague mystical forces that guide and give meaning, and images of war and combat as metaphors for competition and individuality. In the process the film endorses both the traditional structures of racism, sexism and social hierarchy that have helped to create and maintain those frustrations, and the monocular attitudes towards technology that form an important part of the whole ideological package.

FANTASY SYSTEMS AND THE BIAS OF MEDIEVAL ROMANCE

Star Wars is not a science fiction film: it is a combination of what used to be called "sword and sorcery" and "space opera," and is now usually lumped together as "epic fantasy." Lucas says he wanted to make a space fantasy in the genre of Edgar Rice Burroughs rather than Stanley Kubrick's *2001*. He wanted to do a film for "kids" and "the kids in all of us" that would restore "the fairy tales and dragons and

Tolkien and all the *real* heroes'' left out of science fiction and films in general since the 1950s.

Lucas wants to turn ''some ten-year-old kid'' on to outer space and the possibilities of romance and adventure in space exploration: ''What we really need to do is to colonize the next galaxy, get away from the hard facts of 2001 and get on the romantic side of it.'' When we colonize Mars, we will ''go with Stanley's ships but hopefully we are going to be carrying my laser sword and have the Wookie at our side.'' That is, the actual exploration and colonization of space Lucas hopes for in the future will be accomplished by the realistic technology of *2001*, but *Star Wars* will provide the fantasies and motives of the explorers. Lucas says, ''I would feel very good if someday they colonize Mars when I am 93 years old or whatever, and the leader of the first colony says: 'I really did it because I was hoping there would be a Wookie up here.' ''[8]

These ingenuous statements about fantasy and kids and the irrational serve to disguise Lucas's conservative ideological bias, his assumption that humanity's greatest challenge still lies in expansion and the conquest of new territorial frontiers. Space is the new west, the new frontier to be opened and exploited. Instead of using our energies and resources to deal with problems that we have created within the frontiers we already have, we can continue to direct them outward in fantasies of endless worlds and limitless expansion.

Lucas ignores the ideological character of these views by claiming he is working inside an eternal tradition of fairy tales and myths stretching from Homer's *Odyssey* to John Ford's westerns. He says of the kind of adventure he is trying to recreate for kids today:

> I call it the fairy tale or the myth. It is a children's story in history and you go back to the *Odyssey*.... the myths which existed in high adventure, and an exotic far-off land which was always that place over the hill, Camelot, Robin Hood, Treasure Island. That sort of stuff that is always big adventure out there somewhere. It came all the way down through the western.[9]

But Lucas's picture of an unbroken tradition of adventure mythology stretching from Homer to John Ford ignores both the specific meanings these stories had for the societies which created them and the important differences between them. Myths and fantasies are not eternal; they are historical.

To trace the background of its genre briefly, the plot of *Star Wars* is a chivalric *romance* plot, and chivalric romance as a specific form in the European west was first developed in twelfth-century France, by authors such as Chrétien de Troyes, and remained widely popular in Europe throughout the sixteenth century. The form was revived in the nineteenth century by poets such as Tennyson (whose *Idyls of the King* is a reworking of the fifteenth-century *Morte d'Arthur* of Malory), and writers like the socialist William Morris (in his *Well at the World's End*). These works and others like them filtered medieval romances though a gauze of nineteenth-century concerns, and in turn became the sources of the sword-and-sorcery fantasies of the twentieth century, among them Tolkien's *Ring* series, begun in the 1930s, and contemporary works like Michael Moorcock's *Sword Rulers* series. So, even leaving aside the relationship between chivalric romance and romantic (as opposed to realistic) novels, romance has been one of the most successful and long-lived of the fictional structures of western culture.

Romance developed originally in a period when the rigid class structure of the first stages of medieval feudalism began to relax enough for the formation of a commercial middle class and a lower order of nobility within the aristocracy itself. This lower order of nobility was formed primarily by the gradual granting of aristocratic status to the military class, the knights. In the twelfth and thirteenth centuries this class came to share the legal status but not the power and wealth of the great lords, and it filled an increasingly bureaucratic and administrative role in the growing governmental apparatus dominated by the lords.

Within this social framework, Arthurian romances like those of Chrétien (stories about the British King Arthur and his knights) articulated the desires of these lesser nobles for upward social mobility within the rigidly hierarchical feudal system. The fantasy structure of romance in this period depends on a combination of Germanic feudal military codes and the newly rediscovered Roman idea of the state and the Roman conception of imperial power as based on "popular sovereignty." It modifies earlier forms of Christianity, in which God forbade the taking of Christian lives, into a newer style of imperial Christianity in which the state became the supreme moral force on earth and could order men to kill soldiers from rival Christian states in its name. Within this fantasy structure, military action for God and country provides the path to recognition, fame and acceptance (that is, social mobility), and combat becomes a symbolic rite of passage that has social as well as individual implications.

Romance fantasy was potentially revolutionary in the sense that it expressed desires for the overthrow of existing social hierarchies (often expressed through the reversal of male/female roles inherent in courtly love). But it finally served to support the existing hierarchy because the lesser nobility wanted to rise within the system and enjoy the fruits of being at the top rather than overthrow the system entirely, as the social conservatism of romance indicates. So as a genre, romance recognizes and expresses revolutionary impulses, but finally defuses them and renders them harmless to the social structure as it exists.

This fundamental orientation persists within the form. When

medieval romance (and medievalism in general) was revived in the nineteenth century, it was often used to suggest an alternative to industrialism and capitalism and their tendencies towards the destruction of human values. But this alternative had implicit within it a number of conservative and even reactionary strains. As Raymond Williams argues, this particular kind of critique of capitalism, with its nostalgia for past golden ages, knights in armor and flowing robes carries within it a system of received social values which, if they become active, "at once spring to the defence of certain kinds of order, certain social hierarchies and moral stabilities, which have a feudal ring but a more relevant and more dangerous contemporary application."[10]

This implicit conservative and reactionary strain is present in *Star Wars*, and undercuts its tone of youthful rebelliousness. The final scene of the film, in which Luke and Han Solo walk between rows of uniformed soldiers at rigid attention to receive their medals, clearly echoes the march of Hitler, Himmler, and Lutze to the Nuremberg memorial in Leni Riefenstahl's *Triumph of the Will.*[11] The grins that the heroes exchange with Princess Leia are meant to assure us that these three at least aren't taking all this military pomp very seriously. But since the scene and its totalitarian, fascist overtones grow so naturally out of the rest of the fantasies and images in the film, it seems fair to ask whether the grins really undercut this image or simply allow it to function for us in much the same way that Riefenstahl's original image functioned.

The scene confirms all the hierarchical and militaristic values that have characterized the bad guys up to this point, and applies them to the heroes. Martial tones dominate the scene and the music that accompanies it. The military position of attention and the practice of lining troops up in precisely even rows is an attempt to deny the weakness and vulnerability of the human body, to make human beings hard-edged and precise like their weapons. Up to this conclusion, the bad guys have been associated with their rigid body-armor, impenetrable mask-like helmets, and heavily armored Death Star. When so drastic a reversal or transition takes place at the end, it becomes important to try to understand the nature of that transition.

In romance, the generation gap functions as a symbolic representation of the split between upper and lower social levels, or between those with more power and wealth and those with less. The desire to grow up and escape the frustrations and restrictions of childhood by becoming an adult is symbolically analogous to the desire for upward social mobility. This connection falsely attaches the sense of inevitability, which is a natural part of the process of growing up, to the desire for social mobility. Assuming there is no accident, everyone grows up; not everyone rises within the social system.

Luke represents both the youth/age and class splits: he is young, living with his aunt and uncle. As we see him initially (and as he sees himself), he is a farmer, an unsophisticated, rural hick living on an unimportant planet in a backwater of the universe. Luke feels oppressed on the farm. His uncle needs his labor and refuses to let him go to the academy and become a fighter pilot, thus refusing to let him both grow up and move up socially. The youth/age, peasant/aristocrat split takes on another dimension, that of labor/management. Thus Luke's sense of frustration can resonate for the audience on a number of levels, depending on the circumstances of their own lives; any or all three of these levels can be present at the same time. Luke's experience in the film provides a generalized fantasy vehicle through which the real experiences of the audience can be organized, "understood," and solved.

In the course of the film Luke grows up by taking part in military action, moving simultaneously into a more cosmopolitan, aristocratic, big-city world. Indicatively, the language of the rural culture differs from the aristocratic one: Luke, his uncle and aunt speak plainly; aristocratic characters like Princess Leia and Ben (Obi-Wan) Kenobi speak in the highflown, ornamental rhetoric of romance and epic fantasy. This language can seem corny and even campy, but Lucas defends it as straight.[12] Their dialogue gives the aristocratic, cosmopolitan world Luke is trying to enter a heightened reality above that of everyday life, and Lucas's instincts are sound on the point.

But if Luke is to rise socially, his success must be explained. A fantasy system like that of romance, which wishes on the one hand to allow for social mobility but on the other to retain the hierarchical status quo, must contain within it some explanation for the fact that everyone in the society does not rise. If everyone rose to the top, those at the top could no longer feel superior to anyone; but on the other hand, if eligible people do not rise, then the social system itself appears unjust and the hero's success arbitrary and meaningless. These two requirements generate an ideology of individualism. The romance hero can win fame, glory and the boss's daughter and still not threaten the hierarchical status quo because he is a uniquely-talented individual.

In medieval romance the problem is solved by disguise and mistaken identity. The hero is placed in a situation in which his aristocratic identity is not known. He wins his victory and social acceptance through his own strength and courage, and then reveals his identity at the end. This solution serves the dual function of proving that merit alone is enough to succeed but at the same time vindicating the social system by equating rank and merit in his own person. In *Star Wars*, a film which comes out of a U.S. culture that officially denies the importance of class, the problem is solved by racism.

ROBOTS, WOOKIES AND RACISM

The structures of racism in *Star Wars* form an alternative, parallel hierarchy, so that the hero who is oppressed and *inferior* in one system can be *superior* in the other. Luke is on the bottom of the power and age hierarchies, but he is on top in the race hierarchy. He is human, as opposed to the non-human races, and most importantly, as opposed to the robots. And Mark Hamill's blond blue-eyed all-American Wasp good looks reinforce these racial resonances. In his position at the top of the race hierarchy, Luke acts kindly and generously to those under him (specifically in his treatment of the two robots), behaving as he wished his uncle would behave to him, and as the audience wishes their superiors would behave to them. This behavior marks Luke as a good person, and his final success says that good people can, by their own conduct, overcome the unattractive aspects of the hierarchical system and make it function satisfactorily for everyone.

The price paid for this affirmation of the hierarchical system is a corollary dehumanization of those in lower positions. Thus a hierarchy that we perceive as unfair and oppressive when seen from Luke's point of view (the virtual slavery of his position in his uncle's house) becomes fair and matter-of-fact when Luke becomes master of the two robots. The robots (or 'droids for *androids*) are science-fiction Stepin Fetch Its. They do the real work of this society but are discriminated against. This is an issue raised explicitly in the bar scene when the bartender says he doesn't serve their kind, and earlier when C-3PO (See Threepio in Lucas's novel) says he "can't abide those Jawas." The issue of racism has been explicit in science-fiction treatments of androids at least since the early 1950s, when Theodore Sturgeon published a story in *Galaxy* in which scientists had created a race of androids so similar to humans that the only distinction was the androids' lack of a navel. The story revolved around discrimination against the androids and the rape of an android woman who conceived a child as a result. The point here is not that the treatment of robots in *Star Wars* is racist, but that the film makes use of and supports racist habits of thought when it divides its characters up into hierarchical levels based on their physical attributes. The fact that the film is forced to use racism to support and justify its fantasy structure should call that structure into question and make us examine its implications closely.

The robots and the Wookie perform another function in the fantasy system of *Star Wars*. They serve as non-competitive, non-sexual comrades and friends, one of the chief emotional satisfactions of racism. We would like friends and allies who have *our* best interests at heart, but people prefer a leading role in their own play to a secondary one in ours. In fantasy, members of lower classes or races can fill that supporting role because they cannot compete with us. In the fantasy at least, they accept their inferior position without question and assume the role of loyal follower and trusted side-kick. American literature is full of Indians and blacks who fill this role (James Fenimore Cooper's Indians, *Huckleberry Finn*'s Nigger Jim, and so on). In an adventure fantasy you don't want subordinates striking for higher wages while you are being mashed in the garbage crusher, so you make them robots or Wookies who cannot move up in the hierarchy. Wookies and robots are not eligible to court princesses and they do not need money or glory. In the final ceremony only the white male heroes get medals; the Wookie walks down the aisle and then steps aside to join the robots and applauds like everyone else.

This focus on the individual and the recognition of individual merit as a validation of the social system itself requires a plot in which individual (rather than collective or group) action can serve a dramatic purpose. The plot of *Star Wars* hinges on the fact that the imperial space station, the Death Star, has one vulnerable point, the exhaust vent into which one small rocket manned by one heroic pilot can shoot a missile and destroy the entire installation. So the outcome of the rebellion and the fate of the universe hangs on the outcome of one act by one man.

By placing such an apocalyptic weight on the actions of one individual, the film demonstrates both the importance of individualism to the fantasy system and the difficulty in the late 1970s of creating a plot in which individual action can have convincing consequences for the society as a whole. Laser swords and guns and one-man fighters are the weapons of *Star Wars* because they are the weapons of romantic individual combat, the equipment of fantasies in which things can be changed, outcomes significantly affected, by one person. This kind of individualized military combat (like medieval jousts) is an ideal plot vehicle for romance fantasy because it serves as a romantic and morally-justified screen for the more specific forms of competition which are the avenues to success and social mobility in the real world, and which cannot be so easily romanticized. Combat provides a setting for individual victories that singles out the hero and supports him with the moral force of the whole community. By setting things up this way, Lucas denies that people need to work collectively, or long, or even very hard for change. Individual heroism, at one spot, in one heroic moment, can win the war.

The relationship between Luke and Han Solo has particular interest in these terms. Initially Han is smarter, cooler, more sophisticated and more competent than Luke. His cynicism and worldliness serve as a foil for Luke's romanticism and naivete. But as Luke's vague romanticism turns into Force-directed idealism, Han's cynicism turns into a negative kind of individualism which undercuts him and eliminates him as a serious rival for the audience's affection and approval.

Han's withdrawal from the final battle serves two purposes. First, it functions as a criticism of real individualism, the kind of individualism which threatens society because it rejects society's values and imagines the possibility of a life outside its approval, a possibility that romance invariably rejects. Han's decision to take the money and run places him in an inferior position to Luke within the value system of the film and reverses their previous places in the hierarchy. Second, since Han leaves the collective pool of cannon fodder, he can avoid the deaths of the other pilots and return at the last minute to support Luke by keeping Darth Vader off his back while Luke scores.

SEXISM AND THE RESCUE FANTASY

As Princess Leia's withdrawal from the action indicates, this world of romantic combat is structured around male relationships and male-oriented viewpoints. Women exist primarily to provide motivations for male activity, to act as spectators, or to serve as mediators between different levels in the male hierarchy. When Luke's aunt isn't stuffing artichokes into the Cuisinart, she serves as a mediator between Luke and his uncle and then as a motive for revenge when Luke returns home and finds her charred body, in a scene taken from John Ford's *The Searchers* (1956). Princess Leia, despite her attractive spunkiness and toughness, basically fills the same male-oriented roles. She is the traditional damsel in distress — her capture by Darth Vader begins the film and provides the motivation for Ben Kenobi's return and Luke's rescue mission. Although she does grab a laser at one point and fire a few shots, she is dependent on her male rescuers, and the only action she initiates during the rescue almost gets them killed in a garbage crusher. Her most memorable line, repeated over and over by her holographic image, is "Help me, Obi-Wan Kenobi. You are my only hope."

While Luke goes on from his initial helplessness and rescue by Kenobi to take a more heroic role, Princess Leia recedes into the background. During the attack on the Death Star she is merely a spectator. In the final scene, dressed in a décolleté gown, which symbolizes her role as a sexual prize, she stands on the steps between her father at the top and the young heroes at the bottom, mediating the gap between them and mitigating the scene's overt militarism. Her position in the system is clear. Her existence makes the rebel hierarchy a good hierarchy because she is a path to the top. By winning her favor, Luke can rise within the system. But her position is fixed. She is the prize which coerces men into joining the system, and she is the maternal figure who looks on approvingly while boys undergo their rites of initiation and become men.

This role assignment mirrors the ways in which sexism frustrates women in male-oriented societies, but the system is not without its adverse effects on men as well. Women are denied autonomy and a chance to participate on an equal level in the activities valued most highly by the society. They are pushed into the roles of maternal figures or sexual objects, encouraged to see themselves primarily in terms of men and male activities. But by identifying women with the system, men have ensured that when the inevitable feelings of entrapment and betrayal arise, they will be directed at women rather than faced realistically. This identification impels men back into the adolescent, narcissistic male camaraderie which Leslie Fiedler sees as characteristic of American fiction in *Love and Death in the American Novel,* and which Molly Haskell describes as a dominant theme of U.S. films like *Butch Cassidy and the Sundance Kid* in her book *From Reverence to Rape.*

In *Star Wars* the relationships that Luke has with Ben Kenobi and Han Solo are much more important and rewarding than his relationship with Princess Leia. The sexual implications in that relationship are undercut by Leia's maternal behavior to Luke and the focusing of her romantic attention on the older Han Solo. (In Lucas's novel Han Solo is described as "perhaps five years older than Luke, perhaps a dozen — it was difficult to tell.") Princess Leia is most attractive early in the film, when she functions inside this world of male camaraderie as one of the guys, and less attractive and interesting later as she takes on the female roles assigned to her.

In their roles, the two women in the film form two maternal poles that Luke moves between, one middle-class, the other aristocratic. Luke's movement from a lower-class culture into an aristocratic one reflects what Freud called the "family romance," one of the central fantasy structures of the film. Historically, the family romance-fantasy structure first became prominent in medieval chivalric romances in thirteenth-century English works written in or translated into English for audiences that were largely middle-class. In bourgeois romance the family romance-fantasy structure is a substitute for the overt Oedipal rebellion of the adulterous triangles (Tristan, Isolde, and Mark; Lancelot, Guinevere, and Arthur) that characterize French romances written for the aristocracy. But in structural terms both fantasy systems are parallel — both reflect the desire of those in a lower position in the social hierarchy to rise within the system.

Briefly, in the family romance fantasy a child exchanges his or her real parents for more aristocratic ones, imagining himself or herself the orphaned or kidnapped child of royalty. The fantasy reflects the growing child's disillusionment with its real parents and their limitations, and substitutes for them memories from an earlier period in which the parents seemed unique and omnipotent. These idealized figures from the past then become omnipotent parents with whom the child can identify, protectors against the various threats the child is beginning to encounter in the real world, among them the Oedipal issues. The fantasy serves to repress Oedipal conflicts through regression to earlier, less mature conflicts, substituting pre-Oedipal fantasies of parental omnipotence and total identification of the child with the parent for more threatening fantasies of Oedipal sexual desires and rebellion. Rescue fantasies are an inherent part of the family romance, both in the form of rescue of the child by the omnipotent parents, and rescue (or avenging) of the parents by the child. The fantasy has a strong social dimension: lower-class children imagine aristocratic parents, aristocratic children imagine pirate or gypsy ancestors.[13]

In *Star Wars* Luke exchanges his foster parents, who represent the world of middle-class values and dullness, for more aristocratic ones — his dead father (now revealed as a fighter pilot, a Jedi knight) and Obi-Wan Kenobi, who functions as a grandfatherly substitute for his father. His mother is not mentioned since Princess Leia functions as an Oedipal mother, the woman he desires but who treats him like a child — "Aren't you a little short for a Storm Trooper?" — and the woman he rescues but does not possess sexually. The Force then symbolizes the lost sense of parental omnipotence, the child's pre-adolescent, pre-Oedipal sense of his parents as all-powerful and all-protecting.

But sexuality does not disappear entirely — adult sexuality between autonomous equals is replaced by sadistic fantasies of abduction and rape. In order to rescue we must first endanger, and rescue fantasy has a strong, unconscious, aggressive content. There are clear sadistic undertones in Leia's capture — her rough treatment by Darth Vader and the guards, the enormous phallic hypodermic needle that threatens to penetrate her mind, the leather boot-heels of the guards in the corridor as the camera retreats to leave the actual interrogation to our imaginations.

These sadistic elements sexualize Princess Leia's capture and define her as a sexual object, making her helplessness and victimization an essential part of her sexual identity in a way that Luke's early helplessness is not. Vulnerability and the desire to be protected and rescued are not restricted to women, as Luke's capture by the Tusken Raiders and his rescue by Obi-Wan Kenobi indicates. Luke's rescue by Kenobi fulfills the first part of the family romance-rescue fantasy, the desire to be protected by an omnipotent parent. But while Luke can move from the role of victim to that of rescuer, Princess Leia remains trapped inside the role of victim because of her sex, and plays no important role in the action after her rescue. Luke's vulnerability is an aspect of his youth and inexperience, while Princess Leia's is an aspect of her sex.

Women exist as a pool of victims, the fodder for double-edged rescue
fantasies.

TECHNOLOGY, POWER, AND THE FORCE

If *Star Wars* is "about" anything, it is about power — and the source
of ultimate power in the film is the Force. Equally vulnerable and
helpless at the beginning, Luke grows up into possession of power and
the Force while Princess Leia retreats into the background, because
power in *Star Wars* is male power, the patriarchal power of fathers and
sons. Ben Kenobi says the Force is "the energy field surrounding all
living things. . . . it binds the universe together." But as the images
presented in the film show, the force is synonymous with Kenobi himself, the archetypal father and grandfather figure, the rescuer, protector,
magician, master warrior and wise man.

The process of Luke's education and initiation in battle is a rite of
passage into a nostalgic world of patriarchal power that no longer
reflects either our contemporary society or childhood experience. It is a
world in which power (symbolized by the Force) is passed from father
to son. Ben Kenobi is the means for Luke's coming into his true patriarchal heritage. He tells Luke that his father was not just a middle-
class "navigator on a space freighter," but an aristocratic Jedi Knight,
and gives him his father's laser sword, the ultimate phallic weapon (you
carry it in your pocket until you need it, then press a button and it's
three feet long and glows in the dark). It is a technological version of the
Sword in the Stone that makes Arthur king of the Britons. Old Ben
functions as a surrogate father for Luke, instructing him in the ways of
weapons and the secrets of the Force.

Supposedly the collective will of millions of people, the Force is
actually a mystical substitute for the collective action, learning and hard
work needed to effect change. It enables Luke to short-cut the necessarily lengthy process of growing up and acting effectively in the world.
Ben urges Luke to use the Force in his sword practice, a Zen-archery
technique that lets him short-cut years of practice by using his "feelings." Essentially Luke inherits his newfound powers and skills rather
than earning them through learning and practice. The only price he pays
for them is obedience, and Luke internalizes Kenobi after the old
magician's death. When he attacks the space station it is Luke's obedience to Kenobi's voice inside his head, his willingness to give up the
rational control which the radar-scope represents and trust in the non-
rational, mystical Force, which enables him to penetrate the space station's defenses and shoot his missile into the station's one vulnerable
spot — a phallic sexual conquest culminating in the orgasmic fireworks
of the exploding Death Star.

If Luke is Kenobi's "good son" in this Oedipal structure, Darth Vader is the "bad son," the student who rejects the master's teachings, allows himself to be seduced by the "dark side of the Force," and finally fights against and kills Kenobi. Darth Vader is the Faustian man of nineteenth-century literature, the man in black seduced by the pursuit of dark knowledge and experience, unable to deny the definitions of right and wrong by which his community lives, but nevertheless choosing to defy them and place himself outside the society.[14] But whereas in European romantic works like Goethe's *Faust* the Faustian man is the protagonist and represents all of us in his feelings of alienation and rebellion, the U.S. version of the Faustian man, like Cooper's Magua, or Hawthorne's Chillingworth, or Melville's Ahab, is put outside of us as a dangerous Other, leaving us with a sanitized Romanticism that denies self-awareness and an honest confrontation with the destructive forces within. All that's left for the hero is the embrace of the society and its conformist tendencies. While Luke theoretically joins the "rebels," it is really Darth Vader who is the rebel against the orderly succession of patriarchal power that structures the film's psychological fantasies.

These elements of the fantasy structure make the actual political situation in the film, the power relations, confusing and contradictory; but these confusions reflect some of the fundamental contradictions in contemporary foreign policy. The U.S. theoretical fondness for underdogs and rebels, stemming from our own revolutionary history, dictates that the good guys be rebels.[15] However, the film's romance fantasy structure and its support of traditional ideas of hierarchy and obedience demand equally that the bad guys be the rebels. The same confusion is reflected in the contradiction between the U.S. theoretical support of freedom and independence in the world and its actual support of oppressive and dictatorial regimes.

In *Star Wars* this confusion shows up most clearly in the role of Princess Leia, who as a part of the fantasy must be a *princess*, the daughter of the king deposed by evil tyrants, but in plot can only be a *senator* from the planet Alderaan, her father a simple general of the former Republic. In fact, she functions as both. The rebels are actually the loyalists, trying to preserve the old Republic which has been somehow turned into an Empire headed by a ruler who has dissolved the Senate and allows men like Tarkin and Darth Vader to do as they please. Thus the rebels are in fact the restorers of the old order and not creators of a new one. They want to return to the old Republican days of the aristocratic Jedi knights (whatever sense that makes), and it is Tarkin and Darth Vader who are the rebels against the old order.

All these permutations make the political background of the plot almost incomprehensible, but they maintain one of the most fundamental traditions of romance — that the hero cannot rebel against duly-constituted authority, only against tyrannical usurpers. Tarkin and Darth Vader are bad because they use force to seize power; Luke and his new comrades are good because they derive their power and position from the metaphysical sanction of the Force and the moral and legal authority of the Republic.

As one experiences the film, however — without stopping to figure all this out — it seems simply that Luke and his friends rescue the Princess from the bad guys and are rewarded by her father who functions structurally, if not literally, as the Emperor. So the good guys are supporters of a hierarchical, imperial system with kings and princesses on the level of patriarchal fantasy, but supporters of the Republic and democracy on the level of the literal plot, a way to have your authoritarian cake and eat it too.

Because of this contradiction at the center of the film, the distinction between good and evil itself tends to break down. Luke's victory does not revitalize the society or change it fundamentally — it simply replaces one order with another. The old status quo replaces the new one; now Luke is the insider, Darth Vader the outsider. There is no revolutionary change, no reordering of priorities, no new knowledge that fundamentally transforms reality, no alternate vision. All we really have are two basically similar groups competing for power and dichotomized into "good" and "evil." There is no complex understanding of what either good or evil could really mean.

Since there are no real distinctions between groups of characters, the narrative structure derives from a series of parallel sequences in which the good characters do exactly the same thing as the bad ones have done, but are *justified* in what they do. Compare, for example, Darth Vader's use of the Force in the council meeting to control his opponent and Ben Kenobi's use of the Force to get by the storm troopers; or the "bad" guys' destruction of Alderaan and the "good" guys' destruction of the Death Star; or the attack and penetration of Princess Leia's ship by Darth Vader's men firing laser guns, and Luke and Han breaking into the control room on the Death Star in the rescue of the princess; or Darth Vader breaking the neck of the technician on Princess Leia's ship and Ben Kenobi dismembering the alien in the bar scene; or the pursuit of Princess Leia's ship by the enormous ship of Tarkin and the pursuit of the imperial fighter by the Millennium Falcon; and so on.

The common denominators of these scenes are power and violence, and war is an ideal plot vehicle because it sanctions this violence, either to protect the community (Luke must destroy the Death Star before it destroys the rebels' planet), to avenge fallen family and comrades (Luke's family, the planet Alderaan, the other pilots), or to rescue and protect women (Princess Leia). The film makes Darth Vader and Grand

Moff Tarkin as evil as they are *in order to* justify the violent actions of Luke and his comrades. The film pretends to depict the struggle of good against evil, but in fact the evil exists in order to allow the good characters to act violently. In other words, Lucas's desire to make a film about laser guns and abducted princesses and interstellar combat impels him to generate the bad guys; it is not simply that the behavior of the bad guys forces Luke to take up arms. The real relationship between good and evil in *Star Wars* is a symbiotic one: comic book heroes need villains to justify their actions, and in the end the villains are usually more interesting anyway. Darth Vader soon became the most popular character in the *Star Wars* fan mags.

Given this basically symbiotic relationship, the two groups of characters are distinguished primarily by their attitudes towards technology, the *kind* of technology they seem to represent. Lucas himself sees the fundamental difference between *Star Wars* and Kubrick's *2001* as one of attitude towards technology. Lucas says Kubrick is interested in technology, the "hard facts," the "rational side of things," while he is interested in romance and adventure, the "irrational side of things."

What Lucas sees as this fundamental difference in approach is articulated in two basic ways in *Star Wars*. First, the two groups of characters are characterized by what seem to be different approaches to technology or different kinds of technology. Darth Vader and Tarkin represent the large and impersonal, authoritarian, coldly rational forces which threaten us, and they are characterized by the gigantic, impersonal, menacing Death Star, a prison and instrument of destruction by bloodless technocrats. Luke and his companions are characterized by their one-man fighters and personalized robots, by Han Solo's eccentric hot-rod spaceship, and by Ben Kenobi's preference for the more traditionally elegant laser sword over the newer, "clumsier" blaster. This opposition between an individual or a small, coherent group and a large, impersonal, authoritarian force is a common motif in U.S. films, and in *Star Wars* this preference for the individual and traditional reflects the nostalgic, individualistic romance ethos of the fantasy structure.

Second, the Force seems to represent a withdrawal from technology altogether in favor of the irrational and mystical. Luke's 'droid is out of commission in the final attack on the Death Star, and he switches off his radar-controlled bombsight in response to Obi-Wan Kenobi's disembodied voice urging him to "use the Force. . . . let go of the computer. . . . trust me." In the novel Lucas makes Luke's firing of the missile an unconscious act, something he cannot remember doing. The individual and the irrational triumph over the impersonal and the rational.

But Luke's merger with the all-encompassing Force is simply another version of the big, impersonal, authoritarian forces that Tarkin and his henchmen on the Death Star represent, and it prefigures the neo-fascist militarism of the final scene in which Luke and Han are absorbed into the rebel order. This mysticism and irrationality are simply mysterioso smoke screens for the reactionary ideology at the center of the film. *Star Wars* rejects technology in favor of the Force in order to disassociate itself from the more menacing aspects of technology run amok that threaten us. But practically every frame is a hymn to the technology which made the film possible, and Lucas's claim to be interested in "the irrational" is simply an excuse for not looking more closely at the issues he raises. We cannot possibly abandon technology, we need it to survive. Even when Luke turns off the bombsight he still remains encased in his ship, dependent on Han Solo to get Darth Vader's ships off his tail. His giving in to the Force is more a bionic fusion with his ship than a rejection of technology. It is an image of the union of man and machine.

Finally, this union of man and machine in *Star Wars* represents a fantasy of immortality, an assumption by human beings of the hard-edged, replaceable-part nature of machines. The Death Star is a symbol of death, and Luke's destruction of it is a victory over death itself, accomplished with the aid of the Force. The concern with death runs throughout the film, and the robots serve as comic vehicles for the safe exploration of anxieties about death. C-3PO whines continually about his fears of being disconnected or sold for scrap, but both he and R2-D2 articulate bionic resurrection fantasies — for example, the reconnection of C-3PO's severed arm in contrast to the bar scene in which Ben Kenobi kills a "live" by cutting off his arm, or the resurrection of R2-D2 after the final battle in contrast to the more permanent deaths of the human pilots. The return of Ben Kenobi as the voice of the Force is a mythic resurrection which connects the Force and immortality fantasies.

Aside from these fantasies, the real question is not whether or not we should depend on technology but what *kind* of technology we should adopt to solve our problems. Despite the superficial differences between the "good" technology of Luke and his friends and the "bad" technology of Tarkin and Darth Vader, *Star Wars* offers no real alternatives. The differences are stylistic rather than real; both groups are characterized by a high-energy technology of weapons, power, noise, speed and violence. Obi-Wan Kenobi's laser sword is still a weapon; Han Solo's Millennium Falcon is the fastest ship around, "the ship that made the Kessel run in less than twelve standard timeparts"; Luke's flying skill is used to kill "womp-rats in my T-16 back home" and then to destroy the Death Star in his final initiation. There is no difference in the special-effects treatment of the destruction of both the planet Alderaan and the Death Star, or in our reaction to either event, because finally there *is* no difference. Both are explosions, and explosions are fun. As a returned POW in *Hearts and Minds* says in justification of his role as a bomber pilot, ''Almost everyone has blown off firecrackers. The excitement of those explosives hitting their targets is thrilling, deeply satisfying.''

There is no sense in any of this of a truly alternative technology like the ''small is beautiful'' philosophy of E.F. Schumacher, with its orientation away from size, speed and violence and towards ''the organic, the gentle, the non-violent, the elegant and beautiful,'' or like the soft-energy path of Amory Lovins with its emphasis on a technology of energy efficiency and conservation, and dependence on soft energy sources like decentralized solar power and wind.[16] The difference between these technologies and the hard-energy technology of *Star Wars* is the difference between organic farming, 10-speed bicycles, and decentralized solar energy on the one hand, and chemical agribusiness, high-powered gas guzzlers, and nuclear power on the other. The first approach accepts natural limits and works within them; the second recognizes no limits and depends on ever-increasing power and expansion.

The only really alternative approach towards technology present in *Star Wars* is the self-sufficient farming technology of Luke's home. The desert planet Tatooine gives Lucas an opportunity to develop the kind of ecologically sensitive approach to technology that Frank Herbert developed in *Dune*, and the reference to ''spice mines'' and the skeleton of the sand worm which R2-D2 passes are allusions to Herbert's novel. But this alternative is destroyed when the storm troopers burn Luke's home, and its rejection is an important part of the family romance-fantasy structure. This alternative technology is identified with the cast-off bourgeois world of his foster parents, and Luke moves on to excitement, hard-energy technology, and the aristocracy. Thus the desire for social mobility and a technology of power, speed and violence are linked together, a linkage which reflects the film's capitalist ideology.

As Schumacher puts it, the modern private-enterprise system employs greed and envy as its motivating forces, and greed and envy demand continuous and limitless material growth.[17] Unlimited expansion is important to capitalism because only by constantly increasing the size of the economic pie can attention be kept away from the disproportionate and unequal size of the pieces.[18] But the inevitable outcome of this union of capitalism and the hard-energy technology to which it remains committed in order to ensure growth is an increasing concentration of capital, increasing centralization, and an increasingly authoritarian power structure, a combination that Lovins calls ''friendly fascism.''[19]

In the end, *Star Wars* embraces by implication all the things it pretends to oppose. The Nuremberg rally scene is a fitting conclusion in keeping with the film's fascination with speed, size, violence and the mysticism that cloaks the film's patriarchal power structures. The romance plot incorporates sexism and racism and supports a hierarchical social system that glamorizes those at the top and literally turns those at the bottom into machines or monsters. The robots in *Star Wars* do not represent the technology with a human face that Schumacher calls for; they are human beings turned into machines, a metallic Laurel and Hardy, the ultimate workers in a capitalist technology.

The film's commitment to excitement and speed locks it into a hard-energy weapons technology that undercuts its attempts to disassociate itself from the harmful and threatening aspects of that technology. By having no thought-out, consistent position on any of the issues he touches on, Lucas dooms *Star Wars* to repeat all the dominant ideological clichés of our society. That distant galaxy turns out to be not so far away after all.

NOTES

[1] On Nov. 19, 1977, *Star Wars* became (for the moment) the "new all-time top grossing film" in history, nosing out *Jaws* to achieve a cumulative domestic rental tally of $120,286,000 and a domestic box-office rental of $186,924,664 (*Variety*, Nov. 23, 1977).

[2] There is a detailed technical account of these special effects in the July 1977 issue of *American Cinematographer*.

[3] Marshall McLuhan, *Understanding Media* (New York: New American Library, 1973), pp. 284 ff.

[4] Paul Scanlon, "The Force Behind George Lucas," *Rolling Stone* (August 25, 1977) p. 48.

[5] Robert Jay Lifton, *Home From the War: Vietnam Veterans, Neither Victims nor Executioners* (New York: Simon and Schuster, 1973), pp. 26-67.

[6] Ibid., p. 347.

[7] Fred Branfman, "The Wild Blue Yonder Over Laos," *Washington Monthly* 3 (July 1971): 28-43; quoted in Lifton, *Home*, p. 349.

[8] Scanlon, *The Force*, pp. 43, 51.

[9] George Lucas, *Star Wars: From the Adventures of Luke Skywalker* (New York: Ballantine Books, 1976), p. 101.

[10] Raymond Williams, *The Country and the City* (New York: Oxford Univ. Press, 1973), p. 36.

[11] Arthur Lubow, "The Space 'Iliad'," *Film Comment* 13 (July-August 1977): 20-21; Vincent Canby, *New York Times* Arts and Leisure Section, June 5, 1977.

[12] When Lucas was asked about the corniness of Mark Hamill's lines, he said: "There is some very strong stuff in there. In the end, when you know better, it

sort of takes a lot of guts to do it because it's the same thing with the whole movie — doing a children's film. I didn't want to play it down and make a camp movie, I wanted to make it a very good movie. And it wasn't camp, it was not making fun of itself. I wanted it to be real.'' (Scanlon, *The Force,* p. 48).

[13] Freud coined the term "family romance" in 1897 and included a note on it in Otto Rank's *The Myth and the Birth of the Hero* (published in German in 1909), a work which applies the concept to mythology. For a discussion of the family romance and the work done since Freud and Rank, see Linda Joan Kaplan's "The Concept of the Family Romance," *The Psychoanalytic Review* 61 (Summer 1974): 169-202.

[14] See Leslie Fiedler's discussion of the Faustian man in American literature in *Love and Death in the American Novel* (New York: Stein & Day, 1966).

[15] This image of ourselves, which we project to the outside world, helps to explain why Ho Chi Minh initially thought the Americans would be his natural allies in the struggle against French colonialism.

[16] E.F. Schumacher, *Small is Beautiful: Economics as if People Mattered* (New York: Harper & Row, 1973), p. 31; Amory B. Lovins, "Energy Strategy: The Road Not Taken?" *Foreign Affairs* 55 (October 1976): 64-96, and *Soft Energy Paths: Toward a Durable Peace* (San Francisco: Friends of the Earth International, 1977).

[17] Schumacher, *Small,* p. 247.

[18] See Fred Hirsch, *Social Limits to Growth* (Cambridge, Mass.: Harvard Univ. Press, 1977).

[19] Lovins, *Soft Energy Paths,* pp. 91-92, 95.

CHAPTER 5.

Hollywood Transformed: Interviews with Lesbian Viewers

CLAIRE WHITAKER

The women in the following interviews all see themselves as lesbians. Their backgrounds vary. Fannie Freed and J.A. Marquis are Jewish. Gladys is Afro-American. Anna Maria was born in Italy. Gretta was born in Germany. Dagmar, Romaine, Lulu and Ea are of English, German or other European descent. While there may be some difference in class background, no attempt is made here to establish exactly what it is. All of the women are college educated. All work to support themselves.

As a general policy all names are changed, although some women had no objection to use of their actual names.

At the time of the interviews (which took place between 1977 and 1979), Fannie Freed was 37 years old. Romaine and Ea were 34. J.A. Marquis was 33, Gretta 32, Lulu 31, Gladys 29, Anna Maria 28, and Dagmar 24. Fannie, Ea, Romaine, Gretta and J.A. all had their thirteenth birthdays between 1955 and 1959. They are of a 1950s' generation. Lulu, Gladys, Anna Maria, and Dagmar had their thirteenth birthday between the years of 1961 and 1967. They are more of a 1960s' generation.

These interviews are accounts of women growing up in an environment of film and TV, among other things. The interviews are biographical sketches, not sociological or psychological studies. They start with childhood impressions of film and/or TV and work through adolescence up to adulthood. Questions about identification and love and opinions about certain genres appear in all the interviews.

For example, use of the phrase "identify with" is intended by the interviewer to mean "associate closely with." However, that meaning does not stay consistent, as some of the women use "identify with" in a way that could be interchangeable with "love," itself a tricky word. "Love" can have at least three different meanings and shadings: "sexual craving and desire for," the same as lust; "sexual desire for combined with affection for"; and "affection for." The distinctions are important to understand what is really being said. Meaning here is dependent on context.

It can be argued that women's liberation should not only be about fighting oppression but about shedding the repression caused by a "good woman — bad woman" split image. Women's sexuality can be more than an imitation of male sexuality. Women's creativity and integrated well-being are inextricably tied to their finding their own sexual expression: one that is first and foremost for women themselves.

For most of the women interviewed, alienation from predominating heterosexist, sexist and racist values is clear, and so is a vitality and staying power. Transformation and positive self-image are dominant themes in what they have to say. Hollywood is transcended.

TALKING TO ROMAINE, ANNA MARIA, GRETTA, DAGMAR, AND EA

JUDY: What films made an early impression on you?

ANNA MARIA: I loved *All About Eve,* particularly because I had a crush on Bette Davis, a wonderful model. She's a strong bitchy woman who knows what she wants and gets it and yet has stayed human and sensitive. I was particularly interested to see her pitted against another woman and to see a whole bunch of other great tough women, like Thelma Ritter, in the film. I first saw it when I was 12 and have seen it at least eight times.

I came to this country when I was ten and to a great extent learned English by growing up with old films on TV. I fantasized getting into a lot of characters, especially Auntie Mame, who was like a counterculture character. Still, most of those films were upper class, and it was hard to find characters living my kind of life. I identified with *Auntie Mame* not in a class sense but because she was a beatnik. That character really got to me when I was about 11 or 12. Nobody stepped on her feet without her letting them know.

ROMAINE: To the extent that I identified with film characters, it would be with Robin Hood, male characters, cowboys.

JUDY: What about Maid Marian?

ROMAINE: No, she didn't do anything. Women characters were all boring. Later on I liked Katharine Hepburn in *The African Queen* and then Marilyn Monroe, whom I was always caught in a terrible ambivalence about and felt I had to defend because there were so many jokes about her. Marilyn Monroe was almost like a dirty word, yet I found her character and the qualities that came through on the screen appealing. My ambivalence was to like her but hate what she was doing.

DAGMAR: It's hard to reconcile what happened to her with what kind of roles she played. I feel, "This was an exploited woman," and it's hard to ignore that when I see her films.

ROMAINE: Something original, though, came through. If she hadn't been stereotyped, Monroe would have been a great actress. But Bardot did nothing for me.

GRETTA: Well, for me Marilyn Monroe just comes across as a dumb bunny, and boring. But Bardot sparkles.

ANNA MARIA: Monroe was so stereotyped, people couldn't see her as a craftswoman, as a talented practitioner of the art, but only as a symbol.

ROMAINE: During McCarthyism, one of the most repressive periods in American history, Monroe had fewer options than if she'd come out in the 1930s.

DAGMAR: The *fewest* options. Either be "herself" or Doris Day, the eternal virgin.

ANNA MARIA: Doris Day was more protected by the virgin role. At least a virgin doesn't get raped constantly.

ROMAINE: McCarthyism in Hollywood ultimately may have given us Doris Day and Rock Hudson.

EA: I saw *Gone With The Wind,* also from way back then, when I was 12 or 13, after I had read the book, and that film impressed me greatly.

DAGMAR: Me too. Yet I remember in the early seventies when women and some men rejected *Gone With The Wind* as classist and racist. . . .

DAGMAR: And sexist. But growing up with a film like that, you almost excuse it because of your sentimental feelings about it.

ANNA MARIA: You even internalize it. You do more than excuse its problems. You don't recognize them. Part of *Gone With The Wind* is still great for me. But seeing it at age eight made me totally unconscious of all the crap it brought along with it.

EA: Sure, Rhett Butler carrying Scarlett O'Hara up the stairs. That's rape, but how things were supposed to be.

ANNA MARIA: And it was exciting.

GRETTA: I really like Joan Fontaine's 1940s film *Frenchman's Creek.* As an aristocrat leaving her husband, she goes to her country house where a pirate who's put in at the cove has coincidentally been living. She runs away to sea with the pirate, kills a man who tries to rape her, and wears trousers and blousey shirts instead of empire dresses and 50 million skirts. She's in drag, looking like an adolescent boy.

DAGMAR: Did she fall in love? Become feminine?

GRETTA: Still acting out the adventure, she dressed in her lady clothes to entertain her husband and his friends while the pirate was supposed to be escaping. Instead he came back to the house to rob them and kidnap her, but it didn't work out because of her kids.

DAGMAR: I loved TV, which we got when I was 12, and I started eating up adventure movies like *Tarzan* and *Jungle Jim*. As I got older, I started feeling guilty about only liking female characters, having crushes on them, and identifying with them because they were attractive.

JUDY: You were playing in what role? Their role, or were you being a suitor of theirs?

DAGMAR: I thought that these would be the kind of women I would fall in love with. Greta Garbo and Katherine Hepburn stick out in my mind. Through my adolescence, I did try hard to like male characters because I thought I was supposed to, but I found most of them nebishes.

JUDY: If you'd had your choice, would you have been Spencer Tracy?

DAGMAR: No, not to be in that particular role. It wasn't sexuality where I would have fantasies about wanting to sleep with these women, but I thought they were beautiful, and consequently I used to put up pictures of them whenever I could. I idolized someone like Marlene Dietrich, not necessarily even conscious of her as a strong woman but finding something appealing about her: the way she looked. These were beautiful romantic women wearing beautiful clothes. As I got older, I liked the parts they played. But the appeal is hard to put my finger on. I recognize that feeling, too, and as you were talking about it, I thought about which women turned me on and which women didn't. Monroe, Dietrich and Garbo had an aura about them, but certain others like Sandra Dee . . .

ANNA MARIA: You asked, "Did I make myself be Spencer Tracy?" That is the rub about growing up a lesbian and trying to put yourself in the film situation in some way. You're attracted by these women and yet you don't fit in: an incredible contradiction for me. At times I'd identify with a character. Other times I'd float outside the situation, sort of watching the effect this attractive woman was having on me. I'd imagine Katherine Hepburn and Spencer Tracy together, or sometimes I'd be Katherine Hepburn. And I might be sort of behind Spencer Tracy but I wouldn't *be* Spencer Tracy! I felt a tug of war with that. At age 14 or 15 suddenly this gauze or screen got torn away and I realized I could be me, a woman caring about this other woman. There were all sorts of problems with self-hatred, but it became a possibility.

JUDY: It wasn't film that told you it was okay to love women.

ANNA MARIA: No, but it did give me the context in which to play out all these ideas, fantasizing romantic encounters and playing one of many roles, always switching around when it got too hot in one seat. I eventually worked out something acceptable to me. In addition to books, film had a central role in allowing me to come to terms with lesbian sexuality.

EA: I can remember when I was in seventh and eighth grade being riveted to the "Spin and Marty" TV series on *Disney World* and fantasizing that I was Marty and my girlfriend was Spin, both having all kinds of adventures together. No matter that Spin and Marty were boys. And I always identified with cowboys in the westerns who had buddies to ride off into the sunset with.

ROMAINE: I identified with cowboys too, and paid no attention to the sex differences.

ANNA MARIA: I always worried about it. As a matter of fact, I worried about whether Tweety Pie was a girl or boy! I thought, "Oh, my god, I betcha Tweety Pie is a boy! And all this time I thought it was a girl!" I was always really pushed to resolve in some way what just would not fit, and so I found it hard to identify with male characters. I had to change them in some way.

ROMAINE: I identified with male characters even after adolescence, and maybe still do. At a young age nothing seemed to stop me from being anybody I wanted. The cowboy archetype meant being strong and independent, not needing anybody, and moving around a lot. Being free of everything and living with nature were especially important. As a child, independence was something I needed to feel. I had to feel free of society — an attitude I now see as alienated in many ways.

ANNA MARIA: Some women played in those strong roles, like Barbara Stanwyck as Annie Oakley. A film on Calamity Jane starring Doris Day had a good first half which she spends totally covered with dirt, scratching her butt, swearing up a storm, and shooting all the men. But by the end she's horribly cleaned up and in love.

DAGMAR: Then there was the woman with the heart of gold who got knocked off at the end. Or your saloon woman.

EA: Or as in *High Noon:* "Don't go! Don't fight it out! Stay home! Play it safe!"

GRETTA: Actually, sensibly, these women kept saying, "Who are you trying to prove it to?"

DAGMAR: Those women were in the way of the horse!

ROMAINE: They could have exposed the male ego trip but they didn't. The films depicted them as a reactionary force preventing social change.

EA: The shoot-out at O.K. Corral doesn't signify social change.

JUDY: What about lesbian films?

DAGMAR: I think of a "lesbian film" as one where I actually knew two women were in love.

ANNA MARIA & GRETTA: *The Children's Hour*.

ROMAINE: *Chelsea Girls*, a really creepy decadent film by Andy Warhol. This woman wearing jeans kept shooting up heroin in the ass.

JUDY: Were there two women?

ROMAINE: Only two? Warhol wasn't into that. There were five or six women, but they were just talking. It was presumably a documentary.

JUDY: Did you believe that being a lesbian meant you were decadent?

ROMAINE: I think so. That was before I was out. Warhol deals with gay men in a more human way. Yet he has this film with a bunch of gay cowboys doing their super faggot number with each other. But then they ride into town and rape a woman. I felt really ripped off by that movie.

DAGMAR: With *The Conformist* I immediately fell in love with Dominique Sanda's strong character but felt very uncomfortable with the film's defining fascism as the outgrowth of homosexuality.

EA: In *Rome, Open City* the lesbian is also a Nazi.

DAGMAR: *The Conformist*, by depicting the life of a fascist man who had been homosexual as a child and was repressing those feelings, tried to link fascism and repression. But the dance scene between the two women was so strong, and Dominique Sanda was really the only powerful person in the whole film. Although she was married to one of the main characters, I identified with her as a lesbian. She falls in love with a woman, whom she sweeps up in a tango. It's marvelous! That was the most positive screen image of lesbianism for me.

ANNA MARIA: I've never seen a positive lesbian image in commercial film.

EA: It makes me angry that positive roles are so missing and that roles are usually so negative when they do appear.

DAGMAR: We're so starved, we go to see anything because something is better than nothing.

EA: It's a compromise. It's a given degree of alienation.

111

TALKING TO LULU AND FANNIE FREED

JUDY: How did movies affect your coming of age?

FANNIE FREED: I was very confused. I knew I wasn't an Indian, Superman or a cowboy. I was Lois Lane and Wonder Woman a little. I was real fond of Gordon MacRae in *The Desert Song,* who seduced a woman by singing to her.

JUDY: By "fond of" do you mean identified with or were in love with?

FANNIE FREED: Identified with. I was in love with Robin Morgan, who played Dagmar in *I Remember Mama.* The blonde ladies with straight hair and the cowboys were in a world that didn't match what I knew, and I never believed women behaved like Katherine Hepburn. All I saw at home were these big 400-pound women who wore black fur coats and sat in a separate room from their husbands whom they didn't talk to. Katherine Hepburn was out of a play, not like people around me who never played tennis — they'd have turned their ankles. My parents, the most Americanized in my family, tried hard to fit that image but had a lot of trouble. For a long time, because of Hollywood images, I didn't accept myself and felt like I didn't belong, like a failure. Later I invented an image of myself that was apart from all the screen images.

LULU: Not much of a film goer, I am still in love with Anne Bancroft in *The Miracle Worker.* I'd read the book and was already in love with the character when I saw the film. Bancroft attended the opening, and some classmates and I went backstage to meet her. When she asked if we had any questions, I couldn't open my mouth but just froze. Later my friends and I vowed to wear red blouses and black skirts (like she had worn in the film) to school the next day, but only I did — which made me feel odd because I was the only one. I made an Anne Bancroft scrapbook where I pasted in everything I could find about her. My father, a psychologist who was working with a state group that decided to give Bancroft an award that year, said I could go to the award luncheon and then said no — probably because he and my mother thought I was getting too involved. That was a blow. At the time I didn't feel contradictions about sex roles, but I got the message that my parents weren't comfortable with my crush.

JUDY: Were there people that you identified with, as opposed to being in love with?

LULU: James Dean in *Rebel Without A Cause*. I had an absolute identification with him. He was the picture of strength and sensitivity and power and caring. He once played Frankenstein, another great hero of mine. It made sense to me that Dean played him. Dean had a lot of qualities I liked that weren't particularly gender-defined, and his most important relationship in *Rebel Without A Cause* seemed to be not with his girlfriend but with Sal Mineo. I never identified with a female character as much or in the way I did with James Dean. Hepburn and Tracy's relationship seemed dated and not in the least romantic. I liked Dietrich but could hardly identify with her through a whole movie. She played such a horrible character in *The Blue Angel*.

JUDY: What about cowboy movies?

LULU: From westerns I incorporated into myself a strong silent image. Enough that I'd like to get rid of some of it.

FANNIE FREED: You know what a strong image was for me: the one who played the quick-shooting woman, Annie Oakley. Yet she was a blonde woman who missed on purpose — missed the shot on purpose so that the man she loved could beat her. *Annie Get Your Gun* had lines like, "You can't get your man with a gun," and you're supposed to be "sweet and pure as a nursery," etc. Here's this woman working her goddamn heart out, but this schmuck comes, she gives it all up — throws the show. What a message!

LULU: When I started watching TV at age ten, situation comedies gave me a similar message, loud and clear. Basically an oddball appears in the show, often a child, who finally gets corrected. The oddball doesn't conform in gender role. These oddballs were tomboys or sissies or too involved in some interest. *Father Knows Best* was so fascist. Once the father decided that the little girl Kathy had to go out with boys and stop playing baseball with them, even with her good friend who was a boy. The parents set this whole thing up — making her dress up in a dress and keep her feet still and have the boys come in. Crying, she proclaimed, "I don't want it." Horrifyingly, the non-conformists to gender roles got squelched, as did anybody who cared about anything too much.

TALKING TO J.A. MARQUIS

JUDY: In your early memories of film roles whom did you tend to identify with?

J.A. MARQUIS: I've thought about it. I was identifying with men. At age eight, nine or ten and on, when it came to Elvis Presley, I didn't scream, or drool, or cry or really buy records — I wanted *to be* Elvis Presley. For a Hallowe'en party I bought those little sideburns you stick on, had a guitar, and wore my father's flashy shirt. I don't remember even identifying as a child with any female characters.

JUDY: What about cowboys?

J.A. MARQUIS: Well, I liked the Mounties. I also liked Superman. I liked Wonder Woman in the comics but most comic books were male, like *Batman*. Friends of mine and I were into Hitchcock or the Mummy and Dracula, which was great for Hallowe'en. Very soon, though, I got too scared of Dracula movies. I had to invent a way of dealing with that and then I stopped seeing them. I saw *Seven Brides for Seven Brothers* several times for its dancing and stuff, but I really identified with the seven brothers. The female characters were just props. Why the hell identify with that? I did identify with a couple of women, especially the Katherine Hepburn, Spencer Tracy movies and those with Bette Davis. Davis often had undesirable roles but was strong and real, even more than Katherine Hepburn.

JUDY: How did a Jewish background affect your attitudes about film characters?

J.A. MARQUIS: My parents used to point people out to me and say, "He's Jewish," as with Jack Benny. Most of the film characters I remember were blonde, at least a lot of the women were. They were from a world I never had much contact with. That added to the fantasy, the unreality of film. I remember interestingly enough, and she wasn't Jewish, one woman I was always looking for — Lena Horne, the only black woman portrayed as beautiful in film. She had a magnificent presence although few lines. I was pretty attracted to Lena Horne and remember her doing "heat wave" and sashaying around. She appeared as black-identified, with a black band. Somehow I always felt a little better when she or Carmen Miranda showed up. Somebody who's different, not like all the others. But I don't remember too many Jewish characters, only small fat bald men and minor characters. *Gentleman's Agreement,* about the hidden agenda to be anti-Semitic, impressed me very much. It was powerful and scary, about the world that I hadn't much to do with. I was suddenly in there and wasn't welcome.

JUDY: Do you ever remember having a conflict about wanting to be strong and active and then somebody telling you you couldn't be?

J.A. MARQUIS: From film I got a sense of the roles women didn't play. Strong women are aberrant in this society and it's a conflict society hasn't worked out as well as I have. Women were supposed to be goody-two-shoes, beautiful and stereotypically flawless. Being a lesbian was coming to terms with that and it was quite a release. It was like a whole bunch of chains fell off.

JUDY: Would you fall in love with characters you identified with?

J.A. MARQUIS: Marilyn Monroe in *Some Like It Hot* wasn't two-dimensional but nurturing. In both *Bus Stop* and *Some Like It Hot,* she was portrayed as helpless in some respects — a good-hearted victim person — which offered an attractive, "Here, I'll take care of you," kind of thing.

JUDY: What about Sandra Dee?

J.A. MARQUIS: Forget it. None of the Mouseketeers. None of the goody-two-shoes. Not Doris Day. I guess still Lena Horne really stands out, and she didn't even have lines.

TALKING TO GLADYS

JUDY: What early films can you remember responding to?

GLADYS: It may not be the first film I saw, but *The Blue Angel* had the most lasting impact. I was just enthralled with Marlene Dietrich. I didn't get into the professor at all or understand how serious his problems were, like how he might lose his job. I just got into the fact that here was a saloon singer, which is the closest thing I ever saw to a sleazy woman. I can remember her singing with her leg up on a chair. I can also remember vividly the school boys planting her promo cards — not a picture of her naked but nude enough with a little feather covering her bottom half and you blow it and you'd see it all. I just thought that was fantastic. How wonderful it would be to blow it up and see Marlene Dietrich's — pudendum.

That's without a doubt the first film that had a lot of impact on me as a kid. You didn't usually see women being sleazy German barroom singers. You saw women being asinine for the most part. Dietrich had substance. I thought the character was very well developed, as sexist as it was when I think back. But when I was eight years old, sexism didn't mean a thing to me, and I was probably the most sexist person in the audience looking at almost naked Marlene Dietrich on the silver screen. I can remember thinking about it a lot. I'm not particularly a fan of German film, but of Marlene Dietrich. She has a sustaining quality about her that I know has turned on thousands of women in this world. I can't say I identified with her.

JUDY: What was your fascination?

GLADYS: Lust, childhood lust, I'm sure.

JUDY: And love?

GLADYS: Lust. Purely lust. I knew full well that I would never see anyone like Marlene Dietrich in real life. It had to be lust. Like looking at a magazine. You can't call that love. It's lust!

JUDY: Did anybody ever tell you that you shouldn't have those kinds of reactions to a woman?

GLADYS: No, I was a real quiet child. I never really discussed my life. I can remember my mother asking me what I saw but not really discussing it because she never saw the film. I have relatives, honest, who probably haven't seen a movie since *Gone With The Wind* was made.

So I never got trips laid on me that way, at least as a child. I can remember going home and thinking about those movies forever and ever and ever, not modeling myself after them but carrying them around — perhaps I did model myself after them in a lot of ways, but I can't admit to that now. That would take a whole lot of deep thought. I'm positive, being a visual person, that seeing films all my life, I've carried over several portrayals into myself. It would take three years of psychoanalysis to bring it up. I identified with Dale Evans, who was great as a *cowgirl.*

JUDY: Were you into cowboys?

GLADYS: No. I was into robbers more than cowboys. I was into robbers, thieves and murderers more than the clean-cut cowboy. Roy Rogers was so dull. Gene Autrey was the dullest. I would identify with the cowboy who got away with the money and the girl, or who died in the street. I related to Frank Sinatra in *The Man With the Golden Arm,* to his anguish, his leaning in the hallway needing a fix. Marlon Brando in *The Fugitive Kind,* Eartha Kitt in *Anna Lucasta,* Marlene Dietrich, the fugitive — that's the kind of image I identified with more than with the staid member of society. I'd identify with Lex Luther in *Superman.* I'd identify with the smut. I still do. However, I don't see lots of porno films because none of them are women-related. For the same reason I don't see black garbage films; you don't need to pay four dollars to see someone oppressed — just walk outside. But a good amount of smut is always nice in a film. I love Lina Wertmuller. She's just gross! Women have to be gross at times. I think that is real liberating.

JUDY: Did you get into *Rebel Without A Cause?*

GLADYS: I always saw James Dean as being a spoiled kid. He didn't make any impact at all on my life. For a little while I identified with Elvis Presley in those horrible, horrible early movies. He always had money or women hanging on him, was good-looking, etc. I didn't have money or women hanging on me, but it was an ideal.

JUDY: What about your identification with Eartha Kitt as a black actress?

GLADYS: I love Eartha Kitt. *Anna Lucasta* had a great impact on me. It was the first time I had ever seen a black family on the silver screen, not particularly a positive family image but an image. In the film Eartha Kitt had to make up her own mind about marrying a climber or a card shark. She ran away from her family and did what she wanted to do. I can relate to that as far as being a lesbian — doing what you want to do and not really bothering what anybody else said.

In terms of being black, there weren't, and still aren't, many roles to identify with. You could be Hattie McDaniel in the role of Mammy,

Butterfly McQueen in the role of stupid, Eartha Kitt in the role of slut, Lena Horne in the role of light-skinned dark woman leaning against a piano and singing songs. Those are the only images you had or really have! Another one is the strong mother like Jane Pittman. I'm not that, I'm not a slut, and I'm not a rag-on-the-head mammy. Whom can I identify with in terms of a black woman in film? Still the closest would be Eartha Kitt as a slut in *Anna Lucasta*. Even today just try to name ten black actresses. I think of myself as a movie person, and I'm having trouble thinking of five. That's a statement about film. We just can't remember all the names of the maids, that's the problem.

JUDY: You had a special invective talking about *Gone With The Wind* before.

GLADYS: The whole film in its portrayal of black women and men is so blatantly racist. They must have spent hundreds of dollars on glycerine to make *all* the black people look greasy. Every black person looked like they had been in 100-degree sun for hours. Everyone cried on Hattie McDaniel's shoulder — that's bull. Almost all Hollywood films are racist, both when they don't have blacks in them and when they do. And they're sexist. It comes from the minds of the people who make them. It's bad news that we have to pay money to go see this schlock. But I do keep going. We have no alternative. And sometimes horrible movies can be really enjoyable because they hit on a certain level.

JUDY: What kinds of characters do you identify with as a lesbian?

GLADYS: I identify with strong women who are out in the world doing things. I identify with unmarried women but not usually with a married woman unless she's in a crisis trying to get out of the marriage. Then I can identify with that on some lesbian level. I always think these people should come out. *The Turning Point* would have been a much better movie if Shirley MacLaine and Anne Bancroft had come out in the end.

JUDY: What about lesbian characters in film?

GLADYS: *Therese and Isabelle* was the first film I saw with *real* lesbians. I saw it four times and can only remember them screwing behind the altar. Lesbianism was alluded to in *Walk on the Wild Side*, but with no actual lesbian portrayal. I identified with Barbara Stanwyck, who owned a whorehouse and was in love with Capucine. But in the end Capucine left and Stanwyck flipped out. It wasn't a positive image.

When Liv Ullman played Queen Christina of Sweden in *The Abdication,* in the end Hollywood had her fall in love with the Peter Finch character, which I'm sure she never did. I think she went to her grave having sex with women. I'd love to see films where you could say, "I went to see this movie, and it was about two lesbians,'' not about somebody ''who may have been a lesbian.'' We've been alluded to so much. I think it's time people saw a real one. Then they could say, ''That's what one looks like!''

PART TWO

INDEPENDENT FILMMAKING IN NORTH AMERICA

Director Christine Choy (right)

INTRODUCTION

For a radical today, using one's skills making films might be, but does not have to be, a way of doing political work without directly facing or confronting a constituency. Two questions about one's work go a long way in keeping it from being an escape. "For Whom?" and "For What End?"

Norm Fruchter, quoted in *Jump Cut* Editorial No. 3, 1974.

The practical and political issues facing independent filmmakers often seem to demand more attention than the final results of their work: the films themselves. For independent filmmakers, questions of relationship are vital: of independence and accountability between filmmakers and their subjects; of relations with audiences; and of relations to the social movements they are a part of. These questions are not only political, but economic. Together the essays in Part Two explore these concerns and show a growing movement of radical counter-cinema in North America.

In the United States political documentary began in the early 1930s with the Workers Film and Photo League and was from the beginning directly connected to the major social movements of the time. Russell Campbell traces that important work and discusses League films on unemployment, racism, housing fights, labor struggles, and the U.S. government.

This kind of committed documentary continued only sporadically until the mid-1960s, rarely accompanied by critical discussion of the films. Then began a rapid growth that saw the production of hundreds of independent left documentaries. John Hess stresses the role of the anti-war movement and the influence of Newsreel Films as the first catalyst, and also shows how in the 1970s the growing strength of the women's movement forced a reorientation within left cinema. Films such as *Union Maids* and *A Wives' Tale* and the work of Third World Newsreel emerge directly from the activity of the New Left and the women's movement.

Budgets and fundraising take up a good part of a filmmaker's life. Some choose to raise money directly from the constituency they hope will be the eventual audience. For example, the producers of *A Wives' Tale* canvassed the union movement and women's groups for funds — an agonizingly slow process, but one that has political merit as a form of education and audience building. Others choose to tap foundations, TV networks and the state for funds. Sherry Millner's interview with Christine Choy brings out the pros and cons of this approach, showing that political decisions about money often affect film content and style. The process of producing a film affects its eventual shape.

Funding problems are even more acute among filmmakers of color, but the impossibility of working with a big budget has not deterred black film artists. Since the late 1960s, states Clyde Taylor, "Black cinema has arrived to take its natural place beside black music, literature, dance and drama." In the work of Warrington Hudlin, Michelle Parkerson and many others an Afro-American counter-cinema is emerging. It is a movement that not only differs from Hollywood but also challenges many allied forms of political cinema.

CHAPTER 6.

Radical Cinema in the 1930s: The Film and Photo League

RUSSELL CAMPBELL

The Workers Film and Photo League in the United States (known as the Film and Photo League after 1933) was part of an extensive cultural movement sponsored by the Communist International and its affiliated national parties in the inter-war period.* Specifically, it was a section of the Comintern-controlled *Internationale Arbeiterhilfe* or Workers International Relief (WIR), founded at Lenin's instigation in Berlin in 1921.

The WIR's initial function was famine relief in the Soviet Union. After the crisis had passed, the organization — with branches established in most countries of the world — became an international support force for strikers and their families: in the United States, for example, it provided food, clothing and shelter during the Communist-led textile and cotton workers' strikes at Passaic, New Bedford and Gastonia in 1926-29, and during the miners' strikes of 1931-32.

But the WIR's activities extended also into the mass media and many cultural fields. In Germany, under the leadership of the remarkable Communist entrepreneur and propagandist Willi Muenzenberg, the WIR built up a flourishing publishing empire encompassing daily and weekly newspapers, illustrated periodicals and books, all with a left-wing perspective. Elsewhere, with the exception of the Soviet Union, the WIR concentrated on ventures requiring little or no capitalization. Thus in the United States the WIR organized, during the early 1930s, revolutionary drama groups (the Workers Laboratory Theatre), dance groups (the Red Dancers), symphony and mandolin orchestras, bands, choirs and art workshops.

* *I would like to thank Leo Seltzer, Tom Brandon and David Platt for assistance with my research into the League.*

Muenzenberg was especially interested in film. In a 1925 article he decried the fact that ''in the main the labor organizations and even Communist Parties and groups have left this most effective means of propaganda and agitation in the hands of their enemy,'' and called for ''the conquest of this supremely important propaganda weapon,'' which he saw as the monopoly of the ruling class. ''We must wrest it from them,'' he concluded, ''and turn it against them.''[1]

The WIR's first motion-picture activity was in Russia, where in 1922 it began distributing German films. In 1924 it formed the production company Mezhrabpom-Russ (later Mezhrabpomfilm, ''Mezhrabpom'' being the abbreviation for the Russian name of the WIR). This company was to be responsible for many of the more significant Soviet features of the period, including Vsevolod I. Pudovkin's *Mother* (1926), *End of St. Petersburg* (1927), *Storm over Asia* (1928) and *Deserter* (1933), Dziga Vertov's *Three Songs about Lenin* (1934) and the first Soviet sound film, Nikolai Ekk's *Road to Life* (1931). Muenzenberg was to claim credit for the international perspective of many of Mezhrabpom's productions, such as *Storm over Asia*, which he termed ''the first film to thrust deeply into the chaos of imperialist politics.''[2]

In Germany the WIR entered production via the Prometheus company, acquired in 1925. Prometheus produced a number of films with a working-class point of view. The best known are Piel Jutzi's *Mother Krause's Journey to Happiness* (1929) and Slatan Dudow's *Kuhle Wampe* (1932). It also pioneered in the distribution of Soviet films in Europe, scoring a notable success with *Potemkin* in 1926. In 1928 Muenzenberg founded Weltfilm to handle nontheatrical distribution of workers' and Soviet films: this firm first popularized the use of 16mm for such screenings.

Meanwhile, the WIR was active in promoting the formation of workers' photo leagues to provide visual coverage of working-class subjects for the left-wing press. By 1930 or a little later such groups were operating in Germany, the Soviet Union, Great Britain, France, Switzerland, Czechoslovakia, Austria, the Netherlands, Japan and the United States.

THE BIRTH OF THE FILM AND PHOTO LEAGUE

In the United States, the WIR affiliate, at first known as Friends of Soviet Russia, had been involved with film distribution since the organization's founding in 1922. Throughout the decade it arranged nationwide release of documentaries about the Soviet Union, films designed to counteract the hostile propaganda emanating from Hollywood. Beginning in 1926 it also handled nontheatrical distribution (and, effectively, exhibition) of Soviet features. This distribution arm of the WIR was to become closely allied with the Workers Film and Photo League.

In 1930 the breakthrough into production was made. On March 6 a Communist-led demonstration of the unemployed resulted in probably the largest such crowd in U.S. history jamming into New York's Union Square; but the capitalist press minimized the event and commercial newsreels of the demonstration were suppressed at the behest of New York police chief Grover Whalen — no doubt partly because the newsreels exposed the brutality of his officers in action. As the economic situation worsened, protest marches, rallies and manifestations became more frequent and the bourgeois media continued to ignore or distort them. It was clear that there was an urgent need for workers' newsreels.

In May, *Daily Worker* film critic Samuel Brody wrote:

> I want once more to emphasize the news-film is the important thing; that the capitalist class knows there are certain things it cannot afford to have shown. It is afraid of some pictures. . . .
> Films are being used against the workers like police clubs, only more subtly — like the reactionary press. If the capitalist class fears pictures and prevents us from seeing records of events like the March 6 unemployment demonstration and the Sacco-Vanzetti trial we will equip our own cameramen and make our own films.[3]

Less than two weeks later, again in the *Daily Worker,* the call for workers' movie production was reiterated. Radical poet and film critic Harry Alan Potamkin argued:

> The German workers have started well. There is no need to begin big. Documentaries of workers' life. Breadlines and picketlines, demonstrations and police-attacks. Outdoor films first. Then interiors. And eventually dramatic films of revolutionary content. Workers' organizations should support a group to be pioneers on this important front.[4]

Even as the call was being made, the WIR was mobilizing its cinematic forces. The WIR-sponsored Workers Camera League in New York combined with the International Labor Defense (the Communist legal-aid organization) to form the Labor Defender Photo Group. Apart from its still photography activities, this group reportedly possessed two motion-picture cameras and filmed the May Day parade and demonstration in New York City. Other workers' newsreels followed, including film of a Communist Party dance, of the March 6 demonstration leaders in jail, of other Party demonstrations, and of events at a WIR children's summer camp.

Meanwhile the Workers Camera League continued meeting. In the early part of December 1930, apparently absorbing the Labor Defender Photo Group, it was reorganized and renamed the Workers Film and

Photo League. The new group met for the first time at WIR headquarters on December 11, and two days later held a housewarming party with entertainment, refreshments, dancing and a screening of the Soviet movie *In Old Siberia* (probably Yuli Raizman's 1928 film *Katorga*). An organization had been founded under the auspices of the WIR that could sustain political filmmaking and photography on a permanent, ongoing basis.

The key New York WFPL participants at the beginning were Leo Seltzer, Sam Brody (practising what he preached), Lester Balog and Robert Del Duca. Of the group members Del Duca had the most practical experience. He had worked as a newsreel cameraman and laboratory technician. Brody was clearly the theoretician and political overseer. Tom Brandon handled the WIR's film department, and was thus intimately involved with arranging distribution and exhibition of — and often finance for — the League's productions.

This core group was augmented in subsequent years by a larger membership. Outstanding among these members were the writers and critics Potamkin, Lewis Jacobs, Leo T. Hurwitz, David Platt, Jay Leyda (for a short period prior to his departure for the Soviet Union), Irving Lerner and the still photographer and experimental filmmaker Ralph Steiner. For the most part these men were less involved with the League's production work than with its other activities: publications, (program notes, contributions to *New Theatre,* the *Daily Worker,* and *Film Front*); lectures and discussions; film-series screenings; photographic exhibitions; anti-censorship agitation; boycott campaigns; film-school and photo courses.

By 1934 Balog was in California. There, as a member of the San Francisco FPL, he was jailed for showing *Road to Life* (1931) and *Cottonpickers' Strike* (1932) to agricultural workers. And in the fall of that year Hurwitz, Lerner and Steiner broke away to form the Nykino group. Soon after, Seltzer secured work as a filmmaker with the New York City art project, and most of the League's production in the last year or two of its existence seems to have been handled by Del Duca, Julian Roffman (who, like Brody, Brandon, Hurwitz, Platt and Lerner wrote on film topics for the *Daily Worker*), and Vic Kandel. Nancy Naumburg and James Guy did pioneering work, with the League's assistance, on the dramatized political documentary in 16mm.

NEWSREELS FOR THE WORKERS

As Leo Seltzer insists, the group was not challenging Hollywood on its own terms, manufacturing motion pictures as merchandise. Rather than speaking of individual "films," it is more correct to speak, for the bulk of (W)FPL production, of "footage" — news film processed and printed rapidly and then roughly edited for the quickest possible screening and maximum impact. Once the topical moment had passed, of course, the footage became available for recutting into later compilation documentaries, and it is to this class that most of the League's major productions — *National Hunger March* (1932), *Bonus March* (1932), and *Hunger 1932* — belong.

Though the newsreels did sometimes receive theatrical screenings (particularly during 1932-33 at New York's Acme Theatre), they were mostly exhibited by the (W)FPL members themselves, often along with a Soviet film, in a specifically political context. Taking films to the workers became a potent organizing device, as the following quotation from a Communist Party unit organizer indicates:

> Our shop unit in the Caterpillar plant is only about six months old. And while we are getting new contacts on the job (the plant has been working a few days a week and now closed down indefinitely), we found that shop-gate meetings are a great help in approaching workers on their problems.
>
> On March 1st a Party speaker held a meeting at the shop during noon hour. After the meeting the workers discussed a great deal among themselves on how to solve the conditions in favor of the workers. During the same time the Workers International Relief was showing a Russian movie to which the workers were invited. And for the next few days the workers in the plant were discussing the lack of unemployment in Russia and the millions of unemployed here. These discussions among workers gave [the Party members] the opportunity to comment and help them along and thereby find out who is who in the shop.
>
> As a result of the shop-gate meetings outside and our work inside we have now a functioning group of the Metal Trades Industrial League and have recruited seven new members to the Party unit (we started the shop unit with three members).[5]

As might be expected, the content of (W)FPL newsreels and longer films was conditioned by the particular campaigns being undertaken by the Communist Party. Here it is essential to recall that the period 1929-34 was one of militant class struggle for the world Communist movement. Party strategy in the United States (as elsewhere) was to build the strength of the movement by stimulating recruitment into: (a) the "revolutionary" unions — those affiliated to the Trade Union Unity League (TUUL); (b) the Party's "mass organizations," — of which the WIR was one, and; (c) the Party itself.

Thus the footage devoted to the miners' strikes of 1931 and 1932 played its part in assisting the drive to organize the coalminers of western Pennsylvania, eastern Ohio, Kentucky and Tennessee — then destitute and disillusioned with John L. Lewis's leadership of the United Mine Workers — into the TUUL-affiliated National Miners

Union (NMU). On the west coast there was an energetic campaign to build the Cannery and Agricultural Workers Industrial Union, reflected in several of the Los Angeles WFPL productions.

Organization of the unemployed was undertaken via the Unemployed Councils around the demands for immediate relief and a comprehensive program of social insurance. These demands were dramatized by numerous local and two national hunger marches. The national marches, held in December 1931 and December 1932, became occasions for co-ordinated newsreel coverage by WFPL cameramen around the country. The WIR arranged the filmed record along with food, shelter and medical care for the marchers. A hunger march in Detroit on March 7, 1932, filmed by members of the local League, became a massacre when police opened fire and killed four demonstrators; the film survives.

The Bonus March of 1932 was not Communist-led, but the Party did try to extend its influence among the out-of-work veterans through the participation of its "mass organization," the Workers Ex-Servicemen's League (WESL), whose banners are prominent in the powerful League film devoted to the march, camp and eviction.

The Scottsboro Case was used by the Party to focus attention on lynch law in the south and the oppression of blacks generally. The Party conducted a militant defense through its International Labor Defense (ILD) organization and held many rallies demanding the release of the accused men. This activity was reinforced by several newsreels and a short film made by Leo T. Hurwitz for the ILD, with assistance from the League.

Other films, as their titles and descriptions indicate, focused on further pressure points in the class struggle and helped fulfill the League's reported purpose of "the taking of newsreels of demonstrations, meetings, Party activities and other affairs of immediate, daily concern to the U.S. working-class."[6]

THE POLITICS OF FILM FORM

Cinéma-vérité has dulled our appreciation of participant camerawork, but in the 1930s the hand-held, close-range cinematography of street actions which the League footage offered must have struck spectators with great novelty and force. Leo Seltzer stresses the importance for conveying excitement of his physical involvement in the events he was shooting. Writing of his participation in the filming of *Hunger 1932*, Brody makes a similar point. Brody, however, lays emphasis — as Seltzer does not — on the political commitment of the filmmakers:

> I was a member of a group of four cameramen sent by the New York
> section of the Workers Film and Foto League to cover the activities of

Column 8 of the National Hunger March on its way to Washington from New York City.

Soon there will be shown to the workers of New York the evidence gathered by the keen eyes of our cameras. This evidence is totally unlike anything shown in newsreels taken by capitalist concerns. Our camera-men were class-conscious workers who understood the historical signifi-cance of this epic March for bread and the right to live. As a matter of fact, we 'shot' the March not as 'disinterested' news-gatherers but as actual participants in the March itself. Therein lies the importance of our finished film. It is the viewpoint of the marchers themselves. Whereas the capitalist cameramen who followed the marchers all the way down to Washington were constantly on the lookout for sensational material which would distort the character of the March in the eyes of the masses, our worker cameramen, working with small hand-cameras that permit unrestricted mobility, succeeded in recording incidents that show the fiendish brutality of the police towards the marchers.[7]

It is in camerawork and not in editing that the newsreels are distin-guished, but in the longer compilation films there are some striking sequences of montage in the Soviet manner. *Bonus March,* for exam-ple, edited by Leo Seltzer and Lester Balog, opens with a prologue that sketches the background of the contemporary situation; this sequence is a model of savage political comment in film. Without detailing the complete editing of the prologue, it is possible to give an indication of its content, and its power, by listing the shots and groups of following shots, which appear basically in the order given here. Some of these shots appear several times at key points, adding considerably to the drama and commentary of the prologue.

1. A title: "1917 . . ."
2. Swinging sign: "Go Places with the U.S. Army"
3. Sign: "Adventure Over the World" and doughboy
4. Mass parade of troops
5. Battlefield: tanks and troops advance
6. Cannons fire
7. Shell explodes, blows up building
8. Shell explodes on battlefield
9. Tanks, soldiers in battle
10. Battleships (various shots)
11. Interior, ship's gun-barrel
12. Ship's gunfire
13. Turret rotates
14. Explosion, smoking warship
15. Warplane
16. Soldiers advance
17. Explosion in the trenches

18. Dead on battlefield
19. Injured, maimed vets (one stretcher patient, one legless man) line up to be greeted at a garden party
20. U.S. flag
21. Churches
22. Down-and-out unemployed worker on bench
23. Priest
24. Heroic statuary
25. "Catholic Charities" sign
26. U.S. Eagle sign on Bank of the United States building
27. Unemployed man, close-up; and others
28. Salvation Army signs
29. A waterside Hooverville — shacks, one of the inhabitants
30. Breadline (various shots, coming closer to the men)

The film follows this with documentation of WESL agitation, the march to Washington and the encampment, and then begins its sequence of the eviction with a quick reprise of the opening statement — a title "1917..." and shots of marching troops, tanks on the battlefield, an explosion, the wounded given a garden party reception — then "1932..." and the U.S. infantry attacks down Pennsylvania Avenue, backed up by the cavalry and the armored division.

A montage sequence involving Franklin D. Roosevelt in *America Today* offers another example of creative montage used to make a political point forcefully and economically. The Communist Party line at the time was that Roosevelt was preparing for aggressive war and that the New Deal represented incipient fascism. The sequence is cut as follows: troops parade through streets/Mussolini salutes/troops march, give fascist salutes/fascist salute, *pan* to reveal arm is Hitler's/U.S. battleship, *tilt up* to following ship/F.D.R. signing document, reaches for blotter, lays it down, makes a fist to blot/cannons fired on navy cruiser/front view, guns are raised/interior, gun barrel/cannons fired/F.D.R. looks up and smiles/dark cloud, *dissolve* to National Recovery Administration Eagle sign and inscription: "We Do Our Part."

THE DEMISE OF THE FPL

Seltzer was quite content working strictly within a newsreel/documentary mode. By 1934, however, some dissatisfaction was being felt among other League members with this approach. It was in recognition of this and anticipation of arguments to come that Brody wrote the article "The Revolutionary Film: Problem of Form." The riposte came in *New Theatre* three months later, when Hurwitz described the work being done by an experimental group at the League's Harry Alan Potamkin Film School, and stated:

The plan is to develop this experimental group into a production group within the Film and Photo League for the purpose of making documentary-dramatic revolutionary films — short propaganda films that will serve as flaming film-slogans, satiric films and films exposing the brutalities of capitalist society.[8]

The plan encountered rough going, and the issue remains a controversial one among former FPL members. There is not enough space here to develop the ramifications of the dispute, which centered on financial priorities rather than either/or aesthetic commitments, but the upshot was that the FPL did not approve Hurwitz's proposal for a "*shock-troupe* of full time film workers," and in the fall of 1934 Hurwitz, Steiner and Lerner broke away to form the nucleus of a radical filmmaking collective known as "Nykino."

Meanwhile, in September, the FPL rededicated itself to the business of unvarnished newsreel production at a National Conference held in Chicago. Reference has so far been made primarily to the New York section of the League, but in fact branches existed in many cities of the country. Detroit, Chicago and Los Angeles were the most active in production, but there were strong groups also in Boston, Philadelphia, Washington, D.C. and San Francisco, and local FPL organizations were reported at one time or another in Pittsburgh, Hollywood, New Haven, Conn., Perth Amboy, N.J., Laredo, Tex., and the University of Wisconsin.

The Conference resolved that: "The tremendous growth of the working class movement coupled with the increase of strikes and class warfare makes it imperative for the Film and Photo League to concentrate its best film and photo forces on the field of battle, adequately to record the vital events of our time." The Conference also adopted 16mm as the basic stock for local use, and retained 35mm for original photography at the national level. A National Film Exchange was set up, and a National Executive Committee elected, with David Platt as National Secretary and Tom Brandon a member.[9]

Work continued. In 1934-35 Leo Seltzer produced, with Ed Kern, his much-praised *Marine,* and Nancy Naumburg, with James Guy, directed two longish political films (with acted sequences), *Sheriffed* and *Taxi,* the latter of which became an official FPL production. All these films are lost, and reviews provide only frustrating hints as to their content and technique.

It was evident that there were weaknesses in the movement. In November 1934 novelist and *Daily Worker* columnist Michael Gold expressed his disappointment:

Our Film and Photo League has been in existence for some years, but outside of a few good newsreels, hasn't done much to bring this great cultural weapon to the working class.

As yet, they haven't produced a single reel of comedy, agitation, satire or working-class drama.

And invoking *Three Songs About Lenin,* he concluded: "I hope somebody in the Film and Photo League learns how to do a film a tenth as good for proletarian America."[10] In response, Platt admitted that the charge was "very true." He added: "No one knows better how true it is than the Film and Photo League itself, which has been struggling for years to produce films on a budget and with forces that would have wrecked a similar bourgeois organization." He said the Photo League could only promise to do better in the future.[11]

The League members no doubt continued to struggle, but history was against them. The WIR, reeling under the annihilation of its German operations in the Third Reich, suffered a second grievous blow in 1935, when the Communist Party-Soviet Union abolished WIR's Russian section. Muenzenberg, now devoting himself to anti-fascist propaganda from Paris, was no longer with the organization. It managed to survive in several European countries (amalgamated with the International Red Aid), but in the United States its activities seem to have come to a standstill by mid-decade.

The League might have kept going as an independent entity — it did continue into 1937 — but without the organizational backing, financial support or political directions its parent body was able to provide there must have seemed little point in keeping it alive. After editing a feature-length documentary on the Chinese Revolution from commercial newsreel footage as a noble last gesture to the League, filmmakers Julian Roffman, Vic Kandel and veteran Robert Del Duca formed themselves into an independent production company, and a phase in U.S. radical cinema was at an end.

NOTES

[1] Willi Muenzenberg, "Capture the Film!" *Daily Worker,* July 23, 1925, p.3.
[2] Willi Muenzenberg, *Solidarität: Zehn Jahre Internationale Arbeiterhilfe, 1921-1931* (Berlin: Neuer Deutscher Verlag, 1931), p. 513.
[3] S[amuel] B[rody], "The Movies as a Weapon Against the Working Class," *Daily Worker,* May 20, 1930, p. 4.
[4] Harry A. Potamkin, "Workers' Films," *Daily Worker,* May 31, 1930, p. 3.
[5] *Party Organizer* 5, No. 8 (August 1932), 27.
[6] S[eymour] S[tern], "A Working-Class Cinema for America," *The Left* 1, No. 1 (Spring 1931): 71.
[7] Samuel Brody, "The Hunger March Film," *Daily Worker,* December 29, 1932, p. t.
[8] Leo T. Hurwitz, "The Revolutionary Film — Next Step," *New Theatre* 3, No. 6 (May 1934): 15.

[9] David Platt, "The Movie Front: National Film Conference," *New Theatre* 1, No. 10 (November 1934): 30.

[10] Michael Gold, "Change the World!" *Daily Worker,* November 5, 1934, p. 7.

[11] David Platt, "World of the Movies: A Reply to Michael Gold," *Daily Worker,* November 16, 1934, p. 5.

CHAPTER 7.

Notes on U.S. Radical Film, 1967-80

JOHN HESS

In the early 1960s, when a radical cinema began to emerge out of the shadows of cold war America, there was no visible revolutionary working-class movement. There were also no left parties in a position to contest for ideological or political power or to influence and guide young people. Both were crushed during the 1940s, and disappeared seemingly without a trace in the 1950s. Most young people who came to radical and left politics in the 1960s, especially the filmmakers, were from bourgeois and petit bourgeois families. They had little knowledge of or connection to the working class, its history, or its parties.[1] In fact, white working-class people had often opposed, sometimes violently, these young people's early political work in the civil rights movement, in community organizing among blacks and poor whites, and in the peace movement.

As a result there was not a broad base of support (especially in the early and mid-1960s) for a politics based on the working class. Many campus and rural radicals not in the small left parties tended to be actively anti-working class. Those in the industrial cities and in the Socialist Workers Party (a Trotskyist party dating back to the 1930s) or the Progressive Labor Party (which split off from the Communist Party in 1964) were more involved in the labor movement and saw business unionism as an important barrier to working-class development.[2]

Many of these young people were also deeply influenced by the nearly pathological anti-communism of the cold war period. The Korean War, the revolt in Hungary and the revelations about Stalin were played for all they were worth in the press and on TV. The Soviet Union's development made it easy to identify socialism with totalitarianism. Those who had some knowledge of the old left usually rejected it for its passivity, dogmatism, ties to the Soviet Union, and self-defeating policies. Thus there was almost a complete break between the labor and left activism of the 1930s and the student/left/ anti-war movement of the 1960s. It is only recently that we have begun to fill that gap in our knowledge.

The absence of a left tradition, the lack of contact with the working class (or even of a sense of class), anti-communism, the relative under-development of Marxist thought in North America, and the class background of the participants help explain the politics of the new left (I use the term broadly) and its filmmaking. New-left politics were eclectic, containing elements of Marxism, U.S. populism, Maoism (later in the 1960s), existentialism, anarchism, the counterculture, and a moralistic sense of justice and humanitarianism. New-left activists saw themselves as defending the interests of blacks, the poor, the Vietnamese and themselves as students and youth against the white U.S. establishment (of all classes). Their anti-racism was particularly important. They often looked to various oppressed groups to be the vanguard that would lead the revolution to create a free society in which everyone would have a voice in the decisions that affected their lives.

Naturally these politics grew and deepened during the struggles of the 1960s. The new left developed an analysis of capitalism that was very sophisticated, much more so than that developed by the old left, which was dependent on a dogmatic and economics-based Soviet Marxism. The eclecticism and concern for individual and private life created a context in which analyses of racism, sexism, sexuality and family life could develop, thus adding significantly to Marxist thought. As a result of the black struggles during the 1960s — the work of Martin Luther King, Malcolm X, the Student Nonviolent Coordinating Committee (SNCC), the Black Panthers, and the new left — people developed an extensive analysis of racism and of how racism served to divide the working class. Anti-racism, especially the struggles of the Black Panthers, was an important element in Newsreel's films in the 1960s and continued in the work of Third World Newsreel in the 1970s.

An understanding of imperialism grew out of the experience of the anti-war movement and from contact with Cuba (which for U.S. radicals, black and white, in this period, was both an important example of socialism in action and a source of encouragement and support for their work). As the war dragged on, as the evening news and other sources revealed the brutality of the U.S. war effort and the venality and corruption of the South Vietnamese leaders whom the U.S. government was supporting, it became harder and harder to see the war in any other way than as an effort by a capitalist superpower to dominate a Third World country. The idea that Johnson and Nixon were fighting for freedom and democracy was patently absurd. People also began to see the connection between racism at home and imperialism abroad. Thus a Marxist approach, which could explain such interconnections, became more and more acceptable.

During the last years of the 1960s, there was a rethinking of the idea of class. The increasing use of state power — the police, army, FBI, CIA, the draft boards and universities, lending institutions and the courts — against the anti-war movement, students, blacks and anyone else who disagreed with the government, the growing anti-war sentiment of the working class (whose children were doing the fighting and dying) and the growth and influence of the Marxist groups led more and more activists to a Marxist understanding of the central role of the working class in any meaningful social change, and especially in any revolution.

At the same time, from the mid-1960s on, many women broke away from the male-dominated movement in order to deal directly with their specific oppression as women in a patriarchal society. Just as the black movement, which always had a very strong nationalist character, contributed greatly to an analysis of racism and how it served capitalism, the autonomous women's movement developed, and continues to develop, an analysis of sexism. Clearly, had women not created their own autonomous movement, they would not have been able to develop this important analysis.[3]

The 1970s were very different. Whereas the 1960s were dominated by an aggressive mass movement and intense struggle, by the rapid expansion of Marxist thinking, and the development of analyses of racism and sexism, the 1970s were characterized by fragmentation of the movement and an aggressive capitalist attack on the gains that workers, blacks and women made in the 1960s. The economic downturn, the end of the war, the brutal crushing of the Black Panthers and the co-optation of most of the black movement weakened the left to the point that its internal contradictions surfaced and led to fragmentation. Without a cohesive social movement to be part of and to make films for, filmmakers drifted off in many directions. Most Newsreels ceased to exist and the rest split and split again. Only the ongoing strength of the women's movement (in spite of the fragmentation of most of its institutions) provided a base for filmmakers, and women's films dominated the decade.

The political cinema (or any other kind) of blacks, latinos and other Third World peoples in the United States had for obvious class and material reasons not got off the ground by the end of the 1960s. Some Third World people worked within Newsreel, especially Third World Newsreel, in the 1970s, but otherwise the development took place within highly institutionalized settings, especially TV stations and universities, which meant a strict limitation on what kind of films could be made. Nonetheless, the Alternative Cinema Conference in June 1979 and the Chicano Film Festival in August of the same year demonstrate that a great deal was accomplished in the late 1970s. Finally, the Gay Liberation movement, growing out of the Stonewall Rebellion (June 1969), began to produce significant films by lesbians and gay men, work designed to contribute to that movement. A more detailed history of radical cinema would have to treat these minority cinemas in great detail.

THE CONDITIONS FOR LEFT FILMMAKING

The opportunity to make films which go beyond the liberal and social democratic hope of reforming capitalism to explain capitalism as a class system and to advocate socialism was in the 1960s and still remains impossible within the U.S. film industry (that is, Hollywood).

From time to time, because of changing material conditions in the country — the 1930s and more recently are good examples — liberal and left-liberal critiques of the evils of capitalism (the effects of the system, never the system itself) can be found in some Hollywood films (*Blue Collar,* 1978, *F.I.S.T.,* 1978, *Norma Rae,* 1979). But these films remain comfortably within the realm of bourgeois ideology by focusing on the struggles of individuals, leaving systematic oppression and change out of the picture. Also, these liberal films are a tiny portion of a yearly production of films that are primarily racist, sexist, national-chauvinist and appeal to the worst instincts of the film-going audience. Until there is an aggressive left-wing labor movement and a genuinely revolutionary left party with roots in the working class, Hollywood will never make films that support and encourage the class consciousness of the working class. It is important to note here that Hollywood not only controls the production of commercial feature films but also their distribution. As I will discuss below, distribution is the primary problem for radical filmmakers in the United States.

The same situation exists in the commercial television networks. And even the Public Broadcasting System (PBS), which is supported financially by the national government and by large corporations, is conservative politically. Nonetheless, in the last 20 years it has sponsored a small number of progressive documentaries that have exposed gross examples of how U.S. capitalism really works at home and abroad. Even though the PBS audience is small and primarily composed of white, college-educated people, it has managed to make some money available to radical filmmakers, especially Third World filmmakers. But since its support comes from capitalists, it is not likely to become a reliable sponsor of left-wing filmmaking. The medium with the greatest access to the working class, commercial TV, is the least accessible to critical ideas of any kind.

Since the end of World War II the physical and technical requirements for an extensive left film-distribution network have existed. There was a tremendous expansion of production of 16mm cameras and projection equipment during the war. In the pre-TV era, the government turned to 16mm film as one important way to deliver propaganda. By the early 1950s most schools, colleges, churches, unions, community groups and other similar organizations had access to a 16mm projector which was portable and easy to use. In the same period there was a tremendous growth in the production, distribution and use of educational films. Everyone who went to school in the 1950s remembers the anti-communist and fallout-shelter films.

Although an extensive non-theatrical distribution network was available in 1960, it was almost completely closed to radical films of any kind. The distribution of educational films was controlled by large corporations and the school systems that used the films. The films in this system have been until very recently uncompromisingly backward. The few independent distributors who had formed to distribute European art films and 16mm versions of Hollywood classics were unwilling to distribute all but the most innocuous radical films of the 1960s. Even Tom Brandon, one of the founders of the Film and Photo League of the 1930s, was unwilling to have his company, Audio-Brandon, distribute new left films. The American Friends Service Committee (the social action arm of the Quaker church), the "Teach-In" network (of anti-war groups on college campuses), SDS (Students for a Democratic Society) and similar groups used left films in their work but were not really film distributors.

Conscious of this problem, filmmakers saw the need to distribute as well as produce films and it is possible to discuss U.S. radical films by looking at the companies and organizations that were formed to distribute them. American Documentary Films (1966-72) was founded to produce and distribute anti-war films and films from Cuba, Europe and Southeast Asia. Newsreel (founded 1967) always saw distribution of its own and other films as one of its most important functions. New Day Films (founded 1971) was formed as a co-operative to distribute feminist films. Women Make Movies, Iris Films, Odeon Films, Third World Films (later Tricontinental Film Center) and similar groups were all formed to distribute and also usually to produce films.

Although the distribution situation is much better now than in 1965, it is still very primitive, inefficient and incomplete compared to the commercial distribution network. The great number of small distributors and the lack of sufficient capital to advertise films and service customers properly confuse and irritate film users. It is still difficult to get adequate information promptly and to receive well-cleaned and maintained prints when you want them. Even though most of these distributors take into account the fact that many potential users don't have much money, it is still relatively expensive to rent most films. It is still a business in a capitalist economy and there are real conflicts between distributors and users as well as between filmmakers and distributors.

So far most radical films have been documentaries, which has severely limited their audience in two important ways. On the one hand, although documentaries are shown extensively in educational institutions and on "educational" and news shows on TV, these institutions are usually closed to radical films. On the other hand, with few exceptions, documentaries have never done well in theaters — in part, perhaps, because of the educational context in which we come to know them in the first place. Thus radical films in the last 20 years have had access only to the fringes of the potential market. In the last decade some films, such as *Growing Up Female* (1974), *Men's Lives* (1974), the Oscar-winning *Harlan County* (1976), *Union Maids* (1976), and *Controlling Interest* (1978), have made strong inroads into the educational film market. Recently, political filmmakers have been attempting to make feature fiction films in order to overcome the limitation of the documentary format and reach a larger audience (*Over-Under Sideways-Down,* 1977, and *Northern Lights,* 1978, have been made by a group called Cinemanifest). But they have painfully learned that a distribution network set up to handle documentaries is not equipped to distribute features to theaters. And since the politically oriented distributors lack access to regular film theaters, Cinemanifest had to start from scratch in distributing its films.

If distribution were not so weak, it would probably be much easier to raise money for politically progressive films. Indeed, it is usually the case that raising money takes more effort, time, energy, creativity, perseverance, patience and strength than making the film. Although some few politically progressive films have been very successful (*Men's Lives, Union Maids, Harlan County,* for instance), to my knowledge no film has earned the filmmakers enough money to pay off debts, buy needed equipment, and finance the next film.

This means that for each project a filmmaker must go out and raise money. And the sources for these funds are very limited: a few dozen national and local foundations, state and city arts councils, institutions such as churches and unions, and private funds from interested individuals, relatives and friends. Usually filmmakers will go through several cycles of fundraising and filmmaking. They will raise enough money to get started and then take some portion of that unfinished film around to show it to people who might contribute money. Later more will have to be raised to finish the film and get started on distribution. In most cases filmmakers must spend a year or so distributing their film before they entrust it to or can even find a distributor. Many films, especially women's and Third World people's films, never find any sort of distribution.

In 1977 the Film Fund was organized to try to centralize the money available to filmmakers from different foundations and to simplify the fundraising effort. The hope was that the Film Fund would be able to get the foundations to give more money to filmmaking. So far this has not happened. Furthermore, the Film Fund seems less interested in raising funds from foundations and other sources than in getting involved in other projects (that is, ways of spending its money) that seem designed to further the interests of a few, already fairly successful filmmakers whose social-democratic politics (a vague amalgam of sentimental socialism and the liberal desire to reform capitalism, a vision of revolution that includes no pain, suffering or sacrifice and threatens no vested interests) correspond to those of the Fund's leaders. I'm referring to a very expensive survey of radical film distribution that could have just as easily been accomplished by calling up the primary distributors of such films and to an expensive conference for feature "social change" filmmakers held in New York in 1979.

Because the original idea of such a fund was a good one and because radical filmmaking has so little access to money, the founding of the Film Fund created a great many expectations that no such organization could fulfill. But because the Film Fund combined very progressive rhetoric with a practice based on no clearly articulated political principles and because it did not make itself in any way accountable to the left, it created more enemies than it needed to.

I've tried briefly to lay out the political and material conditions of radical filmmaking in the United States in the decades of the 1960s and 1970s. Now I will try to follow the main lines of development of this filmmaking. In what follows, the left wing of avant-garde filmmaking, various left-liberal documentaries made for TV, and the work of Third World people have not been given their due.

NEWSREEL: THE BEGINNINGS

In October 1967 there was a massive demonstration against the Vietnam War in Washington, D.C., right in front of the Pentagon. This demonstration was a turning point in the anti-war movement because it represented an abandonment of non-violent tactics by many parts of the anti-war movement and the beginning of active resistance to the state. It was also the first time that federal troops were used against demonstrators. Many of the mostly student demonstrators not only refused to disperse but aggressively fought back when army troops advanced on them. Many people involved in the movement knew that this demonstration at the Pentagon would be important and many filmmakers, photographers and artists from New York went to Washington prepared to document what would happen.

Informal contacts were made at the demonstration and, once back in New York, people began to discuss the possibility of using all the footage they shot in a collective film. Jonas Mekas, spokesperson for the New American Cinema, editor of *Film Culture*, and critic for the *Village Voice,* called a meeting to discuss this as well as the prospects for forming some sort of production and distribution organization. After several mass meetings, those who were still interested (excluding Mekas, who, however, continued to give support) founded Newsreel in December 1967. In the meantime, much of the footage shot in Washington was given to Marvin Fishman, who soon completed *No Game* (1968), which was distributed by Newsreel.

A great number of the people who formed New York Newsreel (NYN) in the winter of 1967-68 were between 25 and 30 years old, university graduates in the humanities or social sciences, and from mostly middle-class professional families. Many of them had some prior training and experience in filmmaking. Peter Gessner had already made *Time of the Locust* (1966), an anti-war compilation film. Norm Fruchter, Robert Kramer, and Bob Machover had made *Troublemakers* (1965), about an SDS organizing project in Newark, N.J., and several other films. They had also formed Blue Van Films to produce and distribute films. Lynn Phillips had learned filmmaking at a Boston TV station. Allen Siegel and Marvin Fishman had made experimental films. Stu Bird, Eric Breitbart, and Barbara and David Stone had also worked on films. Many other members were practising artists: photographers, painters, writers, actors and actresses. In the early years some 40 to 70 people attended weekly meetings. It was an intelligent and creative group of people who had a profound effect on U.S. left filmmaking and still do: Newsreel continues to function in New York and San Francisco; early Newsreel films continue to circulate; many current political filmmakers got started in or passed through Newsreel.

By the late spring of 1968, Newsreel had spread to Boston, Chicago, San Francisco and Los Angeles. Boston made many of the draft resistance films; San Francisco made the Black Panther films and Newsreel's first film about a labor struggle (*Oil Strike,* 1969); Chicago completed only one film on its own *(April 27th)* in 1968 but contributed footage to several Newsreel films on activities in Chicago.

Although these other Newsreels were usually started by ''organizers'' travelling out from New York, they were all very different. They were mostly composed of people who were younger and had little filmmaking training or experience but who came out of political organizations. Thus these other Newsreels were also better organized and more politically developed than New York. The terrible tension in New York between the individualism of the artists and the need for group discipline expressed by the political activists (and this tension often took place within the same person) was generally absent from these other groups. They were heavily involved in distribution and functioned more as political collectives than as a group of political filmmakers whose individual needs were usually as important as their allegiance to the group.

NEWSREEL FILMS: TECHNIQUES AND DISTRIBUTION

The main impression you get from seeing Newsreel films are both their great excitement and energy and their poor technical quality. Most of the films are short — 6 to 25 minutes — and dynamic. The rock music on the soundtrack directs the editing and because few of the usual editing rules are followed, the films jerk the audience around a lot. Most of the films mix interview/speech material with confrontations with authorities, usually the police. One film, *Pig Power* (1969), contains only street fighting between demonstrators and the police, edited to the beat of a rock-and-roll soundtrack.

Newsreel filmmakers clearly assumed that viewing these confrontations would drive people out into the streets to join in. And there is much evidence that in the highly politicized atmosphere of the late 1960s their assumption was correct. Showings of *Columbia Revolt* (1968), about the occupation by students of Columbia University in New York City, contributed to demonstrations and to building occupations. The films were made at the height of the student and anti-war movements: hundreds of thousands of people were involved in massive, often violent, demonstrations against the authorities. Almost any film depicting and encouraging this activity would have been effective.

Newsreel films are famous for their low technical quality. Unsteady hand-held shots, poor focus, grainy and cloudy images, sloppy framing, unconventional and often confusing editing, and indistinct soundtracks often make watching them a real burden — if you need to see and hear everything. But clearly Newsreel wanted more an emotional than an intellectual response. They didn't care whether you saw or heard every detail as long as you got excited and involved.

Now, it is certainly true that inadequate funds, poor equipment and inexperience, as well as improvised and often dangerous shooting situations caused much of this low quality. But that is not a complete explanation. Newsreel had at least two reasons for consciously making films this way or at least for not making polished films. In the first place, Newsreel (and the new left generally) had a strong desire to shock bourgeois notions of taste. Many of them wanted to be sure their films were not like the slick and polished documentaries and newsreels made by the established media. The studied sloppiness and neglect of bourgeois artistic conventions are typical of much of the countercultural activity of the 1960s, with its strong ties to the avant-garde. In fact, a number of Newsreel filmmakers had come to political activity from the avant-garde. In this tradition, and especially among the Beat poets who influenced many Newsreel filmmakers, anything that outraged the businessman, the politician and the liberal professional was seen as a blow for liberation.

Newsreel had another justification for its kind of filmmaking:

> Our films remind some people of battle footage: grainy, camera weaving around trying to get the material and still not get beaten or trapped. Well, we, and many others, are at war. We not only document that war, but try to find ways to bring that war to places which have managed so far to buy themselves isolation from it.[4]

Although this statement by no means represents a consensus of New York Newsreel participants in the late 1960s (or of the other Newsreels), it was a very strong current.[5] In retrospect it is a strange image for privileged filmmakers living in New York to have. It reflects an identification with oppressed Third World people here and abroad so strong as to hinder rational thinking about one's own situation. It leads to Weather politics* which reject the white part of the U.S. working class as a possible component of any revolutionary change and puts all hope in Third World people. Robert Kramer's *Ice* (1969) is perhaps the best known filmic presentation of where such politics of despair lead white radicals.

All Newsreel people saw distribution of their own and others' films as a primary responsibility and everyone participated in it. And they were very successful. Members would go along with the films to showings and lead discussions of the issues raised by the films. These showings took place in schools of all different kinds, in community centres, offices during lunch, churches, street corners (using the cinemobile, a truck with projection facilities in the back). The practice of participating actively in film showings greatly increased the effectiveness of the films and provided invaluable political training for the people who did it. It is something that many political filmmakers continue to do. Not only does it increase the effectiveness of films but it also provides the filmmakers with important feedback about how audiences respond to their films.

Between 1970 and 1973, Newsreel went through profound changes. SDS suffered a serious split at its June 1969 convention between the Weatherman faction, which saw imperialism as the primary contradic-

---

*"Weather politics" was a type of radical confrontation activism practised by a small group of white radicals in the late 1960s and early 1970s.

tion, and those forces wanting to focus on the U.S. working class. This split heralded the disintegration of the student-based radical movement of which Newsreel was a part. In spite of the split, the school year 1969-70 was a high point of student activism and of Newsreel as well. In the following few years, however, most of the Newsreel chapters disappeared. New York and San Francisco remained but went through a series of changes typical of the times. At some points they found themselves down to one or two people who would barely manage to do a minimum of distribution.

Finally, with all new people (except for Allan Siegel, who had edited many of New York Newsreel's original films), Third World Newsreel began making and distributing films in New York City about Third World people living in the United States. *Teach Our Children* (1972), *In the Event Anyone Disappears* (1974), *We Demand Freedom* (1974), *Inside Women Inside* (1978) explore various aspects of the prison system and racism. Other films include *From Spikes to Spindles: A History of the Chinese in New York* (1976), *Fresh Seeds in the Big Apple* (1976), which looks at childcare problems, *Percussions, Impressions, Reality* (1978), which examines Puerto Rican life in the city through its music, *Mohawk Nation*, about native Americans, and *A Dream is What You Wake Up From* (1979), which deals with both middle-class and working-class black family life.

San Francisco Newsreel became California Newsreel and began distributing films and working with labor unions, churches and community groups. Their film on multinational corporations, *Controlling Interest*, was one of their most notable successes. But the 1970s also saw the development of other filmmaking collectives, such as Cinemanifest in San Francisco, Lucha Films in Los Angeles, Kartemquin Films in Chicago, and Pacific Street Films in New York.

THE WOMEN'S MOVEMENT AND FILM

Although feminist filmmaking as we know it today began in Newsreel, women such as Maya Deren have long been active in avant-garde filmmaking. It has always been easier for women to learn filmmaking skills in the liberal, anti-technology atmosphere of art schools than in the film-industry-oriented film schools. This fact may explain the strong urge towards formal innovation among feminist filmmakers and the great overlap between the formalist, avant-garde, and the more directly political branches of feminist filmmaking in the United States.

Within New York Newsreel the oppression and marginalization of women was extreme: an exclusively male leadership dominated the organization. Most of the women in Newsreel had no filmmaking skills and were relegated to menial jobs, especially office work. Lynn Phillips learned filmmaking at a Boston TV station, worked with Richard Leacock and D.A. Pennebaker in New York and was mainly responsible for Newsreel's most successfully distributed film in the 1960s, *Columbia Revolt*. But in spite of (or perhaps because of) her skills, she found it very difficult to do important work in Newsreel.

Women with fewer skills found it almost impossible to learn them. A few men controlled access to money and equipment. They would let women help and support their projects, but they never shared much of their knowledge and experience with them. New York Newsreel never had formalized training sessions. However, at one point Bob Machover taught several informal classes which were very important to the women in Newsreel, who had no other way to learn these skills.

Nonetheless, women were able to work together to make several films on women's events and issues: *The Jeanette Rankin Brigade* (1968), *Up Against the Wall, Miss America* (1968), *She's Beautiful When She Is Angry* (1969), *Childcare* (1969), and *Makeout* (1970). Finally, in San Francisco, where sexual politics were dealt with much earlier and more thoroughly and successfully than in New York, the major Newsreel film by and about women, *The Women's Film,* was produced in 1970.

In the years 1970-71 six more important women's films appeared: *I Am Somebody* by Madeline Anderson, about a strike by primarily black and female hospital workers; *Wanda* by Barbara Loden, a cinéma vérité-style fiction film about the oppression of a lower-class woman; *Woo Who? May Wilson,* a short documentary about an older woman artist who begins a new life in New York City, by Amalie Rothschild; *Janie's Jane,* which was made by Geri Ashur and Peter Barton within New York Newsreel and portrays the evolution of a white welfare mother; *Growing Up Female,* by Julia Reichert and Jim Klein, which analyzes female socialization; and Kate Millet's *Three Lives,* portraits of three women.

These seven films cover most of the basic concerns that feminist filmmaking developed in the next 10 years, except for lesbianism. They include portraits of individual women who in their own words tell about their lives in a patriarchal society where they lack voices or articulated histories. The films deal with women's sexuality and how it has been shaped, defined, distorted, repressed and abused by men. The traditional female role of wife and mother comes under scrutiny and is revealed as a kind of enforced drudgery rather than a freely chosen and embraced avocation. Great attention is paid to women's economic position as wife and worker. Women can choose between unpaid labor in the home and low-paid labor in the service industries. Most of the films clearly show the various ways in which women have fought back and, by example, suggest a new way — organization as women.

From that point on into the 1970s, feminist filmmaking greatly expanded. Barbara Hammer, Jan Oxenberg, Iris films and others made films about the lesbian experience in a homophobic society. Many films were made about rape and women's self-defense. The area of women's health, self-examination, and medical care produced a large number of films. Women also made films not specifically about women, for example Cinda Firestone's *Attica* (1973). Finally, and in part a continuation of the portrait films, women made films about activist women in the labor movement: *Union Maids, Harlan County,* and *With Babies and Banners* (1978).

As the list of feminist and political films made by women in the 1970s makes clear, women have produced a large proportion of the most influential and most used radical films in North America since the high point of Newsreel in the late 1960s. Women have also founded several significant distribution companies to distribute their own and others' films. How can we explain this productivity and political success within a radical movement dominated by men and a patriarchal ideology? It seems clear that the political strength and creativity of the autonomous women's movement and the interaction between that movement and women filmmakers have given them the space to make this valuable contribution to women's consciousness and to the U.S. left in general.

Many women filmmakers became active in the women's movement before they became filmmakers. Many of them were active in a feminist political project, such as abortion counselling (which was a criminal activity) and in struggles against institutions, such as universities and city governments, for childcare facilities and better medical care for women, against sex discrimination, for equal pay and union recognition in the service industries to which women and Third World people have been relegated. Because of this practical organizing experience. These women were able to make films based on the real needs and aspirations of other women, not on wishful thinking or abstract theories about what should be. Also because they have roots in the women's movement and make their films for this movement (if not always exclusively), they have a tremendous rapport with their audience.

These filmmakers' success demonstrates the correctness and need for separatist politics within many parts of the women's movement. Many of these filmmakers were able to develop politically, intellectually, emotionally and artistically within the context of an all-women's movement. For many, this same sort of development would probably not have been possible within the male-dominated left. The success of these films, which have radicalized more people than most other political films made in the United States in the last 20 years, also demonstrates that the issues they tend most to deal with — healthcare, rape, wife and child abuse, abortion, homosexuality and sexuality, sexism, patriarchy and the family — are of vital interest to a great number of people.

Even if many of these films seem to have been made exclusively for women, they are nonetheless important for the left both because the issues dealt with *are* left issues, issues any socialist revolution will have to deal with, and because they show how to move people with films. On the whole the films have not drawn women away from political activity, as some men often charge; they have, instead, drawn large numbers of U.S. women of all classes, ages and races into direct confrontation with capitalism. Of course, the films have not done this alone. The tremendous growth of the service industries since World War II and the influx of women into these industries and out of the home have created material and social conditions that have made many women open to radical ideas and activity.

In addition, after ten years of political filmmaking experience, some women went on to make more and more subtle and sophisticated films for women, films that examine various aspects of women's consciousness and experience. These more recent films are based on social and psychological research and often use sophisticated formal techniques — optical printing, mixed media (film and video), and a variety of distancing devices to disrupt the linear narrative or documentary flow of the film. These formal devices, rather than being used for their own sakes, help both to clarify complex problems and to communicate a more complex message.

Jo Ann Elam's *Rape* (1974) is based on a group discussion of rape which was first recorded on videotape and then transferred to film. The film also includes titles that comment on what the women are saying, and a variety of other 16mm materials: cinéma vérité street scenes of men ogling women, pans of downtown buildings to represent male institutions, and a variety of art works representing conventional views of women's role. Much of the latter material is in humorous counterpoint to the seriousness of the discussion which often continues on the soundtrack.

Michelle Citron's *Daughter Rite* (1978) is a 50-minute color film that interweaves the stories of two nuclear families, concentrating on the relationship between mothers and daughters. One story consists of 8mm home-movie footage of the interaction of a mother and daughter. The footage is manipulated by optical printing and slow motion to bring out the violence and domination of very common gestures, and on the soundtrack the audience hears excerpts from a daughter's diary (it may or may not be the daughter in the movie). The second story consists of the interactions of two sisters and their reflections on their mother, shot in imitation cinéma vérité style (it is actually scripted and acted).

Both these films have produced very intense personal and political discussions among women. Although neither film expresses much class consciousness, they both clearly describe and analyze the domestic and social ideologies that oppress women in patriarchal society and demonstrate the physical power (men and mothers) which backs up these ideologies. Thus they both clearly demonstrate that human liberation is not simply a matter of getting one's head together. Only revolutionary social change will change the power relations revealed in such films.

FILM AND THE LABOR MOVEMENT

The relationship between radical filmmakers and the labor movement in the 1960s and 1970s was an uneasy one. The various left groups that did consider labor to be of primary importance and sent their members into (or had members in) factories often neglected culture, especially film.

Throughout the period, however, documentaries on labor subjects were produced by National Education Television (NET) and the other networks. Examples are Harvey Richards's *The Land Is Rich* (1965), about agribusiness and farm workers in California, and Susan Racho's NET documentary, *Garment Workers in Southern California,* (1975). Also, the farm workers union made several organizing films for themselves, such as *Nosotros Venceremos* (1971).

While these films do make people aware of certain issues and have sometimes been useful in specific organizing drives, they tend to show workers as helpless victims and call at the most for various reforms of capitalism. However, there were also people in Newsreel who were interested in labor issues; they were usually people from working-class backgrounds or people with connections to the old left. San Francisco Newsreel made *Oil Strike* (1969) about a strike by oil refinery workers in Richmond, Calif. Peter Gessner, Stu Bird, and Rene Lichtman made *Finally Got the News* (1970) in Detroit about the Revolutionary Union Movement among black auto workers.

Although labor as a subject was by no means new, there was an intensification of interest in the subject through the 1970s as many leftist filmmakers tried to revive a labor and left tradition. *Union Maids* and *With Babies and Banners* focus on past struggles of women both as workers/organizers and as wives of workers. *Harlan County, On the Line* (1977), and *Song of the Canary* (1978) all focus on current labor issues. All of these films helped to educate people about past and present labor struggles. *Union Maids, Harlan County,* and *With Babies and Banners* made important links between feminism and labor issues.

However, these films tend to show and interpret union struggles and activities for a predominantly intellectual audience and have not, with the possible exception of *Harlan County*, been used very much as part of labor struggles themselves. To meet this more agitational need, a new trend in film and video-making appeared to be developing. In the San Francisco Bay Area, several groups of left film and video makers began to work closely with unions, rank-and-file dissident groups within unions, and with unorganized workers (80 percent of workers in the United States) to make films and tapes designed to aid the workers themselves, or designed to raise class consciousness. It was a trend that held out the possibility of a kind of film and video production speaking directly to the needs of the working class and taking the issue of class as a central concern.

CONCLUSION

In the 1960s and 1970s radical filmmaking in the United States changed considerably. *Harlan County* won an Oscar and *Union Maids* was nominated for one. These and several other radical films appeared on TV. As a result, radical filmmaking received increased media attention — including film reviews in the *New York Times* and *Wall Street Journal* — and more access to audiences outside the metropolitan areas. By the end of the period radical filmmakers were spending more money, making longer and more sophisticated films, and developing their skills to a higher degree than ever before. As a result there developed a large pool of skilled and experienced filmmakers who considered themselves "on the left."

At the same time, however, the mainstream of radical filmmaking grew less militant. There was still no viable left or labor movement able to guide and sustain filmmakers. There was no student movement to push them to the left. The absence of a movement, a party and a structure for film funding and distribution encouraged filmmakers to temper their politics in order to obtain a more secure basis from which to work.

There also seemed to be a success syndrome (called Hollywooditis) in which filmmakers who are successful and obtain a more secure basis grow to want larger budgets in order to make more grandiose films or to move into fiction filmmaking. By doing this they tended to move away from their political roots and to a certain extent betray their responsibility to the movement which, in great part, gave them their success. Without the women's movement, for example, *Growing Up Female, Union Maids, Harlan County* and *Men's Lives* would never have been made. It is usually only those filmmakers working within political collectives and women who hold themselves accountable to the women's movement who have maintained a sharp political focus and who have continued to make films that engage people politically.

Finally, in the 1970s there was a steady development of political film and video-making within the black, latino, and Asian communities as well as in the lesbian and gay community. In the last decade a few individuals from these various oppressed groups have been able to learn skills and work in the film and TV industries. Groups like Newsreel and Kartemquin made films about them. But until recently they have not had the opportunity to make political films and tapes about themselves, expressing their aspirations to the fullest. Along with labor-oriented film and video-making, lesbian, gay, black, latino and Asian films and video-making would become politically important in the next period.

NOTES

[1] This is clearly an oversimplification. There was a fairly large countercurrent of people who came out of left and progressive families — often sons and daughters of people who were in or around the Communist Party during the Popular Front period in the last half of the 1930s. Often the parents had left the Party during the persecution of leftists in the late 1940s and early 1950s and sometimes the children only found out about their parents' political activity after they themselves became active. It is important to keep in mind, too, that the kinds of people who became politically active in the 1960s changed over the decade.

[2] "Business unionism" refers to the structure and ideology of the U.S. trade-union movement. The union bureaucracies are fully integrated into the state apparatus and accept the basic premises of capitalism: need for profit, a market economy, labor discipline, and "productivity."

[3] Other women remained within mixed organizations and fought for feminist demands there, often with the help of men who were equally disgusted with the style and content of movement leadership. The New American Movement, for example, in 1972 consistently raised feminist demands internally and externally. In trade-union work feminists have tended to gravitate towards unions with a larger number of women. But the basic point is that the autonomous women's movement was and still is a tremendous source of inspiration and support for women no matter where they do their political work.

[4] Newsreel, unpublished typescript, December 1967, p. 4.

[5] I want to emphasize this point because even though the current I am describing dominated the early years of Newsreel and many of the films, there was a wide variety of people and tendencies in Newsreel. A yippie tendency produced such early films as *Garbage* (1968) and *Mill-In* (1968), about the Negro Action Group's attempt to set up a meat co-op. *Herman B. Ferguson,* about the Peace and Freedom Party's black candidate for Senate from New York, and *Community Control* (1968), about a struggle for community control by black and Puerto Rican New Yorkers, show a much more sober and rational side of Newsreel's membership.

CHAPTER 8.

Union Maids: Working-Class Heroines

LINDA GORDON

Union Maids (1976) is an important, compelling and happy film, product of a new class-conscious socialist movement that is emerging out
of the strengths of both the new and old lefts.* The film should also help
to build that movement by making it possible to understand and use our
history.

Union Maids is thus a film about working-class history made to
become part of the working-class future. It is carefully researched
(although it contains some misleading implications) and it is easy and
accessible. It is about the emotional and personal — as well as the
objective and political — reality of its heroines. As a film about heroics,
it is therefore in the optimistic tradition of socialist realism; it reasserts
the potential of leadership by people who are at once exceptional and
ordinary.

The film, a collective portrait of three women labor organizers
active from the 1930s to the present, focuses on the Congress of Industrial Organizations (CIO) organizing drive of the 1930s. The three
women were part of a community of working-class Chicago socialists.
They all came to Chicago in their youth, two from farms and one from
New Orleans. All of them entered industrial jobs in the early 1930s and
rapidly became rank-and-file activists, union organizers and socialist
leaders.

Their stories first appeared, told by themselves, in Alice and
Staughton Lynd's book, *Rank and File: Personal Histories of Working
Class Organizers*.[1] Thus it is possible to find out even more about them
than the movie tells us. In content as well as in conceptualization the
movie is in some ways a cinematic version of the book, and this is no

* I am indebted to Rosalynn Baxendall, Peter Biskind, Nancy Falk,
Allen Hunter and Ann Popkin for helpful comments and ideas.

slight to the film. Rather, it suggests the importance of the kind of class conscious, political, oral history that the Lynds are doing.

I am writing about this film mainly as an historian. I bring in "extraneous" information, from the Lynds' book and from other sources, because I want to evaluate the film as a form of historical and political communication. Many of my comments are more questions than criticisms, for being neither filmmaker nor film critic, I am unsure of the possibilities of filmic communication.

THE WOMEN, THE HISTORY

Sylvia Woods was born in New Orleans in 1909, the daughter of a black craftsman roofer, a man proud of his skill. She is conscious of the political legacy left her by her father, an ardent union man and a Garveyite.* As a schoolgirl she was already fighting racism and refusing to accept the accommodationist ideology her school offered.

Stella Nowicki also apparently sees herself mostly as her father's daughter. She grew up on a midwestern farm, leaving there in 1933 at age 17. Her father had been a coal miner, a socialist who read Lenin and Gorky in Polish. Her mother was a practising Catholic. Stella learned Polish from her father's revolutionary books, yet she also had to struggle against her father's patriarchal control.

Kate Hyndman immigrated to Iowa from Croatia at age five, in 1913. Her father was also a coal miner. But she is the only one of the "union maids" who speaks in the film of her debt to her female ancestors' rebelliousness and toughness. Since in the Lynds' book Hyndman too speaks mainly of what she learned from her father and how she struggled against him, I wonder whose decision it was, or whether it was merely chance, that in the film she talks about the women in her family. This is one of several instances when the viewer senses that the filmmakers are not entirely in control of what their film says.

Visually we meet these women only through contemporary interviews. We do not see them at their work — neither factory work nor organizing. These are not famous or rich people, and there are no old newsreels of them, only a few old snapshots. The viewer imagines them as young women in the 1930s by drawing on their current liveliness and vitality as they describe their past work. Those who already know some of this history can add to the film mentally, enthusiastically participating in the historical reconstruction.

That the film works so well and is so gripping even to those who are

---

*Marcus Garvey (1887-1940) was a Jamaican black leader active in the United States from 1916 to 1925. He advocated racial separation and emigration of American blacks to Africa, and was eventually deported.

not familiar with this history is, I think, largely due to Julia Reichert's and James Klein's wonderful editing and use of old still and documentary photography. On second viewing it is surprising to realize that this energetic movie is composed only of interviews edited together with historical images. We see what Chicago looked like during the depression; we see mass strikes, sit-downs, demonstrations, eviction resistance, class violence. The film shows — it doesn't just talk about — the force of the class struggle of the 1930s. One feels inside this energy, and the music is important to this. Taj Mahal, the Pointer Sisters, Howie Tarnower, Pete Seeger and the Almanac Singers help set the mood and pace.

But the specific political content of the film, the history that it teaches, is not as precise as its more general communication of mood. I found myself wishing for more explicitness in many areas, especially considering how few of the film's viewers can be expected to know working-class history (given the deliberate suppression of that history in our education).

The film is about a period of great working-class power. The three organizers reveal nostalgia for the feeling of that power. Sylvia Woods describes how in the laundry where she first worked (it was only rarely that black women could get industrial jobs at that time), the workers conducted what she believes may have been the first sit-down strike of the depression era. She is proud of those women, full of respect for their and her own militancy and bravery. Stella Nowicki's face is luminous with delight when she describes how often the packinghouse workers would stop the line, shutting down production. There is an important lesson here: when workers, for a change, feel powerful, it is fun — even elating. This emotion is a large part of what makes people militant and gives them confidence in their own and other people's power to make radical social changes.

Yet this respect for the reality of working-class power in the industrial cities of the 1930s contains a misconception of women's reality. The film's whole conception — the story of three women CIO organizers — denies the larger reality, which is that the CIO did very little for women. Most women did not then and still do not work in heavy industry; the CIO's efforts to organize the large numbers of women in clerical and service work were puny. The exceptions came as a result of bottom-up pressure, rank-and-file local organizing drives, like the early actions in Sylvia Woods's laundry, which virtually forced the CIO to respond. The unions did not initiate significant drives to organize women's employment sectors. Furthermore, most employed women did not work in mass employment situations at all. Until 1940 the largest job category for women was domestic service. Domestic and personal service workers represented 20 percent of the female labor force. Thus, partly owing to the sexism of the CIO, partly to the structural sexism of the labor market and the family, the women who, like the ''union maids,'' were involved in the great working-class rising of the 1930s were exceptions. To miss this basic fact would be not only to misunderstand history but potentially also to mistake some of the problems of organizing women today.

These qualifications do not lessen the legitimacy of choosing the ''union maids'' as the topic for a film. Their very strengths and achievements show what women can do. But even a brief piece of narrative in the film, spoken or written, could have placed the three women in a better historical context.

SEXISM, RACISM AND POLITICAL STRATEGY

The views about women that the ''union maids'' held in the 1930s reveal a sensitive understanding of women's special problems. Sylvia Woods tells a moving anecdote about encouraging women to resist employers' efforts to intimidate them about absenteeism. The women would refuse to give specific reasons on the form supplied for that purpose; they all wrote in ''tired'' as their reason for absence.

Kate Hyndman tells about how, when she was a CIO staff organizer, the men all ate lunch without her, and her union boss complained that it was inappropriate for her to eat with the staff stenographers. Yet all three women are insistent on the necessity of working with men, struggling with them, and educating them, though understanding that this means double work and double struggle for the women.

Kate's personal sense of her womanness, symbolic perhaps of the whole generation, comes through in a story she tells us about her farm grandmother. The first morning after her grandmother's wedding night, the whole extended farm household assembled, expecting grandmother to serve them breakfast as usual. She announced, however, that she would not be their servant and would not wait on them. Instead, she would work in the fields and challenged any man to do more than her. The point is, the women were to be super-women. They were to prove their merit by being better than the men. This was not an unusual attitude; it was characteristic not only of women on the left but also of a large part of the late nineteenth- and early twentieth-century feminist movement. And yet we must be critical of this. It not only avoids a direct attack on male supremacy, but it also is not an effective strategy for organizing women. After all, it's not much of an appeal to say: join us so you can work twice as hard.

Could the film have found some way to offer a critical view of this, to contrast it with other possible feminist strategies? Could the film at least have pointed out that though there were many precedents for autonomous women's labor organizations before the 1930s, they were not seriously considered by any of the radicals of the 1930s?

The film's confrontations with racism are equally tentative and limited, merely reporting the problems and analyses of the organizers. The three women seem to understand the fact of black vanguardism, that black workers were the most militant and led the others. They all struggled with the racism of white workers as well as that of the capitalist system. They are also unwavering in their certainty that interracial class unity is essential to a strong workers' movement and that integrated organization is the only way to get it. Indeed, black Sylvia Woods, in her warm, personal but very didactic style, chooses to tell us about overcoming her own racism. That is, she says at first her loyalty and her political commitment were exclusively to black workers and that she slowly learned that there were whites whom she could trust to fight for racial justice.

This story no doubt reflects the positive experience of many black radicals of the period, but it is hardly more common than the experience of betrayal by whites. And looking back on the 1930s today, we experience a certain sadness that the interracial unity fought for by these radicals did not predominate, and that racism continues as a powerful, perhaps the most powerful, disunifying force within the working class. Could the film have put the optimism of the 1930s on this question into some perspective? Without that perspective one wonders if that historical optimism is not meant to seem unconvincing and naive.

I am a bit disturbed by the reportage-like stance of the film, its backing off from interpretation. There is too little narrative, too little historical context, too little comment from the point of view of the present. It would not diminish the contribution and acumen of the three heroines to suggest that their historical era was different, that 40 years later we could learn from their mistakes as well as from their victories.

The film's documentary stance is perhaps most disturbing on the question of leadership and socialist organization within the CIO. I believe that all three women were members of the Communist Party. However, the film masks their Party membership. The three women speak of themselves as "radicals," not socialists or Communists, and say nothing about their organizational connections. Stella Nowicki refers in the film to "Herb," whom we know from the book as a CP activist, but in the film he is entirely unidentified.

Having had Communist Party parents myself, I suspect that the reticence may be the preference of the women themselves, the caution resulting from years of persecution, and the filmmakers may have been powerless to change their minds. Their discretion is understandable, but it is a mistake. It is a mistake, first, because when the issue does come up, as when Kate Hyndman is denounced as a Red in the 1940s, she is in a defensive position. Thus, the film viewer sees being a Communist as an accusation of wrong-doing before we have encountered it as a strength and a source of pride. Furthermore, this avoidance potentially confirms widespread fears and stereotypes of Communists as habitually devious and manipulative. By contrast, the personal qualities of Woods, Nowicki and Hyndman would have made it possible for the film to show that it was a good thing to be a Communist in the 1930s.

Secondly, a failure to discuss the discipline, support, comradeship and strategic consultation these women got from their Party comrades suggests that somehow they became effective leaders magically, through their innate individual talents. One response to that kind of understanding would be politically pessimistic, to think, "I could never be like them." The truth is that good leadership is created by a combination of individual qualities, learned skills, and connective organization and support.

Furthermore, the relationship between leaders and the rank and file is mystified by the lack of clarity about the role of the Communist Party. For example, Sylvia Woods criticizes the CIO leadership for failing to lead, for remaining behind the understanding and demands of the masses of workers. Yet given her overall evaluation of the CIO — its bureaucratism, sexism, conservatism — this criticism makes no sense without the additional information that there were organizations of socialists that could have educated and challenged workers to a more radical understanding of what could be done.

Again, I am not sure how the film could have been otherwise, given what I suspect might have been the women's reluctance to discuss their CP affiliations. Yet even had there been no way of confronting the CP issue, there could have been a clearer sense of the collective nature of the leadership that these "union maids" offered.

One of the strengths of the film is the great attractiveness of the three women. They are so witty, happy, energetic and handsome; I would like to hang out with them. At the very end of the film there is a still picture, posed, of the three together. I imagine they might be reminiscing about their work, the countless meetings they must have gone to, their experiences of sharing personal and public problems with others if not with each other. Conversation among the three might have brought out more hindsight observations and criticisms, lessening the burden of the narration to provide this. Here too there may have been reticence to overcome, not only about past politics but also about the relevance of "personal life." One of the three women points out that most women activists were unmarried, and clearly she views this fact as socially significant, whereas a feminist today thinks immediately of women's labor in the family and men's exploitation of women as factors that prevent women's political activity. But the woman in the film does not wish to elaborate. Apparently she does not view these problems as political issues. Choosing not to comment, the film again limits us to seeing the story through three individual narratives.

Despite their existence in the film as separate individuals, the women do not seem isolated. This is largely because of the skill with which filmmakers Reichert, Klein and Miles Mogulescu put together sounds and images of the collective force of the CIO drive. Yet beyond this, the very attractiveness, magnetism and dignity of Kate Hyndman, Stella Nowicki and Sylvia Woods show that their lives have been lived in an intensely social manner. Ultimately the film is theirs, and they are its strength. The film lets us see them, and the view is clear due to the filmmakers' craft. Perhaps one of the most wonderful things about *Union Maids* is that it marks the beginning of film being used to let us learn from the activists of an earlier period. If we rely on historians to build this communication, or even on the written work of our now scanty movement press, we will lose too much.

NOTES

[1] Alice and Staughton Lynd, *Rank and File: Personal Histories of Working Class Organizers* (Boston: Beacon Press, 1973).

CHAPTER 9.

Third World Newsreel: Interview with Christine Choy

SHERRY MILLNER*

Third World Newsreel has the distinction of being the oldest independent political filmmaking organization in the country. Christine Choy's long-continued participation in Newsreel has equipped her with the necessary historical perspective to draw some needed and, in part, overdue conclusions about the state of contemporary U.S. political filmmaking.

NEWSREEL HISTORY

CHRISTINE: In the early 1970s Newsreel was making films like *The Black Panther Party* and *The Young Lords,* and the majority of Newsreel people felt they should work at recruiting more non-whites into the organization. Two Third World men began working with the organization and I, a Chinese woman, began about the same time.

In New York, we started a Third World Caucus within the Newsreel chapter, recruiting 12 people. (No one got paid, with the exception of the one person who worked in distribution for $50 per week.) At this time, most people in Newsreel — called the White Caucus — were going through tremendous turmoil as they split into two groups — the haves and the have-nots, and everyone wanted to be a have-not instead of a have. The have-nots felt sympathy with the Third World people's oppression. Six months later the haves all left Newsreel, and the have-nots debated working-class issues, working-class filmmaking, defini-

* with the assistance of John Hess and Ernest Larsen

tions of and strategies for cultural work, filmmaking, and organizing work.

Meantime the Third World Caucus began to work on a film called *Teach Your Children.* The white section was going through such chaos that they decided to dissolve themselves, leaving the organization with the 12 Third World members but no money or equipment. We had a lot of films and debts but no catalogue. At the same time, among the minority members, people didn't know how to produce but everybody wanted to get paid. Internally we faced rip-offs and stealing.

Newsreel was left with three people, Sue Robeson, Robert Zelner and myself. Fortunately, at that time Allan Siegel, an early Newsreel member, came around to help us reorganize, which sparked debate because he was white and we were operating with nationalist tendencies.

When we began demanding training and skills from former members, only one or two were sincere enough to teach us how to use the camera. The rest wouldn't have anything to do with us. So it was out of anger that we called ourselves "Third World Newsreel." More and more, as we define the term, we find it's not appropriate to our situation. The term Third World in the international sense is more applicable to an underdeveloped country, and domestically speaking, it applies to a national minority struggling for equality. When we use the term Third World we use it superficially, since we distribute films from Latin America, Africa and Asia. But the production we do does not relate to Third World issues but to conditions in the United States, especially among minorities and working-class people as a whole. So the term has to be revised, but we haven't gotten around to it yet, and it's become an established trademark for our market.

JUMP CUT: Were you able to start making films right away, teaching each other skills?

CHRISTINE: We were mostly self-taught, which is reflected in our films. In our first film, *Teach Your Children,* a film about Attica, we eliminated everything that had to do with whites. This film, made by two women all about men, contains only images of blacks and latinos. It represented our gut feelings about what had happened in that prison revolt. When first shown at UCLA, it had a tremendous impact because there was a struggle going on there around minority students entering film school; and then it was shown in a black film festival. Later on we began concentrating on prison issues. We started making *In the Event Anyone Disappears,* on men's prisons in New Jersey. And the following year, 1974, a New York Arts Council grant enabled us to start filming *Inside Women Inside.*

With all the films about men's prisons, we thought one should deal with women in prison. We didn't even know how much film cost, so we applied for a $4,000 grant. Then, operating from an ultra-democratic approach, we called for a city-wide meeting, where 50 women showed up to work on this film but could not agree. Everyone wanted to do the cinematography and direct, all with conflicting approaches and ideologies. From 50 the number fell to 12, and from 12 to 5. Then Sue Robeson left the organization, and I was left with the film. I believe that once a film is started, it should be finished — both for the people who worked on it and for those filmed. The film may not be perfect but it should be finished, because you cannot just take advantage of people.

When we recruited more minority women in 1974, problems arose because of a lack of class analysis and class definition in most of the women who started to work with us. They either came from a very petit bourgeois or lumpen background. The same thing applied to the women's movement in general, so the same contradictions would arise among the Newsreel women. Also I think sexism has always existed in our organization, so women have a hard time sticking through. Often in filmmaking a woman feels more comfortable working with other women, and this problem was never worked out very well on the production teams. And then we began to realize we couldn't afford to train people on the job, because of the very little amount of money we got — in 1974 we received $10,000 for three films: *Inside Women Inside, Fresh Seeds in the Big Apple,* and *Spikes to Spindles.* It was ridiculously low, but we made them all.

On *Inside Women Inside,* women were trained on the job, yet due to this fact, high shooting ratios increased our budget. Since our distribution could not yet support the production, it became a financial drain to the organization.

However, as an organization, when the money comes in, we decide collectively how to spend it. If we get $10,000 for two films but cannot make two films for $10,000, we decide collectively which film has priority. Still, people with skills and techniques tend to dominate the discussion, especially about style and approach.

We try to make three films a year, one major film and two shorts. It's a difficult goal but we do it.

TELEVISION PRODUCTION

JUMP CUT: Did you stop training other people since you couldn't do on-production training?

CHRISTINE: A major aim is to train people on the job as much as possible. For the television film I did in Philadelphia, *Loose Pages Bound,* we took on three trainees. I would get very frustrated because

I'd get deadlines and quality pressures very directly from the station. It's ironic, within the traditional family the man gets the pressure from the job and comes home and takes it out on the wife and children. Here I felt the same, being in a producer situation and responsible to the station. I would yell at other people and often I'd be wrong or just didn't want to do it anymore. I hated myself for being in that kind of contradictory situation. Fortunately, we had a meeting every night and were able to discuss the problems as they arose. Political filmmakers, minority filmmakers and women filmmakers should have more work within the system so they are able to produce. It's very important for political filmmakers to be able to have some understanding about the network and get their films shown on television.

Through working with the system I've learned about myself and found I could now provide other people with information — about who to see, etc. — which makes it easier for other filmmakers to approach television. Of course I had to go through a year and a half of battling with them before actual production started. You can get really sucked into the idea of working in television, but they don't care about quality, just a product. We artists have to find a way to combat our dependency. As the federal and state governments organize us, grants become the base for doing work, so the product comes before the politics. This recent tendency typifies the capitalist system; art becomes a commodity, and the artist does too.

And the more money a filmmaker has, the more it dictates point of view. When I worked on that film in Philadelphia for TV, which I got a lot of money for, I began to be more cautious about saying anything provocative because someone else was putting out the money.

JUMP CUT: Did you start to worry about your audience doing that film, wanting to reach more people?

CHRISTINE: Yes. Now I look at TV very differently. At first I looked at it romantically, thinking we could make a documentary for TV that could be aesthetically and politically strong, and at the same time reach a mass audience. We also thought that after we produced it for TV, Newsreel could distribute it on a community level.

It didn't work out. First, the film was designed for commercial TV, so it was cut that way. Secondly, contractual time limitations affected the project's depth and left us with a shallow analysis. Since it *is* so desperately important to provide an analysis as a political filmmaker, we superficially injected one that didn't quite make it. Then, we thought that since it was a semi-political film, Newsreel should distribute it. Yet, because of the money Third World Newsreel had to invest in prints, negatives, and promotions, we wound up losing money and not being able to distribute the film well.

JUMP CUT: Do you think it's possible theoretically to make a really good political film for TV, knowing what you do now?

CHRISTINE: If you go in as an independent producer for TV, you get a big chunk of money, including a big salary. Regardless of quality, you have to deliver. That's how payment comes: 50 percent to start up, 75 percent on the rough cut, 100 percent on delivery. What we're doing is an experiment to see if we're able to work with TV or not. We did a show for ABC and people liked it. It was about Asian-Americans in the Delaware Valley — five nationalities in 42 minutes. Every seven minutes there's a commercial break, so you cut for that. You end each section with a hype to keep people tuned in. Those are the requirements. If you have that kind of mentality you can do it, but I was not ready for it.

The censorship is tremendous. I needed to say something to tie the five nationalities together, so I had a song written by a political musician saying essentially that oppressed peoples are going to rise. This was towards the end of the film. They wanted me to cut that line out. There was a struggle about that. They said straight out it was too political. And prohibiting people's curse words immediately eliminates most people's vernacular.

Overall, they accepted the film and aired it. My personal feeling is that independent producing represents an opportunity to get into network TV without working up the ladder as a secretary, etc. Yet you're still working within the system. And I was kidding myself about that. I was very romantic and idealistic.

What happens is the project itself becomes such a secondary issue. Within the system, first of all you write a proposal, get it accepted, get a budget, go into board meetings several times all dressed up — because they want to see what a producer-director looks like (I got myself a little blazer). And people say things they don't believe — that you're great, blah-blah — and there's a lot of backstabbing from other producers. All this affects your mentality. If I go in to do some xeroxing a secretary says, "I'll do it for you." Wait a minute, I can do my own xeroxing! They offer you superficial status while they've got you by the neck.

Although there are a lot of good people working in television, they're not organized. The network hires me because non-union help is cheaper. It costs them $60,000 for a 24-minute in-house film; I did it for $25,000. That's why they hire independent producers. A context like this makes TV workplace-organizing all the more necessary.

THE POLITICS OF FUNDING AGENCIES

CHRISTINE: For five years we got pretty good funding from the

National Endowment for the Arts (NEA) and New York State Council on the Arts. Then there were cuts, as they funded experimental films more. The funding agencies want to support social and political films that will make a big splash. When we went to a foundation for funding for our violence against women film, *To Love, Honor and Obey*, the first thing they asked was "Will it be on PBS?" More and more multinational corporations are investing money in documentaries for PBS programming. Visibility on the largest scale — through PBS or the U.S. film festivals — is all that matters. How the film, the product, gets circulated, how it really affects people, becomes secondary. That's what hurts. And a lot of filmmakers gear to that approach in order to get grants.

JUMP CUT: That's clear. A non-political PBS mentality has come to represent alternative cinema. It tends to make what you're doing here, for example, less visible and have less credibility.

CHRISTINE: I agree with you. It affects us a lot and is depressing. There are not enough outlets for showing independent films. Yet, if your films get shown at the Whitney's American Film Series, there's a pretty good chance that you'll get a grant next cycle from the American Film Institute.

JUMP CUT: This process creates an establishment for alternative filmmakers, which makes it very much harder for everybody else.

CHRISTINE: Nowadays fewer political films are being made. Partially, within the logic of the economic situation, people just write grants for $50,000 to $100,000 before they touch a camera. They want fame overnight, and they shoot for PBS.

JUMP CUT: There's a real loss of immediacy when the most important part of the filmmaking process is raising the money. Yet one can't be an idealist. We have to deal with material reality.

CHRISTINE: Yes, there are things you should do just for money, like some TV shows. There are films that should be produced for $5,000, $10,000. There are films that should be produced for $50,000 and make a profit so you can make other films. But proposal writing takes time, and every foundation runs on different cycles. So you spend a whole year just writing proposals and circulating sample work. All of which perpetuates individual filmmakers' competitiveness, and people writing grant proposals become cautious about their political statements. At Newsreel our strategy is to get the distribution to sustain itself, to support our production. But it's very difficult.

At the same time social films are becoming more legitimate, which means the institutionalization of women's issues, the institutionalization of racism, and the institutionalization of social change issues.

JUMP CUT: Which gives arts administrators a whole new field to start administering... cleaning films up, making them slick, and professional.

CHRISTINE: I think that has affected our whole organization. In terms of content we still manage to produce a certain level of politically oriented films, but in order to have marketability, in order to have sales, we have to be tremendously technically sophisticated. Also we have to gear into the demands of the TV market, and to edit in a certain way to fit the market.

In our recent work, our style has changed. The cinematography is better and we have a better sense of post-production work. Old Newsreel film used to be called workprint: you shoot it, cut it, and show it — basically as a workprint. Now, some of our films have ten tracks of sound. Much slicker work. But it works both ways. Most American audiences are conditioned to see slick films; sloppy films do bother them. Both aspects have their own values. The films that have the immediacy, the roughness, have a different type of emotional impact, and a different type of consciousness.

Films like *Inside Women Inside* hit you very hard, whereas films that are slicker are too comfortable to watch and content becomes secondary. The visual element is so pretty that the prettiness tends to dilute what we're really trying to say. Also, from the filmmaker's viewpoint, if we have film that's really well shot and we edit it, we are more reluctant to throw any of it away.

NEWSREEL'S ORGANIZATION

JUMP CUT: What is the structure of Newsreel?

CHRISTINE: We decided we had to have a division of labor to function: distribution, production, and theatre. In production, we train in techniques and filmmaking theory. A small core of staff members works day-to-day and makes a commitment to Newsreel. We used to demand of Newsreel members a lifetime commitment, so many people left, instead of working with people on the basis of whatever they could contribute. Now we have a larger body considered part of the Newsreel network, who work only on specific projects and share in the organization's benefits.

Originally, maybe 10 or 20 people would produce a Newsreel film but nobody got a credit. This eliminated a hierarchical system between producer, director, editor, but 10 years later people felt resentful about the lack of credits.

JUMP CUT: But that's something created by material conditions. We all have to go get jobs.

CHRISTINE: And you have to have track records.

JUMP CUT: At that time we didn't think we'd have to go out and operate in those same old ways. We thought that would change.

CHRISTINE: Resentment developed against the organization, and because a lot of people here are new, it's hard to remember who worked on what films. Our solution is that whoever has been part of Newsreel can get prints at lab cost and splice in their own credits.

JUMP CUT: You want to be a stable organization that a lot of people can connect to and put their energy into. But you can't always do that. It's not realistic financially, or for the needs of the organization. You wind up being a social service agency — a political social service agency.

CHRISTINE: The only way an organization works is through the individuals themselves within the organization, who must have some kind of understanding of their needs from the organization. Everybody felt they were serving the organization, but what they were getting out of the organization was never even questioned. That became a large contradiction.

We've talked about possible solutions to the lack of money. Take myself, for instance, I have skills and can go out and get a job. Is that the way to solve the problem? Getting a job to support yourself? Then the organization doesn't have to pay anybody's salary. Another way is to bring jobs into the organization. That's what we've been doing recently. Before we were saying — you go out and get a part-time job to make money, but that alienated people much more.

JUMP CUT: If you want to make films and you want to be able to finance them and have some credibility, you can't struggle on every front, so you put individual credits on the films. Now, 10 years later, we understand the work it takes to keep going, making films that people will understand, finding a style that people will be receptive to. But Newsreel has survived.

CHRISTINE: Well, that's the miracle. There've been many transitions, so many new people. Sometimes all the checks bounced, and the IRS pressured us. We survived, I think, because we have political unity. People here still believe in making films independently from the system. They still have idealism, which keeps the organization moving. Second, Newsreel does provide an opportunity for people who really want to make films, because its organizational structure can offer more stability than independent individual filmmakers often have.

CHAPTER 10.

Decolonizing the Image: New U.S. Black Cinema

CLYDE TAYLOR

The best approach to black cinema as art is to see it in intimate relation to the full range of Afro-American art expression. The urgent need at this point is to recognize that black cinema has arrived to take its natural place beside black music, literature, dance and drama. By black cinema, I am speaking of the independent films made since the late 1960s by determined, university-trained filmmakers who owe Hollywood nothing at all.

If the Harlem Renaissance or, better yet, the New Negro Movement that began in the 1920s were to take place under today's conditions, many of its major creative talents would be filmmakers. They would celebrate and join a contemporary black renaissance in films.

Consider: Paul Robeson's struggle to bring dignity to the Afro-American screen image is well documented. Richard Wright's interest in films extended beyond the filming of *Native Son* (1951) to include his search for work as a screenwriter for the National Film Board of Canada and the drafting of unused film scripts. Langston Hughes co-authored the script for *Way Down South* (1939) with Clarence Muse and continually sought creative opportunities in Hollywood. In 1941, he wrote with great clarity to his friend Arna Bontemps, "Have been having some conferences with movie producers, but no results. I think only a subsidized Negro Film Institute, or the revolution, will cause any really good Negro pictures to be made in America."[1]

In 1950, Arna Bontemps tried to stir up interest in the production of black films in the manner of Italian Neorealism.[2] About this same time, the Committee for Mass Education in Race Relations was set up with the intent to "produce films that combine entertainment and purposeful mass education in race relations.'' Among the consultants and members of this committee were Katherine Dunham, Paul Robeson, Richard Wright, Eslanda Robeson, Langston Hughes and Countee Cullen.[3]

I pinpoint the film involvement of some of the central artist-intellectuals of the New Negro era in order to contrast the lack, with some important exceptions, of a comparable interest among their successors. This short-sightedness is both ironic and painful, for over the last decade a body of Afro-American films has emerged comparable to the flowering of the ''Harlem Renaissance'' in its cultural independence, originality and boldness. The appearance of these films marks perhaps the most significant recent development in Afro-American art.

This body of films, which I call the new black cinema, is distinct from four prior episodes of filmmaking about Afro-Americans: Hollywood films portraying blacks before World War II, Hollywood films after that war, films made by black independents like Oscar Micheaux and Spencer Williams before World War II, and the black exploitation movies of the late 1960s and early 1970s. What separates the new black cinema from these other episodes is its freedom from the mental colonization that Hollywood tries to impose on all its audiences, black and white.

The new black cinema was born out of the black arts movement of the 1960s, out of the same concerns with a self-determining black cultural identity. This film phenomenon drew inspiration from black-subject films made by white directors in the 1960s, films such as *Nothing but a Man* (1964), *Cool World* (1963), *Shadows* (1959), and *Sweet Love, Bitter* (1967). But it was also fired by the creative heresies of Italian Neorealism (following Arna Bontemps's early interest) and ultimately by an expanding international film culture, with a particularly deep impression being scored by African and other Third World filmmakers.

The new black cinema is a movement with many separate beginnings in the late 1960s. One was the gathering of a nucleus of young black filmmakers at ''Black Journal,'' a weekly television magazine aired on PBS under the leadership of Bill Greaves in New York. Another was the tragically brief career of Richie Mason who, without training, took cameras into the streets of New York to make dramatic street films (*You Dig It?*; *Ghetto*). Still another was a pathbreaking exhibition of historical and contemporary independent black films in New York organized by Pearl Bowser. By the time films of great innovation and energy began emerging from UCLA in the early 1970s from Haile Gerima, Larry Clark and Charles Burnett, it was clear that a new path had been broken towards a liberated black screen image.

What gives this new cinema its particular unifying character? In truth, little more than its determined resistance to the film ideology of

Hollywood — but that, as we shall see, is a great deal. Under that broad umbrella of kinship, these filmmakers have produced work of considerable diversity, pursuing various goals of aesthetic individualism, cultural integrity or political relevance. Despite this diversity, some core features, or defining aesthetic principles, can be seen to underlie many works of the new black cinema: its realness dimension, its relation to Afro-American oral tradition, and its connections with black music.

THE REALNESS DIMENSION

Indigenous Afro-American films project onto a social space, as UCLA film scholar Teshome Gabriel observes in noting the difference between that space and the privatistic, individualistic space of Hollywood's film theater. It is a space carrying a commitment, in echoes and connotations, to the particular social experience of Afro-American people. It establishes only the slightest, if any, departure from the contiguous, offscreen reality.

While shooting *Bush Mama* (Haile Gerima, 1976), for instance, one camera crew was accosted by the Los Angeles police. What was there in the sight of black men with motion-picture cameras filming in the streets of south-central Los Angeles (Watts) that prompted the police to pull their guns, spread-eagle these filmmakers against cars, and frisk them? Did they mistake the cameras for weapons — did they sense a robbery in progress, a misappropriation of evidence? Did they suspect the cameras were stolen, being in the inappropriate hands of the intended victims of cinema?

The paranoia of such questions belongs to the mentality of the Los Angeles Police Department. The evidence of their actions is recorded objectively in cinéma vérité as the establishing shots of the film. These shots make a fitting prologue because *Bush Mama* is about the policing of the black community by school officials, in and out of uniform, who intrude their behavioral directives into the most intimate reaches of its residents. From such a documentary beginning, one is more easily convinced that the daily actions of the black community's inhabitants are constantly policed, in the sense that all actions are regarded with hostility and suspicion except those that reproduce the cycles of victimization and self-repression.

The social space of many new black films is saturated with contingency. Simply, it is the contingency of on-location shooting. But what a location. It is a space where invasion is immanent. A street scene in these films is a place where anything can happen, any bizarre or brutal picaresque eventuality, as in *A Place in Time* (Charles Lane, 1976). An interior location attracts the feeling of prison, or refuge. A door is a venue through which there may suddenly burst an intruder, either police or madman. The folklore surrounding this school of adventuresome filmmaking is replete with art-life ironies: a film about a black man trying to live his life without going to jail is interrupted when the actor interpreting the role is put in jail for nonsupport.

The intensities of such dilemmas, sometimes the events themselves, become interwoven into the text of the film. Everyone knows that the anthropologist with a camera alters the village reality he/she records. Similarly, "reality" arranges itself differently in North America for an independent black filmmaker. Nor does this filmmaker always maintain a cool detachment in the face of these rearrangements. The hot rage that suffuses *Sweet Sweetback's Baaadass Song* (Melvin van Peebles, 1971) is one clue that the film itself is an allegory of the furious ordeal of a black person trying to make a mentally independent film against the resistances society will mount in reaction. By Larry Clark's testimony, the sharp-edged racial portrayals in *Passing Through* (1977) reflect his frustrations in getting his film completed against such resistance.

So the space occupied by an independent black film is frequently tempered by the values of social paranoia, volatility and contingency, and by a more knowing acquaintance with these values, rather than by the stable tranquillity and predictable unpredictability of a U.S. movie set, even when that set is background for a commercial black movie.

The screen and theatrical space of the new black cinema is one the spectator can enter into and exit from without carrying away the glazed eyes and the afterglow of erotic-egotistic enchantment that identifies the colonized movie-goer. In it, both filmmakers and spectators can move easily and interchangeably before and behind the camera without drastic alterations of character. This is a rare circumstance for Afro-Americans, for as Walter Benjamin notes of another cinema,

> Some of the players whom we meet in Russian films are not actors in our sense but people who portray *themselves* — and primarily in their own work process. In Western Europe the capitalistic exploitation of the film denies consideration to modern man's legitimate claim to being reproduced.[4]

It is a space open to wide-ranging possibilities, yet free of the illusionism whose effects make mainstream commercial films so superficially enchanting. To take one convention of the Hollywood cinematic code, for example, consider the double pyramid that describes the individualistic perspective. One of these imaginary pyramids extends from the four corners of the screen towards a vanishing point within the scene, reproductive of the depth perception of Renaissance painting. The other pyramid extends from these same points, converging on the eye-screen of the single observer. Such a perspective has great potential for focusing attention at hierarchically staged points of meaning, which seem to individual observers to be channeled directly to their mind-screens, the chambers of privileged voyeurism.

The camera of the new black cinema is not similarly obsessed. The focus of its attention is wider, more open to diverse, competing, even accidental impressions. The basic palette of the indigenous Afro screen is closer to that of Italian Neorealism and Third World cinema than to Southern California. Charlie Burnett, in *Killer of Sheep* (1977), for instance, makes effective use of the open frame, in which characters walk in and out of the frame from top, bottom and sides — a forbidden practice in the classical code of Hollywood (but common in the European and Japanese films Burnett saw as a UCLA student). One further encounters fewer close-ups, suggesting less preoccupation with the interior emotions of individual personages.

The techniques of the new directors do not exclude inventive camera movements and placements, but these are dictated more often by the needs of social reflection than by the demands of individual fascination. The treatment of space generally reminds us that linear perspective was an invention and once the exclusive preoccupation of postmedieval western art. By contrast, in Afro cinema one often finds the nonlinear, psychic space of medieval paintings, oriental scrolls and other non-western media. In *Child of Resistance* (1972), to take another example from the prolific Haile Gerima, the camera follows the central figure, a woman dressed in a robe, hands bound, as she is transported through a barroom into a jail cell, directly outside of which later appears a jury box filled with jurors. Linearity is rejected as space is treated poetically, following the co-ordinates of a propulsive social idea — the social imprisonment of black women.

Techniques associated with nonfictional cinema appear frequently in indigenous Afro films. One of the most piercing scenes in Ben Caldwell's poetic and literary *I and I* (1978) is staged as a documentary interview. Similarly, the dramatic action of *Torture of Mothers* is launched from the setting of a group pooling testimony before a tape recorder. An off-camera voice-track supplants dialogue in *Child of Resistance.* And Larry Clark, in making *Passing Through,* goes beyond the typical use of archival footage as historical flashback by inventing a documentary-looking sequence that places his hero, Womack, in the midst of the eruption at Attica.

Another support of the realness dimension in Afro cinema is its use of cultural-historical time. The cultural identity of the people in these films may be expressed as that of a people with a certain history. Dramatic time is never wholly divorced from historic time.

Both black and white independent filmmakers sometimes forsake explicit cultural and historical reference but usually for different reasons. It has been said of the affecting documentary, *The Quiet One*

(1948), made by Sidney Meyers, that "the boy's blackness was not given any special significance."[5] And *Nothing But a Man* (1964), directed by Michael Roemer, omitted reference to the civil rights movement taking place at the time and place of the film's action. In these respects, the themes of these two films, both respected by black cineastes, would probably have received different treatment by indigenous filmmakers. For example, when Haile Gerima downplays the particulars of the legal case in *Wilmington 10, USA Ten Thousand* (1978), it is to subsume that travesty within a broader historical framework, that of the continuous struggle of Afro-Americans for liberation, in which 10,000 people have been victimized in the manner dealt to the Wilmington freedom fighters.[6]

Even where concrete historical reference is absent, where the action is set in an unspecified present tense, the idea of who black people are historically is implicitly reflected in every communicative action and reflected most consistently with the self-understanding of the cultural group portrayed. This is true despite variations in the sense of history among individual filmmakers.

In Hollywood portrayals of blacks, there is also an historical dimension, but this sense of history is "vaudevillainous" — the play history of musical comedy, costume spectaculars and sentimentalized biographies. It is not noted often enough that the liberties taken with history for the sake of a more entertaining story in this vaudevillainous cinema have an important connection with ethnic distortions. For when a people are distorted on screen, their history, their collective cultural memory, is disfigured at the same moment.

The subtly implanted sense of who these people are and where they are coming from is thus a major source of the greater internal authority of the new black cinema — because it is a cinema in which Afro-Americans are both the subject and the object of consideration, and the relations of those considerations are least tampered with by extraneous manipulations.

ORAL TRADITION

In one of the most rudimentary film situations, the "talking head" sequence of nonfiction film, lies a key to another source of the character of indigenous Afro films. When our attention is riveted by the information given by the speaker, as in television newscasts, we may think of the speaker as an interviewee. When this attention is split between the information imparted and the personality of the speaker, the manner of speech, the cultural resonance of the words and images, the social and cultural connotations, the art of the message spoken, when, in short, speech takes on the character of *performance,* we may likely think of the speaker as an oral historian.

One finds oral historians in all segments of North American cinema, from the Appalachian coal miners of *Harlan County, USA* (1976) to the interviews inserted in *Reds* (1981). But the Afro speaker in films is more likely to speak as an oral historian, if only because of inadequate assimilation of the bourgeois broadcast orientation that leaves one voice interchangeable with another. The significant contrast is between the Afro-American oral tradition, easily the most vital vernacular tradition surviving in the United States, and the linearized speech dominated by western literacy. In Afro oral tradition, filmmakers of the new black cinema find one of their most invaluable resources.

Because it brashly transgresses the barriers of standard communication, Afro oral tradition is also a magnet for those inclined to vaudevillize, minstrelize or sensationalize it. *Cotton Comes to Harlem* (1970) is typical of the exploitative use of black speech with its gratuitous vaudeville jokes that harken back to the slack-mouthed asides of Willie Best. The humor of *Putney Swope* (1969) relies mainly on a leering treatment of black hipspeech and profanity.

But the real thing is abundantly available in documentaries and ethnographic films made by black and white filmmakers about the Afro oral tradition or its related expressions — in films such as *No Maps on My Taps* (1980) (tapdancing); *American Shoeshine* (1976), *Ephesus* (1965) and *Let the Church Say Amen* (1972) (folk preaching); *The Facts of Life* (1981) (blues), and *The Day the Animals Talked* (1981) (folktales), both by Carol Lawrence; and the southern folklore films of William Ferris; and particularly in jazz films like *But Then She's Betty Carter* (1981), *Mingus* (1966) and *The Last of the Blue Devils* (1980). In such films one might find a saturation of black values and therefore an edge towards the definition of black identity in films after Stephen Henderson's approach to black poetry.[7]

Contrasting postures towards the representation of Afro oral history are seen in two carefully positioned nonfiction films, Warrington Hudlin's *Street Corner Stories* (1978) and Haile Gerima's *Wilmington 10, USA Ten Thousand.* The orientation of *Street Corner Stories* is *observational.* Hudlin used cinéma vérité techniques, exposing his films in and around a New Haven corner store where black men congregate before going to work. Hudlin caught their practice of black storytelling and uninhibited rapping, not entirely unobserved, as their occasional straining for effects reveals. The orientation of *Wilmington 10* is *committed.* This is nowhere more apparent than in the powerful, impassioned speeches of the women who dominate its text, the wives and mothers of some of the Wilmington defendants who recount chapter and verse of liberation struggles past and present together with their uncensored opinions, directly into the camera.

It is not simply the case of one approach being more political than the other, for both are necessarily ideological and reflective of the ideological diversity and oppositions *within* the indigenous Afro film movement. Nor is it narrowly a question of technique: neither film, for instance, uses a voice of God narration. Finally, as is usual with nonfiction cinema, it is a question of selectivity. *Street Corner Stories* derives its Afro oral energies from the witty irreverence of black crackerbarrel humor, its rhymes and jibes merely transposed from the porch of the country store to the city. *Wilmington 10* is much like an updated escaped-slave narrative, with all of the intense political sermonizing familiar to that genre. Both films are valid, essentially successful deployments of black verbal creativity in different occasional modes.

As black oral history, many of the scenes in *Wilmington 10* are unsurpassed in the projection of strong, committed black speech and personality, offered straight from the soul with earthy articulateness. The folk songs and prison blues of its soundtrack are hauntingly supportive of the film's eloquence. Yet the film is excessively rhetorical, specifically in its last sequences where unidentified black activists of no clear connection with the Wilmington struggle make political speeches while sitting in abstract isolation on pedestals. Their inclusion is gratuitous, an inorganic code to the Wilmington scene from which the earlier speakers drew their spontaneous vitality. Ironically, the ideological tendencies of both films are pushed towards enervation by their urging too much of one kind of text without sufficient, balancing context.

In Afro-American "orature" one can generally find many distinctive and richly expressive characteristics, including a tolerance for semantic ambiguity, a fascination with bold, extravagant metaphor, a "cool" sensibility, a funky explicitness, and a frequently prophetic mode of utterance. The centrality of this tradition to the new black cinema is only understood when we realize its presence not only in the speech and "performance" of the participants in nonfiction films but within the total configuration of both nonfiction and dramatic works, in characterization, camera strategies, principles of montage, tempo, narrative structure and so forth. One can even find its features in Charles Lane's wittily silent tragi-comedy, *A Place in Time*.

As in Afro orature, narrative structure in the new films is often more episodic and nonsequential than the well-made plot dear to western popular drama and more concerned with tonal placement and emphasis. In its search for its own voice, for a film language uncompromised by the ubiquitous precedents of the dominant cinema, the new black cinema is making productive explorations into the still undominated speech of black people.

THE INFLUENCE OF BLACK MUSIC

To turn from black oral tradition to black music is really not to turn at all but only to allow one's attention to glide from the words to the melody of a people's indivisible cultural expression. But what has been said about the influence of oral tradition has been inferential; the impact of black music on the new black cinema is clearly intentional and well documented. Of about 20 black filmmakers I have interviewed recently, roughly three-fourths of them stressed black music as a formative and fundamental reference for their art.

The involvement with black music probes deeper than laying a rhythmic soundtrack beneath images of black people (tom-toms for the rising redemptive energies of the collective), though the musical soundtrack is a good place to begin.

Western music will menace a non-western film with cultural compromise. Not intrinsically, not inevitably — Charles Lane, for one, uses "classical" music effectively in his silent farce, *A Place in Time,* with no loss to its Afro character. But who can have escaped the subsidized imposition of European superiority as communicated by its musical "classics" which are hawked and hustled everywhere, underwriting, for instance, the insistent Europeanness of so many, say, French new wave films with their Bach and Mozart scores, or not noticed the introduction of nonclassical music for comic or pastoral diversion? For the new black filmmaker, the technical invention and development of the art of cinema in the West poses a burden and a challenge to her/his creative independence that is lifted once she or he turns to the question of music. Being artists, living under cultural domination, they will be privy to the open secret that the definitive musical sound of the twentieth century originates from their people.

What is more revealing is the *way* music is used. Ousmane Sembène, Africa's most independent film innovator, accurately observes that "the whites have music for everything in their films — music for rain, music for the wind, music for tears, music for moments of emotion, but they don't know how to make these elements speak for themselves."[8] But, recognizing in their music an invaluable precedent of cultural liberation, Afro filmmakers have not pursued, with Sembène, a "cinema of silence." (Although Woodie King effectively omits music from *The Torture of Mothers,* a taut reliving of a series of brutal racist incidents.)

Instead, their use of music in films is less sentimental and less literary than conventional western practice. To get to the core of the difference, we should recall Richard Wright's contrast between the false sentiment of tin pan alley songs and lyrics, with their twittering about *moon, croon, June,* and the more adult, realistic directness of the blues.

Mass film entertainment in America has never outgrown the musical shadow work of the silent film era where piano or organ sententiously telegraphed the appropriate emotion to the viewer regarding the character, place and event on the screen, channeling the viewer's aural responses towards a self-pitying individualism, much as the visual cinematic code cultivates egocentric perspective.

In Afro film music relates to screen action more like the relation of guitar accompaniment to sung blues, broadening the primary narrative statement with commentary that sometimes modulates its directness but just as frequently establishes an ironic, parallel or distancing realism. When used as sympathetic accompaniment, the music in Afro cinema frequently shares connotations with its audience of collective, cultural-historic significance, in contrast to the music of bourgeois, commercial egoism. Though subject to abuse, the motif of tom-tom signifying communal resurgence nevertheless illustrates this less privatistic musical intention.

The deeper possibilities of black music for furnishing a creative paradigm for Afro cinema have been advanced in Warrington Hudlin's film concept of "blues realism," a defining attitude and style of life.

> It seems to me that if black films are to continue to be called black films, they will have to develop an aesthetic character that will distinguish them in the same way that Japanese films, Italian neo-realist films, or even the French new wave films are distinct. I think the blues provides an aesthetic base and direction. At the risk of sounding pretentious, I feel my efforts in *Street Corner Stories* and the achievments of Robert Gardner in his exceptional short film *I Could Hear You All the Way Down the Hall* (1976) are the beginnings of a new school of filmmaking, a new wave, if you will.[9]

In retrospect, Hudlin's formulation of blues realism betrays the adventitiousness of artistic theory developed in the course of resolving particular aesthetic problems, then promoted too broadly as a vehicle of self-definition.

Blues realism as articulated by Hudlin needs to be respected, nevertheless, as a premature sally onto sound grounds. We do not need to discard it but to amplify and extend it to many different blues sensibilities and many different registers of black musical sensibility which help us realize an understanding of Afro films in their variety. *Street Corner Stories,* for instance, captures the tonal reference of an amoral, all-male blues world moving from country to city on a trajectory roughly parallel to the course from Lightnin' Hopkins to Jimmie Witherspoon. Alternatively, *Wilmington 10,* as already noted, vibrates most completely to the blues of the southern prison farm but also realizes on the screen the equivalent of its soundtrack employment of the woman-supportive, acapella country/folk singing of "Sweet Honey in the Rock."

Many of the new filmmakers attempt to transpose the tonal/ structural register and cognitive framework of several varieties of black music. The works of others seem attached to specific black musical worlds by virtue of having tapped dimensions of black experience congruent with certain musical precedents. (One must understand music in Afro-American culture as a constituent element of thought, perception and communication.[10]) Hugh Hill's *Light Opera* (1975) offers an example from the "pure" end of the visual music spectrum with his exposures and editing of light and images in New York's Times Square, orchestrated nonnarratively to the music of Ornette Coleman and to the more abstract explorations of New Jazz. The fictive-emotional world of Bill Gunn's *Ganja and Hess* (1973) is embedded in the resonances of a literary, self-conscious form of gospel music. The visual imagery of Barbara McCullough's experimental *Water Ritual #1* (1979) emerges out of a funky New Jazz, saturated in African cosmology.

Ben Caldwell's *I and I*, another film deeply implicated in black music, is best understood as a meditation in blues mode on identities of Africa in America. Its title further notes a debt to reggae-Rastafarian consciousness. Framed by the passage of a spirit-woman protagonist from Africa through experiences and revelations in America, its structure rests principally on three "stanzas" or "choruses." First, the protagonist becomes a black man mourning/cursing his coffined white father. Next, she witnesses the oral narration of an old black woman, recounting the lynch-murder of her grandfather. Finally, she metamorphoses into a contemporary black woman, imparting a cosmological heritage to her son.

The distinct contribution of *I and I* to the repertory of music-based black cinema is its impact on improvisation. Still photos of urban and rural black life are interspersed among explicitly funky dramatic vignettes and lyrical-prophetic stagings in an order hovering between narrative closure and abstract association, one idea or image giving birth to another in the manner of an instrumental jazz soloist's far-flung, highly colored variations on a traditional blues theme. The semantics of this film are akin to those of the instrumental jazz theater in which the performer calls the audience together to celebrate shared passages of life through her/his voicing of a familiar tune. In *I and I*, blues realism is extended to blues prophetism in a register my ears would place close to the spiritualized, Africanized blues of John Coltrane or Coltrane-Ellington.

The idea of black film as music is also given wide syntactical exploration in Larry Clark's dramatic feature, *Passing Through*. Here, the dramatic theme is black music, the struggle of musicians against the exploitations of gangster entrepreneurs. More subtly fulfilled than its story is its visual exposition through musical montage. Each sequence is introduced or segmented by music. Musical cues dominate its architecture. Typically, in the middle of a tenor saxophone solo played by the protagonist, Womack, the camera closes in on the bell of the horn, which becomes an iris perspective, framing the documentary flashbacks mentioned earlier: the dogs of Birmingham, black nationalist/police shootouts in Cleveland and Attica. Clark's montage suggests visual references for the solo's non-verbal expression, offering a visual exegesis of the way improvised jazz solos reflect individual and group experience.

I and I and *Passing Through*, together with the briefer explorations of Barbara McCullough and Hugh Hill, offer the widest, most far-reaching illustrations of the integral relation of black music and film. In these works, we recognize the representative palette of the new black filmmaker as a keyboard. The greater dimension of performance in the identity of the African and Afro-American artist also extends to the new black filmmakers. We should visualize them as shaping their compositions by selectively *playing,* with more or less emphasis, the available elements of documentary realism, the several modes of Afro oral tradition, musical structure and coloration, and dramatic intention.

Two useful perspectives can be gained by viewing the new black cinema as a creative ''renaissance.'' Some fruitful bearings can be found in considering the recent film movement alongside the Harlem Renaissance, the best-known art movement launched by black Americans. One is then further drawn to the fundamental relatedness between this body of films and other forms of black art.

The independent films of Afro-Americans since the late 1960s, it should be clear by now, have made a departure from all prior examples of black imagery sharp enough to be considered a distinct aesthetic phenomenon. History has not favored the new film movement with a reverberating social and artistic era in which it might achieve its full resonance. Many Afro-Americans have lamented the virtual adoption, as pets, of the writer of the 1920s by white patrons and faddists, yet ironically remain mute when an indigenous film movement emerges without benefit of such dubious blessings.

Without the buoyancy of a vogue or the nostalgia of an era consecrated in popular mythology, the new black cinema has managed a transformation of imaginative possibilities comparable in scope, diversity and creative verve to the literary 1920s. Over the last decade, Afro independents have produced over 200 films of varied length, including a score of dramatic features and an equal number of documentary features — an output rivaling the literary output of the Harlem Renaissance.

The singular accomplishment of the literary awakening of the 1920s was to establish an Afro-American voice for literary art, the recreation of a cultural identity in literary form, more solidly in poetry than prose, and principally through the reappropriation of Afro vernacular in speech and music. The writers of that period advanced a fertile decolonization from western aesthetic norms. Almost without notice, the contemporary filmmakers have gone further towards decolonization of a more blatantly colonized medium. They have not only planned a new body of Afro-American art, they have done this while freeing that art of colonial imitation, apology or deference. And while the observations made here fall far short of exhausting the characteristics that give these films their cultural identity, they might point the way to the realization that the new cinema, unlike any other, is a representative expression of Afro-American line.

NOTES

[1] *Arna Bontemps — Langston Hughes Letters, 1925-1967,* ed. Charles H. Nichols (New York: Dodd, Mead & Co., 1980), p. 89.

[2] *Ibid.,* p. 273.

[3] From a brochure in the files of the Schomburg Library, New York City.

[4] Walter Benjamin, *Illuminations* (New York: Harcourt, Brace and World, 1968), p. 232.

[5] Lewis Jacobs, *The Documentary Tradition* (New York: Norton, 1979), p. 187.

[6] The Wilmington 10 were defendants in a celebrated case of official misjustice. The 10 North Carolina political activists were charged with firebombing a grocery store during a time of racial tension in 1971 and convicted on the basis of pressured testimony, later recanted by some of the supposed witnesses. They were given unusually harsh sentences. At the time of the film, all but the Reverend Ben Chavis has been released. Chavis himself is now free.

[7] Stephen Henderson, *Understanding the New Black Poetry* (New York: Morrow, 1973). By saturation, Henderson means a density of reference and tone by which the observer can recognize the cultural Afro-ness of a work, even in the absence of explicit verbal clues. Henderson finds saturation, for instance, in Aretha Franklin's "Spirits in the Dark."

[8] "Film-makers Have a Great Responsibility to Our People: An Interview with Ousmane Sembène," *Cineaste* 6, no. 1, p. 29.

[9] "Interview: Warrington Hudlin," by Oliver Franklin, program brochure for Black Films and Film Makers, Afro-American Historical and Cultural Museum, Philadelphia, Pa.

[10] See Clyde Taylor, "Salt Peanuts: Sound and Sense in African/American Oral/Musical Creativity," *Callaloo,* June 1982.

CHAPTER 11.

A Wives' Tale:
Rewriting Working-Class History

• Interview with the Filmmakers

PETER STEVEN WITH SARA HALPRIN
AND CHUCK KLEINHANS

On September 15, 1978, 11,700 mine and smelter workers, local 6500
of the United Steelworkers of America, voted to strike against the
International Nickel Company (Inco). For the following eight and a half
months the city of Sudbury, Ont., was the site of Canada's most important labor struggle since World War II.

Inco was the first major producer of nickel in the world and remains
the largest. It has been operating in Sudbury for over 75 years, but like
many other multinational corporations it has operations in both North
America and the Third World. This leaves it in a position where it can
threaten to leave the Sudbury area entirely for its Guatemala or
Indonesia operations if the Canadian labor force doesn't buckle to its
demands. The company has laid off over 6,000 workers since 1970.

The Sudbury strike ended in June 1979, with a victory for the
miners and the whole working class of Canada and Quebec. At the same
time the struggle in Sudbury was significant for many of the women in
the city, who played a large role in the victory by organizing a militant
support-group known as the Wives Supporting the Strike Committee
(WSS). Their efforts shed new light on the role of women in times of
labor conflict.

A Wives' Tale, a 73-minute film completed in 1980, documents the
role of the Wives' Committee. The filmmakers, Sophie Bissonnette,
Martin Duckworth and Joyce Rock, went to Sudbury in March 1979,

about mid-way in the strike. They lived with the women ''on a daily basis'' and the resulting film tells the story of the strike from a woman's point of view. The following interview with the filmmakers took place in June 1979, before the film was completed.

CHUCK: How did you become involved in making this film? Could you tell us how you arrived at the point you are at now?

MARTIN: I went to a Sudbury strike benefit in Ottawa in February 1979, one of dozens across the country. At that time I saw three women speaking from the Wives Supporting the Strike Committee, and it struck me right away that there was an important film to be made.

Within three weeks after that Ottawa benefit, I contacted Sophie and Joyce — and that's how it got started.

PETER: Why is the Sudbury strike so important?

MARTIN: This strike has had more Canadian working-class support than, oh God, since maybe the Ford Windsor strike of 1945. That's because Inco is one of the dozen biggest multinational companies in the country, has one of the most anti-union managements, and is the corporation with the most visibly damaging effect on the environment. It spreads acid rain all over northern Ontario's lakes.

It also became a national strike because it was a rank-and-file strike. The workers voted to strike against the advice of the United Steelworkers hierarchy. Outrage against the steel hierarchy had been building up.

PETER: Tell us about the 1958 strike and the women's role then. The myth about what happened then bears on this latest struggle.

SOPHIE: The whole Sudbury community had maintained the mythology about the women being to blame for the '58 strike's failure, always in the context of the women having forced the men back to work.

So when the women started organizing the Support Committee, around the union local they faced a lot of skepticism and a certain hostility from the husbands about their intentions. One activity gained them an enormous amount of respect and credibility — a great Christmas party, held before we actually got involved.

SOPHIE: None of the strikes in Sudbury prior to this held out past Christmas. It was difficult for families to imagine going through Christmas without a pay check. When we arrived in Sudbury, there was this mixture of the 1958 myth that the women were to blame, and yet an increasing respect for the Support Committee and their activities.

SARA: So, there's another story about '58, right?

· SOPHIE: Right. The women started asking themselves about what role women had really played in '58.

JOYCE: In '58 the strike had begun about the same time, had gone from mid-September to just before Christmas. A number of organizationally and politically naive women (about 900) had gone to the mayor of Sudbury, whom history records as totally corrupt, asking him to put pressure on the company to give the men a fair deal and end the strike. But of course he was in cahoots with Inco and other business interests. He eventually suggested a meeting in the city ice arena. There he placed the women in the bleacher seats, himself and other local officials on the ice, and in the audience "plants" of many non-strikers' wives. Then after he had the plants read proposals, he asked any women who were *still* opposed to their husbands going back to work to come down onto the ice. It was a totally intimidating environment for the women to express any objections.

When the current Christmas party was being planned, many people were saying, "Ha, ha, this is never going to happen. Who do they think they are kidding? It's going to be a big flop. A handful of women preparing Christmas for 11,700 families? Never!" But it was such a mind-boggling success, so rich in spirit, that the men started saying, "Well, I guess we have to give the girls a pat on the back."

SARA: Are you planning on having something in the film about 1958?

JOYCE: The film must include rewriting that history, putting it straight. But it was equally important to be filming while this strike was happening, while the wives were organizing, while they could still say, "How *are* we going to do . . ." with no past tense.

SARA: What is the platform of the WSS group? How do they speak about their activities and how do they want the platform presented on film?

SOPHIE: The first leaflet they handed out to invite other women to join their group outlined principles which differ from the way women usually organize around strikes. They appealed that the union was a family affair. They started the leaflet with, "You work for Inco, too. You raise the kids. You reproduce your husband's labor force so he can go back every day and continue to produce for Inco." And since Sudbury is basically a one-company city, the families are also reproducing the future labor force for Inco.

Their work centered on providing moral support for the men. The support group was crucial in building community backing for the strike because in Sudbury the entire city was paralyzed since Inco is the major industry and most other industries sub-contract from them. It's important that people who are laid off as a result of the strike understand who their real enemy is. That was clear in the community because Inco had been laying off workers for some time. The wives sustained solidarity with their community contacts, for instance, where shopkeepers and banks extended credit to enable the strike to go past Christmas.

Struggling with family tensions was also crucial. The wives have to cope with the usual workload of the children and housekeeping in addition to having husbands at home who find it hard to deal with suddenly being out of work. Then they have to manage a reduced budget which, in this case, for a family of four was $34 a week. These things create a lot of tensions. So one of their most important contributions was maintaining the family unit and holding the community together — setting up social activities to keep everybody in solidarity.

They've done other things. They set up a crisis centre for pregnant women. They had family pickets. They went outside Sudbury to factory gates and spoke at fundraising benefits. They published a comic book for children, to explain the strike. They set up a wives' chorus and organized community suppers to decrease food costs.

Inco had a huge stockpile when the strike started. It was clear to the workers that the company had made them an offer they couldn't accept (a four cent increase, for instance), and Inco went back on gains workers had made on the previous contract.

The strikers were always faced with the threat of court injunctions. This threat seemed to hold the men back over what they could do — other than maintain the nominal picket shacks with a few fellows in it. The wives added a spark. They were able to say, "We'll organize, we'll bring other wives and even our children out, we'll send the chorus to sing our repertoire of union and strike songs." They burned the effigy of the personnel manager at a dawn picket rally.

The company had sent the workers letters telling them to go back to work, and the workers' and wives' eloquent response was a collective letter-burning. The wives don't have a vested interest in the standard union thinking, such as, "We mustn't do anything because we have to wait for word from above." The wives constantly felt, "Why *not* do something? Isn't this a strike?"

SOPHIE: I wouldn't say the union thinking is so standard — it was a rank-and-file strike and there was lots of militancy from many of the men. The crucial point was that the wives educated themselves politically. In most labor struggles women are kept ignorant about the issues, so that a strike means to them no pay check coming in and a husband out of work, period. The women in Sudbury knew what was at stake and they wanted to participate in that struggle. And they knew that they were fighting for more than themselves. Of course, there were divisions in the women's group, and not everyone saw the situation as simply as I've discussed it.

JOYCE: Feminists in Canada helped organize many of the strike benefits. Also, the women insisted that we film their conflicts as well as the good moments: the difficulties of organizing, of getting together, of learning about and trusting each other *specifically as women* — things that were new to them.

CHUCK: What kind of film are you making?

JOYCE: It's a 90-minute color film, shot in 16mm. There will be two versions, one French, one English. We are working in the tradition of cinéma-direct (sometimes referred to as candid-eye in English Canada).

MARTIN: We want to do another week or two of shooting on the after-effects of the strike on the Wives group. There was an interesting meeting of the group within three days of the union's acceptance of the company's offer, which we filmed. Here an older woman who had been active in the old Steelworkers Women's Auxiliary (defunct since 1975) proposed that they reconstitute the women's auxiliary in the union local. She was massively outvoted. All but three of the others supported the idea that they could be more effective if they had their own autonomous organization. They also realized they had to change their name from Wives Supporting the Strike to something new.

As a group they're now going through a period of redefining their roles. One of the ideas they were discussing during the strike was that they demand the right to attend union meetings as observers, which has never happened. They'll be discussing that soon and we hope to be there to film it. And while that's happening, the individual women we have been filming (approximately ten) will be going through an important period of self-discovery and self-examination with their husbands about how to avoid returning to their old roles as housewives, bedmakers and childraisers and how to remain community activists. We hope to film some of those transitions.

SOPHIE: One of the reasons we wanted to stay there so long is they've gone through so many changes in the nine months of the strike, and those changes have continued. We are quite hopeful the women won't go back to the kitchen. They have to prevent the unions and their husbands from sending them back to the kitchen.

SARA: Could you go into more detail about the politics of the film? Martin, I'm really curious to know what's happened to your thinking in the course of working on this film. You've made many films from a left perspective, but this is the first made from a fully feminist perspective. How do you see those things coming together?

MARTIN: Well, first of all, it's not my film. That's the main thing I've learned — how to work with other people. I think that's the most exciting part — to learn how to be equal partners in the feminist and socialist movements. Because I think if we're going to build movements, it has to be done in this kind of working partnership.

SARA: It sounds like a description of the content of the film.

JOYCE: We want this film to be widely distributed within both the union movement and the women's movement and to be used as a departure point for discussion and action. What's been costing a lot of money and time is the fact that the film follows in the tradition of cinema-direct, a tradition of being there and watching and listening and paying attention. That tradition demands more footage, and it's a tradition that agencies like the Canada Council* don't respect in terms of the norms of your budget. For them budgets should conform to norms that correspond to a more manipulative documentary tradition.

PETER: What ideas do the Sudbury women have for the film? How wide an audience are they thinking of, or are they more concerned with it as a specific tool which they could use in Sudbury?

JOYCE: They're very interested in this film being made so that what they have learned in this strike other women can learn from. They had to start from zero and go through the ABC's. We hope other women can use the film and not have to start from scratch. The women filmed hope that other people can get clued in even faster about how to organize against a multinational, not just during a strike but in daily living when you, too, as a wife, work for a multinational.

MARTIN: They don't use terms like working-class consciousness or feminist consciousness, but that is what they've evolved during these strikes, not only in Sudbury but in plant-gating and in speaking at benefits for the strike throughout Ontario. The wives' chorus has travelled, met women in other parts of the country, and they have become aware that they're not isolated.

CHUCK: Why is this strike so different? It's an inspiring pattern. What conditions do you think led these women to achieve this remarkable unity and determination in pushing forward that they either didn't have before or that women in similar situations haven't been able to manifest?

JOYCE: Necessity! And a general social climate that's theirs in 1979.

SOPHIE: The women's movement!

JOYCE: These women live in this company town where every three years a new contract is negotiated. They've had a lot of strikes before '58 and since.

Many women tell you openly how before the strike they sat at home

* The Canadian government's funding agency for the arts.

and watched soap operas all day. Now they are just as openly looking around apprehensively, thinking, "What will I do now?" because they know they can't go back. Many of them married very young, and are now in their early twenties with several children to raise.

MARTIN: There were three women who first broached the idea of setting up a support committee and they belonged to a feminist consciousness-raising group established three years earlier, called Women Helping Women, designed to help women meet their own problems. The existence of the earlier group was one reason for such a good response to the call for setting up a support committee. I think that the remarkable unity achieved in Sudbury at this time was due mainly to the tremendous hatred which had built up against Inco and a real profound determination to win this goddamned strike — against the advice of the international union. They were very angry against the company and they still are.

SARA: Would it be true to say that a lot of the analysis of the support group comes from a re-evaluation of traditional women's skills, which had never been previously valued?

JOYCE: This film is being made from the women's point of view. I think we're being really thorough in what we shoot, whom we listen to — that it's the women who have center stage. We don't turn to their husbands or the union leaders for approval, asking, "Are *they* doing it right, boys?" The women have more often than not a higher consciousness than the men.

SOPHIE: I've learned a lot from these women. We've had many discussions about the film on a daily basis, deciding what we should film and the meaning of specific events. They're rarely formal discussions. It usually happens because we've been living there on a daily basis. The film is on many people's minds (specifically the ten women we focus on), so there's a lot of interaction back and forth.

CHUCK: How are you financing the film? How do three young, broke people make a film? (laughter)

SOPHIE: That's an exciting thing. We've almost been operating in the same way that the strike's been operating in terms of gathering support. On the one hand, we've appealed to individuals and politically or socially involved organizations to give us donations, so that we could shoot on a day-to-day basis. Grants take a long time and we couldn't wait. The wives have helped us in that respect, too — one form of their involvement has been giving us a hand with fundraising. We made sure there was no overlap in our fundraising efforts.

Our second route has been grant money. We've received $25,000 from the Canada Council and $40,000 from L'Institut Québécois du

Cinema which invests in Quebec productions. We should emphasize again that we're making both an English and a French version, because a good 35 percent of the population in Sudbury is of French origin and are trying hard to resist assimilation in northern Ontario.

Many people became involved in supporting the film. That's exciting and crucial, especially in Canada and Quebec where activists aren't familiar with the potential uses of a political film. Film isn't being used very much yet. And scarcity of money and funding sources leads filmmakers into competing for that money, which creates a fairly unhealthy climate at times.

SARA: What about the issue of communism and redbaiting? Is it possible that the women you're filming might be ostracized through redbaiting in the city?

SOPHIE: The Communist Party and individual CP members have not played a role in this strike. That situation would relate more to the events of 1958. In '58 the sides were described by many as the Roman Catholic Church and the company against the Communists. I think the problem now is the way communism is used to blame something on someone and how the women deal with that. Several women have said to us, on film, ''I don't care if I get called a Communist; I don't care if I work with radicals; we're in this because we want to move on to get a good deal out of Inco and we want to tell Inco what we think of them.''

They don't care if they get called Communist or not, but some of the women and some husbands and some union people especially are using that label of communism and putting it on the women. If I may speculate as to what's happening: often the women aren't threatening because they have anything to do with communism, they're threatening because they're stepping out of order, and anything that's stepping out of its ordered role gets labelled communism. More often than not ''feminism'' would be the more important label. Often what the people who are redbaiting really mean is, you're not acting like a woman, you're not playing a traditional woman's role. What threatens people is the fact that the women in the Wives group are feminists. We've also been redbaited like this.

SARA: That still leaves the issue untouched. You understand the kinds of fears that lead to that accusation, but you also want to deal with the putdown itself. Feminists similarly face the putdown ''lesbian.'' The solution does not lie in denying that one is a lesbian. I was wondering what your politics around dealing with the issue of communism is — both in terms of the union and among the women in the film.

JOYCE: At a certain point in the struggle, as strike tensions mounted, redbaiting started from a small number within the Wives group. That's a part of our film.

MARTIN: They were the same women who voted for the Ladies' Auxiliary.

JOYCE: Yes, three or four in the entire group. Someone first said to us, "This film will never get passed if you put a Communist in or if we talk about communism at all." We soon decided that our political integrity or the political integrity of the film depended on our going ahead and including that fact if we had to. Otherwise, it's just feeding into this whole network where you only have to mention the word *communism,* and we all go scurrying into our corners and go, "Right, we don't mention communism." That response just keeps redbaiters going no matter what the situation, the city, or the sex of those involved. We hope to talk with those three who have resisted being in the film. They view us very suspiciously and think Martin is a Communist because he spends so much time away from his family and doesn't believe in God. Now that's interesting, because he's considered a Communist, but Sophie and I aren't; he's the man up there and so they count him as "a person away from home" — we don't count anyway. I mean, I'm glad you get the brunt of it, Martin, because it's the shits. (laughter)

SOPHIE: We have to maintain our integrity. If we're trying to rewrite the women's history of 1958 in order to demystify it, we also have to do the same thing with communism. The women get scapegoated and blamed for the failure of the '58 strike at the same time as communism is also used to justify failures. So it's important for the worker also, not only getting rid of all those false ideas but also starting to see, "Well, if I can't blame my wife, if the community's not to blame, then who is to blame?" Then the workers have to start doing the analysis.

SARA: What's your accountability to them?

SOPHIE: We have an agreement that they have a majority vote. There's a geographic problem in that the editing will be done in Montreal. We'll be organizing screenings at intermediate stages of the editing to get feedback from some women and their impressions, then a final meeting to show the finished film.

JOYCE: Of course, when we press ahead and include the mention of communism, I flash forward to that majority vote agreement's determining whether this film gets out or not. It adds a whole subtext to the problematic side of this kind of democratic participatory filmmaking.

Whenever I hear filmmakers talking about accountability and how they showed people all the stages of the work, I think at the same time there's some hoodwinking there, some skipping over the positive value that your distance, your outsidedness, does bring.

CHUCK: It seems to me that you're being put in that situation whenever you come in because of the skills you have as filmmakers, but you're also coming in as political people who are committed to documenting this struggle and to making a film out of it which will be useful to other people. That puts you in a position of leadership which you don't want to be irresponsible about. You want to listen to what people are saying, yet you also want to influence them to some extent. You don't want to abrogate your responsibility completely.

JOYCE: I understand what you're saying, Chuck, but it's not possible with these women, and luckily so, because we'd feel very awkward. I don't think any of us are suited to being leaders. Also, it's because we arrived five months into the strike. They had already proved their own leadership talents to one another. They're very smart and organized, and they're not bashful in front of a camera. It's not just that they say, "This should be on film to help women in other situations." They're more apt to say, "Oh, you've got a camera. Well, that's nice. What else is new?"

CHUCK: I don't mean you were being leaders in the strike. I was referring to the position you're in as filmmakers, not that you're making the policies of the strike.

JOYCE: I guess the reason why that has not been a problem with the specific ten women we're focusing on is because we did become friends, living in their homes and providing our "shared accountability" on a personal level. We trusted each other to talk about issues.

SOPHIE: I think also that using the style of cinéma-direct sets up an interesting situation. In a sense it's a very manipulative style, but on the other hand it gives us more room to start making links and providing analysis. In cinéma-direct there seems to be very little intervention on the part of the filmmakers. I think its appeal to audiences depends on their inclination and what they want to see.

For example, there's a possibility of making something out of the mention of communism and how it's used to scapegoat that will click for some people while other people won't respond to it in that way. We can use it just as recording an historical event, but I think several people in the audience who are listening to what happened in '58 will start coloring in how they perceive the strike of 1979. Others won't be able to make that link.

CHUCK: Here's another side to my question. I've heard filmmakers say, "Well, I'm out there to serve the community. I make films." Sometimes I think the medium is being used passively: the filmmaker goes in and simply records other people's views. I don't think that's really appropriate.

JOYCE: This whole issue has a lot to do with feminism. It's not just that we went in there like some kind, generous filmmakers from the big city. Part of our creating a rapport has to do with what feminism is stylistically, based on how you approach people and how you don't approach people — whether it's with a camera and sound equipment walking into a room, demanding or recording a situation, or just sitting eating breakfast bleary-eyed with somebody.

SOPHIE: It took us a very long time and many discussions in the women's kitchens before we got some of these things on film, because when you're making a film about women's personal lives and some of the discussions that go on in kitchens, then you have to spend a long time listening before you can build a sort of trust and rapport. You must get to the point where you feel you're not abusing the women and they feel they're not being abused.

JOYCE: The film focuses on the women, and at the same time the perspective is theirs. They're the ones that are legitimizing themselves — that combined with our feminist politics. They have grassroots, working feminism, but it doesn't get called that, and we have big city, more intellectual feminism. We have more labels, more analysis. They're organizing around this strike. They take these basic skills they learned in the women's auxiliary many years ago or in kitchens or in raising families — the whole survival network that they know — and they're applying it around the strike.

In dealing with us as people, well, you're someone in the kitchen, and how you deal with them across the kitchen table determines how they decide how much of themselves they're going to give to you and the film.

• In Review: Voices and Visions

SARA HALPRIN

As the women became increasingly involved in the strike, they questioned more and more their traditional supportive role. This provoked many heated discussions among the women and obviously not without upsetting husband, family, union — and company.

This situation forced us as filmmakers to find a cinematic approach that could capture this reality. It is difficult (impossible) to take "pretty pictures" under these conditions: kitchens are small and don't well suit the movements of a film crew; children scream and cry in the microphone, making it hard to hear....

We often packed up our equipment and decided not to shoot...

because we felt it would be a betrayal of the trust we had established with the women. You may perhaps be disappointed not to witness a family feud. . . .

So we shot a film that doesn't in fact show "everything," hoping that what is not obvious comes from between the lines, between each frame of the film.

The strike lasted eight and a half months. We stayed four and a half months in Sudbury, living with strikers' families. We returned six months later to "finish" *A Wives' Tale*. Later still we returned to show the wives the film. The voted unanimously to release it.

— *the filmmakers: Sophie Bissonnette, Martin Duckworth, Joyce Rock*

As an employer and as an environmental influence, Inco's record is impressively atrocious — a paradigm of patriarchal capitalism. The Sudbury smokestacks of Inco belch polluting agents into the air, resulting in acid rain across the province. Men die in the mines. Women live lives of patient desperation caring for, fearing for, and fearing the miners ("he's not always easy to live with"), raising future miners and miners' wives. And the Board of Directors annually raises the required profit margin for the company. There is some change as the world turns — now a few women are employed in the mines (30 out of 11,700), and recently one of those women died in a foundry accident. Equality of opportunity.

Against this background, *A Wives' Tale* (1980) is the most ambitious labor film to be shot in Canada in recent years, certainly the most ambitious in English-speaking Canada since the early days of Evelyn and Lawrence Cherry and their agrarian populist films of the 1940s in Regina.[1] Although shot in Ontario, *A Wives' Tale* is not an English Canadian production. Sudbury has a large francophone population, a fact strongly reflected in the structure of the film. *A Wives' Tale* is a bilingual film, released first in French in Montreal, and very much in the tradition of militant Quebec cinema. The executive producer was Arthur Lamothe, whose film *Le Mepris n' aura qu' un temps* (*Hell No Longer,* 1969) remains a landmark of radical documentary.[2] However, unlike most Quebec militant films and unlike most labor-oriented documentaries made in English in Canada and elsewhere, *A Wives' Tale* is pre-eminently, self-consciously, happily, and proudly a feminist film, insisting on the priority of women's experience and women's wide-ranging voices and visions as its perspective on the strike.

The Inco strike made labor history in Canada. It was originally provoked by the company in order to dispose of a nickel stockpile, on the evident assumption that a few months on the picket lines would deplete the union treasury and the energies of the workers so that they would crawl back to work whenever Inco offered some paltry concessions. This did not happen — the strikers held out for eight and a half

months, until they were offered a contract that made the strike worthwhile. The main reason they were able to hold out for so long was that
they were solidly backed by the Wives Supporting the Strike Committee.

The Wives raised money for special needs. They organized a Christmas party that gave out 10,000 toys, held suppers and sales and ran a
thrift shop. They developed a clear analysis of the reasons for the strike
and gave financial, emotional and physical support, which for once they
themselves understood to be invaluable. But the most important
accomplishment of the women who organized in Sudbury, as the film
shows, was the validation of the work women do, and the skills women
have, and the right of women to speak on their own behalf.

The most difficult challenge for the filmmakers, aside from the
usual hardships faced by radical artists here and everywhere, was to
make this self-validation interesting and accessible on film. Mines and
foundries make wonderful material for film documentarians — the colors and sounds of the molten metal, the awesome machinery, the
physical courage of the workers daring the fury of the elements. The
filmic problem is how to move from this audio/visual spectacle to the
subject matter of *A Wives' Tale* — two or three women arguing around
a kitchen table about how far they can press their desire to keep
informed about strike matters and have their say about issues that
directly affect their lives.

One solution found by the filmmakers was simply to juxtapose these
disparate elements. Near the end of the film, when the strike is over,
one of the women is shown doing her laundry, "helped" by her toddl-
ing child. As the woman reaches for the controls of the washing
machine, the scene cuts to one of the most dramatic sequences of the
film, starting in the foundry, ending with a shot of molten metal stream-
ing golden down the hillside from great vats tipped against the indigo
sky.

A woman's voice, humming, connects this scene of men and their
machines back to the familial reality that makes the drama possible. Cut
to an early-morning scene of a miner eating breakfast, a woman talking
about her life since the strike ended six months earlier, how she tries to
get out some evenings to see other women. Another younger woman
tells one of the most important stories of the film. Sitting in a rocking
chair, as she did at the beginning of the film when she told how she first
became involved in the Wives' group, she now, 14 months later, talks
about how involvement changed her. "I'm not scared to go out by
myself anymore." Before, she was terrified that someone might talk to
her and she would have nothing to say. She is the same young woman
seen earlier in the film speaking at a mock trial of the Inco Board of

Directors, speaking of being a miner's daughter and a miner's wife and a miner's mother. She says she hopes someday she'll be able to hold her head high when she says, "My son is a miner."

Cut from the rocking chair to a picket line for another strike and familiar faces — some of the women in Wives Supporting the Strike have been politicized by that experience. They have formed support groups, and go out to work in their community. Of these, the most militant is the francophone group, who have been shown in the course of the film to be aware of triply oppressed status as working-class francophone women. The women form a circle, dancing, and I remember the words of Anne Sylvestre's song, sung earlier in the film by Quebec folk star Pauline Julien at a benefit for the strikers. Singing of women who have borne and suffered and buried men throughout the ages, Pauline Julien pays tribute to *"une sorcière comme les autres"* (a witch, like all the others).

The heart of the film is the growth of these women, these potential witches, picketers, organizers, mothers, wives, movers and shakers. They argue, they yell bitterly at each other. An older Scots woman, paying homage to her husband's "thirrrty years of serrrvice," announces that she will abide by his decision, whatever it is. And what of her own 30 years of service to him? That is my question, but it is raised, in other ways, by other women in the film. One woman says firmly, "My husband is the one who works and brings home the pay check, but I'm the one who balances his bank account." Another woman, who is seen earlier in the film reporting on her research about the management of Inco (the Board of Directors, she announces, is composed entirely of men connected with banks, men in their sixties and seventies who seem to be suffering from "hardening of the heart as well as hardening of the arteries"), says now that she is "not for the strike, I'm for my husband . . . and if my husband decides to go back to work, then fuck the strike!" Other women applaud. Cathy, one of the 30 striking women, retorts: "It's not your strike, it's everybody's . . . this is history in the making."

A number of recent feminist documentaries have used historical material (photographs, old footage, oral testimony) to pay tribute to women who were active in the labor movement (*Union Maids* 1977, *With Babies and Banners* 1978, *Rosie the Riveter* 1980). *A Wives' Tale* also uses this sort of archival material, to very different effect, as it serves to validate the work and experience of women as working-class wives and mothers, and it brings their rich and untapped history directly into the present, showing the unbreakable connection between working-class struggle and feminism. When this connection is denied, as it has repeatedly been denied in practice by socialists around the world, the result is betrayal of the struggle — men and women all suffer.

The opening sequence of the film moves from a scene in the mine to an overview of the city of Sudbury, with a woman's voice providing factual information which is then rooted in personal experiences as she speaks of "our labor" as the source of Inco's profit. Over footage of the strike she brings the film home: "The strike has now been going on for about six months . . . we, as wives of strikers . . . our history is a forgotten one." Credits: *A Wives' Tale*. Tracking shot: railway tracks, music, old pictures, old footage, women's voices recounting their history, their arrival in Sudbury, their lives as pioneers, as miners' wives and daughters and mothers — always spoken in the first person, the story of one woman and of many — as paid workers during the war, women who joined the first union in 1944, who were laid off when the war was over and returned to their customary unpaid work at home, as wives of miners who spoke out against the hardships of a previous bitter strike in 1958 and were then blamed for the poor contract the miners accepted soon after.

Cut now to present-day footage, the Wives of 1979, haunted by the shame of 20 years earlier, an undeserved shame with implications that recur throughout the film — if we speak out now and they take a bad contract we'll be blamed . . . but we're speaking out *against* the settlement . . . they're afraid we'll turn out to be smarter than them . . . they're afraid of us . . . they don't trust us . . . our own husbands. Nervous, shy, brassy, tough as old sinew, organizing, collecting money, phoning, speaking, arguing, cooking, washing, cleaning, bright as new pennies, learning new skills, learning the value of skills they already have.

Balancing the family bank account means they can balance the group's account very well, thank you — but still the union insists that checks be signed by a union officer. And the women agree, after an argument, with one dissenting vote. But a woman who argued against the decision later pipes up and informs her pontificating husband that he is a male chauvinist pig. She explains to the camera that she grew up in a family where father was the boss — she thought it was natural and right. Now she's having other thoughts.

In a written statement accompanying the film's Toronto opening, the filmmakers refer to the Wives' insistence that "we record their 'lows' as well as their 'highs', their tensions and conflicts — all that would keep them 'real', even on the big screen, and far away from being 'heroines'."

A Québécois film, still and always an act of faith.

Briefly, *A Wives' Tale,* seventy-three coloured minutes where the sound and image belong to women.

It is a different cinema . . . why hesitate to name it? It is a militant film, a feminist film, a tale of women.

— the filmmakers

NOTES

[1] Evelyn and Lawrence Cherry were a husband-and-wife team who first made films in England, went to Ottawa to work with John Grierson at the National Film Board, and finally moved to the prairies where they set up an independent production company. Evelyn Cherry is still active in filmmaking.

[2] Since completing *Hell No Longer* in 1970 Lamothe has gone on to make a series of eight films on the Quebec Amerindians, *Carcajou et le péril blanc* (1973-77). For a thorough analysis of Quebec filmmaking see Michel Houle's "Themes and Ideology in Quebec Cinema" in *Jump Cut* 22.

PART THREE

WOMEN'S COUNTER-CINEMA

Shirley MacLaine in Sweet Charity

INTRODUCTION

Feminist filmmakers... have shown it is possible to reach new audiences
— in women's groups, libraries, and public schools — with films that
combine personal statement and political analysis with experimental and
innovative means.

Jump Cut Editorial No. 3, 1974

In 1973 Claire Johnston wrote an influential essay, "Women's Cinema
as Counter-Cinema," in which she argued the need for women in film
to "operate at all levels."* Rejecting conventional definitions of
realism and criticism based only on empirical study of women's roles,
she called for the "development of collective work" and for a women's
cinema that is not merely *"captured"* from the world but "constructed." The allusion to images being captured indicates her rejection
of conventional realism, because to be content with capturing reality
means that one also adopts the ideology of the social status quo. The
work included in Part Three represents in many ways the kind of collective work Johnston was calling for.

Critical debate over "positive images" of women has been one of
the key issues for women's counter-cinema and remains central in the
1980s. Women who use films for consciousness raising and workplace
organizing are constantly searching for representations that act as strong
"role models" to encourage confidence and collective spirit. Yet many
women film critics have pointed out hidden dangers in this search for
positive images. The debate here between Linda Artel and Susan
Wengraf on the one hand and Diane Waldman on the other illustrates
this issue in a clear and succinct way. It shows that the Artel and
Wengraf book obviously functions as a valuable resource, yet also
invites criticism about its theoretical base. The career of Shirley Mac-
Laine opens up the positive images debate in another arena, leading
Serafina Bathrick and Patricia Erens to take opposing approaches to
Hollywood's star system.

Women's cinema as something that needs to be constructed is demonstrated clearly by Ruby Rich's "In the Name of Feminist Film Criticism." Rich makes a strong case for the need to foster the avant-garde,

*See Claire Johnston (ed.) *Notes on Women's Cinema* (London, S.E.F.T.),
reprinted in Bill Nichols, *Movies and Methods* (Berkeley, University of California Press, 1976.)

but her main aim is to encourage critical practice for all types of feminist film. Her essay provides a thorough history of the movement since 1970, and offers a detailed critique of major feminist filmmakers such as Yvonne Rainer, Chantal Ackerman, and Marta Mészáros.

Whereas Rich suggests categories for understanding recent films, Julia Lesage returns to one of the most famous films of the silent era, Griffith's *Broken Blossoms,* considered a progressive and humanitarian art film when released in 1919. Lesage asks, "How is it I can be emotionally involved in a work that victimizes women?" By probing her own feelings as a viewer she is able to explore her enjoyment of the film even while recognizing the sexist and racist elements at work in the fiction.

Finally, Michelle Citron and Ellen Seiter talk about their experiences teaching film production. Their article usefully summarizes a number of this book's themes in concrete terms and contains many practical ideas for teachers who would like to be sensitive to the needs of women students. But Citron and Seiter also introduce debate on wider pedagogical issues concerning creativity and the artist. They state, "We consider it very important to debunk the romantic myth of the artist." The opposite of this romantic genius myth is a more collective art practice; the writings collected here demonstrate how women's counter-cinema will continue to be constructed and to grow.

CHAPTER 12.

The Politics of Positive Images

• Positive Images: Screening Women's Films

LINDA ARTEL AND SUSAN WENGRAF

As feminist educators we are committed to facilitating young people's awareness of alternatives to sex-stereotyped behavior.* As feminist *media* educators we recognize the powerful ability of film and video to present positive role models that encourage this awareness. In an effort to provide easy access to non-sexist media, we have compiled *Positive Images,* an annotated guide to over 400 short 16mm films, videotapes, slides and filmstrips in educational distribution.

The primary aim of *Positive Images* was to evaluate media materials from a feminist perspective. We looked for materials that had at least one of the following characteristics:

• presents girls and women, boys and men with non-stereotyped behavior and attitudes: independent, intelligent women; adventurous, resourceful girls; men who are nurturing; boys who are not afraid to show their vulnerability.

• presents both sexes in non-traditional work or leisure activities: men doing housework, women flying planes, etc.

• questions values and behavior of traditional male/female role division.

• shows women's achievements and contributions throughout history.

• deals with a specific women's problem, such as pregnancy, abortion or rape, in a non-sexist way.

*This article is is a revised version of the introduction to Linda Artel and Susan Wengraf's *Positive Images: Non-Sexist Films for Young People* (San Francisco: Bootlegger Press, 1976).

• contains images of sexist attitudes, behavior and institutions that can be used for consciousness raising.

While many films contain important non-sexist elements, few fulfill an ideal standard. A number of films deal with feminist issues but are sexist in the way they treat the subject matter. For example, *Rape: A Preventative Inquiry* (1974) uses male police as experts but ignores knowledgeable female experts such as rape-crisis-center workers. Some films present women who talk about non-sexist ideas or do non-sexist work, but we see them acting in a way that limits their credibility, as with Mary Tyler Moore in the women's history film, *American Parade: We the Women* (1974). On camera, Moore behaves in a coy manner that suggests she doesn't really want to be taken seriously.

Other films undermine women's credibility by using a male narrator who makes condescending remarks about the women in the film. Thus, *Persistent and Finagling* is a fascinating study of Montreal housewives who mount a successful grassroots campaign against air pollution. However, the value of what the women are doing is continually diluted by paternalistic comments from one of the husbands. Some dramatic shorts portray a strong and independent female protagonist until the final scene, when she is suddenly rescued by a man. For example, in the history drama *Mary Kate's War,* Kate, a newspaper publisher, develops as a courageous character with ethical integrity until the end when a male friend saves her from political harassment.

Some films are class biased: they present a viable alternative for upper-middle-class women and men but have little relevance for people in other economic situations. *Joyce at 34* (1972) shows a husband and wife — one a writer, the other a filmmaker — equally sharing childcare responsibilities. But this documentary shows no consciousness that this alternative serves only the few who have the luxury of flexible work schedules.

Some films cover women's subjects but lack a feminist perspective. We discovered several film biographies on women that failed to show the subject's strength. For example, a film on Louisa May Alcott depicts the author as a selfless, weepy woman. We also found films that were erroneously (and widely) publicized as non-sexist. In a prime example, *How to Say No to a Rapist — and Survive* (1974), Frederic Storaska, a self-appointed expert, lectures women on how to avoid physical harm from rape. He stereotypes women by dwelling on the use of feminine wiles as the best way to outsmart attackers and recommends several defense tactics that other rape experts have found to be ineffective and even dangerous.

Other films portray a strong female protagonist in a non-sexist way yet stereotype secondary characters. In *Madeline* (1950),the animation based on Ludwig Bemelmans's book, the title character is adventurous, but the other girls behave in a very conventional "good little girl" manner. A growing number of "career" films, especially those on vocational training, include a "token" girl or woman while the rest of the film presents the standard view of men in that field.

A number of excellent films — in content — have diminished effectiveness because of technical inferiority: poor sound, aimless visuals, slow pacing. In *Hey Doc* (1971), a film about a black woman doctor committed to healthcare for the poor, the camera does nothing more than trail after Dr. Allen, much as in a home movie.

Although we did find over 400 examples of what we call non-sexist films, we found that positive images still need to be created in the following areas:

• films for young children: only a handful of films present positive images at the preschool or primary grade levels. For example, adventure stories with exciting plots and strong female protagonists are rare.

• biographies of women: though there are three or four film biographies of Helen Keller and Eleanor Roosevelt, there are none of such women as Emma Goldman, George Eliot, Mother Jones, Rosa Bonheur, Sacagawea, Maria Mitchell, Simone de Beauvoir and Elizabeth Blackwell.

• women's role in history: several films present a general survey of women's role in U.S. history, but very few deal with their role in specific historical movements and events (such as settling the west or the world wars). Even fewer deal with women's contributions to world history.

• women in non-traditional jobs: although a number of films survey women working in non-traditional occupations, new films focus on a particular occupation to give an in-depth view. Films about women scientists and mathematicians are notably absent.

• Third World women: while there are several films about black women, very few focus on women from other ethnic backgrounds. Furthermore, too many of the existing films treat their subjects as victims rather than as strong women who survive hardship.

• male liberation: few films offer meaningful alternatives to traditional masculine values. We did find several films in which boys express tender feelings, but those emotions are most often directed at pets, not people. Also, the sensitive male protagonists in these films are usually from minority ethnic groups — leaving the stereotype of the macho white male unchanged.

• changing definition of "family": although the number of single-parent families is steadily increasing, few films deal with divorce or show alternatives to the nuclear family, such as communal living or single parenthood, let alone explore the way these alternatives affect sex roles.

The school curriculum needs non-sexist visual media used in conjunction with books in every course. In addition, classroom visits from women and men working in non-stereotyped jobs can present effective and immediate role models. When students read texts and library books or watch films that perpetuate sex role stereotypes, teachers should promote that kind of discussion essential to develop critical thinking. The curriculum should also include discussions about TV programs, commercials and Hollywood films that students can watch in order to develop such an awareness.

A public film program of non-sexist films can effectively be presented at libraries, women's centers or other community centers. We attracted enthusiastic audiences to a series in which the program each week focused on a particular aspect of sex-role liberation, such as new roles for work, sexuality, women's history and childcare. Knowledgeable speakers from the feminist community led discussions after the films and helped make the programs an active experience for the audience.

We would like to see a time when films showing positive images of women will not require special notice but will be an integral part of our culture. As a means to that change, educators, librarians and others involved with young people need to seek out and screen films that can educate them about non-sexist ways of thinking and behaving.

• There's More to a Positive Image Than Meets the Eye

DIANE WALDMAN

Reviewing the book *Positive Images* is a deceptively simple task, for one would not expect much controversy to be generated by a catalogue, a resource for teachers and librarians, a book not designed to be read from cover to cover. The authors, Linda Artel, film consultant at the Pacific Film Archive, and Susan Wengraf, a filmmaker and educational media consultant, spent over two years in research previewing films and talking with teachers and librarians. The project culminated in this guide to over 400 films, videotapes, slide shows, filmstrips and photographs, which in some manner deal with the problem of sex roles.

As such, *Positive Images* seems to be an extremely valuable resource. Not only do the authors cite films that have received attention in recent years, such as *Growing Up Female* (1971), *Union Maids* (1977), *The San Francisco Women's Film* (1971), they also unearth many unusual films that do not make the usual circuit of Women in Film courses and film festivals. (For example, I was unaware of the existence of *What Eighty Million Women Want,* 1913, an early suffrage film produced by Emmeline Pankhurst, much less of its rental cost or where it could be obtained.) The authors perform another service in that they have included a few films they do not recommend *because* "they are being widely and erroneously publicized as non-sexist."

Positive Images, then, performs the valuable function of helping teachers supplement and plan their courses. In addition, as the authors themselves note in their preface, they discovered:

> that some of the most exciting and effective non-sexist media are being distributed by independent filmmakers, feminist groups, and small, alternative companies. Providing information about these little known resources has become an important aspect of the guide, since such sources do not have the financial means for large-scale publicity campaigns.

Having stated what I find to be valuable and useful about the book, I now wish to state my reservations. My criticisms fall into two categories: first, the criteria involved in determining what is to be considered a "positive image," and second, the limits of the very notion of "positive image" itself.

In their foreword, the authors describe the "guidelines for selection and evaluation." This immediately introduces a problem on the theoretical level: what are "positive" characteristics, and what is the relationship of these images to the social reality? This problem can be articulated more explicitly if we look at the contradictions embodied in the pun that constitutes the title *Positive Images*.

When we speak of a "positive image" in film or photography, we mean that the lights and shades correspond to those of the original subject; indeed, by extension, one meaning of the word "positive" in a general sense is "concerned only with real things and experience; empirical." On the other hand, "positive" also means "affirmative," or "tending in the direction regarded as that of progress," or "constructive." Judging from the above criteria, both meanings are employed, but then we must ask, in ascribing "positive characteristics" to certain depictions are we claiming a truth value for them? Do they depict things as they really are, or as we think they should be? How do we deal with the reality of sexism as it currently exists? Because these questions are not raised by the authors, a tension between "things as they are" and "things as they should be" informs many of the film descriptions.

Let us see how the above criteria work in practice. At times they seem to be applied too narrowly, without regard for specific cultural situation or historical context. For example, the entry for *Boran Women* (1975):

> In a cattle raising community in Northern Kenya, the women perform the traditional tasks of child-rearing and food preparation while the men manage the herds. Although the women are also responsible for building the cowhide covered dwellings, this too is viewed as "women's work."

Does the term "traditional tasks" refer to a western tradition of sexual division of labor? Is the film included, then, because women are responsible for the "non-traditional" (in the western sense) task of building the dwellings, but then critiqued because even this is viewed as "women's work"? Is this a critique of the film, or a critique of the Boran culture?

In addition, this measuring of a film's worth against a checklist of "positive" characteristics can seem silly, as in the case of *Janie Sue and Tugaloo:*

> Eight year old Janie Sue lives on a farm and wants to become an accomplished rider. Her goal is respected by her grandfather who teaches her how to control her horse and how to herd cattle. Janie Sue handles her horse well and demonstrates perseverance in learning this skill. Unfortunately, the film shows her several times trying to corner a cow, but never gives us the satisfaction of seeing her succeed.

The authors seem to fault the film for leaving us with a sense of struggle or process instead of supplying the inevitable "happy ending."

The authors can also be humorless, as in the case of their description of *Free to Be You or Me* (1974).

> One animated sequence, "Ladies First," by humorist Shel Silverstein, is actually misogynist. A prissy little girl has always insisted that "ladies go first." When she and her friends are captured by hungry tigers, [the animals] say, "Ladies first," and eat her first. This story is an inappropriate way to convince little girls or boys that chivalry is ridiculous and even destructive.

Or they can be even cruelly absurd, as in *A Day in the Life of Bonnie Consolo:*

> Bonnie Consolo introduces herself and tells us that she was born without arms. We see Bonnie do an amazing array of tasks with her feet and legs. She cooks dinner, bakes bread, cans fruit, drives, shops, kills a fly, puts on a necklace, cuts her son's hair and then hugs him. Although performing domestic duties that do not challenge the traditional female role, Bonnie does present the image of a woman who has overcome her particular obstacle with immense strength and courage.

One wonders whether Bonnie Consolo would have to operate a fork-lift before presenting a totally "positive image" in the authors' terms.

Similarly, we might question the authors' tendency to critique a film for presenting a woman in relation to history in lieu of concentrating on biographical information. Take, for example, *The Eleanor Roosevelt Story* (1965): "The film loses sight of Mrs. Roosevelt as it chronicles historic events." Or *Margaret Sanger* (1972):

> Unfortunately, this film spends very little time on the life of Margaret Sanger, the courageous, vital woman who defied societal taboos to create family planning clinics in America. Rather, the film documents the development of family planning and the problem of population explosion, using historic photographs along with early and contemporary motion picture footage.

Do we, as teachers, want to convey a history composed of the lives of "great women" merely to replace or supplement the dominant bourgeois histories of "great men?" Incidentally, by 1916 this "courageous, vital woman" was presenting birth control as the solution to working-class misery and as a means of controlling the birth rate of the "unfit."[1]

This brings me to another major point: the book employs a pluralistic conception of what constitutes a "positive image." The authors often lump together films that clearly represent different class interests, different types of role models, and discuss all with equal enthusiasm. I am reminded of the scene in *Adam's Rib* (1949) in which three women are brought into court by Katharine Hepburn to demonstrate women's equality and/or superiority over men: a forewoman in a factory, an incredibly strong acrobat, and a scientist with various degrees from prestigious universities and a specialty in biological warfare.

In *Positive Images* for example, on p. 119 we find the *Are You Listening?* (1976) videotape series described as "a series of sincere and direct discussions among groups of people who are often talked about, but rarely listened to, in our society." Although these groups include "Black High School Girls" and "Welfare Mothers," they also include "Men Who Are Working with Women in Management," a group of male executives at AT&T, "Women in Management," and "Women in Middle Management." These latter two videotapes, ironically juxtaposed with an entry on *Women and Children in China* (1975), include a "discussion among women in management — a general in the army, a university president, corporation executives, and government officials. The wide-ranging discussion covers many important issues: the need to bring a new kind of humanism to management; to avoid playing by 'men's rules' ."

On the following page we have *Women Workers* (1974), in which the director of trade union women's studies at the New York State School of Industrial and Labor Relations at Cornell talks with a union organizer for the Distributive Workers of America. "They believe that there is a new consciousness among office workers who are banding together for better wages and job conditions." How would this "new consciousness," one wonders, accord with the "new humanism" of the women in management?

In all fairness to the authors, both of these entries contain the "Not Previewed" designation. The authors in their introduction do note that "certain films present a viable alternative for women and men in the upper-middle class, but are of less relevance to people in other economic situations" and do include critical comments covering assumptions about class in films such as *Art of Age* (1971) and *Careers: Women in Careers* (1973). It is possible that a more critical analysis would have been included had they previewed a film such as *Women in Management* (1976).

However, something about the phrase "are of less relevance to people in other economic situations" seems to be slightly amiss: it accepts as a given the structure that permits those "other economic situations" to exist, and fails to distinguish those role models that serve to perpetuate it from those that actively challenge it. This failure to distinguish between types of "positive image" is, of course, not unique to this catalogue but has plagued the feminist movement from its inception, splitting those feminists who sought liberation and equality through solidarity with other oppressed groups and a radical transformation of society from those who wanted an equal share in the power structure as it existed, often at the expense of other oppressed groups. (For example, certain members of the suffrage movement consciously appealed to racist, nativist and class sentiments in attempting to obtain the vote for women: "There is but one way to avert the danger [of the influence of 'undesirables']," argued Carrie Chapman Catt in 1894, "Cut off the vote of the slums and give it to women."[2])

Positive Images seems to be predicated upon a notion of a sexist society and media, but with little analysis of how this sexism functions in an advanced industrial capitalist society. In the authors' introduction, they describe the media as "controlled by men" and "notoriously sexist," but this is the extent of the analysis. It is little wonder, then, that the authors state, "The powerful effect of media can be refocused to question destructive patterns and demonstrate credible options," and that "Film and video can be highly effective tools for introducing new, non-sexist values and encouraging awareness of alternative possibilities for growth," without any indication of the magnitude of the problems involved: ownership of production, access to distribution networks, or transformation of society at large.

But this brings me to my second major criticism of this catalogue — the very notion of "positive image" as a critical concept and a pedagogical tool. The notion of "positive image" is predicated upon the assumption of *identification* of the spectator with a character depicted in a film. It has an historical precedent in the "positive hero" and "heroine" of socialist realism. It assumes that most of what children see are "negative images," distorted stereotypes, and that the corrective to this is exposure to "positive images" or non-sexist role models.

Yet the mechanism of identification goes unchallenged and unchanged, and introduces, I think, a kind of complacency associated with merely presenting an image of the "positive" hero(ine). That this attitude informs this catalogue can be demonstrated by quoting from the authors' instructions on "How to Use Visual Media for Greatest Effectiveness." We are told that "non-sexist visual media used in conjunction with books should be integrated into every part of the curriculum" and that "when students read texts and library books or watch films that do perpetuate sex role stereotypes, discussion is essential to develop critical thinking." I would strongly emphasize this last sentence, but would extend the "necessary discussion" to those materials deemed "non-sexist" as well. For if the mechanism of identification goes unchallenged, how are students to distinguish between "positive" and "negative" images?

And more importantly, does this concept allow or does it mitigate against the development of those critical tools so necessary for dealing with the dominant media and society? If, as the authors say, "children spend more time watching TV than going to school," and, as a friend who teaches in a daycare center remarked, "Two minutes of the Six Million Dollar Man can counteract the effects of my teaching of non-sexist values for both boys and girls," then perhaps, as teachers, we should stress analysis, critical distance and discussion of *any* material we use rather than rely upon the identification implied by the "positive image" concept.

Put another way, we should remember that meaning is to be located in the interaction between reader and image and not in the images themselves. This is stressed in an article by Elizabeth Cowie in *Screen Education·*

> Sexism in an image cannot be designated materially as a content in the way that denotative elements such as colours or objects in the image can be pointed to. Rather it is in the development of new or different definitions and understandings of what men and women are and in their roles in society which produces readings of images as sexist; the political perspective of feminism produces a further level of connotative reading.[3]

This latter point can be affirmed by anyone who has had the curious experience of re-reading or re-viewing a book or film and reacting in disgust and amazement not only at the representations but at one's former neutrality or even delight in those same representations.

We certainly should attack blatant sexual stereotypes and applaud "positive images" when they do appear: that these media images *do* serve to shape children's attitudes, behaviors and expectations is undeniable. And I don't want to diminish the work which went into the compilation of this catalogue or the potential usefulness of *Positive Images*. My criticisms are intended to indicate the limits of the "positive image" concept, and to demonstrate some of the important pedagogical issues that underlie such a compilation.

NOTES

[1] From David Kennedy, *Birth Control in America: The Career of Margaret Sanger* (New Haven, Conn: 1970), p. 112, quoted in Eli Zaretsky, *Capitalism, the Family and Personal Life* (New York: Harper and Row, 1976), p. 123.

[2] Cited in Ailen Kraditor, ed., *Up From the Pedestal* (Chicago, 1970), p. 125, quoted in William H. Chafe, *The American Woman: Her Changing Social, Economic and Political Roles, 1920-1970* (New York: Oxford Univ. Press, 1972), pp. 14-15; see also Catharine Stimpson's " 'Thy Neighbor's Wife, Thy Neighbor's Servants': Women's Liberation and Black Civil Rights," in Vivian Gornick and Barbara K. Moran, eds., *Women in Sexist Society* (New York: Basic Books, 1971), pp. 622-657.

[3] Elizabeth Cowie, "Women, Representation and the Image," *Screen Education* 23 (Summer 1977): 19.

CHAPTER 13.

In the Name of Feminist Film Criticism

B. RUBY RICH

> Whatever is unnamed, undepicted in images, whatever is omitted from biography, censored in collections of letters, whatever is mis-named as something else, made difficult-to-come-by, whatever is buried in the memory by the collapse of meaning under an inadequate or lying language — this will become not merely unspoken, but unspeakable.
>
> — Adrienne Rich[1]

The situation for women working in filmmaking and film criticism today is precarious.* While our work is no longer invisible, and not yet unspeakable, it still goes dangerously unnamed. There is even uncertainty over what name might characterize that intersection of cinema and the women's movement within which we labor, variously called "films by women," "feminist film," "images of women in film" or "women's films." All are vague and problematic.

I see the lack of proper name here as symptomatic of a crisis in the ability of feminist film criticism thus far to come to terms with the work at hand, to apply a truly feminist criticism to the body of work already produced by women filmmakers. This crisis points to a real difference between the name "feminist" and the other names that have tradi-

---

*Earlier versions of this article appeared in *Jump Cut* 19 (1979) and *Heresies* 9 (1980)

Many of the ideas in the section on "Towards a Feminist Film Glossary" originated in the context of a germinative discussion published as "Women and Film: A Discussion of Feminist Aesthetics," *New German Critique* 13 (1978), pp. 83-107. I am grateful to the other participants in that discussion, including Michelle Citron, Julia Lesage, Judith Mayne, Anna Marie Taylor, and the three *New German Critique* editors, for their support.

tionally been applied to film (that is, "structuralist" for certain avant-garde films or "melodrama" for certain Hollywood films).[2]

"Feminist" is a name that may have only a marginal relation to the film text, describing more persuasively the context of social and political activity from which the work sprang. Such a difference is due, on the one hand, to a feminist recognition of the links tying a film's aesthetics to its modes of production and reception; and, on the other hand, to the particular history of the cinematic field which "feminists" came to designate — a field in which filmmaking-exhibition-criticism-distribution-audience have always been considered inextricably connected.

THE HISTORY

The great contribution of feminism, as a body of thought, to culture in our time has been that it has something fairly direct to say, a quality all too rare today. And its equally crucial contribution, as a process and style, has been women's insistence on conducting the analysis, making the statements, in unsullied terms, in forms not already associated with the media's oppressiveness towards women. It is this freshness of discourse and distrust of traditional modes of articulation that placed feminist cinema in a singular position vis-à-vis both the dominant cinema and the avant-garde in the early 1970s.

By the "dominant," I mean Hollywood and all its corresponding manifestations in other cultures; but this could also be termed the Cinema of the Fathers. By the "avant-garde," I mean the experimental/personal cinema which is positioned, by self-inclusion, within the art world; but this could also be termed the Cinema of the Sons. Being a business, the Cinema of the Fathers seeks to do only that which has been done before and proved successful. Being an art, the Cinema of the Sons seeks to do only that which has not been done before and so prove itself successful.

Into such a situation, at the start of the 1970s, entered a feminist cinema. In place of the Fathers' bankruptcy of both form and content, there was a new and different energy; a cinema of immediacy and positive force now opposed the retreat into violence and the revival of a dead past which had become the dominant cinema's mainstays. In place of the Sons' increasing alienation and isolation, there was an entirely new sense of identification — with other women — and a corresponding commitment to communicate with this now-identifiable audience, a commitment which replaced, for feminist filmmakers, the elusive public ignored and frequently scorned by the male formalist filmmakers. Thus, from the start, its link to an evolving political movement gave feminist cinema a power and direction entirely unprecedented in independent filmmaking, bringing issues of theory/practice, aesthetics/meaning, process/representation into sharp focus.

Since the origin and development of feminist film work are largely unexamined, the following chronology sketches some of the major events of the 1970s in North America and Great Britain. Three sorts of information are omitted as beyond the scope of this survey: (1) European festivals and publications, although some have been extremely significant; (2) beyond the first entry, the hundreds of films made by women during the decade; and (3) the publication in 1969-70 of key feminist writings such as *Sexual Politics, The Dialectic of Sex,* and *Sisterhood is Powerful,* which must be remembered as the backdrop and theoretical impetus for these film activities.

1971: Release of *Growing Up Female, Janie's Janie, Three Lives* and *The Woman's Film:* first generation of feminist documentaries.

1972: First New York International Festival of Women's Films and the Women's Event at Edinburgh Film Festival. First issue of *Women & Film* magazine; special issues on women and film in *Take One, Film Library Quarterly* and *The Velvet Light Trap;* filmography of women directors in *Film C.*

1973: Toronto Women and Film Festival, Washington Women's Film Festival, season of women's cinema at National Film Theatre in London, and Buffalo women's film conference. Marjorie Rosen's *Popcorn Venus* (first book on women in film) and *Notes on Women's Cinema* (first anthology of feminist film theory), edited by Claire Johnston for British Film Institute.

1974: Chicago Films by Women Festival. First issue of *Jump Cut.* Two books on images of women in film: Molly Haskell's *From Reverence to Rape* and Joan Mellen's *Women and Their Sexuality in the New Film.*

1975: Conference of Feminists in the Media, New York and Los Angeles. *Women & Film* ceases publication; *The Work of Dorothy Arzner* (BFI monograph edited by Johnston), and Sharon Smith's *Women Who Make Movies* (guide to women filmmakers).

1976: Second New York International Festival of Women's Films (smaller, noncollective, less successful than first) and Womanscene, a section of women's films in Toronto's Festival of Festivals (smaller, noncollective, but comparable in choices to 1973).

1977: First issue of *Camera Obscura* (journal of film theory founded largely by former *Women & Film* members, initially in opposition to it); Karyn Kay and Gerald Peary's *Women and the Cinema* (first anthology of criticism on women and film).

1978: Women in Film Noir (BFI anthology edited by E. Ann Kaplan); and *New German Critique;* Brandon French's *On the Verge of Revolt: Women in American Films of the Fifties* (study on images of women).

1979: Alternative Cinema Conference, bringing together over 100 feminists in the media for screenings, caucuses and strategizing within the left; Feminism and Cinema Event at Edinburgh Film Festival, assessing the decade's filmmaking. Erens's *Sexual Stratagems: The World of Women in Film* (anthology on women and cinema).

It is immediately apparent from this chronology that the 1972-73 period marked a cultural watershed that has not since been equalled and that the unity, discovery, energy and brave, we're-here-to-stay spirit of the early days underwent a definite shift in 1975, mid-decade. Since then, the field of vision has altered. There is increased specialization, both in the direction of genre studies (like *film noir*) and film theory (particularly semiotic and psychoanalytic); the start of sectarianism, with women partitioned off into enclaves defined by which conferences are attended or journals subscribed to; increased institutionalization, both of women's studies and cinema studies departments — twin creations of the 1970s; a backlash emphasis on "human" liberation, which by making communication with men a priority can leave women-to-woman feminism looking declassé.

Overall, there is a growing acceptance of feminist film as an area of study rather than as a sphere of action. And this may pull feminist film work away from its early political commitment, encompassing a wide social setting; away from issues of life that go beyond form; away from the combative (as an analysis of and weapon against patriarchal capitalism) into the merely representational.

The chronology also shows the initial cross-fertilization between the women's movement and the cinema, which took place in the area of practice rather than in written criticism. The films came first. In fact, we find two different currents feeding into film work: one made up of women who were feminists and thereby led to film, the other made up of women already working in film and led therein to feminism. It was largely the first group of women who began making the films which were naturally named "feminist,"[3] and largely the second group of women, often in university film studies departments, who began holding the film festivals, just as naturally named "women and/in film." Spadework has continued in both directions, creating a new women's cinema and rediscovering the antecedents, with the two currents feeding our film criticism.

The past eight years have reduced some of the perils of which Adrienne Rich speaks. No longer are women "undepicted in images": Bonnie Dawson's *Women's Films in Print* lists over 800 available films by U.S. women alone, most depicting women. No longer are women omitted from all biography, nor are letters always censored. (In this respect, note the ongoing work of the four-woman collective engaged in "The Legend of Maya Deren Project" to document and demystify the life and work of a major, underacknowledged figure in American independent cinema.) No longer are women's films so hard to come by: the establishment of New Day Films (1972), the Serious Business Company (c. 1973) and the Iris Films collective (1975) ensures the continuing distribution of films by or about women, although the chances of seeing any independently made features by women in a regular movie theatre are still predictably slim (with Jill Godmilow's *Antonia* and Claudia Weill's *Girl Friends,* 1978, among the few U.S. films to succeed).

Returning to Rich's original warning, however, we reach the end of history's comforts and arrive at our present danger: "Whatever is unnamed . . . buried in the memory by the collapse of meaning under an inadequate or lying language — this will become, not merely unspoken, but unspeakable." Herein lies the crisis facing feminist film criticism today; for after a decade of film practice and theory, we still lack our proper names. The impact of this lack on the films themselves is of immediate concern.

FILMS AND THE POWER OF NAMING

One classic film rediscovered through women's film festivals indicates the sort of mis-naming prevalent in film history. Leontine Sagan's *Maedchen In Uniform* (Germany, 1931) details the relationship between a student and her teacher in a repressive girls' boarding school.[4] The act of naming is itself a pivotal moment in the narrative.

Towards the end of the film, the schoolgirls gather at a drunken party after the annual school play. Manuela has just starred as a passionate youth and, drunk with punch, still in boy's clothing, she stands to proclaim her happiness and love — naming her teacher Fraulein von Bernburg as the woman she loves. Before this episode, the lesbian substructure of the school and the clearly shared knowledge of that substructure have been emphasized; the school laundress even points to the prevalence of the Fraulein's initials embroidered on the girls' regulation chemises as evidence of the adulation of her adolescent admirers. This eroticism was *not* in the closet. But only when Manuela stands and names that passion is she punished, locked up in solitary — for her speech, not for her actions.

Such is the power of a name and the valor of naming. It is ironic that the inscription of the power of naming within the film has not forestalled its own continuous mis-naming within film history, which has championed its anti-fascism while masking the lesbian origins of that resistance. The problem is even more acute in dealing with contemporary films, where the lack of an adequate language has contributed to the invisibility of key aspects of our film culture — an invisibility advantageous to the existing film tradition. Monique Wittig writes:

> The women say, unhappy one, men have expelled you from the world of symbols and yet they have given you names . . . their authority to accord names . . . goes back so far that the origin of language itself may be considered an act of authority emanating from those who dominate . . . they have attached a particular word to an object or a fact and thereby consider themselves to have appropriated it. . . . The women say, the language you speak poisons your glottis tongue palate lips. They say, the language you speak is made up of words that are killing you . . . the language you speak is made up of signs that rightly speaking designate what men have appropriated. Whatever they have not laid hands on . . . does not appear in the language you speak. This is apparent precisely in the intervals that your masters have not been able to fill with their words . . . this can be found in the gaps, in all that which is not a continuation of their discourse, in the zero.[5]

The act of mis-naming functions not as an error, but as a strategy of the patriarchy. The lack of proper names facilitates derogatory name-calling; the failure to assign meaningful names to contemporary feminist film eases the acquisition of misnomers. Two key films of the 1970s reveal this process and the disenfranchisement we suffer as a result.

Chantal Akerman's *Jeanne Dielman* (1975) is a chronicle of three days in the life of a Brussels housewife, a widow and mother who is also a prostitute. It is the first film to scrutinize housework in a language appropriate to the activity itself, showing a woman's activities in the home in real time to communicate the alienation of woman in the nuclear family under European post-war economic conditions. More than three hours in length and nearly devoid of dialogue, the film charts Jeanne Dielman's breakdown via a minute observation of her performance of household routines, at first methodical and unvarying, later increasingly disarranged, until by film's end she permanently disrupts the patriarchal order by murdering her third client. The film was scripted, directed, photographed and edited by women with a consciously feminist sensibility.

The aesthetic repercussions of such a sensibility are evident throughout the film. For example, the choice of camera angle is unusually low. In interviews, Akerman explained that the camera was positioned at her own height; since she is quite short, the entire perspective of the film is different from what we are used to seeing, as shot by male cinematographers. The perspective of every frame thus reveals a female ordering of that space, prompting a reconsideration of point-of-view that I had felt before only in a few works shot by children (which expose the power of tall adults in every shot) and in the films by Japanese director Yasujiro Ozu (where the low angle has been much discussed by western critics as an entry into the "oriental" detachment of someone seated on a tatami mat, observing).

Akerman's decision to employ only medium and long shots also stems from a feminist critique: the decision to free her character from the exploitation of a zoom lens and to grant her an integrity of private space usually denied in close-ups, thereby also freeing the audience from the insensitivity of a camera barrelling in to magnify a woman's emotional crisis. Similarly, the activities of shopping, cooking and cleaning the house are presented without ellipses, making visible the extent of time previously omitted from cinematic depictions. Thus, the film is a profoundly feminist work in theme, style and representation; yet it has been critically received in language devoted to sanctifying aesthetics stripped of political consequence.

Shortly after *Jeanne Dielman*'s premiere at the Cannes film festival, European critics extolled the film as "hyper-realist" in homage both to the realist film (and literary) tradition and to the super-realist movement in painting. Two problems arise with such a name: first, the tradition of cinematic realism has never included women in its alleged veracity; second, the comparison with super-realist painters obscures the contradiction between their illusionism and Akerman's anti-illusionism. Another name applied to *Jeanne Dielman* was "ethnographic," in keeping with the film's insistence on real-time presentation and non-elliptical editing. Again, the name negates a basic aspect by referring to a cinema of clinical observation, aimed at "objectivity" and non-involvement, detached rather than engaged. The film's warm texture and Akerman's committed sympathies (the woman's gestures were borrowed from her own mother and aunt) make the name inappropriate.

The critical reception of the film in the *Soho Weekly News* by three different reviewers points up the confusion engendered by linguistic inadequacy.[6] Jonas Mekas questioned: "Why did she have to ruin the film by making the woman a prostitute and introduce a murder at the end, why did she commercialize it?" Later, praising most of the film as a successor to *Greed* (1923-25), Mekas contended that the heroine's silence was more "revolutionary" than the murder, making a case for the film's artistic merit as separate from its social context and moving the work into the area of existentialism at the expense of its feminism. A second reviewer, Amy Taubin, considered the film "theatrical" and, while commending the subjectivity of the camerawork and editing, she attacked the character of Jeanne:

> Are we to generalize from Jeanne to the oppression of many women through their subjugation to activity which offers them no range of creative choice? If so, Jeanne Dielman's pathology mitigates against our willingness to generalize.

By holding a reformist position (that is, Jeanne should vary her menu, change her wardrobe) in relation to a revolutionary character (that is, a murderer), Taubin was forced into a reading of the film limited by notions of realism that she, as an avant-garde film critic, should have ordinarily tried to avoid: her review split the film along the lines of form/content, annexing the aesthetics as "the real importance" and rejecting the character of Jeanne as a pathological woman. Again we find a notion of pure art set up in opposition to a feminism seemingly restricted to positive role models.

Finally, Annette Michelson wrote a protest to Mekas which defended the film for "the sense of renewal it has brought both to a narrative mode and the inscription *within it* of feminist energies" (my italics). Yes, but at what cost? Here the effect of inadequate naming is precisely spelled out: the feminist energies are being spent to create work quickly absorbed into mainstream modes of art that renew themselves at our expense. Already, the renaissance of the "new narrative" is underway in film circles with nary a glance back at filmmakers like Akerman or Yvonne Rainer, who first incurred the wrath of the academy by reintroducing characters, emotions and narratives into their films.

The critical response to Rainer's films, especially *Film about a Woman Who . . .* (1974) adds further instances of naming malpractice.[7] Much of the criticism has been in the area of formal textual analysis, concentrating on the "post-modernist" structures, "Brechtian" distancing or cinematic deconstruction of the works. Continuing the tactic of detoxifying films via a divide-and-conquer criticism, critic Brian Henderson analyzed the central section in *Film about a Woman Who . . .* according to a semiological model, detailing the five channels of communication used to present textual information.[8] The analysis was exhaustive on the level of technique but completely ignored the actual meaning of the information (Rainer's "emotional accretions") — the words themselves and the visualization (a man and a woman on a stark bed/table). At the opposite extreme, a *Feminist Art Journal* editorial condemned Rainer as a modernist, "the epitome of the alienated artist,'' and discounted her film work as regressive for feminists, evidently because of its formal strategies.[9]

Rainer's films deal with the relations between the sexes and the interaction of life and art within a framework combining autobiography and fiction. Whatever the intent of Rainer's filmmaking in political terms, the work stands as a clear product of a feminist cultural milieu. The films deal explicitly with woman as victim and the burden of patriarchal mythology; they offer a critique of emotion, reworking melodrama for women today, and even (*Kristina Talking Pictures,* 1976) provide an elegy to the lost innocence of defined male/female roles. The structure of the themes gives priority to the issues over easy identification with the ''characters'' and involves the audience in an active analysis of emotional process.

Yet little of the criticism has managed to reconcile an appreciation for the formal elements with an understanding of the feminist effect. Carol Wikarska, in a short review for *Women & Film,* could only paraphrase Rainer's own descriptions in a stab at *Film about a Woman Who . . .* seen in purely art-world terms.[10] More critically, the feminist-defined film journal *Camera Obscura* concentrated its first issue on Rainer but fell into a similar quandary. While an interview with Rainer was included, the editors felt obliged to critique the films in the existing semiological vocabulary, taking its feminist value for granted without confronting the points of contradiction within that methodology. The lack of vocabulary once again frustrates a complete consideration of the work.

Lest the similarity of these mis-namings merely suggests critical blindness rather than a more deliberate tactic, an ironic reversal is posed by the response to Anne Severson's *Near the Big Chakra* (1972). Silent and in color, the film shows a series of 36 women's cunts photographed in unblinking close-up, some still and some moving, with no explanations or gratuitous presentation. Formally the film fits into the category of ''structuralist'' cinema: a straightforward listing of parts, no narrative, requisite attention to a predetermined and simplified structure, and fixed camera position (as defined by the namer — P. Adams Sitney). Yet Severson's image is so powerfully unco-optable that her film has never been called ''structuralist'' to my knowledge, nor — with retrospective revisionism — have her earlier films been so named. Evidently any subject matter that could make a man vomit (as happened at a London screening in 1973) is too much for the critical category, even though it was founded on the ''irrelevance'' of the visual images. Thus a name can be withheld by the critical establishment if its application alone won't make the film fit the category.

''Whatever they have laid hands on . . . does not appear in the language you speak,'' writes Monique Wittig. Here is the problem: not so much that certain names are used, but that other names are *not* — and therefore the qualities they describe are lost. Where patriarchal language holds sway, the silences, the characteristics that are unnamed, frequently hold the greatest potential strength. In Chantal Akerman's work, what is most valuable for us is her decoding of oppressive cinematic conventions and her invention of new codes of non-voyeuristic vision; yet these contributions go unnamed. In Yvonne Rainer's work, the issue is not one of this or that role model for feminists, not whether her women characters are too weak or too victimized or too individualistic. Rather, we can value precisely her refusal to pander (visually and emotionally), her frustration of audience expectation of spectacle (physical or psychic) and her complete reworking of traditional forms of melodrama and elegy to include modern feminist culture. Yet these elements, of greatest value to us, are not accorded critical priority.

The effect of not-naming is censorship, whether caused by the imperialism of the patriarchal language or the underdevelopment of a feminist language. We need to begin analyzing our own films, but first it is necessary to learn to speak in our own name. The recent history of feminist film criticism indicates the urgency of that need.

IN TWO VOICES: BRITISH AND AMERICAN

There have been two types of feminist film criticism, motivated by different geographical and ideological contexts, each speaking in a different voice.[11] According to Gilles Deleuze:

> History of philosophy has an obvious, repressive function in philosophy; it is philosophy's very own Oedipus. "All the same, you won't dare speak your own name as long as you have not read this and that, and that on this, and this on that." . . . To say something in one's own name is very strange.[12]

Speaking in one's own name versus speaking in the name of history is a familiar problem to anyone who has ever pursued a course of study, become involved in an established discipline, and then tried to speak out of personal experience or nonprofessional/nonacademic knowledge, without suddenly feeling quite schizophrenic. Obviously it is a schizophrenia especially familiar to feminists. The distinction between one's own voice and the voice of history is a handy one by which to distinguish the two types of feminist film criticism. At least initially, these two types could be characterized as either American or British: the one, American, seen as sociological or subjective, often a speaking out in one's own voice; the other, British, seen as methodological or more objective, often speaking in the voice of history. (The work of the past few years has blurred the original nationalist base of the categories: for example, the Parisian perspective of the California-based *Camera Obscura*.)

The originally American, so-called sociological, approach is exemplified by early *Women & Film* articles and much of the catalogue writing from festivals of that same period. The emphasis on legitimizing women's own reactions and making women's contributions visible resulted in a tendency towards reviews, getting information out, a tendency to offer testimony as theory. Although the journal was fruitful in this terrain, the weakness of the approach became the limits of its introspection, the boundaries established by the lack of a coherent methodology for moving out beyond the self. An example of this approach is Barbara Halpern Martineau's very eccentric, subjective and illuminating analyses of the films of Nelly Kaplan and Agnes Varda.[13] A dismaying example of the decadent strain of this approach is Joan Mellen's mid-1970s book *Big Bad Wolves,* which offers personal interpretations of male characters and actors in a move to shift attention to the reformist arena of "human liberation."

The originally British, so-called theoretical approach, is exemplified by the book *Notes on Women's Cinema* edited by Claire Johnston, by articles in *Screen,* and by the initial issues of *Camera Obscura* (which, like the British writing, defers to the French authorities). Committed to using some of the most advanced tools of critical analysis, such as semiology and psychoanalysis, this approach has tried to come to terms with *how* films mean — to move beyond regarding the image to analyzing the structure, codes, the general subtext of the works. The approach has been fruitful for its findings regarding signification, but its weakness has been a suppression of the personal and a seeming belief in the neutrality of the analytic tools. The critic's feminist voice has often been muted by this methodocracy.

Two of the most important products of this approach are pieces by Laura Mulvey and Claire Johnston.[14] Johnston critiques the image of woman in male cinema and finds her to be a signifier, not of woman, but of the absent phallus, a signifier of an absence rather than any presence. Similarly, Mulvey analyzes the nature of the cinematic spectator and finds evidence — in cinematic voyeurism and in the nature of the camera look — of the exclusively male spectator as a production assumption.

Another way of characterizing these two approaches would be to identify the American (sociological, or in one's own voice) as fundamentally phenomenological, and the British (theoretical, or the voice of history) as fundamentally analytical. The texts of Johnston and Mulvey taken together, for example, pose a monumental absence that is unduly pessimistic. The misplaced pessimism stems from their overvaluation of the production aspect of cinema, a misassumption that cinematic values are irrevocably embedded at the level of production and, once there, remain pernicious and inviolable. Woman is absent on the screen and she is absent in the audience, their analysis argues.

And yet here a bit of phenomenology would be helpful, a moment of speaking in one's own voice and wondering at the source in such a landscape of absence. As a woman sitting in the dark, watching that film made by and for men with drag queens on the screen, what is my experience? Don't I in fact interact with that text and that context, with a conspicuous absence of passivity? For a woman's experiencing of culture under patriarchy is dialectical in a way that a man's can never be: our experience is like that of the exile, whom Brecht once singled out as the ultimate dialectician for that daily working out of cultural oppositions within a single body. It is crucial to emphasize here the possibility for texts to be transformed at the level of reception and not to fall into a trap of condescension towards our own developed powers as active producers of meaning.

The differences implicit in these two attitudes lead to quite different positions and strategies, as the following selection of quotations helps to point up.[15] When interviewed regarding the reason for choosing her specific critical tools (auteurist, structuralist, psychoanalytic), Claire Johnston replied: "As far as I'm concerned, it's a question of what is theoretically correct; these new theoretical developments cannot be ignored, just as feminists cannot ignore Marx or Freud, because they represent crucial scientific developments." In contrast to this vision of science as ideologically neutral would be the reiteration by such theoreticians as Adrienne Rich and Mary Daly that "You have to be constantly critiquing even the tools you use to explore and define what it is to be female."

In the same interview as Johnston, Pam Cook elaborated their aim: "Women are fixed in ideology in a particular way, which is definable in terms of the patriarchal system. I think we see our first need as primarily to define that place — the place that women are fixed in." In marked contrast to such a sphere of activity, the Womanifesto of the 1975 New York Conference of Feminists in the Media states: "We do not accept the existing power structure and we are committed to changing it by the content and structure of our images and by the ways we relate to each other in our work and with our audience." In her own article, Laura Mulvey identified the advantage of psychoanalytic critiques as their ability to "advance our understanding of the status quo," a limited and modest claim; yet she herself went beyond such a goal in making (with Peter Wollen) *The Riddles of the Sphinx* (1976), a film which in its refusal of patriarchal codes and feminist concerns represents in fact a Part Two of her original theory.

I have termed the British approach pessimistic, a quality which may be perceived by supporters as realistic or by detractors as colonized. I have termed the American approach optimistic, a quality which may be viewed by supporters as radical or by detractors as unrealistic, utopian. It is not surprising, however, that such a dualism of critical approach has evolved. In *Woman's Consciousness, Man's World,* Sheila Rowbotham points out: "There is a long inchoate period during which the struggle between the language of experience and the language of theory becomes a kind of agony."[16] It is a problem common to an oppressed people at the point of formulating a new language with which to name that oppression, for the history of oppression has prevented the development of any unified language among its subjects. It is crucial for those of us working in the area of feminist film criticism to mend this rift, confront the agony and begin developing a synthesis of maximally effective critical practice. Without names, our work remains anonymous, insecure, our continued visibility questionable.

TOWARDS A FEMINIST FILM GLOSSARY

Without new names, we run the danger of losing title to films that we sorely need. By stretching the name ''feminist'' beyond all reasonable elasticity, we contribute to its ultimate impoverishment. At the same time, so many films have been partitioned off to established traditions, with the implication that these other names contradict or forestall any application of the name ''feminist'' to the works so annexed, that the domain of ''feminist'' cinema is fast becoming limited to that work concerned only with feminism as explicit subject matter. ''Feminist,'' if it is to make a comeback from the loss of meaning caused by its all-encompassing overuse, requires new legions of names to preserve for us the inner strengths, the not-yet-visible qualities of these films still lacking in definition.

Because this need is so very urgent, I here offer an experimental glossary of names as an aid to initiating a new stage of feminist criticism. These names are not likely to be an immediate hit. First of all, it's all well and good to call for new names to appear in the night sky like so many constellations, but it's quite another thing to invent them and commit them to paper. Second, there's the inevitable contradiction of complaining about names and then committing more naming acts. Third, there's the danger that, however unwieldy, these new names might be taken as formulae to be applied willy-nilly to every hapless film that comes our way.

The point, after all, is not to set up new power institutions (feminist banks, feminist popes, feminist names) but rather to open the mind to new descriptive possibilities of non-patriarchal, non-capitalist imaginings.

• *Validative:* One of feminist filmmaking's greatest contributions is the body of films about women's lives, political struggles, organizing, and so on. These films have been vaguely classified under the cinéma vérité banner, where they reside in decidedly mixed company. Since they function as a validation and legitimation of women's culture and individual lives, the name "validative" would be a better choice. It has the added advantage of aligning the work with products of oppressed peoples (with the filmmaker as insider), whereas the cinéma vérité label represents the oppressors, who make films as superior outsiders documenting alien, implicitly inferior cultures, often from a position of condescension.

The feminist films of the early 1970s were validative, and validative films continue to be an important component of feminist filmmaking. They may be ethnographic, documenting the evolution of women's lives and issues (as in *We're Alive,* 1975, a portrait and analysis of women in prison) or archaeological, uncovering women's hidden past (as in *Union Maids,* 1977, with its recovery of women's role in the labor movement, or Sylvia Morales' *Chicana,* 1978, the first film history of the Mexican-American woman's struggle). The form is well established, yet the constantly evolving issues require new films, such as *We Will Not Be Beaten* (1981), a film on domestic violence culled from videotaped interviews with women. By employing the name "validative" in place of cinéma vérité, we can combat the patriarchal annexation of the woman filmmaker as one of the boys, that is, a professional who is not *of* the culture being filmed. It is a unifying name aimed at conserving strength.

Correspondence: An entirely different name is necessary for more avant-garde films, like those of Yvonne Rainer, Chantal Akerman, Helke Sander or Laura Mulvey/Peter Wollen. Looking to literary history, we find a concern with the role played by letters ("personal" discourse) as a sustaining mode for women's writing during times of literary repression.

The publication of historical letters by famous and ordinary women has been a major component of the feminist publishing renaissance, just as the long-standing denigration of the genre as not "real" writing (that is, not certified by either a publishing house or monetary exchange) has been an additional goad for the creation of feminist alternatives to the literary establishment. A cinema of "correspondence" is a fitting homage to this tradition of introspective missives sent out into the world.

Equally relevant is the other definition of "correspondence" as "mutual response, the answering of things to each other," or, to take Swedenborg's literal Doctrine of Correspondence as an example, the tenet that "every natural object symbolizes or corresponds to some spiritual fact or principle which is, as it were, its archetype."[17] Films of correspondence, then, would be those investigating correspondences, between emotion and objectivity, narrative and deconstruction, art and ideology. Thus *Jeanne Dielman* is a film of correspondence in its exploration of the bonds between housework and madness, prostitution and heterosexuality, epic and dramatic temporality.

What distinguishes such films of correspondence from formally similar films by male avant-garde filmmakers is their inclusion of the author within the text. *Film about a Women Who...* corresponds to very clear experiences and emotional concerns in Rainer's life and *Jeanne Dielman* draws on the gestures of the women in Akerman's family, whereas Michael Snow's *Rameau's Nephew* (1974) uses the form to suppress the author's presence. (Of course, there is a tradition of "diary" movies by men as well as women, but, significantly, the presence of Jonas Mekas in most of his diary films — like that of Godard in *Numéro deux* — is of the filmmaker rather than the "man" outside that professional role.) Similarly, Helke Sander in *The All Around Reduced Personality* (1977) revises the ironic, distanced narration of modernist German cinema to include the filmmaker in a same first-person-plural with her characters, unlike her compatriot Alexander Kluge, who always remains external and superior to his characters.

It is this resolute correspondence between form and content, to put it bluntly, that distinguishes the films of correspondence. Such films are essential to the development of new structures and forms for the creation and communication of feminist works and values; more experimental than validative, they are laying the groundwork of a feminist cinematic vocabulary.

• *Reconstructive:* Several recent films suggest another name, located midway between the two described above, and dealing directly with issues of form posed by the political and emotional concerns of the work.

One such film is Sally Potter's *Thriller* (1979), a feminist murder mystery related as a first-person inquiry by the victim: Mimi, the seamstress of Puccini's *La Bohème,* investigates the cause of her death and the manner of her life, uncovering in the process the contradictions hidden by the bourgeois male artist. Michelle Citron's *Daughter Rite* (1978) probes relations between women in the family, using dramatic sequences to critique cinéma vérité and optical printing to re-examine home movies, that North American index to domestic history.

Both *Thriller* and *Daughter Rite* are reconstructive in their rebuilding of other forms, whether grand opera or soap opera, according to feminist specifications. At the same time both Potter and Citron reconstruct some basic cinematic styles (psychodrama, documentary) to create new feminist forms, in harmony with the desires of the audience as well as the theoretical concerns of the filmmakers. By reconstructing forms in a constructive manner, these films build bridges between the needs of women and the goals of art.

• *Medusan:* Humor should not be overlooked as a weapon of great power. Comedy requires further cultivation for its revolutionary potential as a deflator of the patriarchal order and an extraordinary leveller and reinventor of dramatic structure.

An acknowledgement of the subversive power of humor, the name "Medusan" is taken from Helène Cixous's "The Laugh of the Medusa," in which she celebrates the potential of feminist texts "to blow up the law, to break up the 'truth' with laughter."[18] Cixous's contention that when women confront the figure of Medusa she will be laughing is a rejoinder to Freud's posing the "Medusa's Head" as an incarnation of male castration fears. For Cixous, women are having the last laugh. And, to be sure, all the films in this camp deal with combinations of humor and sexuality.

Vera Chytilova's *Daisies* (1966) was one of the first films by a woman to move in the direction of anarchic sexuality, though its disruptive humor was received largely as slapstick at the time. Nelly Kaplan's two films, *A Very Curious Girl* (1971) and *Nea* (1976), also offer an explosive humor coupled with sexuality to discomfort patriarchal society (even though her fondness for "happy" endings that restore order has discomfited many feminist critics). Jan Oxenberg's *A Comedy in Six Unnatural Acts* (1975) is an excellent example of a Medusan film, attacking not just men or sexism but the heterosexually-defined stereotypes of lesbianism; its success has been demonstrated by its raucous cult reception and, more pointedly, by its tendency to polarize a mixed audience along the lines not of class, but of sexual preference. It is disruptive of homophobic complacency with a force never approached by analytical films or those defensive of lesbianism.*

Another highly Medusan film is Jacques Rivette's *Celine and Julie Go Boating* (1974). This may be somewhat curious, as it is directed by a man, but production credits indicate a total collaboration with the four actresses and co-scenarists. In the movie, Celine and Julie enter each

*Michelle Citron discusses *A Comedy* . . . in her article in Part Four.

other's lives by magic and books, joined in a unity of farce; once they are together, each proceeds to demolish the other's ties to men (an employer, a childhood lover) by using humor, laughing in the face of male fantasies and expectations and thus "spoiling" the relationships with a fungus of parody. The film has been criticized as silly, for Juliet Berto and Dominique Labourier do laugh constantly — at the other characters, themselves, the audience, acting itself — yet their laughter ultimately proves their finest arsenal, enabling them to rescue the plot's ultimately proves their finest arsenal, enabling them to rescue the plot's girl-child from a darkly imminent Henry Jamesian destruction simply through a laughing refusal to obey its allegedly binding rules. Again, *Celine and Julie* has consistently divided its audience according to whom it threatens: it has become a cult feminist movie even as the male critical establishment (except for Rivette fan Jonathan Rosenbaum) has denounced the film as silly, belabored and too obvious.

• *Corrective realism:* As mentioned earlier, the tradition of realism in the cinema has never done well by women. Indeed, extolling realism to women is rather like praising the criminal to the victim, so thoroughly have women been falsified under its banner. A feminist feature cinema, generally representational, is now developing, with a regular cast of actresses, a story line, aimed at a wide audience and generally accepting of many cinematic conventions. The women making these films, however, are so thoroughly transforming the characterizations and the narrative workings of traditional realism that they have created a new feminist cinema of "corrective realism."

Thus, in Margarethe von Trotta's *The Second Awakening of Christa Klages* (1977), it is the women's actions that advance the narrative; bonding between women functions to save, not to paralyze or trap the characters; running away brings Christa freedom, while holding ground brings her male lover only death. The film has outrageously inventive character details, an attention to the minutiae of daily life, an endorsement of emotion and intuitive ties, and an infectious humor. Marta Mészáros's *Women* (1978) presents a profound reworking of socialist realism in its depiction of the friendship between two women in a Hungarian work hostel. The alternating close-ups and medium shots become a means of social critique, while the more traditional portrayal of the growing intimacy between the two women insistently places emotional concerns at the center of the film. Both films successfully adapt an existing cinematic tradition to feminist purposes, going far beyond a simple "positive role model" in their establishment of a feminist cinematic environment within which to envision their female protagonists and their activities.

These, then, are a few of the naming possibilities. However, it is not only the feminist films that demand new names, but also (for clarity) the films being made by men about women.

• *Projectile:* One name resurrected from the 1950s by 1970s criticism was Molly Haskell's recoining of the "woman's film," the matinee melodramas which, cleared of pejorative connotations, were refitted for relevance to women's cinematic concerns today. Wishful thinking. The name was Hollywood's and there it stays, demonstrated by the new "woman's films" that are pushing actual women's films off the screen, out into the dark.

These are male fantasies of women — men's projections of themselves and their fears onto female characters. The name "projectile" identifies these films' true nature and gives an added awareness of the destructive impact of male illusions in the female audience. It is time the bluff was called on the touted authenticity of these works, which pose as objective while remaining entirely subjective in their conception and execution.

The clearest justification for this name can be found in director Paul Mazursky's description of his *An Unmarried Women* (1978):

> I don't know if this is a woman's movie or not. I don't know what that means anymore.... I wanted to get inside a woman's head. I've felt that all the pictures I've done, I've done with men. I put myself inside a man's head, using myself a lot. I wanted this time to think like a woman. That's one of the reasons there was so much rewriting.... There were many things the women I cast in the film ... wouldn't say. They'd tell me why, and I'd say, "Well, what would you say?" and I'd let them say that. I used a real therapist; I wanted a woman, and I had to change what she said based on what she is. In other words, the only thing I could have done was to get a woman to help me write it. I thought about that for a while, but in the end I think it worked out.[19]

Films such as this one (and *The Turning Point, Pretty Baby, Luna,* and so on, ad infinitum) are aimed fatally at us; they deserve to be named "projectile."

Certainly the names offered here do not cover all possibilities, nor can every film be fitted neatly into one category. But I hope their relative usefulness or failings will prompt a continuation of the process by others. The urgency of the naming task cannot be overstated.

WARNING SIGNS: A POSTSCRIPT

We are now in a period of normalization, a time that can offer feminists complacency as a mask for co-optation. Scanning the horizon for signs of backlash and propaganda, the storm clouds within feminist film criticism are gathering most clearly over issues of form.

It has become a truism to call for new forms. Over and over, we have heard the sacred vows: you can't put new revolutionary subjects/ messages into reactionary forms; new forms, a new anti-patriarchal film language for feminist cinema, must be developed. While certainly true to an extent, form remains only one element of the work. And the valorization of form above and independent of other criteria has begun to create its own problems.

There is the misconception that form, unlike subject matter, is inviolate and can somehow encase the meaning in protective armor. But form is as co-optable as other elements. A recent analysis by critic Julianne Burton of the *cinema novo* movement in Brazil raised this exact point by demonstrating how the Brazilian state film apparatus took over the forms and styles of *cinema novo* and stripped them of their ideological significance as one means of disarming the movement.[20] If we make a fetish of the long take, the unmediated shot, etc., as feminist per se, then we will shortly be at a loss over how to evaluate the facsimiles proliferating in the wake of such a definition.

Furthermore, the reliance on form as the ultimate gauge of a film's worth sets up an inevitable hierarchy that places reconstructive films or films of correspondence at the top of a pyramid, leaving corrective realist or validative approaches among the baser elements. This itself is a complex problem. First, such a view reproduces the notion of history as "progress" and supposes that forms, like technology, grow cumulatively better and better; some believe in that sort of linear quality, but I don't. Second, criticism by Christine Gledhill (of film) and Myra Love (of literature) has questioned the naturalness of the Brechtain, postmodernist, deconstructive model as a feminist strategy, pointing out the real drawbacks of its endemic authoritarianism and ambiguity.[21] Third, our very reasons for supporting such work must at least be examined honestly. Carolyn Heilbrun's point should be well taken: "Critics, and particularly academics, are understandably prone to admire and overvalue the carefully construed, almost puzzlelike novel [read: film], not only for its profundities, but because it provides them, in explication, with their livelihood."[22] Just as a generosity of criticism can provide the strongest support for feminist filmmakers, so acceptance of a variety of filmic strategies can provide the vigor needed by the feminist audience.

For we must look to the filmmaker and viewer for a way out of this aesthetic cul-de-sac. Aesthetics are not eternally embedded in a work like a penny in a cube of Lucite. They are dependent on and subject to the work's reception. The formal values of a film cannot be considered in isolation, cut off from the thematic correspondents within the text and from the social determinants without. Reception by viewers as well as by critics is key to any film's meaning. As my chronology indicates, feminist cinema arose out of a need not only on the part of the filmmakers and writers, but on the part of the women they knew to be their audience. Today we must constantly check feminist film work to gauge how alive this thread of connection still is, how communicable its feminist values are.

We are in a time of transition now, when we still have the luxury of enjoying feminist work on its makers' own terms, without having to sift the sands paranoiacally for impostors. But this transitional period is running out: as the cultural lag catches up, the dominant and avant-garde cinema may begin to incorporate feminist success before we recognize what we've lost. The emphasis on form makes that incorporation easier. Burton ended her article with a call for the inscription of modes of production within the body of Third World film criticism. Therein lies a clue. Feminism has always emphasized process; now it's time that this process of production and reception be inscribed within the critical text. How was the film made? With what intention? With what kind of crew? With what relationship to the subject? How was it produced? Who is distributing it? Where is it being shown? For what audience is it constructed? How is it available? How is it being received? There is no need to establish a tyranny of the productive sphere over a film's definition, or to authorize only immediately popular films, but it will prove helpful in the difficult times ahead of us to keep this bottom-line of method and context in mind, to avoid painting ourselves into a corner.

Formal devices are progressive only if they are employed with a goal beyond aesthetics alone. Here, finally, is the end of the line. Feminist film criticism cannot solve problems still undefined in the sphere of feminist thought and activity at large. We all are continually borrowing from and adding to each other's ideas, energies, insights, across disciplines. We also need to develop lines of communication across the boundaries of race, class and sexuality. In Cuba, I heard a presentation by Alfredo Guevara, founder and director of the Cuban Film Institute. He explained its efforts to educate the Cuban audience to the tricks of the cinema, to demystify the technology, to give the viewers the means with which to defend themselves against cinematic hypnosis, to challenge the dominant ideology of world cinema, to create a new liberated generation of film viewers. I will never forget his next words: "We do not claim to have created this audience already, nor do we think it is a task only of cinema." The crisis of naming requires more than an etymologist to solve it.

NOTES

[1] Adrienne Rich, "It Is the Lesbian in Us," *Sinister Wisdom* 3 (1977) and "The Transformation of Silence into Language and Action," *Sinister Wisdom* 6

(1978); see also Mary Daly, *Beyond God the Father* (Boston: Beacon Press, 1973) for her pioneering analysis of naming as power.

[2] "Melodrama" and "structuralist" cinema were the two names analyzed in papers presented by my co-panelists, William Horrigan and Bruce Jenkins, at the 1978 Purdue Conference on Film, where the ideas in this paper were first presented.

[3] Women artists working in film continued, as before, to make avant-garde films, but those without feminist material lie outside my present concerns.

[4] For a fuller discussion of the film, see my "Maedchen in Uniform: From Repressive Tolerance to Erotic Liberation," in *Jump Cut* 24/25 (1981).

[5] Monique Wittig, *Les Guérillères* (New York: Avon, 1973), pp. 112-114.

[6] See *Soho Weekly News,* Nov. 18 (p. 36), Nov. 25 (p. 31), and Dec. 9 (p. 35), all 1976.

[7] See also my article, "The Films of Yvonne Rainer," *Chrysalis* 2 (1977).

[8] Presented at the International Symposium on Film Theory and Practical Criticism, Center for 20th-Century Studies, University of Wisconsin at Milwaukee, in 1975.

[9] Cindy Nemser, "Editorial: Rainer and Rothschild, An Overview," *Feminist Art Journal* 4 (1975): 4; the same issue contained Lucy Lippard's "Yvonne Rainer on Feminism and Her Film"; Lippard, however, is the exception in her ability to handle both the formal value and feminist strengths of Rainer's work.

[10] *Women & Film* 7, p. 86; also, *Camera Obscura* 1 (1977).

[11] Here I am considering only English-language feminist film criticism; there are other complex issues in French and German criticism, for example.

[12] Gilles Deleuze, "I Have Nothing To Admit" in *Semiotexte* 6 (Vol. II, No. 3, 1977): 112.

[13] See Barbara Halpern Martineau, "Nelly Kaplan" and "Subjecting Her Objectification, or Communism Is Not Enough," in Claire Johnston, ed., *Notes on Women's Cinema* (London: Society for Education in Film and Television, 1973).

[14] See Claire Johnston, "Women's Cinema as Counter-Cinema," in Johnston *Notes,* and Laura Mulvey, "Visual Pleasure and Narrative Cinema," in Karyn Kay and Gerald Peary, eds., *Women and the Cinema* (New York: E.P. Dutton, 1977), pp. 412-428.

[15] Quotations are taken from: E. Ann Kaplan, "Interview with British Cine-Feminists," in Kay and Peary, *Women and the Cinema,* pp. 400-401; Barbara Charlesworth Gelpi and Albert Gelpi, *Adrienne Rich's Poetry* (New York: W.W. Norton, 1975), p. 115; Barbara Halpern Martineau, "Paris/Chicago," in *Women & Film* 7, p. 11; Laura Mulvey, "Visual Pleasure," p. 414; as well as personal communications; see also E. Ann Kaplan, "Aspects of British Feminist Film Theory," in *Jump Cut* 12/13, 1976, for an in-depth examination of the British theories and their implications.

[16] Sheila Rowbotham, *Woman's Consciousness, Man's World* (London: Penguin, 1973), p. 33; see also her statement, p. 32, that language always is "carefully guarded by the superior people because it is one of the means through which they conserve their supremacy."

[17] *The Compact Edition of the Oxford English Dictionary.*

[18] Helène Cixous, "The Laugh of the Medusa," *Signs* 1 (1976): 888.

[19] "Paul Mazursky Interviewed by Terry Curtis Fox," *Film Comment* 14, (1978): 30-31.

[20] These remarks by Burton are taken from memory of her talk at the 1979 Purdue Conference on Film. As stated, they are a simplification of complexities that she was at pains to elucidate without distortion.

[21] Christine Gledhill, "Recent Developments in Feminist Criticism," *Quarterly Review of Film Studies* 3 (1979); and Myra Love, "Christa Wolf and Feminism: Breaking the Patriarchal Connection," *New German Critique* 17 (1979).

[22] Carolyn G. Heilbrun, Introduction to *Mrs. Steven Hears the Mermaids Singing* (New York: Norton, 1974), p. xii.

CHAPTER 14.

Starring Shirley MacLaine

• A Beauty and a Buddy

SERAFINA K. BATHRICK

Patricia Erens, *The Films of Shirley MacLaine* (New York: A.S. Barnes, 1978)

Why does a feminist film critic write a book about a contemporary female movie star whose single most important personal and professional attribute must be an infinite capacity for action? The answer may lie in the assumption by both Patricia Erens and her publisher that it is time for film audiences to question the objectified qualities of the star as beauty-queen. *The Films of Shirley MacLaine* certainly represents a promise to update that passive symbol of perfection. But why does our new model have to be a hyper-activist actress, a self-made dynamo with a perfect body who also keeps everyone happy, if not laughing?

It is indeed a disturbing fact that between Erens's insights into The Modern Woman and her publisher's desire to promote a star, the persona of Shirley MacLaine is a repellent concoction of the benign and the bionic. If in fact that actress deserves recognition for creating and living a part that "paved the way for changes for all women" (p. 20), it is also significant that her power as a comedienne-dancer confines her to the use of "gentle humor" (p. 65), and that her offscreen dedication to "the simple life" (p. 35) also keeps her humble: a "conspicuously nonconsuming celebrity" (p. 27). Compared to Jane Fonda, our heroine comes off as a Total Woman, if not a Pollyanna. In this text, the Good Woman is aligned against the Bad Woman, just like in the movies.

Unlike Jane Fonda, another prominent actress deeply involved in public agitation, MacLaine never alienated her public. Reflecting on this phenomenon, MacLaine stated recently, "For one thing, I've worked inside The Establishment, and always will.... And another thing is, I don't hate anybody."[p. 37]

This new-star hype, in both format and emphasis, fits into the old tradition of star-making practised by gossip columnists, fan clubs and fan critics. Even the formula by which the private lives of the stars remain totally relevant to, if not in perfect harmony with, their screen roles, is never questioned by Erens. Instead, Shirley MacLaine's private and public lives are juxtaposed and interwoven to reveal how one can in fact neutralize the other, so that Shirley will not be another Jane. "On-screen MacLaine perfected the role of the affable mistress or down-trodden prostitute who was short on brains but long on common sense. Offscreen she proved herself an independent, intelligent woman" (p. 14). Thus the modern movie star gets her credentials as an autonomous person, not by the roles she plays, but by the difference between those roles and the life she leads.

"Being an actress is what I do; not what I am" (p. 14), MacLaine is quoted as stating. And it is this pronouncement of self which perhaps best marks the actress's real power today — the capacity and determination to create her *own* star-persona. Thus her desire to define and maintain a split between work and life is consistently reinforced by the critic-biographer who uses it as the basis for a portrait of an artist whose dependence on the film industry leaves her "womanly" — untouched by her work.

Because MacLaine has already published two autobiographies, and has been the subject of much feminist film criticism, the challenge for Erens is particularly interesting and complex, although certainly her freedom to develop a systematic critique of The Star, or an analysis of woman as actress, is severely hampered by the cult-value of the enterprise itself. The book is divided into two major parts, which inhibits a critical approach by separating the woman-star from her production. The opening chapters introduce MacLaine's "Image" and "Career," while the latter two-thirds of the book is devoted to a chronological account of the films she appeared in, with detailed plot summaries, comments on reviews, and some insights and interpretations of MacLaine's roles. There is the standard filmography and bibliography at the end, which apparently permits Erens to cite reviews and articles at random throughout her text, often without references to the dates, kinds of publications or qualifications of authorship.

The form and content of the early chapters create a number of myths about MacLaine. These myths contribute to the impossibility of examining her films themselves with any critical consistency or feminist acumen. The dictates of star-worship are surely incompatible with an understanding for the politics of women in Hollywood cinema, and although Erens has edited a collection of essays, *Sexual Stratagems: The World of Women in Film,* in this particular effort her admiration for Shirley MacLaine is dependent on mythmaking, and her jargon-packed prose is finally more of an apology for a strong woman than an honest look at that woman's work.

NATURAL TALENT AND THE BUDDY SYSTEM

The first 40 pages of *The Films of Shirley MacLaine* are intended to introduce us to the "real" woman, and the verbal clichés that abound in the creation of this modern star are matched only by the use of dozens of slick photos of the actress clowning in a tuxedo. The pictures, like the studio stills that illustrate the section on the individual films, are never explicated in terms of their coded origins: comic as Chaplin-tramp, or comedienne as Maurice Chevalier. They simply exist to provide "mood" for the flat description: "MacLaine's droll wit and extraordinarily expressive face were spontaneous. On camera she seemed totally un-self-conscious, her performance flowing naturally, effortlessly" (p. 13). In this section the author establishes several myths (apparently fostered by MacLaine as actress-author) which typify the old ideology of the star: her humble birth, simple life, natural talent and good luck. We must read between the lines when Erens mystifies the "discovery-of-the-genius" to find indications of the real professional, although the disjunctive transitions and the super-rhetoric ("self-educated, self-opinionated, and self-propelled" [p. 15]) leave the reader reeling, if not skeptical.

First, there is the myth of MacLaine's class and parentage. The facts are sparse and ambiguous since the self-made woman myth requires MacLaine to be fully responsible for her upbringing, education and career breaks. She is forever "taking herself in hand" (p. 25), so that the information about her successful real-estate father who had been a professional musician, or her actress and drama-teaching mother, is eclipsed in favor of personal details about Warren Beatty, the "soul brother." In fact, MacLaine's only acknowledgment of her sibling as a potential competitor, "we both liked to be King of the Mountain" (p. 23), remains as unexplored as her parentage. Erens shifts away from this critical responsibility to a meaningless summary that tells little about the complex of class and family circumstances that helped shape this 1934-first-born daughter. The mystification of family life remains inviolate:

No doubt a fortuitous confluence of ingredients worked to nurture the two

233

future talents. A combination of native intelligence, boundless energy and physical good looks prepared each to succeed in the years ahead. [p. 23]

No less troubling is Erens's determination to abdicate as feminist critic when she describes how MacLaine got her start as a dancer. MacLaine apparently started dancing at the age of two and appeared publicly at four. The "natural talent" myth is supplemented by the author's contention that young MacLaine's ballet lessons "were not oriented towards a career," but were merely a "pleasant pastime" (p. 23). No Shirley Temple, she! But in the tradition of the best of bourgeois ideology-for-girls, "dancing quickly raced through Shirley's blood" (p. 23), and there is no questioning of the importance of classical ballet for a future movie star. Instead, safe homilies explain MacLaine's early years as a dancer: "Perhaps things have a way of going right for the wrong reasons" (p. 24). Her beginnings in show business are treated by Erens in much the same way that Hollywood film depends on "seamless" techniques by which transitions are as easy as fades and dissolves. The questions relevant to current feminist criticism never arise. Why comedy? Why are dance and comedy a significant combination? Why does Erens keep harping on MacLaine's "great pair of legs" (p. 25)? Does her "perfect figure" somehow have to "offset" her red hair and freckles? What is the meaning of this description: "Shirley's comic bent made her a natural for the musical stage where she could freely express her feelings" (p. 24)? Is being "natural" a way by which a woman retains her status as a non-professional?

The myth of the "self-taught" star also prevents us from understanding the reasons for MacLaine's dependency on a succession of successful men in the business, just as the "natural talent" myth keeps hidden the many parental-teacher calculations that went into the decision to encourage MacLaine's particular career. There is also no attempt to suggest that the actress had any important associations with individual women, or with any female group of performers or friends. Her advice and support comes entirely from her producer-husband, and later from her bond with the "Rat Pack" (Dean Martin, Frank Sinatra, Peter Lawford, etc.).These two relationships imply that MacLaine needed powerful men in the industry to help her become a confident actress and entrepreneur. Instead of taking a straight look at the economics of male hegemony in Hollywood, Erens mystifies her subject with some "perfect match" ideology that leaves MacLaine "more than human" as she ascends the traditional ladder to stardom.

On the eve of her first film-acting job, the 20-year-old MacLaine married Steve Parker. And while the "lucky break" (Erens even cites the backstage musical as "proof" [p. 26] — that *really is* how show biz works!) explains how she was "found" by Hitchcock, the myth of the "kindly patron, critic, and coach" explains her marriage to a man 13 years her senior. Erens further capitalizes on the "magic" between the two by suggesting all the ingredients needed for the "happy ending." Erens writes: "He was cultivated, articulate, serious, and well-traveled. She was provincial, earthy, and spontaneous. But in the end his sophistication matched her naivete" (pp. 25-26). Is writing the life of a Hollywood comedienne just like writing a classical Hollywood comedy? Where is the critical complexity or the feminist understanding in this account?

The details about MacLaine as a member of "The Clan" are also disturbing from a feminist point of view. For instead of an analysis of the star system, which might help explain why a young actress would require the protection of and affiliation with such powerful men as Sinatra or Lawford, MacLaine's own term is used to explain her place in the group. Surely the notion of "mascot" might induce Erens to comment on the irony of MacLaine's self-image in this context. But no, the biographer continues to admire MacLaine's capacity to join in and be another good old boy in the circle. The whitewash job on this particular aspect of male culture within the film industry is painful: "They were free-thinking, spontaneous performers who may have had their professional hangups, but who on the whole enjoyed an uninhibited good time" (p. 30). Golly, what fun for a woman!

Dean Martin was particularly enthusiastic about their new pal: "She loves to laugh. I'd be the biggest hit in the world if I had only 500 like her in every audience" (p. 30). At moments like this, the possibility that the biography is a subtle parody of power and pretence in Hollywood does enter my mind. But no, the author is simply telling us more about the success of the comedienne — today's actress makes it by laughing for the male comic. While we learn little about the buddy system in film business, we are forced to validate Shirley-the-new-star as a buddy herself.

MacLaine's hyperactivity — presumably a sign of natural energy — and not her ambition to be a rich or famous public figure also helped her to support many liberal causes in the 1960s. "Obviously she saw no discrepancy between a high salary and a commitment to the simple life," writes Erens (p. 35). Thus the author misses yet another opportunity to examine the importance of a movie star whose screen roles and visibility help her to help politicians, orphans, blacks and Sino-American diplomacy. It seems clear that MacLaine's established stardom, her familiarity with travel and with film production, all granted her a particular authority to attack the "ugly American" or to praise the noncompetitive Chinese. "It's like having 800,000,000 in group therapy," MacLaine says (p. 40). Once again the biography of the star depends on invisible editing and dissolves that smooth and mystify her passage from ebullient tomboy (Uncle Tomboy?) to a mature and charitable woman.

Quoting MacLaine's own rhetoric, Erens grants her the right to decide whom she will be — today's star is her own author, as the critic abdicates (in the name of sisterhood?). "Becoming committed is commensurate with maturity. I don't think of myself as an actress, as a movie star. I'm a person. I'm involved in society — American society. The basis of our democracy is individual commitment" (p. 37).

The tone even sounds like a political speech, and indeed MacLaine has changed places with our new idols: she speaks to the people at presidential campaign rallies, while the male politicians become media celebrities, a new breed of movie star. What is the particular function of a woman as facilitator in this process? It is a recent development that has been observed by media critics who see politics as TV drama. Instead of noting the real power that is available to the performer-turned-reformer, Erens applauds MacLaine for her capacity to alienate no one with that potential. Consistent with her youthful good cheer as a buddy in Hollywood, the older activist MacLaine must continue to be "nice," even above reproach, while she serves politicians who require her glamor and charisma — the presence of the star-as-mascot. Erens's attempts to keep her subject's reputation as an "original" intact seem feeble indeed at this point, and it is difficult to believe that an active life is the necessary proof of woman's autonomy or integrity.

THE PROSTITUTE AND THE HETAIRA

In order to discuss Erens's approach to the films themselves, it is important at this point to formulate a position on the modern star and her roles, so we can understand why the inadequacies of the critic's biography lead to similarly disappointing explorations of Shirley MacLaine's work. The fact that, in a great number of her film roles, MacLaine plays a prostitute is revealing.

In *The Second Sex,* Simone de Beauvoir makes a distinction between the prostitute and the hetaira. The prostitute needs two kinds of men, client and protector. "In her environment man is enormously superior to woman, and this setting apart favors a kind of love-religion which explains the passionate abnegation of certain prostitutes."[1] The hetaira, on the other hand, seeks a life of her own.[2] "Beauty and charm or sex appeal are necessary here, but are not enough: the woman must be publicly *distinguished* somehow, as a person."[3]

De Beauvoir sees a parallel between the hetaira and the modern movie star as a professional who does not "reveal the world" like a real artist might, but rather tries to "captivate the world for her own profit."[4] The French feminist comments on the enormous power that this new hetaira-female possesses through her capacity to satisfy a new level of male fantasy: for her pride, her independence and her money mean that she will never be "taken" like the prostitute — no man will be her absolute master.

And yet de Beauvoir points out, with characteristic compassion for the female dilemma, that even the hetaira, who understands that her entire personality is her capital, remains hopelessly dependent on her beauty. And for the Hollywood actress, "the struggle against growing old assumes its most dramatic form."[5]

At this point de Beauvoir speculates that of the two, "the prostitute who simply yields her body is perhaps less a slave than the woman who makes a career of pleasing the public."[6] The insistent descriptions of MacLaine's projects, past and future, all in the name of her "boundless energy," might thus indicate an increasing need to compensate for her decreasing value as an aging woman. Instead, this biography asks that we admire the proliferation of new plans and careers (MacLaine is writing a novel, and will write the script and star in a film about Amelia Earhart), rather than question the compulsion that keeps her ever-active. A feminist analysis of the star requires an examination of both her own career choices and the conditions that necessitate such decisions. Why did this astute hetaira-star combine her business savvy with a determination to play the role of prostitute on the screen?

The challenge for a feminist critic is to find a method of inquiry whereby these essential questions of sexual politics can be raised and discussed. In this case that goal is heightened by the narrow dictates of Erens's publishers. On the jacket copy the editors have summarized their own limits for understanding the problem: "Ms. Erens charts the growth and development of the MacLaine persona — a warm-hearted, dumb broad who is used and abused by men. Ms. Erens shows how MacLaine's private life contradicts this image and points out films that offer another perspective on this versatile actress."

Up to this point I have tried to show how the language and ideology of star myth-making have shaped Erens's approach to MacLaine, so that the author has had to neglect all the difficulties and compromises which a woman must experience in Hollywood, or more generally, as a public commodity in the United States today. Erens's analysis of the MacLaine mystique provides us with little understanding or even admiration for the star's life as an entrepreneur (perhaps the male-impersonator par excellence). Furthermore, at the point when the author's project might involve some critical insights into the recurrent narrative structures and techniques in the films themselves, as well as some speculation as to the actress's abiding desire to play the whore, she abdicates again. This time it is because (and the jacket copy sets out the paradigm) she must show that it is the versatility of the actress that qualifies her to play the prostitute, rather than MacLaine's extensive experience as a modern hetaira — the star who learned to promote her whole self, to use her charm as capital, and to "captivate the world for her own profit."

Classical Hollywood narrative films have consistently denigrated the importance of women's work, as wage earners or as houseworkers. The professional woman appears most often on screen as a broad-shouldered caricature of a man, her hair pulled back, her eyes and feet denied their fetish values by the use of glasses and practical shoes. Characteristically, the Good Woman who gets the man *and* the happy ending is portrayed as a sexual child, a dependent who prefers to wait at home while her profit-minded sister-in-a-suit burns herself out doing public work.

Erens suggests the difficulty of changing this formula, and refers often to "the absurdity of traditional role-playing" (p. 61). But her approach to each film as an individual product requires that she, and we, must repeatedly experience the possibility and then the denial of that possibility for these films to promote the independent woman as loveable. There is a curious sense of naive surprise engendered by the retelling of plot after plot, as though the "selling out" by the strong woman, or the sad resignation by the older and wiser woman, are disappointing "twists," rather than part of a systematic way by which narrative film consistently operates — to offer and then withhold the potential for change, equality or sexual liberation.

The mechanisms that make this tantalizing offer renewable with each decade of genre-innovations are not explored by Erens. Just as she preserved for us the "image" of the star-above-reproach, she seems intent upon the same non-critical affirmation of Hollywood's narrative tradition. What this tradition has done to women, and to our understanding of alternatives, cannot be uncovered by an apologist mode of criticism. The prostitute is no answer to our search for the independent woman on screen, and I have suggested that the entrepreneurial hetaira may be no answer to our need for the public woman.

For instance, *Some Came Running* (1969) provided an important beginning for MacLaine's role as prostitute, "the prototype for all the subsequent hookers" (p. 66) she would play on screen. Half of what Erens includes in her two pages on the film is a plot summary, parts of which are as provocative to the feminist critic as MacLaine's character Ginny was to her tough lover:

> In the supporting role of Ginny, MacLaine plays a good-natured but unintelligent tramp whom Dave "picked out" while on a drunken spree. Decked out in a low-cut, short dress, she tumbles off the bus with

disheveled red hair, rosy cheeks, and bright red lipstick. Part hussy, part child, she munches on chewing gum, uses the broad "a" typical of Chicago's lower classes, and carries a few belongings in a stuffed animal that serves as a purse. [p. 66]

After this description, the story is traced to its conclusion, with the observation that Ginny "becomes the tool of Dave's revenge" (p. 68) followed by praise for MacLaine's skills as an actress. She was able to use her facial expression and her body movements "to imply more than she stated" (p. 68), but we do not gain an understanding from this recommendation. How, structurally, does the sacrifice of Ginny the child-whore serve to reinforce certain attitudes about male privilege and power? Both MacLaine, who wrote about the role in her autobiography, and Erens the deferential critic treat the character of Ginny the prostitute *not* as a victim but as a pure spirit. The actress's own perception of the role is cited, again granting her the ultimate authority on herself: "She knew how to love. To me, that's all important" (p. 68). However, this saccharine additive is qualified when the biographer momentarily engages the star in a kind of dialogue, if not debate:

Despite MacLaine's comments about Ginny's "femininity", her walk, her manners, and her language all reveal a manner typical of little girls who learn to play with and be accepted by the boys. This freedom from conventional ladylike behavior becomes the trademark of many Mac-Laine roles. [p. 68]

But both the star and her critic seem intent upon preserving the image of the female, either as loving creature or tomboy, in this film about a prostitute who is shot trying to shield her protector-husband from the bullets of her ex-client-boyfriend. The fact that MacLaine's opportunity to be in this film, and to star with Dean Martin and Frank Sinatra, had a great deal to do with her propitious connections with the Rat Pack, makes the analysis just that much thinner.

It is not enough to praise the modern star for acting in films that deal with "the complexity of adult sexual relationships" (p. 86). Erens looks neither at the ideological aspects of the narrative conventions which are instead naturalized as detailed stories, nor at the economic implications of prostitution as they relate to class, ethnic and female stereotypes. This omission leaves the "complexity" intact, if not further mystified.

Many of the prostitutes played by MacLaine are French, Japanese or simply working-class women who cannot make a sufficient wage as elevator-girls. Surely we need to question the appropriateness of the comic potential that this star brings to these characters. Perhaps this is part of her capacity to be free of "conventional lady-like behavior," which is seen in this book as a sign of versatility and thus indicates a woman's chance to be free. The adaptability of the narrative film is infinite, and the conventions which brought us aggressive career women in the 1940s, or bland blondes in the 1950s, can do wonders with the spunky but dumb working girl whose willingness to charge for her services tells more about the commodification of sex than about the liberation of women.

Erens's deference to MacLaine the woman and to the roles that constitute her work ensures that she remains among the stars; she is not understood as a professional in her life, or as a worker in her film personae. We do not get close to her as a *woman* with considerable energy and even good will, because this account suggests that those traits become her market-value as a new kind of *star*. We are not allowed to fathom the real complexity of what the culture industry does to promote and prostitute the second sex — and to keep it that way.

NOTES

[1] Simone de Beauvoir, *The Second Sex,* trans. H.M. Parshley, Bantam Edition (1949 orig., NY: A. Knopf-Bantam, 1970), p. 529.
[2] Hetaira is defined as the feminine form of the male word in Greek for comrade or companion (hetairos). "One of a class of highly cultivated courtesans in ancient Greece" (*Webster's Third New International Dictionary,* 1976).
[3] De Beauvoir, *Second Sex,* p. 533.
[4] *Ibid.,* p. 533.
[5] *Ibid.,* p. 537.
[6] *Ibid.,* p. 537.

• In Defense of Stars: A Response

PATRICIA ERENS

In her review of my book *The Films of Shirley MacLaine,* Serafina Kent Bathrick raises several provocative questions, including what approach should be taken to the star system and classical Hollywood cinema, the purpose of feminist criticism, the function of stereotypes within the Hollywood narrative, the relevance of star studies, the concept of stars as role models, and the U.S. success ethic. But central to Bathrick's reactions is the expectation that *The Films of Shirley MacLaine* is a critique aimed at film scholars.

In truth the book was written for a popular, non-film-oriented public with the hopes of providing some perspectives along with the prerequisite plot summaries. It falls into that category known as ''the films of...'' Like genre films until recent times, this species of book has never been held in high esteem. I believe that Bathrick was hopeful of a self-reflexive film book and was disappointed to find a genre film book instead. Many of the theoretical issues Bathrick raises are not dealt with because of the limitations of this type of work. Other issues of feminist interpretation are a matter of differing positions.

So to the matters at hand. Despite the low reputation of the star study, I believe that like auteur and genre studies, there is much to be gained by viewing an entire opus, unified in this case by the appearance of one performer. On one end it tells us much about the creation of a screen persona. On the other, it reveals considerable information about latent aspects of our culture.

In *The Films of Shirley MacLaine* I attempt to do both things, with greater emphasis on the first. Before rescreening the films I already held certain notions. MacLaine had portrayed a considerable number of prostitutes. The question posed was how had these images changed over the years, how were her interpretations different from those of other actresses in similar parts, and what characteristics constituted the Mac-Laine persona (the person on the screen).

In dealing with the body of work produced by MacLaine from 1955 to 1978, there emerged certain themes, which I felt were revealing of the star in particular and of the place of women in U.S. society. In film after film — *Artists and Models* (1955), *Ask Any Girl* (1959), *My Geisha* (1962) and *The Gambit* (1966), to name a few — there emerged a pattern of masking and unmasking. A female character (Shirley Mac-Laine) is introduced, events occur, she finds it necessary to adopt an alternative image or personality (usually at the instigation of the male protagonist), and eventually she sheds her false image and reverts to her original (genuine) self. I felt this pattern represented something very strong in the MacLaine persona, a pull towards self-determination. I also felt that the pressure to mask and to assume artificial identities reflected the situation of women, a kind of schizophrenic split that results from the way women are treated in U.S. society: ''The films exposed the false dichotomy that had always existed between what male society expected and envisioned woman to be and what she really was.''[1]

Closely allied with the theme of masking is the prevalence of multiple roles in MacLaine films. These occur in such works as *What a Way to Go!* (1964) and *Woman Times Seven* (1967). This pattern is another manifestation of the split referred to above, and it is a point that I feel is central to my work. Unfortunately Bathrick did not touch on this aspect of the study.

THE MAKING OF THE PUBLIC WOMAN

The first major objection that Bathrick raises seems aimed at MacLaine the public woman, or at least at my presentation of her in the book. In the first sentence of her review Bathrick questions my emphasis on MacLaine's "infinite capacity for action" as her "single most important personal and professional attribute." She queries the image of the "self-made dynamo."

Before addressing myself to the "truth" of my presentation and the merits or limitations of such characteristics, I should comment on three distinctions: I shall call them Shirley MacLaine, MacLaine, and Shirley. These equate to the screen image, which is carried from film to film with some, but not total, consistency; to the public woman written about in newspapers, magazines and books; and the private woman, whom few have come to know. *The Films of Shirley MacLaine* deals with the first two.

Bathrick was quite right in sensing that she was reading about a star. Herein lies some of the confusion. It was never my intention to present the "real" (private) MacLaine. My book deals with the actions of a public woman. The question raised is why would a seemingly intelligent, independent-minded actress play dumb, dependent women on the screen? The fascination lies with the discrepancy between the public woman and the screen persona, a disjuncture that I believe does not become neutralized as Bathrick has stated, but rather reflects the same schism already noted in MacLaine's movie roles. The relationship between star and image needs to be examined. I feel that the enormous gap that existed between the on-screen/off-screen image in MacLaine's early films represents a form of repression and suppression and that the films of the last decade, made when she had increasing control over her career, demonstrate a healthy shift.

For me, Bathrick's objections to MacLaine are hard to comprehend. In recent years women have been encouraged to forgo their acculturated tendencies towards passivity and here is a woman who is ambitious in several directions, but whom Bathrick finds inherently dislikeable (or unbelievable). Bathrick calls into question MacLaine's efforts at writing and producing. Why does Bathrick assume such activities are neurotically motivated (she refers to her project as a "compulsion that keeps her ever-active")? For me this seems a healthy response for an intelligent woman in the entertainment field, who has within her means opportunities to fulfill her creative powers. The move from performer to producer or director has been a common route for many actors (Chaplin, Newman, Redford and Eastwood, for example), and has always been praised as artistic growth. Why then does Bathrick portray this same effort as derogatory in MacLaine's case?

No doubt at the base of Bathrick's reservations is an implicit critique of the whole success ethic. But Hollywood is not a 1930s gangland where only one person succeeds to the top of the apex at the expense of everyone else. Nor is MacLaine's success destructive. Rather it lies in the development of artistic potential. Yes, Hollywood is a commercial industry wherein images are sold, so all the more admirable to find a woman who seeks to control the "selling" of her talent. Bathrick shows an inconsistency when she lashes out against women's victimization in the film industry, sympathizes with their positions as *hetairos* (actors suffer from this situation too),[2] and then criticizes their efforts to become anything in life besides fading film stars. In an era when women have fought for the opportunity to achieve on an equal basis with men, I find the objections to MacLaine's success slightly peculiar.

I may reveal a higher than average regard for MacLaine (why else would I write the book?), but I do think some credit is due the woman who came to Hollywood in the mid-1950s when actresses were considered properties and who refused to mold herself into the ready-made star image with cheesecake photos, expensive wardrobes and a glamorous social life. Certainly MacLaine played a large part in redefining our concept of a "star." Perhaps the new star image was eventually co-opted and merchandised, but the model *had* changed. Less glamorous, more critical of established traditions and more open to alternative life styles, she provided a healthier image for those women (and there were millions) who looked to actresses as standard bearers. In a later generation Barbra Streisand would reduce annual expenditures on plastic surgery by implying that it's okay to have a bumpy nose — that's the way you were born.

Lastly, with regard to MacLaine's position within the film industry, I feel her aggressive opposition to the "seven-year contract" which tied up all performers and her willingness to take action by going to court were positive forces which made a difference to the position of all performers within the system. All this was in the days before the establishment of the women's liberation movement, wherein female solidarity has provided strength and support to many younger, creative women.

I do not fault Jane Fonda "for alienating her public," but at the same time I think that working within the establishment is not a dirty word. There are many kinds of feminists and certainly MacLaine is free to choose between reformism and radicalism. And it is likely that as a reformist MacLaine did reach a broader audience with her message, "change is possible."

This brings me to one last point with regard to MacLaine, the public figure. Bathrick challenges what she regards as myths. Among these are the following: the "self-taught" star myth, the "natural talent" myth and the "lucky break" myth. In part this needs to be clarified; elsewhere, I am stymied in the face of the facts. Bathrick cites my reference to MacLaine as "self-educated, self-opinionated, and self-propelled." This sentence, referring in context to her later career, in no way implies that MacLaine was "self-taught," a term proposed by Bathrick. "Self-educated" refers to book learning, not dance training. I think the passages describing the "exhausting physical demands of ballet class[11] (p. 24) should have made that clear. No dancer is "self-taught," just as no dancer I know reached artistic maturity through the pressures of a pushy stage-mother. A dancer has to want to dance and to be willing to put up with physical hardships and social limitations. S/he must find sufficient rewards to make these sacrifices meaningful. S/he must be "self-propelled."

Bathrick raises an eyebrow at the notions of "natural talent" and "good legs." I think that I adequately indicated the long hours of training and daily lessons which comprise the dancer's preparatory years. But even that is not sufficient for those without the natural propensities, and legs are part of it. I was not creating sexist distinctions. Legs, for both male and female dancers, constitute their equipment, a muscular tool which enables them to stretch longer, jump higher and to be more visible.

As to the "lucky break," I agree that the term sounds like a backstage musical, but from all accounts that seems to be the facts of the case. Compared to other careers, I would say that for a 20-year-old chorus dancer who had spent two years on Broadway to get a starring role in an Alfred Hitchcock film (*The Trouble with Harry*, 1955) was pretty nigh instant success.

FROM PROSTITUTE TO INDEPENDENT WOMAN

As two-thirds of my book dealt with the films, I would like to conclude with a discussion of MacLaine's roles within these films, although the majority of Bathrick's comments are focused on MacLaine the public person. Bathrick makes several points. First, she cites my failure to treat the screen prostitute as victim. And second, she raises the problem of Hollywood's depiction of "the independent woman."

That a prostitute is a social victim seems so obvious that it hardly bears stating. More interesting from my perspective was an analysis of the fictional prostitutes who made up the Shirley MacLaine canon and how these had changed over the years. Broadly speaking, MacLaine's approach to her subject falls within the category of "the whore with a heart of gold." Such a presentation automatically possesses advantages and disadvantages. On the positive side, it tends to humanize the character, placing in the foreground her individual worth in a non-sexual capacity and eliminating her relegation purely to sexual object. Compared to the blatant misogynist attitudes that are a common feature in crime films and melodramas, "the whore with a heart of gold" emphasizes society's mistreatment of a basically worthwhile character. On the other hand, such a portrait tends to romanticize the character (a figment of male projection like the Happy Hooker) and to suppress social reality.[2]

I think it is necessary to look at the changes that occur in the Shirley MacLaine roles from *Some Came Running* (1958) to *Two Mules for Sister Sara* (1970) — her first and last films as a whore — and to the films beyond. During this 12-year period, MacLaine became an established star and one of Hollywood's top-grossing female actresses. By buying out her contract with Hal Wallis, she also gained control over which films she would appear in. After 1970 her image changed. Not only did she refuse to play a prostitute, but I believe that in films such as *The Bliss of Mrs. Blossom* (1968), *Desperate Characters* (1974), *The Possession of Joel Delaney* (1972), and *The Turning Point* (1977), she portrayed characters whose lives carry relevance for modern women. She has also established that actresses over 40 need no longer settle for supporting, character roles. It is a welcome relief to see a female who has a wrinkle or two and perhaps an extra layer of fat, but who is appealing and still commands the title "star." Certainly the John Waynes, Henry Fondas and Marlon Brandos had monopolized that arena for long enough.

In *Some Came Running,* MacLaine plays Ginny, a dumb, childlike whore who willingly allows people to use her. In the end, she is rewarded with a bullet in the back. Some 12 years later, in *Two Mules for Sister Sarah,* MacLaine impersonates a sharp-tongued revolutionary and whore, disguised as a nun, an equal match for hero Hogan (Clint Eastwood). To a degree this performance reflects another manifestation of masking (although the schism is not as great as in earlier films); and the ending is another variation on "the taming of the shrew." But the dominant characteristics of the image are different. As I pointed out in my book, director Don Siegel had enormous difficulty dealing with an actress who had "too much balls" (p. 160). It is my contention that much of this strength is inscribed in the film text.

This leads to Bathrick's second point, the depiction of "the independent woman,'' or rather Hollywood's inability to ''promote an independent woman as loveable.'' Bathrick, along with many feminist critics, attacks Hollywood's consistent tendency to recuperate the independent heroine. I would like to challenge this reading.

Some feminist critics have begun to re-examine positions first stated in the early and mid-1970s, especially by British feminist critics. In a recent article on current feminist film theory, Christine Gledhill elaborates on a comment by Molly Haskell, to wit, that though the independent woman stereotype is ''rejected and humiliated by the end of the film, she has one and a half hours of struggle and self-assertion before this defeat, and it seems possible that aesthetic play with such an image might be very risky for patriarchal ideology.''[3] Gledhill then posits that even classical Hollywood films, with their ''seamless'' techniques, do not remain static or fixed in the coding system which produced them. She proposes a triple relationship (subject/reader/audience) for critics to consider and develops the notion that even within the traditional film text, there are multiple readings and that feminist consciousness provides the ground upon which new readings are manufactured.

For me, Gledhill's method provides a meaningful approach to the films of Shirley MacLaine in light of the work that I have done. It is not sufficient to conclude, as Bathrick does, that ''the selling out by the strong woman is a systematic way by which narrative film consistently operates.'' I think individual factors within each film need to be analyzed in context and that we can now begin to assume a more conscious viewer, one who is capable of making these distinctions.

NOTES

[1] Patricia Erens, *The Films of Shirley MacLaine* (New York: A.S. Barnes, 1978), p. 16.

[2] MacLaine comments on this in her description of the making of *Irma La Douce:* Shirley MacLaine, *Don't Fall Off the Mountain* (New York: Bantam, 1971), chapter 9.

[3] Christine Gledhill, ''Recent Developments in Feminist Film Criticism,'' *Quarterly Review of Film Studies* 3 (Fall, 1978): 490.

CHAPTER 15.

Artful Racism, Artful Rape: Griffith's Broken Blossoms

JULIA LESAGE

Sexist and racist films and television programs continue to engage women as viewers, women of all classes and races. The mass media catch us up in their violence and sensuality. As a woman I must ask how the media can so seduce me that I enjoy, either as entertainment or as art, works that take as one of their essential ingredients the victimization of women. The immediate answer is that historically, from the silent film era to the present, bourgeois film has developed various mechanisms for structuring in ambiguity and for keeping us emotionally involved; one of film's hallmarks as a "democratic" art form is its ability to allow for and co-opt an oppressed group's response. Feminist film criticism takes as its task the exposure of these ideological mechanisms and the analysis of how they function in ways both internal to a film and in a broader cultural and political context.

Specifically, if we look closely at narrative films, with the intent of decolonizing our minds, we will find a similar "story" about sexual relations running below the surface of film after film. Over and over again, male and female film characters are assigned certain familiar, recognizable sexual traits, which provide a ready way of expressing the culture's commonly-held sexual fantasies.[1] The way these fantasies are expressed varies, of course, from film to film, where they are manipulated and often displaced or condensed according to the exigencies of the plot and/or the social acceptability of directly expressing a given fantasy.[2]

Strikingly, the same kind of sexual-political "story," or assignation of sexual traits, is repeated from film to film, no matter how much the manifest content differs. This repetition is not ideologically neutral.

Persistent configurations of assigned sexual traits, deriving perhaps most directly from nineteenth- and twentieth-century literature, have a vitality in contemporary film because these patterns emerge from and serve to reinforce patriarchal social relations in the world outside the film.[3] Fictional sexuality parallels the real options that hegemonic male culture would like to continue offering men and women today, and real power differentials exist between the sexes. The emotional options for both men and women — the patterns of characterization — are, in fact, usually oppressively perverse.

BROKEN BLOSSOMS: CHARACTERS, PLOT AND SEXUAL TRAITS

The sexual-political structures in film are not only perverse, but exceedingly durable. D.W. Griffith's *Broken Blossoms* was one of the first films in the United States received as high art and as a progressive and emotionally moving statement against both masculine brutality and racial prejudice. The film was released in 1919, one of a number of poetic and intimate depictions of domestic life that followed Griffith's monumental epics of 1915-16, *The Birth of a Nation* and *Intolerance*. *Birth of a Nation*, originally entitled *The Clansman*, had valorized the founding of the Ku Klux Klan, depicting it as a paternalistic, semi-feudal organization bringing order to a south suffering under the "chaos" of reconstruction. Consequently, the film provoked a national scandal because of its racist content. *Broken Blossoms* was Griffith's cinematic rejoinder to the charges against him.

Broken Blossoms deliberately tried to counter the then dominant racist ways of depicting Asians in popular literature, magazines and film. In reaction to the importation of masses of Asian laborers and congruent with U.S. imperial ambitions in the Pacific, the United States had seen waves of anti-Asian prejudice in the late nineteenth and early twentieth centuries. Newspapers sensationally editorialized on and presented stories about the "yellow peril." Fictional narratives often used "inscrutable orientals" as villains, or located vices such as drug addiction or white slavery in a U.S. Chinatown. In the decade before *Broken Blossoms*, films treated what seemed the most dangerous threat of all: "miscegenation."[4]

Within this context, *Broken Blossoms* was perceived as a sensitive and humanitarian film. It daringly presented a chaste and ideally beautiful love between an immigrant Chinese man and a young white girl. The plot of the film was derived from Thomas Burke's short story, "The Chink and the Girl," from his *Limehouse Nights*, tales of lumpen criminal life. Griffith changed Burke's Chinese protagonist from a schemer and "worthless drifter of an Oriental" to a poetic, peaceful Buddhist lover of beauty.[5] Ostensibly, *Broken Blossoms* has a moral message: Asian Buddhist peacefulness is superior to Anglo-Saxon ignorance, brutality and strife.

Griffith embodies his moral message in his two male protagonists, who both live in London's Limehouse slum district: a gentle Chinese storekeeper, played by Richard Barthelmess; and a working-class brute, Battling Burrows, played by the large-framed, muscular actor Donald Crisp. Burrows prides himself on masculine prowess. He is master both in the boxing ring and at home, where he bullies his housekeeper and daughter, the 15-year-old Lucy. Lucy, played by Lillian Gish, is a poverty-stricken, beaten child who awakens for one brief moment to emotional life before she is killed.

The plot of the film is simple. The film opens in a Chinese port city with Barthelmess in his ornate robes saying goodbye to his Buddhist mentor and trying unsuccessfully to break up a fight between brawling U.S. sailors. The Chinese man is going out to the West to bring a message of peace. The setting shifts to a London Limehouse slum, where we find out that the young Chinese man has become a disillusioned shopkeeper and opium addict. Elsewhere in the slum, Battling Burrows sits in his shack reminiscing about a fight he has just won and is reprimanded by his manager for drinking and womanizing before his next fight.

The film introduces Burrows's daughter Lucy sitting huddled on a coil of rope on the wharf outside their house. Here the set plays its part as well. As Charles Affron points out in *Star Acting,* all the sets in this film are claustrophobic, even the outdoor ones. Departing from the epic scope of *Birth of a Nation, Broken Blossoms* formally accepts and uses the edge of the frame as limiting the scope of the action and incorporates within the frame many other boundaries such as walls, arches and corners to enhance a claustrophobic effect.[6]

Two sequences, showing either Lucy's reverie or perhaps moments recently experienced, present Lucy's "education" about women's lives. First, a woman in a crowded one-room apartment is cooking a meal for her huge family and fighting with her husband. The woman advises Lucy never to get married. Then Lucy is seen on the street retrieving a compact dropped by one of two prostitutes, who also warn her about men. Lucy gets up and enters the shack.

Still smarting from his manager's rebuke, Burrows bullies Lucy. Before he goes out on the town again, he demands that she have tea ready when he gets back and also that she put a smile on her face. Lucy makes a pathetic gesture, using her fingers to turn up the corners of her mouth — it is a gesture she will repeat four times in the film.

In Burrows's absence, Lucy takes a few treasures out from under a brick on the floor, puts a new ribbon in her dirty hair, and goes out to shop. She looks longingly at the dolls in the Chinese man's shop window, buys a few essentials from a street stand, and wants to trade in some tinfoil to buy a flower but does not have enough foil. She is harassed on the street by another Chinese man, Evil Eye, but is protected by Barthelmess. When she goes home, her father, irritated by his manager's restrictions on his social life, bullies her again. In nervousness, she drops hot food on his hand. Burrows angrily takes a whip out from under the bed and beats her into unconsciousness. He then goes to work out in the gym, preparing for his big fight.

Lucy staggers to her feet, leaves the house and weaves down the Limehouse streets. She falls unconsciously through the door of the Chinese man's store. He has prepared himself an opium pipe and sits and gazes at her as if she were a vision from his drugged dream. She stirs and startles him into full awareness. He bathes her wounds, takes her upstairs to his living quarters, gives her his robe to wear, and puts her on his bed as on an altar. He surrounds her with all his beautiful things, gives her a doll, and it becomes clear that he is sexually attracted to her. As he moves to kiss her, he sees her fear and kisses the sleeve of her robe instead. The sequence is intercut with shots of Burrows slugging it out and winning his big fight amidst the wild cheers of a working-class male audience.

One of Burrows's friends, while shopping at the Chinese man's store, discovers Lucy asleep alone upstairs and runs to tell Burrows of the daughter's "sin." The boxer and his friends agree to wait till after the fights to settle the affair. When they get to the store, the Chinese man is away on an errand. Burrows hits his daughter, forces her to change back into her rags and come with him, and destroys everything in the upstairs room. His friends downstairs keep Lucy from escaping. Once back at home, Burrows chases Lucy, who takes refuge in the closet. When she refuses to come out, Burrows smashes in the closet door with an axe; the sequence is shot from inside the closet, showing Lucy's hysterical reaction and absolute fear. The claustrophobic visual composition and Gish's acting indicate that we are intended to be "inside" Lucy's experience in this cinematic equivalent of rape. When Burrows chops through the door, he pulls Lucy through it and throws her on the bed, where he beats her to death.

When he discovers the destruction in his room and Lucy's abduction, the Chinese man throws himself on the floor and sobs hysterically. He takes a gun, goes to Burrows's shack, finds Lucy dead, acknowledges the challenge Burrows gives him to fight, and shoots and kills the brute. Taking Lucy's body with him, the Chinese man goes back to his room and lays her body once again on his bed as on an altar.

Burrows's friends discover the boxer's body and get the police to round up the Asian killer. Before they can do so, however, in a last act of tranquil and sorrowful love, even ectasy, the "yellow man" prays before his Buddha and stabs himself, joining his child-woman in death. This is the "plot" of *Broken Blossoms*.

THE ABUSES OF MASCULINITY

When we analyze the story line closely, looking particularly at the visual elements and cinematic tactics, it becomes clear that the film is *about* sex roles as much as *about* race. In particular, it is about masculinity. In the figure of Battling Burrows, the film presents the potential *evil* of masculinity, here safely attributed to a grotesque Other from the lower classes. Projected onto the Chinese man's character are all the traits of the nineteenth-century sensitive outsider, the romantic hero — a self-destructive dreamer who never lives out the fulfillment of his dreams. I wish to examine how and why such traits have been divided and assigned to the two major male characters in the film, and also what it means that the narrative places both men in relation to a "virgin." Finally, I wish to look at the kind of role assigned to Lillian Gish and Gish's impact on/attraction for me as a woman viewer both drawn to and distressed by this film.

In *Broken Blossoms,* if we look closely at the gestures, clothing and course of events in any given sequence, we see that our interpretation of the character's behavior relies on and indeed underscores many popular notions about masculinity and the abuses of masculinity. Donald Crisp as Battling Burrows uses exaggeration to delineate the attributes of a working-class bully and macho brute, carrying the traditional attributes of masculinity to an abusive extreme. In contrast, Barthelmess plays the Chinese man as being in many ways not fully a man, as woman-like. Compare, for example, our judgments on the costumes and gestures of the two men as we first see them. We notice the ornateness of Barthelmess's robe, his facial gestures, especially his acts of looking upward with half-closed eyes or of carrying a fan, his small movements, and his semi-static poses and stance.

The opening titles and the choice of content in the film's early shots — the initial contrast between a port in the Far East and a Limehouse slum — emphasize a social and moral point, namely that Asian civilization and altruism outshine European and American immorality and grossness. Yet another set of reflections is simultaneously elicited from the audience — an evaluation and comparison of effeminacy and brutal manliness. In his scripted role and in his physical movements and appearance, Barthelmess as the young Chinese man elicits from the audience a common social accusation: effeminacy. Time and time again the viewer seems led to conclude, "That's an effeminate man — or effeminate gesture, or article of clothing, etc." His robe is excessively ornate; in the exterior shots, its shirts conspicuously blow in the wind. It is shapeless, making the shape beneath androgynous in form. When he is in the Buddhist temple with his mentor, the temple itself filled with flowers, exotica and ornate design, Barthelmess acts "girl-like": holding a fan, moving only with slight restrained gestures, and standing with eyes cast down.

In contrast with the Chinese man's demeanor, these sequences also present other men self-consciously proud of their masculinity. These are the U.S. sailors whom Griffith calls in one intertitle, "barbarous Anglo-Saxon sons of turmoil and strife." They swizzle down liquor, stuff food grotesquely into their mouths, make large gestures and swagger around as ugly Americans totally insensitive to their milieu. They seem incapable of being together without violent physical discord, and foreshadow Griffith's critique of Battling Burrows.

In the Limehouse environment, we first see the Chinese man huddled against a wall, one foot up against it, arms wrapped around himself, eyes cast sadly down. The soft curve of Barthelmess's body seems to "catch" the contrasting, harsh linear angles of the architecture. For a man to have his arms wrapped around himself is to assume a typical "woman's" gesture of depression, insecurity and even sad self-hatred. The Chinese man takes a stance which is as far from that of a masculine doer, a self-determining agent of one's own life, as it is possible to present. In his store we see him semi-statically posed, smoking his opium against a background of meager beauty. The life he creates for himself is one of melancholy, contemplation and escape.

The opium den that the Chinese man frequents suggests not only moral but sexual derangement. As a matter of fact, fictional films usually "signal" moral derangement by showing women in sexually transgressive roles. Here, we see mannishly dressed women in sexually active poses or in compositions of sexual self-sufficiency or dominance, often with a man of another race. In one composition, an Anglo woman is sitting above a totally self-absorbed, opium-smoking Turk and looking down on him. Another shot shows a blonde woman interacting with a black worker; another, an Anglo woman flirting with a Chinese man we later know as Evil Eye. We see a woman lying on a couch, filmed either as if she wishes to seduce someone or as if the opium is giving her an orgasmic experience on her own. She is panting slightly, wetting her lips, and looking towards the camera with an expression that suggests illicit ecstasy. This shot parallels a later one of Barthelmess stretched out full length on a couch, with the opium seller tending this completely passive figure. The equation of the protagonist's vice with sexual derangement and a suspiciously feminine passivity could not be more explicit.

In contrast, the figure of Battling Burrows is a study in established norms of masculine dress, gesture, attitudes and behavior. Every aspect of Burrows's character is heightened to make us reflect on the falsity or brutal consequences of those norms. What do we see Burrows doing? In the ring he fights strictly by heavy slugging. After winning, he is proud and struts about. Before the fight he makes faces at his off-screen opponent, juts his chin out, and pounds his gloves up and down on his legs — indicating that he thinks a fight will clearly prove to the whole world who is the "better man."

Back home, he drinks and entertains the advances of a Loose Woman. The signs of her looseness are many: her activity, her smiling, her friendliness, and her initiative to visit a man in his house. She walks in, hands in her pockets, looks Burrows in the eye, immediately moves over to where he is standing, receives a quick embrace from him, and then goes back out, still looking at him with a flirting glint in her eye, presumably having made a date to meet him later.

Burrows's typical posture asserts macho self-confidence in a socially coded way, particularly in the use of cinematic gestures normally assigned to figures supposedly from the working class. He stands with feet spread apart, lets his eyes sweep around the room possessively, pulls his vest down, puts his hands in his pockets to pull his pants tight across his crotch, and sways back and forth from one foot to another. Such a stance is a way of declaring himself master of a given space, and especially master over the woman in his domestic space.

When angry, Burrows knocks one fist against the palm of the other hand, and when proclaiming his opinion he gestures with his hand open and palm down. Although he is characterized as stupid, he is also shown as having the prerogative of having his emotions and opinions respected as law in his house — a witty cinematic comment on the nuclear family — the place where all of us can observe patriarchy as insane.[7] To portray this man's physical excess, which culminates in beating his daughter, Griffith has Burrows pick up a chair and swing it around, eat like a pig, throw a spoon at Lucy's rear-end and then oblige her to smile, upon which pathetic act he passes judgment. There are many such gestures of dominance towards Lucy before Burrows beats her. Indeed, all of Burrows's gestures in the film form part of a brutal whole.

Burrows's male friends reinforce for him the rightness of his behavior and attitudes. They form a Boys' Club, the kind of thing all socially successful men use to protect their men's rights in a man's world. When the men go to the police station to report Burrows's death, the police's co-operative interaction with them reveals an unusual degree of male cohesiveness, for in another context we might expect more of a conflict to be presented between the police and the fight-loving element of a portside slum. The conflicts among Burrows's associates function well within the confines of the boys' club, for the manager only wants the fighter to fight better; and the associates band together to get the woman back for their friend once the joke of telling him about it has been sprung.

In fact, the tale is told to Burrows just as if it were a spicy story of local adultery. The man who had spied on Lucy paces his account to arouse Burrows's sexual curiosity, to bring forth laughter and contempt for any cuckolded man who would lose a woman to a weakling and a "Chink." In a competitive fashion, his friends found it great fun to see the boxer's chagrin at "losing" both to a girl, his own daughter whom he was supposed firmly to possess, and to a man who seemed Burrows's inferior because that man would not fight and because he was of another race. There is no love between Burrows and his associates but a lot of mutual self-protection. When they "recover" Lucy, they all assume that Burrows will — and should — beat her, both to assuage his wounded masculine pride and to put her firmly in her place.

POSSESSING A VIRGIN AND A CHILD

Certain perversities in the film are labelled as such by the intertitles and the story line: namely, racism, opium addiction and physical violence. Yet equally important to the development of the film are other perversities: rape, incest and the seduction of a child. It is testimony to the force of the intertitles and the declared narrative line — the overt story of racism and child abuse — that few critics have looked closely at the specifically sexual perversity of this film.[8] In fact, if we look at the mise-en-scène and composition, in visual terms it is clear that both the brutish father and the gentle, dope-smoking Chinese man "get" the girl. Visually we see both men symbolically consummating sexual contact with Gish. The film allows both men to possess a virgin, a child.

It is clear that Burrows's breaking into the closet with an axe and dragging the cowering Lucy out through the broken boards visually symbolizes rape. Indeed, this is one of the most emotionally powerful sequences of sexual assault on film. Yet there are many other indications in the film that Burrows's relation to his daughter is a sexual one. He abuses her for the same reasons and in the same way that a working-class man is supposed to abuse his wife. That is, when the world is down on you, if you are a married man you can always take it out on the wife and kids at home. Aside from one intertitle introducing Lucy, there is no other indication of a father-daughter relation, and all of Burrows's actions towards Lucy would appropriately be those of a man towards a wife.

More explicit in visual composition and mise-en-scène is the role of the bed in the Burrows household. Sometimes, especially when Burrows is alone drinking or with his manager, the composition is cast towards the room's center, with the bed predominantly visible behind Burrows. When Lucy is alone in the house doing her domestic chores, looking at her treasures or looking in the mirror, the composition is cast towards the right side of the room, the domestic corner that includes the hearth. On the opposite side, the bed and closet form an angle, which compositionally becomes a trap.

The first time Burrows beats Lucy, he grabs a whip from under the mattress and stands in the center of the room, holding the whip at penis height. The lighted areas in the composition form a triangle, with the pillow and Lucy's and Burrows's faces forming the triangle's corners, and the whip-phallus aligned midway between the pillow and Lucy's face. Lucy cries, cowers by the door, and clings to the far right wall away from the bed. Burrows is filmed in a symmetrically-composed medium-shot, whip prominently in the center, and he points for her to move away from the right wall, that is, towards the direction of the bed.

Lucy tries to create a diversion by telling him there is dust on his shoes. She bends down to wipe off his shoes with her dress. Here, the change in composition from one shot to another connotes the act of fellatio. In the long shot before Lucy wipes the shoes, the whip hangs almost to the floor. But in the close-up of her wiping the shoes, the whip's tail is at the height of Burrows's penis, and as Lucy raises her face the whip swings past her lips. As Burrows grabs Lucy's arms and throws her towards the bed near the closet, the whip is again between his legs at penis height. We see blurred, orgiastic shots of him beating her senseless.

In the film's final beating sequence, the same connotative devices are repeated, but in a more exaggerated way. Burrows beats Lucy's face with the whip handle, and the bed becomes the site of her death.

Finally, the way Burrows dies emphasizes that his relation to the Chinese man was one of sexual competition after all. When the Chinese man discovers the dead Lucy on the bed and is about to shoot Burrows, both men face off and tacitly acknowledge the other's "manly" challenge to fight to the death over the "cause" of this woman. Posed next to a fight poster on the wall and standing with his back to the angle formed by the bed and closet (the trap-like locus of Lucy's rape and death), the Chinese man shoots Burrows, discharging the gun held at penis-height.

In paradigmatic contrast to sexual violence is the sensual completeness of Lucy's one night at the Chinese man's home. And yet that relation is not only tender and beautiful, but also explicitly perverse. We see this most clearly in the sequence where the Chinese man overcomes his lust just after the girl Lucy has received her first doll. Lucy, wrapped in her new protector's ornate, "womanly" robe, cuddles the doll with delight. However, her friend with the gentle eyes now wears a look of acquisitive passion, and he is seen moving in on Lucy, his eyes in shadow. Shots of Burrows at his big fight are intercut with this sequence: we see Burrows slugging heavily and an all-male audience, primarily working-class, on their feet wildly cheering. When we see the Chinese man and Lucy again, there is fear in her eyes as she clings to the doll. He picks up the hem of her sleeve and kisses that instead, his face moving to the light where we see his illuminated, gentle, ecstatic smile as he goes away.

Significantly over-apologizing for the man's sexual intent, the intertitle announces: "His love remains a pure and holy thing — even his worst foe says this." In fact, the title makes no sense, because no one at the time knew that Lucy was there, and later her father and his friends just assumed that a sexual relation had taken place. Griffith seems to use the title to deny the sequence's visual explicitness, yet this very denial creates suspicion about and thus confirms the reality of that sexual passion which the sequence has both presented and repressed.

After the Chinese man withdraws, we see Gish examining the sleeve that had been kissed and then stirring in bed. Both gestures indicate the child's emotional, indeed sexual, involvement with this gentle yet seductive man. The visual lushness of this sequence, the child's gestures of preening and of loving the doll, the advances of the Chinese man, and the child's awakening to both maternal and sexual emotion: all these visual details offer a clear erotic message, a message that is then ambiguously denied.

MALE OPTIONS UNDER CAPITALISM

Two men, a brute and an effeminate beauty-lover, "get a virgin." This is the sexual plot of *Broken Blossoms*. What does that mean? What is the power of such a plot? Why did Griffith construct his story that way?

First of all, their slum environment, brutality and opium-smoking cast the male protagonists as Others. Griffith safely assigns perversity to other races and to the poor. Onto the working class are displaced Griffith's unconscious, artistic insights about the problems of the nuclear family under capitalism, an understanding he never could have admitted to since he was very much the patriarch, a man who fondly recalled the paternalistic and militaristic values of the Old South and who always had a love for pretty young women.[9]

In fact, the film presents two key aspects of male life under capitalism. A man can be socially successful and conventionally masculine, or he can cultivate his sensitivity and imaginative capacity and live as an outsider. Since the last century, middle-class men have had as a model of emotional success either the role of "breadwinner" and thus possessor of a home, wife and family; or the role of "free-spirited" (in fact petit-bourgeois) rebel, usually an artist or intellectual. *Broken Blossoms* utilizes and heightens the contrast between these two emotional options. It reduces the outlines of these male roles to a schematized emblematic form, and it displaces the whole "problem" of masculinity onto a story about the lives of the very poor. The film is thus particularly useful to feminist critics, to show how popular art transmits patriarchal assumptions. The roles of the two major male characters not only set out two contrasting sides of a single sexual-political configuration, but the film also makes the emotional implications of each kind of role totally explicit.

The figure of Burrows represents conventional notions of masculinity as enacted by a socially successful man. Within that formula, the corollary to a "real man's" aggression in taking what he can in the social and economic world is his "wearing the pants" at home. That is, he is the boss or the possessor of a wife and family, and his woman must always know her place. In *Broken Blossoms*, Battling Burrows seemingly has no wife, only a daughter. Yet multiple notions of women's servitude, dependency and helplessness — and reception of sexual abuse — are condensed in the figure of Lucy.

Women's role in the nuclear family under capitalism was classically described by Friedrich Engels using the metaphor of prostitution.[10] Across class lines and cultures and across historical periods, we have sold our bodies for sustenance. Furthermore, the ideological compensations given to "good" women in western culture — the romantic love myth and the courtly "woman-on-a-pedestal" or Victorian "wife-as-moral-focus" myth — are, as Kate Millett wrote,

> grants that the male concedes out of his total power. Both forms of compensation have the effect of obscuring the patriarchal character of western culture and, in their general tendency to attribute impossible virtues to women, have ended by confining them to a narrow and often remarkably conscribing sphere of behavior.[11]

Symbolically, in *Broken Blossoms* Lucy functions as the Good Wife. But what is most daring about this film is that it pushes Engels's metaphor of prostitution, used to describe the way women are possessed

257

in the nuclear family, one step further. *Broken Blossoms*'s metaphor equates the possession of women in the family with incest. Many works of literature, especially from the nineteenth century on, deal with the relation of father-figures and sons as the sons come into their patrimony or struggle to become self-made men. This has also been a favorite theme in contemporary film (*The Apprenticeship of Duddy Kravitz,* 1974, *Star Wars,* 1977, and *The Godfather,* 1971, immediately come to mind). But *Broken Blossoms* is unusual in the way it faces the opposite question, not the coming into patrimony but the servitude of women, a servitude enforced by threats of deprivation, emotional bullying and the potential or actual use of physical force.

In *Broken Blossoms* the father rapes his daughter: what does that mean? In Burrows's case, murdering Lucy is clearly the ultimate abuse of his prideful masculinity. In real life, we know that on the individual level rape is not an act of sexual desire but one of possession.[12] On the social level, as Susan Brownmiller points out, rape is analogous to lynching. It is an act supposedly committed by lumpen proletarian men or a crazy few, but in fact rape performs a more general social function as a reminder and brutal enforcer of women's "place."[13]

When we take the second half of the term, "the father rapes his *daughter,*" and ask what *incest* means to the sexual-political structure underlying the film, we arrive at the same answer: possession. The challenge to patriarchy that this film poses (or can pose through a feminist reading) is the following: if a man's social world consists primarily of a boys' club, of a nexus of economic and power relations conducted principally among men, how can a man ever set his daughters free or even conceive of what their freedom might mean? For the emotional implication *Broken Blossoms* dares to draw out is that for a man to be the possessor at home means to be incestuous towards his girl children as well as towards his wife.[14]

Griffith is perfectly clear about Burrows's excesses and is morally righteous in disliking abusive masculinity, here safely assigned to the working class. We all see what Burrows is like and know why the brute is wrong. More interesting to me, and more ambiguous, is Burrows's complement, the Chinese man. On the superficial level, the film is an anti-racist text, but the film says nothing from an Asian person's point of view, just as it says nothing from a woman's point of view. The images of the East, of Buddhism, of racial traits and of an oppressed person's reaction to oppression are all drawn from hegemonic, white stereotypes. In fact, not only is Griffith working with received opinions and prejudices about Asians, women and the working class, but when he sets up his basic opposition of brute vs. sensitive man, he is also working with a set of oppositions that has nothing to do with race.

THE MAN OF ACTION VS. THE SENSITIVE OBSERVER

What are these oppositions set up by the use of two contrasting male figures — the boxer and the opium smoker?

The one character is a violent, selfish, insensitive man of action. Burrows moves with large gestures and commands a large space wherever he is. He is self-assured and demanding, even to the point of being physically and emotionally destructive to others around him. The other male figure in the film is a gentle, altruistic lover of beauty. He is a soft person, often emotionally paralyzed into inaction. He burns his days up in reverie and opium. But even though he would waste himself with drugs, he is basically fatherly and tender. He is totally self-sacrificing for a child-woman that he would wish to, but cannot, possess. Furthermore, he understands the hypocrisy of most social values in the capitalist West; his solution is to surround his own life with beauty and otherwise to withdraw. In his love life, the yearning is all.

The character whom Griffith can demean by calling ''Chinky'' has all the traits of a male cultural persona which has been valorized in western literature for several centuries now — a persona Griffith himself surely must have identified with. ''Chinky'' is no less than our old friend, the romantic hero. He is the sensitive lover of beauty and the pursuer of unattainable women. The Chinese man could have stepped right out of Thomas DeQuincey's *The Opium Eater,* and it is indeed likely that the author of *Limehouse Nights* was influenced by DeQuincey's depiction of London poverty and a young man's opium addiction and friendship with a girl waif. That Griffith, the artist who always thought of himself and his role in idealized terms, identified with the Chinese man can be seen in the way that *Broken Blossoms*'s plot and mise-en-scène constantly valorize the young man's tenderness, aesthetic sensibility and moral superiority. Indeed, all the Chinese man's virtues are conflated in a romantic way: to recognize beauty and to surround oneself with beautiful things are indices of moral superiority that people enmeshed in the workaday world do not recognize. Only artists, fellow outsiders and women can recognize such a virtue for its worth.

To carry my analysis of sexual politics in *Broken Blossoms* one step further, I think we should ask why this figure is characteristically male and what his social role is. In fact, the romantic hero and the sensitive outsider (or, to use a more familiar equivalent, the filmmaker and the professors of literature and film) have a specific class position under capitalism; their chance to *choose* that position is the escape valve that capitalism allows for dissatisfied male members of its petite bourgeoisie.

To put it schematically, there are three roles available to men in capitalist society: outsider, worker, or boss. If you pursue profit and power, you also exploit others. To avoid facing that, you have to dull your emotional sensibility as you move up in social position. That is what *Duddy Kravitz, Godfather II* (1974), and *Room at the Top* (1959) were all about. The capitalist has to believe that the profit motive serves society the best and cannot look with regret either at how he is exploiting others or at how his emotional and social forms of interacting with others might be better. Possession and dominance become embedded in a way of life. Or a man may be a worker, putting in time at a stultifying job for a weekly pay check, suffering humiliation both from superiors at work and from the threat of unemployment and/or illness — the threat of not being able to take care of one's own. Both for male workers and for bosses, most of whom are male, there are many reasons why men continue to suffer from rigid notions of sex roles, emotional paralysis, moral compromise and a crippling of the imagination — and also why they oppress women.

The one "out" that has traditionally been offered to men since the last century has been to be the artist, the outsider, the rebel. This person has the insight and the inner drive to reject social respectability and emotional sterility. He can turn to creating art, living alone in nature, or taking drugs — often doing all these at once. Instead of pursuing money, success and power in bourgeois terms, the romantic hero idealistically lives by virtues that seem to be precluded if one searches for social success: these virtues include creativity, passion, love, authenticity, honesty, sincerity, beauty, innocence, spontaneity and contemplation of nature. At the same time, the romantic hero in his self-gazing is also like Hamlet, often paralyzed into inaction, usually ineffective, yearning for the unattainable woman, and inevitably self-destructive. That this is a *male* role can be seen from the fact that the rebel goes off to the woods or into dope, but not back into the domestic sphere to raise a bunch of kids. That has just not been one of the options that men have imagined for themselves.[15]

DISPLACEMENT

Furthermore, Griffith's "ruse" of using the Asian man as the romantic hero hides the social reality of racism. The romantic hero is more like Griffith's image of himself; Griffith wrote that he sought to live by the pen as a way of identifying with his earlier and most beloved image of his father, that is, of a man brandishing a sword (and in fact, it was brandishing a sword against a black servant to teach the man his place).[16] When Griffith came of age in the South, the illustrious days of the Civil War and family prosperity were for him sadly a part of the legendary past. To be a writer was for Griffith to find a more modern, petit-bourgeois way of being a real man in a culture not instinctively his own, of being socially functional yet still maintaining his felt identity as an Outsider, and of devoting himself to Creativity and Art.[17]

Perhaps reacting against the charges of racism that *Birth of a Nation* had provoked, Griffith clearly wanted *Broken Blossoms* to be considered anti-racist, but the film represses all understanding of the real mechanisms of racism. Griffith did not embed his depiction of doomed interracial love within an artistic structure that would clarify understanding of race and racial oppression. Instead, he assigned to the Asian man the traits of his own class, that element of the petite bourgeoisie who feel themselves as individuals to be above economic and social constraints — sensitive outsiders morally superior to the bosses and brutes.

If the artistic structure of *Broken Blossoms* deals only superficially with race, it deals profoundly with sexual politics, especially masculinity. In particular, it implies that all three ''types'' of men under capitalism desire the same type of woman: the unattainable or nonsexually active woman.[18] Battling Burrows represents the ''family man.'' Because he is an entrepreneur, an aggressive boxer, he represents the self-made man, and because of his economic level, he also represents the working class. Thus Griffith has condensed onto the figure of Burrows traits of both the capitalist and the worker. In this context, Burrows possesses his blonde virgin and good wife and child within the context of a man's possession of his family.

As I mentioned before, Griffith condensed and displaced all his notions of the potential evil of family life onto the figure of a lower-class man both for his own protection and that of his audience. Similarly, projected onto the figure of the Chinese man are all the traits of the romantic hero, living only for the pursuit and never living out the fulfillment. The woman that both men need, each for different reasons, is played by Gish in a way that collapses virgin, child and wife all into the same role. For the father, she is the traditional good woman and also the virgin child. For the Chinese romantic hero, she is like Faust's Gretchen and DeQuincey's waif or even Werther's Lotte: a figure desirable from afar.

When I first saw *Broken Blossoms,* I asked myself, what does it mean that both men have to get a virgin? Griffith's emblematic schema of the sexual possibilities for men in the West, that is, under capitalism, makes the answer clear. The men in the film live in a world of men, and Burrows embraces that world while the Chinese rejects it. None of the men in the film can enter into or even imagine a world where women are sexually active, initiators and agents of actions and decisions, and bearers of social power.

Coming to the same conclusion, but in a contrasting way, G.W. Pabst's silent film *Pandora's Box* (1928) also took up the theme of the capitalist's and the romantic hero's sexual decisions, but that film traced the fate of two men who aligned themselves with the seductress, the dark woman. Lulu, played by the dark-haired Louise Brooks, is the mirror opposite of Gish. Lulu is a destroyer of men and the bearer of chaos. In *Broken Blossoms,* the function of the good woman, the virginal woman, is to be put on a pedestal and yearned for, and after marriage or within the family, she is to be possessed. It is not Lucy's own vision, for Griffith early included scenes which showed Lucy losing all illusions about her future as a woman, either in marriage or as a prostitute.

That all the main characters must die at the end of *Broken Blossoms* and that the sexual-political situation as Griffith presents it is so static and despairing is no accident. Griffith presents a sparse yet emotionally charged outline of what happens when men cling to established norms of masculinity or rebel against those norms as a romantic hero would. *Broken Blossoms* has the vision to present both kinds of emotional possibilities that men in capitalist culture can allow themselves as, at worst, murderous in their consequences, and, at best, as crippling to men and oppressive to women.

A WOMAN VIEWER'S RESPONSE

To conclude, I would like to try to analyze why I liked the film. First, as I pointed out, Griffith's films have many ways to pacify our superego while promulgating a racist and sexist ideology. *Broken Blossoms'* s intent seems to be to combat racism. The fact that the Chinese man has the outlook of the romantic hero more than the point of view of someone from a non-white race does not at first seem racist, since the romantic hero has long been a figure women have found sympathetic. Sheila Rowbotham in *Woman's Consciousness, Man's World* spoke for my whole generation when she exposed the basic infantile selfishness of that figure as encountered by women in real life. But even so the sensitive, often androgynous man in fiction still has his appeal. Male authors give him "womanly" virtues and also a man's right to be agent of his own destiny. *Broken Blossoms* takes a clear stand against violence and male brutality and, in the figure of the Chinese man, it valorizes male tenderness, gentleness, and appreciation of beauty and innocence. No matter how many times I see the film, its simple praise for virtues I too prize in men comes through with an emotional power.

For most viewers, the other side of that message, that Brutality is Wrong, is conveyed not through the caricature of masculinity as enacted by Donald Crisp as Battling Burrows, but through the pathos elicited by Lillian Gish. *Broken Blossoms* established Gish's critical reputation and was part of a series of films Griffith made in this period which looked lovingly at the small detail and at women in the domestic sphere. Griffith's films were famous for their female roles, and Griffith was admired for the performances he drew from actresses and the way he filmed them. *Broken Blossoms*, for example, featured Griffith's first use of the irregular ''Sartov'' lens, which resulted from then on in his dramatically exploiting softly-blurred close-ups of Gish.[19] It was also one of the first commercial films in the United States to be promoted successfully as high art.[20]

Although our attention is constantly being drawn to Gish, she is not playing a woman seen on women's terms or from a woman's point of view. Her role is reduced to the depiction of a virgin, a ''vision'' of women often manipulated in male or, rather, patriarchal art. Within the narrative structure, the figure of Lucy is a term or a marker in a male story about male concerns.

The critical question that remains unresolved for me as a feminist viewer is this: where does Lucy's pathos, which affects me so strongly, derive from? Are my eyes constantly on Lucy in the way that a male viewer's would be, insofar as traditional feature films constantly have us look *at* women as objects in stories told through men's eyes?[21] Do I or can I stay on the film's surface and admire it as anti-racist and/or as art? Do I respond to the figure of Lucy primarily because I appreciate this virtuoso film role for an actress, one which demands a range from childlike ingenuousness to complete hysteria? By extension, do I admire other of Griffith's films for such roles and for women's acting in them?

Most students I have taught remember specific Griffith films through ''what happens'' to the female lead and the actresses' performances. *Broken Blossoms* is seemingly ''about'' Lucy's plight, her moment of love, and her murder. The surface emphasis on Lucy's story is enhanced both by Gish's acting and the close-ups of her face and glowing hair. Such an emphasis on the waif, Lucy, gives the film an appeal to both men and women. Although, for me, the device of Lucy's making a smile with her fingers is repulsively saccharine, the way Gish captures Lucy's limited emotional experience and the way her figure is filmed seem so ''right'' for this sad tale. For example, Griffith brilliantly assigns Gish the prop of a doll to represent Lucy's awakening to her childhood, sexuality and maternal emotion all at once, and he maintains a visual emphasis on the child clinging to that doll while she is attacked in the closet. While seemingly fixed in a rigid stance, Gish can let her eyes, posture or fluttering hands express a whole range of emotions, and when she is attacked in the closet, she can let her body totally respond to the hysteria of impending death.[22]

Gish draws us in and holds us, and our sympathy for the child's plight both pacifies our superego and assures us that such things happen only to poor waifs and not to us. The other drama, that of masculinity and of men's need to get a virgin, is enacted on a level of the film which I think many people can observe but which goes by relatively uncommented on either by the overt story line or by the intertitles. And on this level, the film leads us all to participate in Lucy's rape by her father and her seduction by the Chinese man, the seduction in fact of a child who has just been given her first doll.

The film depicts interracial love yet hides the ways it makes that love "safe." It protests male brutality yet draws us into male violence and child-abuse. I cannot speak for a Third World person's reaction to the film's ambiguous combination of anti-racism and racism. I do know that, as a feminist, the fact that I am drawn into cinematic depictions of this kind of sexual perversion disturbs me the most. It seems a gauge of my own colonized mind.

Lucy's pathos draws me into identifying with a cinematic depiction of woman as victim.[23] On the one hand, as a viewer, I want to protect this girl as a motherless child. Her helplessness calls out to me. As a girl and also as a woman, I have both felt helplessness (even been addicted to it) and nurtured others from helplessness to independence (the teacher's role, the lover's role, the mothering role that I have learned in my female socialization).

On the other hand, *Broken Blossoms*'s patriarchal, extreme depiction of father-daughter relations also reflects my own internalized and eroticized fears of male authority, dominance and control: fears that also derive from my girlhood in this culture. I have to ask myself: in what ways as a viewer do I "participate" in Lucy's brutalization and rape? I know how many levels of culture (from the structure of language to the structures of fiction to the structures of the economy) operate in a way that would encourage me to turn female submission into something erotic.[24]

In her key work on the presentation of women in male pornography, Angela Carter compares *Broken Blossoms* to de Sade's *Justine*:

> Sometimes this waif, as in Griffith's *Broken Blossoms,* is as innocently erotic and as hideously martyrized as Justine herself, and, as a sexual icon, the abused waif allows the customer to have his cake and glut himself upon it, too. She could be as enticing in her vulnerability and ringletted prettiness as she was able but the audience knew all the time

that the lovely child before them was a mature woman whom the fiction of her childishness made taboo. The taboo against acknowledging her sexuality created the convention that the child could not arouse desire; if she did so, it was denied. A sentimental transformation turned the denial of lust into a kitsch admiration of the "cute."[25]

Carter discussed the mechanism of denial by showing the response of male spectators to Gish's roles. I would also apply that mechanism to my own response. My response may include a denial of "lust," that is, my own erotic reaction to my preferred female stars. But more clearly, Gish's role as waif-woman both elicits my own Oedipal fears and fantasies and allows me to deny them. The extremity of Lucy's condition allows me to deny that there is an internalized, "masochistic" drama of the brutalized girl child that I, the mature woman, still carry around with me emotionally. Furthermore, Gish, acting the desired and abused girl, represents the vision I as a "good girl" had to have of my sexuality: it was there but denied, and I long thought that its destiny was to be possessed.[26]

Broken Blossoms openly teaches that its configuration of male dominance/female submission is destructively perverse. Do woman viewers who identify strongly with Gish's role sense that *Broken Blossoms* has artistically presented their own problems in such a way that it has brought sexual-political problems to the surface for conscious consideration? I suspect not. As a viewer, pathos has overwhelmed me. When I identify with women on the screen as victims, it is difficult to move away from "feeling" to a more active, self-aware response.

Even with this caveat, my response to *Broken Blossoms* is ambiguous. I cannot help but admire it. In a visual style fully adequate to expressing the complex interrelationships between romantic striving and male brutishness, the film offers a symbolically complete, although schematized and condensed, representation of masculine options under capitalism. Like most bourgeois, patriarchal narrative art, it provides a social and superego "cover" for its viewers so that they can immerse themselves in its flow.

Yet here the "cover" is honorable and exhaustive: high art, anti-racism, anti-child abuse, male idealism and tenderness pitted against brutishness, female pathos and admirable women's screen roles. Below this manifest content, *Broken Blossoms* demystifies the romantic hero as a semi-paralyzed pursuer of unattainable ideals. And it creates a daring metaphor — based on incest — to describe the patriarch's possessive role in the nuclear family.

NOTES

[1] How films assign characters recognizable traits and how connotations are "readable" in film because they are reinforced in the action and in the narrative development are two topics I deal with extensively in the following articles, where I apply the methodology of Roland Barthes's *S/Z* to film: "*S/Z* and *Rules of the Game,*" *Jump Cut* 12-13 (Winter 1976-77); "Teaching the Comparative Analysis of Novels and Films," *Style* 9 (Fall 1975).

[2] For a discussion of the mechanisms of *condensation* and *displacement* in Hollywood film, see Charles Eckert, "The Anatomy of a Proletarian Film: Warner's *Marked Woman,*" *Film Quarterly* 17, No. 2 (Winter 1973-74).

[3] Kate Millett's *Sexual Politics* (New York: Avon, 1970) deals precisely with this topic and remains a model of feminist criticism which moves fluidly back and forth from historical to literary analysis.

[4] The historical background here comes from Vance Kepley, Jr., "Griffith's *Broken Blossoms* and the Problem of Historical Specificity," *Quarterly Review of Film Studies* 3 (Winter 1978).

[5] *Ibid.*, p. 41.

[6] Charles Affron, "The Actress as Metaphor: Gish in *Broken Blossoms,*" in *Star Acting* (New York: E.P. Dutton, 1977), p. 12.

[7] I use the term "insane" in the sense of a *system of oppression.* R.D. Laing in *The Politics of the Family* (New York: Random House, 1969) views this systematic oppression from a psychological perspective. Rayna Rapp offers an analysis of the family from a multi-class, social and economic perspective in "Family and Class in Contemporary America: Notes towards an Understanding of Ideology," *University of Michigan Papers in Women's Studies,* Special Issue, May 1978; and Lillian Breslow Rubin in *Worlds of Pain: Life in the Working-Class Family* (New York: Basic Books, 1976) presents through interviews a poignant and telling analysis of the systematic deformation of emotional life in white working-class families in the United States.

[8] The major exception is Marjorie Rosen, whose discussion of "Griffith's Girls" in *Popcorn Venus* (New York: Avon Books, 1973) inspired me to go back and take another look at Griffith from a feminist point of view.

[9] Marjorie Rosen, Gary Gordon, "The Story of David Wark Griffith" (a biography of Griffith based on interviews), *Photoplay* (June and July 1916), excerpted in Harry Geduld, ed., *Focus on D.W. Griffith* (New York: Prentice Hall, 1971).

[10] Friedrich Engels, *The Origin of the Family, Private Property and the State* (New York: International Publishers, 1967).

[11] Kate Millett, *Sexual Politics,* pp. 60-61, citing the work of Hugo Beigel.

[12] For a discussion of feminist cinematic treatment of rape, see Lesage, "Disarming Rape: JoAnn Elam's *Rape,*" *Jump Cut* 19 (Winter 1978).

[13] Susan Brownmiller, *Against Our Will: Men, Women and Rape* (New York: Simon and Schuster, 1975).

[14] Some readers may find this conclusion outrageous, so I shall add a few examples from daily life. We have all observed fathers' discomfiture at the thought of their daughters' sexual activity; at the same time male adolescents are excused for "sowing wild oats." And with girls of a younger age, when a father

yells, "Wipe that lipstick off your face!" or challenges, "Where were you so late?" his reaction is a sexually as well as paternally possessive one. It is the sexual connotation of the girl's action that is disturbing to him, and his excuse for his reaction is often that he knows "how men are."

[15] For a psychoanalytic explanation of the cross-cultural and trans-historical division of male and female roles into the "public" and the "domestic" sphere, see Nancy Chodorow, *The Reproduction of Mothering: Psychoanalysis and the Sociology of Gender* (Berkeley: Univ. of California Press, 1978).

[16] D.W. Griffith, "My Early Life," in Geduld, *Focus,* p. 33. That such an act was a lesson in masculinity as well as racism is implied in Griffith's comment that his father winked at the terrified child to assure him all was a joke. What was the black servant feeling? Griffith's inability to ask that question in relating this, his most sacred memory, parallels his inability to depict the real mechanisms oɪ racism in *Broken Blossoms* or *Birth of a Nation.*

[17] D.W. Griffith, "My Early Life," in Geduld, *Focus,* p. 35.

[18] Kate Millett traces the close relation between an esteem for virginity and the fear and desire that women provoke as the "dark force," seen as part of uncontrolled nature and destructive to male-defined culture. (*Sexual Politics,* pp. 72-82). Thus, a paradigmatic variation to *Broken Blossoms* in the treatment of the nuclear family in fictional film is to depict a dark-haired siren destroying families and individual men and social cohesion.

[19] Lillian Gish and Billy Bitzer, in their respective autobiographies, describe the introduction of the Sartov lens; Gish discovered this flattering way of being photographed and promoted it after she first had her passport picture done by Sartov. Lillian Gish (with Ann Pinchot), *The Movies, Mr. Griffith, and Me* (New York: Prentice Hall, 1969); G.W. Bitzer, *G.W. Billy Bitzer, His Life* (New York: Farrar, Straus and Giroux, 1973).

[20] For a discussion of how *Broken Blossoms* was exploited commercially as high art, see Arthur Lenning, "D.W. Griffith and the Making of an Uncoventional Masterpiece," *Film Journal* 1.

[21] Key essays on this subject are Laura Mulvey, "Visual Pleasure and Narrative Cinema," *Screen* 16 (Fall 1975), and Pam Cook and Claire Johnston, "The Place of Women in the Cinema of Raoul Walsh," in Phil Hardy, ed., *Raoul Walsh* (London: Vineyard Press, 1974). A discussion among feminist critics that deals extensively with the subject of how women are presented in dominant male cinema and how this affects us as women viewers can be found in "Women and Film: A Discussion of Feminist Aesthetics," *New German Critique,* 13 (Winter 1978).

[22] Charles Affron's *Star Acting* provides a good formal analysis of this sequence.

[23] For discussions of the adverse effects of presenting woman as victim in a portrait intended to elicit audience sympathy, see my article, "Disarming Rape" and Charles Kleinhans, "Seeing through Cinema-Verité: *Wanda* and *Marilyn Times Five*," *Jump Cut* 1 (May-June 1974).

[24] Ellen E. Morgan, "The Eroticization of Male Dominance/Female Submission," *University of Michigan Papers in Women's Studies* 2 (September 1975).

[25] Angela Carter, *The Sadeian Woman and the Ideology of Pornography* (New York: Harper and Row, 1978), p. 60.

[26] See my extended discussion of *Celine and Julie Go Boating* and that film's relation to female fantasies in "Subversive Fantasies," *Jump Cut* 23/24 (Spring 1981).

CHAPTER 16.

The Perils of Feminist Film Teaching

MICHELLE CITRON AND ELLEN SEITER

> A man has an argument with his girlfriend. The man leaves. The woman gets ready for bed. Later that night, the man returns, breaks into the apartment, stabs the woman to death and stuffs her body into a plastic garbage bag. The man carries the bag downstairs to the alley where he dumps it into a large metal trash receptacle. The man walks off into the night.
>
> — *Plot synopsis, proposed three-minute student film project, Fall 1979*

This fairly typical synopsis of a student film treatment in a university film-production class indicates a learning environment generally hostile to women. Such ideas for films are only one of a complex matrix of elements that contribute to the adversities women face as student filmmakers. Other inhibiting elements include women's access to fundamental skills, cultural myths about art and the artist, traditional pedagogical approaches used to teach filmmaking, and established hierarchies in the university and media institutions. As women film-production teachers we have been working on strategies to combat these many elements, which discourage women from entering filmmaking.

Women frequently drop out of filmmaking, or they never pursue it as a subject for study at all. There are several reasons for this. First, women film students lack visible role models. Students usually enter production classes motivated either by the overwhelming mythic presence of Hollywood or by film-history classes. In either case, they encounter few examples of women in the media. If the male student has an unrealistic dream of being the next Francis Ford Coppola or George Lucas, the female student may find such a dream inconceivable. Sexism, reinforced by the economic structure of the U.S. film industry, has excluded women from becoming directors. Recent attention given to Dorothy Arzner and Ida Lupino reinforces even further these women directors' exceptional status and points out Hollywood's pervasive discrimination against women.

The situation is similar in film-history classes. Documentary and avant-garde film history, as established through texts, museum showings, and college curricula, recognizes only a handful of women. And inclusion of a few women filmmakers in film courses depends even now on the teacher's gender and orientation. On the film department faculty, men outnumber women in the areas of history and criticism, and overwhelmingly so in production. Even in the university, then, women students are unlikely to encounter alternative role models.

PROBLEMS FOR WOMEN PRODUCTION STUDENTS: AN ANALYSIS

Production classes often treat filmmaking as pure technology, as having no intellectual tradition. Or at least many students perceive it that way. The production-class reputation may discourage women who believe their talents are verbal and visual, but not mechanical, from entering the field. Women's hesitation is further aggravated by the widespread belief that women cannot handle heavy and often clumsy equipment. We have been asked countless times, ''What's a little girl like you doing with a big camera like that?'' Both male and female students over-value men's physical strength. What does it matter whether or not men are stronger than women when both are quite capable of handling the equipment?

To really solve these problems, we need broad social changes in both attitudes and opportunities. But some of the difficulties women face in filmmaking classes can be directly improved by responsive pedagogy. First of all, teachers should present technology in a way that recognizes the unequal distribution of technical knowledge in the culture and the negative socialization of women in relationship to technical skills and information. Teachers must be aware of men's particular cultural privilege regarding technology, and they should show an active concern about privileges that they do not share with the students, whether these be the result of class, race or sexual status. In film study, class privilege may have granted some students previous access to equipment — in their homes or in better-funded suburban school districts — and also with money to spend on film stock and processing, which are very expensive and rarely subsidized by university film courses.

Second, teachers should be aware of behavior — their own or their students' — that fosters male domination of the classroom and excludes women from full participation. Third, teachers must reject any approach to film teaching that separates form from content. Such a formalist division is ideological. In particular, it creates an environment where sexism and other reactionary attitudes go unchallenged.

Three power hierarchies affect women's situation in filmmaking classes: male dominance, whether from the teacher or other students; the teacher's position of authority over the student; and the power of technology — knowledge that has traditionally been accessible only to men. Girls' socialization about technology frequently serves to convince them that they are by nature mechanically inept. Their unfamiliarity with many kinds of technical equipment often leads to great anxiety when operating a camera, and sometimes excessive and paralyzing concern about breaking or damaging film equipment.

The conscientious production teacher faces these problems: how to communicate technical information, confront students' attitudes towards technology, and control classroom dynamics that lead to women's feelings of inferiority. When lecturing on film technology, the teacher must create an atmosphere where students can ask questions without embarrassment or self-effacement. The teacher should always avoid unnecessary jargon, especially when working with women who are encountering a technical language for the first time. In some classes, especially with adolescent students, men may continually laugh or talk when women ask questions. Then the teacher should confront the group as a whole with the situation. Discussing the problem openly encourages students to control such offenses through peer pressure, and the discussion also acknowledges as legitimate the women's anxiety. If, for instance, concerned lab instructors initiate these kinds of discussions, this in effect gives women permission to confront male students in the lab who persist in this kind of behavior. Such a supportive atmosphere in the classroom further encourages the women to discuss such problems among themselves outside of class and to form support groups of their own.

A more complicated issue involves the way that the film teacher treats ideas about creativity and the artist. As teachers and filmmakers ourselves, we consider it very important to debunk the romantic myth of the individual artist. A cultural stereotype about artists exists very strongly in the minds of the students. This stereotype has an historical genesis and varies slightly from art to art. Since the Romantic period western artists have tended to define themselves as outsiders, alienated and misunderstood. Such artists (including filmmakers) are stereotypically eccentric, obsessive and seemingly unconcerned with daily material realities or the profit potential of their work. Additionally, in the visual arts, an incapacity to discuss one's work becomes the hallmark of a "genius." The experience of making art seems so personal and complex it cannot possibly be articulated. In the Romantic tradition, art and creativity are perceived as the result of uncontrollable urges and they seemingly have nothing to do with work. This myth of the artist is especially damaging to women.

Historically, culturally recognized artists are men. Clearly all of the above characteristics of the romantic artist are undesirable for any filmmaking student. Each attribute, if adopted by students in their concept of their own role, serves to close students' minds in a learning situation and restricts any sense of community developing in the classroom. By tacitly allowing male students in a filmmaking class to act out this stereotype of the artist, the teacher may be perpetuating an image of artistic production that excludes women. Adverse kinds of behaviors attributable to the Artistic Role must be examined and criticized in the classroom situation, particularly since historically women are excluded from participating in them (and may not want to participate in them).

As teachers, we encourage the idea that in their daily lives everyone makes some form of art. But in learning filmmaking, where technical competence increases student confidence in ideas, men students often feel "naturally" superior. To explicitly criticize this stereotype of creative genius is crucial to establishing a non-sexist pedagogy in filmmaking classes. Socially, we see it as a step towards opening up filmmaking (and art in general) to women, blacks, latinos, working people — all those who have been excluded by the historical and social definition of the artist as white, male and alienated middle class.

We find it effective to begin a semester by discussing how students define the word "create." (We developed this tactic to deal with the particularly imposing title of our freshman course: "Creative Processes in Sight and Sound.") Students write a variety of definitions on the board. Their list usually includes the full range of cultural assumptions about artistic production, especially notions about genius, inspiration, mysticism and originality. The teacher can then suggest the earliest and simplest definition of the word: that is, to make. We stress that in the class students will learn how to make something, and that capacity to make art does not reside with a small number of "talented" individuals. The students' initial assignment leads them to become first aware and then critical of all of the other cultural connotations of the word "create."

Another crucial pedagogical issue in filmmaking is how to teach responsibility. The teacher can never ignore that filmmaking is a powerful social tool. The course must not only impart technical information and skills, but it also must make students aware of filmmakers' accountability for the ideas and implications of their work.

Traditional film teaching emphasizes aesthetics and technique and ignores content. However, in a production class film form cannot be divorced from film content. The film theory which deals with visual coding, narrative conventions of realism and invisible editing certainly should mean as much to the production student as to the criticism student. Because so much of the production teachers' job involves teaching conventions, they must learn to present film techniques as historical and constructed within ideology.

In many production classes a concept like "suspense" is discussed by talking about editing, composition or lighting, and an example from a Hollywood narrative film is shown to illustrate the techniques; for example, the shower sequence from Hitchcock's *Psycho* (1960). Yet "suspense" here hardly comprises a neutral formal concept. Structures of suspense have developed within a particular cultural context, within established genres, and a major part of cinematic suspense depends on depicting woman as victim. When teachers use "classic" Hollywood films like *Psycho* in a production class, they limit their students' intellectual perspective and promote sexism both in the classroom and the media if they neglect to discuss and emphasize specific narrative and formal techniques that perpetuate cinematic violence against women.

In our course, students present their film treatments orally to the entire class and are held accountable for both form and content. We suggest that students make films about something they know or have thought about. And we actively discourage films that merely imitate Hollywood and television. Not promoting merely personal filmmaking, we do advocate content that is important to the student.

Mainstream films and television, which tend to be class biased, racist and sexist, consistently attract our students, who for the most part are white and from middle-class professional families. Most consider themselves to be political liberals and have enough consciousness about racism to censor their own scenarios for overtly racist content. However, many male students submit film treatments that are extremely sexist. Violence against women is a favorite student theme. That male students have such a lack of consciousness about these issues alarms us.

We often receive proposals for student projects like the one described at the opening of this article. Certain patterns recur in these film treatments: revenge films using explicit violence against women; placing women in seemingly dangerous situations which the narrative resolves as merely a flirtatious game; and using violence against women as part of slapstick comedy. In one proposed film, a burglar is shown breaking into an apartment and terrorizing a woman. The film consists of an elaborate chase through the apartment with extreme close-ups of the woman's screaming face intercut with scenes of rats crawling through garbage. The accelerated editing ends with a shot of the woman backed into a corner, screaming as the man approaches wielding a billy-club. Another film treatment shows a woman walking alone at night. A car driven by a man follows and passes her three times, ominously. At the end of the film, the car pulls up next to her and stops; she is shown getting in and smiling. Another film idea, for a "slapstick comedy," portrayed a man hiding behind bushes and repeatedly jumping out to attack women joggers on campus; such images were accompanied by an upbeat Scott Joplin soundtrack.

In class discussions we try to point out the way that such films confirm dangerous social myths, trivialize violence against women, sensationalize this violence, and deny the seriousness of rape. Ideally, the students themselves collectively question these films' content. Often a student filmmaker learns with amazement how many women and men in the class find his film offensive. To discuss film content thoroughly in class is to enlist peer pressure. This can be the most powerful factor in influencing students to change offensive film ideas and in teaching them to recognize their responsibility to the audience. Discussing scenarios accomplishes an object lesson in both film and ideology at the same time.

PRACTICAL TACTICS FROM OUR TEACHING EXPERIENCE

We constantly evaluate both the level and our pacing of the presentation of technical material. We have to make sure that all students comprehend technical information. Surprise quizzes that students hand in but do not sign help us keep track of how well they have absorbed the material. Because filmmaking involves so many "numbers" and brand names, students must understand the categories of film terminology, know where they can look up unfamiliar words, realize that there are often different terms for the same thing (like fullcoat and mag stock), and do a certain amount of memorizing. We often use analogies from more familiar fields, such as the water-faucet explanation of exposure factors in the Time-Life Photography series book, *The Camera*. Frequently, we explain an underlying principle. For example, before outlining the three factors that affect depth of field, we review with the class the concept of the inverse relationship. Often we simply reassure students that we ourselves did not always possess a perfect understanding and knowledge of filmmaking. Such reassurance helps in allaying the students' anxieties.

When demystifying art, the artist and creativity, we find that a good alternative is to emphasize process. If teachers use as an example a film that they made themselves, they can trace the making of that film from the original idea, through treatments and storyboards, rewrites, test shoots, editing and mixing. We emphasize the many changes that occur between the conception of a film idea and the complete film. And we stress that filmmaking is not an individual activity. Crew members, friends and colleagues contribute to a film, as well as subjects or actors who give the filmmaker input. Such an emphasis on *process* gives students a better sense of the time element in making a film, of how filmmakers often change their minds about certain aspects of a film, or of how production may be delayed while raising money or applying for funding. Such a pedagogical tactic gives students a more flexible approach to the filmmaking process than do most production textbooks, and prepares them better for the amount of frustration and disappointment that often accompanies beginning filmmaking.

We structure an emphasis on process into the course by requiring each student to present a film treatment to the class. This helps acquaint students with each other's projects and requires them to articulate their film ideas and present them in summaries or scripts accompanied by storyboards. The storyboards are mimeographed so that each student in the class has a copy of everyone else's treatment. Because we place an importance on these treatments, we show that we stress conceptualization as well as technical performance as criteria for grading. This means all students have one assignment, at least, where the more familiar skills of writing and drafting are important. Discussion of the treatments also serves to diffuse the teacher's authority in giving criticism. Students are encouraged to critique their own work and each others', to think of improvements for projects other than their own, and to anticipate problems with films. Thus, the entire class benefits from the experience of criticism and learns to accept new ideas or critiques from a variety of sources. These benefits do not occur if the students only discuss final projects individually with the instructor.

The assignments for each class, whenever possible, consist of a series of filmmaking exercises, which the students screen and discuss in class. We stress the idea that these are *exercises*. This makes any single lengthy project impossible, and it subverts the students' ideas about themselves as "auteurs" and their films as "masterpieces." We've found that the more specific the assignment for the exercise, the more interesting the students' projects.

Two assignments particularly interesting to women students have been to make a self-portrait in which students must describe themselves without actually appearing in the film, and to film an interaction between two people, which need not be verbal, or spatially and temporally continuous. We advocate these kinds of assignments rather than an exercise to shoot a sequence "à la Hitchcock", or in the manner of film *noir,* because these approaches tend to encourage the student to mimic the kind of ideology expressed in these films as well as the style.

The more often students handle equipment, especially in a trial shooting situation where the teacher is present to answer questions, the more they gain confidence. In all classes whenever possible, the teacher should arrange groups projects and trial shoots. These are the most important factors in equalizing the levels of knowledge and self-assurance with the equipment for men and women students. When dividing into groups for shooting, it is sometimes helpful to form same-sex groups. The advantage for women is that the absence of men reduces the amount of tension they experience when using the equipment, and it prevents the more experienced or aggressive men in the class from taking over the project. Although dividing into same-sex groups may meet with some resistance from the students initially, women students in the class quickly recognize this system's advantages.

In our own experience we have seen significant and encouraging changes in students' attitudes towards and understanding of filmmaking. Yet we have also encountered a great deal of hostility. Women teaching in a non-traditional field initially encounter enormous distrust and disrespect from students who don't expect to find a woman teaching a technical subject. And directly confronting sexism in the classroom often provokes even greater hostility and skepticism towards us as teachers. The problems women teachers face when confronting these issues are increased because we experience such isolation and lack of job security in the university.

Yet all film-production teachers can do much to improve the situation for women students in a film-production class. Dealing with these issues will lead to the increased enrollment of women in filmmaking classes, and eventually to more women teaching film production and making films. What we offer are some partial solutions — until broader solutions and ideological changes take place.

PART FOUR

GAY AND LESBIAN CINEMA

Director Dorothy Arzner

INTRODUCTION

> When the topic is the "image of" the *lesbian* in film or the "function of" the *lesbian* in the text, then whole different issues have to be approached and whole new critical methodologies must be found to deal with those issues.
>
> "Lesbians and Film," *Jump Cut* No. 24/25, 1981

Gay and lesbian film criticism presents a real challenge to straight men and women, beginning with the fact that so little criticism has been published from this perspective.

The collectively written article "Lesbians and Film" in this section represents a major effort to bring a lesbian orientation into the center of feminist criticism. Similarly, when Tom Waugh states that "leftists often see the gay struggle as a civil rights struggle and nothing more" he is making the case for radical changes regarding cultural politics. The articles in Part Four exemplify that case and contribute to the beginning of a serious gay-lesbian critical practice.

Jump Cut No. 16 (1977) carried a special section on gays and film that attempted to survey the basics of gay criticism, to challenge straight readers to examine forms of homophobia in the culture, and to push left culture generally towards a serious incorporation of gay politics and aesthetics. In 1985 Tom Waugh looked back on that work:

> Published in November 1977, the special issue pioneered in an important way dialogue between the gay liberation movement and the left, and focused on the then work-in-progress *Word Is Out* which was to become a watershed in the evolution of gay cinema in the U.S. In retrospect the issue appears to have been timely for other reasons, appearing as it did at the height of the Anita Bryant backlash against gay and lesbian civil rights, one of the first inklings of the New Right's imminent agenda of scapegoating minorities and feminists.

The discussion between Tom Waugh and Chuck Kleinhans, which opens Part Four, provides a good introduction to these issues and offers a brief look at how one of the editors of the magazine evolved in his thinking.

While Waugh and Kleinhans concentrate on the general issues of gay politics, Richard Dyer digs deeply into the recent history of gay representation in the dominant cinema. His focus on four problematic aesthetic concepts — gayness should express itself; gays as ordinary human beings; realism; and stereotyping — allows us to make sense of Hollywood's views of gays. Perhaps more importantly, his rejection of heterosexual aesthetic values turns us in the direction of more appropriate questions for gay art, and for all the issues surrounding representation and gender.

Jump Cut's Lesbian Special Section appeared in 1981. It represented at least two year's preparation and contained both collective discussion on general issues and examples of specific critical work. The introduction to that section, included here as "Lesbians and Film," is both a survey and a manifesto calling for films and theory built on a "more inclusive foundation." As an example of a consciously lesbian cinema, Michelle Citron points to the inventive and comic work of Jan Oxenberg. Citron's appreciation of Oxenberg's films brings us back to the problems outlined earlier by Ruby Rich: when new forms and content remain unnamed, they become lost.

In the 1980s gay and lesbian characters have become somewhat more visible in Hollywood and the avant-garde. Films such as *Personal Best, Making Love, Lianna* — and a rash of TV dramas — plus the radical and controversial *Born in Flames* require the kind of political criticism featured here.

CHAPTER 17.

Gays, Straights, Film and the Left: A Discussion

TOM WAUGH AND CHUCK KLEINHANS

In 1977, *Jump Cut* 16 carried a special section on "Gays and Film" which opened with the following discussion between magazine editor Chuck Kleinhans and gay activist Tom Waugh.

TOM: It's only in the last ten years that the left has re-evaluated its attitude towards women. Similarly, until now the left's attitude towards gays has reproduced the attitudes of the dominant institutions in the most retrogressive ways. For that reason, most gay leftists have more or less dissociated themselves from the left movement and worked only in the gay movement, often abandoning the left after years of scrapping and humiliation. Leftists at best often see the gay struggle as a civil rights struggle and nothing more and fail to see the connection between the oppression of gays and that of women and minorities and the working class.

CHUCK: It's often very hard for any of us to understand the systematic nature of our oppression . . . that it is understandable as a system and not just as what happens to us as individuals. Both gay and straight men have to understand sexism, as a system of oppression, as part of patriarchal capitalist society, not just in terms of how it affects them psychologically or materially but also how it affects women. I'm critical, for example, of the film *Men's Lives* [Dir. Josh Hanig and Will Roberts, 1975] for not making that connection. While it's very good at showing the surface level oppression of men, it never connects that to the operation of sexism within our whole capitalist culture. It fails to see that all men benefit from the oppression of women, whether they want to or not. We need to move to a much more comprehensive analysis and political action. Straight men have to be active in fighting in the interests of gay men. Both gay and straight men have to understand and fight against the oppression of women. And all of us have a stake in replacing capitalism with socialism. Whatever our immediate priorities, we have to realize we're fighting a whole system of exploitation.

In examining my own attitudes, I realize that in the past few years I've tended to think of gays in terms of those who are able to live a relatively open gay lifestyle in several hip professional areas in Chicago. Because those men are "visible," I've tended to think of gay issues more in terms of lifestyle and also to assume that indeed there has been a gradual improvement in the situation — that gays are accepted, or at least tolerated. I've had to see that was a pretty superficial attitude. I was really wrong. The depth of the problem is more apparent, and from what I've seen in Chicago, I think gays and straights who had counted on gradual reform are rethinking their politics.

TOM: There was a lot of illusory "progress" in the early 1970s. What really happened was not so much a liberalization of social attitudes, but an accelerated ghettoization of the gay community in large urban areas where there was a kind of anonymity and defense in numbers. These were ghettos with a definite economic and cultural vitality which led to a false sense of well-being, a kind of complacency on the part of middle-class, unpoliticized gays. People failed to see that the gay community extended far beyond those ghettos and that the liberation of the ghetto was every bit as tenuous as the security of the closet. Now we can see how premature the euphoria of "ghetto-liberation" really was.

Movies made in the atmosphere of so-called liberation might have shown us the same thing — that the new hip tolerance was really a new form of homophobia. I get the feeling that Hollywood and European filmmakers who openly and frankly portray gays really think they're being liberated. It's as if the frankness about rape in a film like *Lipstick* (1976) actually made that film a progressive one. Or as if the brazen affrontery it took to make all of the villains in *The Deep* (1977) black indicated a progressive attitude towards race. It's incredible: popular films like *Scarecrow* (1973), *Slapshot* (1977), *Funny Lady* (1974), *Cross of Iron* (1977), *The Man Who Fell to Earth* (1976), *Barry Lyndon* (1975), instead of being liberal in their use of gay characters, actually perpetuate the most vicious of stereotypes.

Look at *Slapshot*. The movie comes across as hip, realistic and liberal because of all the "frank" homophobic language in the script and the introduction of a "sensitive" lesbian character (actually an insidious stereotype — all she needed was to be satisfied in bed by Paul Newman). But the anti-gay language of the hockey players, which the scriptwriter probably thought would be taken ironically, as signs of macho sexual fear or whatever, actually caters to homophobia. Audiences lap it up. They think it's cute and original to be able to queer-bait openly and without guilt. When Paul Newman tells a widowed businesswoman that she better toughen up her pre-teenaged son or else she'll find him with a cock in his mouth, one of the oldest stereotypes in the book is confirmed, legitimized because it's said by hip, liberal Paul Newman.

CHUCK: I think there's a similar danger within the left, within *Jump Cut,* that we'd run this Special Section on gays and then congratulate ourselves and in effect ghettoize gays by either stopping at that point or saying, "Well, now we have some people who will write about gay films and we'll run them from time to time," rather than really dealing with issues of sexism and gay struggles in all of our criticism. It would reproduce the way men have sometimes dealt with the women's movement, saying, "Well, we'll have a women's page" or letting women write feminist criticism and acting as if that absolves men from dealing with their own sexism or with sexism in the films they make, write about, or teach about.

TOM: You're right that that's a dangerous kind of tokenism, but film culture hasn't even gotten to the stage of tokenism yet. There are all kinds of areas which should be impossible to discuss without dealing with the gay question. But it's never dealt with; it's politely ignored.

I'm not talking only of films like *Dog Day Afternoon* (1976), where the subject is obvious: the main character is gay. But those areas where a gay reference is obviously suppressed or visible just below the surface. Male buddy films, for example, and most male action genres. I'm not saying such films have consciously touched on any truths about homosexual components of male-to-male relationships, but the fear of such truths is usually clearly articulated; those films show the repression of such truths, whatever they may be.

Another area where the gay question is a crucial one but is always suppressed is that whole stream of European cinema which expresses a kind of "decadent" or androgynous sensibility, regardless of whether it deals explicitly with gayness. I'm thinking of the Italians of course — Fellini, Bertolucci, Visconti, Zeffirelli, Pasolini, but also of Fassbinder, Daniel Schmid, Losey, Ken Russell, Jansco, and Roeg, etc., etc. Gayness is never raised in criticism of those films, leftist or otherwise. The fact, for example, that *The Conformist* (1970) is positing some vague and ambiguous connection between fascism and homosexuality is not interrogated in any criticism of Bertolucci that I've seen.

The erotic cinema and pornography are another area where the gay perspective is suppressed. I thought it was shocking when *Cineaste* magazine ran their survey on "Pornography and the Left," and they invited comments from five or six "authorities" and it never occurred to them to ask an openly gay person for his or her opinion. Particularly since the gay pornography industry is such a huge one and pornography has had such a formative influence on gay culture, a progressive influence even, according to many people.

CHUCK: In what sense progressive?

TOM: Before the days of an openly visible gay movement, the only way for many gay people to discover and explore their own homosexuality was through pornography. That's how they recognized certain things about themselves, about their own bodies, that there were other people out there like themselves, that they were not alone. . . . It was so typical of leftist cultural attitudes for *Cineaste* to have this glaring omission in their "comprehensive" treatment of the issue of pornography. I think the feminist attitude to pornography is often quite different from the gay male one.

With a few important exceptions, I think that gay men are almost always opposed to any form of censorship, because they remember what it was like in the closet, and they know that censorship will always be applied to their own legitimate cultural expression as soon as it's permitted anywhere. That's what's happening in New York right now: no sooner does the *New York Times* makes its hypocritical, puritanical decision to refuse advertising for porno films than they take it upon themselves as well to decide what gay cultural manifestations are decent enough to be advertised in a family newspaper, refusing to run an ad for a gay theatrical piece called *Gulp* — with no pornographic content whatsoever — because somebody didn't like the title. It's the same with the Canadian government's decision to block the import of a gay sex manual while admitting a real flood of the comparable hetero manual, *The Joy of Sex*. Or the U.S. prison system's refusal to allow gay prisoners to receive gay publications. The issue of censorship is far from closed.

CHUCK: Another aspect of the liberalism that I talked of before can manifest itself in straight men accepting gay men or gay film criticism but without learning what gay men have to say to them as men. I think straights can often be passive and smug about it. But they should become more active in learning about gay liberation. What do you think straight men should do to become more active in coming to terms with their own sexism and fighting it?

TOM: Rather than telling straight men what they should or should not do, I think I'd rather say how important it is for gays within the left to come out and form a visible and vocal presence within both the straight left and the unpoliticized gay movement. It's up to straight men to choose their own methods of self-criticism and activism.

CHAPTER 18.

Rejecting Straight Ideals: Gays in Film

RICHARD DYER

Since the gay movement began we have insisted on the centrality of the media (understood in its widest sense) as a carrier, reinforcer or shaper of our oppression. Sometimes we have gone overboard in blaming the mass media — they are only one of the instruments of oppression. More important, we have tended to condemn images of gayness in the name of aesthetic concepts and values that are highly problematic.

We've tended to demand that gay characters and themes be represented according to certain ideas and ideals about what art is, without seeing that such ideas and ideals are *straight* ones, not neutral or transparent but imbued with a sexual ideology that has anti-gayness as one of its cornerstones. When those notions are applied to films, what appears to be "given" aesthetic principles are, in however ambiguous a way, also principles of heterosexual hegemony.

"GAYNESS SHOULD EXPRESS ITSELF ON FILM."

Many critics, especially in gay publications, are concerned with how gayness expresses itself on film. I am thinking particularly of Jack Babuscio's articles in *Gay News,* a leading gay rights magazine in England. (And let me make it clear right now that what follows is not an "attack"; Jack's articles raise central issues in a widely available non-pornographic forum, and his articles have helped me enormously in trying to think through these issues.) Running through all of these articles is the notion of the "gay sensibility," which he defines as

> a creative energy reflecting a consciousness *different* from the main-
> stream, a heightened awareness of certain human complications of feel-

ing that spring from the fact of social oppression; in fact, a perception of the world which is coloured, shaped, directed and defined by the fact of one's homosexuality. (GN 82; p. 15.)

Many of his articles are concerned with the way this sensibility "surfaces" in films — for example, his pieces on John Schlesinger (GN 74) and James Dean (GN 79).

There is already a problem here with the notion of a gay sensibility. Jack tends to write as if the very fact of being oppressed, and of being able to pass as straight because one's stigma need not show, automatically produces the gay sensibility. I am certainly happy to acknowledge the fact of the gay sensibility, but it has to be understood as something that has been and is produced and praised in history and culture: it is the specific way we (or rather, a relatively "out" minority) have found of coping with and resisting our oppression and our peculiar situation as "invisible" stigmatized people. Oppression does not just "produce" a subcultural sensibility; it merely provides the conditions in relation to which oppressed people create their own subculture and attendant sensibility.

A second problem is that it is in fact rather hard for an individual sensibility to surface in a film. This is partly because of the sheer numbers of people who work on a film, in an often fragmented and long-drawn-out organization of production; even the director has limited room for manoeuvre.[1] But it is more importantly because any artist in any medium whatsoever is working with a tradition, a set of conventions imbued with meanings that she or he cannot change, and indeed of which she or he is most likely not aware. Even if films did have individual authors (as most "underground" films do),[2] it would still not alter the problem. The author may have any qualities you like; but the cinematic language has connotations and conventions that escape the author.

Take a film like *The Detective* (1968) which sets out to be sympathetic, puts a major star (Frank Sinatra) as a liberal defender of gays (in what he says, if not altogether in what he does) and details some of the forms our oppression (and self-oppression) take. That film cannot, all the same, help but reproduce the dominant image of gays. The actual conventions of the film are more powerful than the intentions of scriptwriter and star. Thus the star's unassailable heterosexuality and centrality to the action enforce a narrative function of gay passivity, requiring a straight to act for us. The bleak view of sexual relations in thrillers like this means that gayness is seen as part of a web of sexual sickness, equated especially with the hero's wife's nymphomania (that is, she fancies men other than him). The gay scene can only legitimately be shown at points in the plot relating to crime (why else would Sinatra be interested?), and so enforces the link between gayness, deviancy and crime. And the actual visualization of the gay scene can find no way around the impression of the grotesque. The milieu is sketched in by cutting from bizarre face to bizarre face, accompanied by snatches of dialogue lifted out of context, as the protagonist supposedly looks around and takes in the gay environment. This is a convention of representing the gay scene: compare similar scenes in *The Killing of Sister George* (1968), *PJ* (1967), *The Naked Civil Servant* (1976), and so on.

Nor is this problem confined to commercial cinema. (Indeed, as Claire Johnston has pointed out, the very obviousness of the conventions in commercial cinema may mean that it is easier to manipulate in progressive ways than the hidden conventions of ''art cinema''.)[3] Thus in contemporary French cinema there is really little to choose between the lesbian in *Emmanuelle* (Jaechlin 1974), an obvious exploitation film, and those in *Les Biches,* directed by critically acclaimed Claude Chabrol (1967), and the feminist film *A Very Curious Girl* (Kaplan, 1969) — except that she is actually rather nicer in *Emmanuelle*. This is because in every case the film is made within a straight framework, women seen only in relation to men, and the lesbianism is there as a facet of the heterosexual world view. In the case of the first two, the attraction of lesbianism is evoked the better to assert the superiority of heterosexuality. In the case of *A Very Curious Girl,* the lesbian seems to represent a ''sick'' way of being an independent woman over against the heroine's independence via prostitution (which both allows her to revenge herself on men and gives her enough money to leave the village). In no case is lesbianism expressing *itself.*

In this perspective, Jack Babuscio's article on James Dean is instructive. He bases his argument on the hints of gayness in Dean's recent biographies, and suggests that Dean's gayness informs his three screen roles, giving them ''depth,'' ''warmth'' and ''sensitivity.'' Thus *Giant* (1956), for instance, allowed him to express ''the inability of adolescents to relate to the sexual roles played out by parents.'' Now in terms of how a particular screen image happened to come about, the role of Dean's gay sensibility in modifying and shaping it may well have been crucial, and it is polemically important to say so. But at the same time one has to see that, as an expression of gayness, the role is deformed. There is never the slightest suggestion in any of his roles that Dean is gay; Plato's ''crush'' on him in *Rebel Without a Cause* (Ray, 1955) is by no flicker of recognition reciprocated by him, and there is no other such attachment in the other two films.

At one level of course, Dean, quite possibly through his gayness, did help launch a way of being human and male on film without being particularly ''masculine'' — as did also, perhaps, Montgomery Clift and Anthony Perkins — and that is a contribution to the struggle against the sex roles. But this struggle could only be shown at the expense of the character's gayness: he had to be seen as emphatically heterosexual. Moreover, the narrative frameworks of the films implicitly reinforce the heterosexual, sex-role norms. The point about Dean's roles as *roles* (rather than the qualities his performance suggests, which may well be in contradiction with the roles) is that he is, in *East of Eden* (1955) and *Rebel Without a Cause*, the son of, in the first case, a strong mother, and in the second a weak father. The stress is on the "extraordinary" quality of these parents: Jo Van Fleet in *Eden* was photographed in shadow and with dramatic "expressionist" techniques of lighting and camera angle; Jim Backus played for laughs and pathos in *Rebel*. This presentation implies the properness of the ordinary parental roles of "weak" mothers and "strong" fathers.

Dean of course had a following, and it was undoubtedly linked to the kind of non-butch image of being a man that he incarnated. This was an image that gay men have been in a particularly good position to imagine and define — I don't want to deny his contribution or its gay roots. But this contradiction is, inevitably, at the expense of gayness, and it is moreover in an artistic form where the function of his role in the narrative and the construction of other characters through performance and filming contradict the implications of his image. People may have taken away an image of gentle sensitive ways of being a man, but they may also have taken away a sense of neurosis born of inadequately performed sex roles. Films, and most art, are usually as contradictory and open to alternative interpretations as this; and as long as it is a question of inserting gayness into films as they are, any full, undeformed expression of the gay sensibility will tend within any film to offer a weak counterpoint to the reinforcement of heterosexual and sex-role norms.

"GAYS AS ORDINARY HUMAN BEINGS."

A very common stance of straight critics, and alas of many within the gay movement (for we so easily take over straight notions without realizing how inapplicable they are to our situation), is that films should show that gay people are just ordinary human beings. In this line of thought, highest praise is granted to those films where it is apparently "incidental" that the characters and milieu are gay.

Now it may be true that we are still at the stage where we need to assert, to others and to ourselves, that we are part of the human race. But such assumptions assume that there is no real difference between being gay and being straight. Yet, from a materialist standpoint, gayness is different physically, emotionally and socially from hetero-sexuality.

It is physically different not in the sense of involving different genetic factors (the equivalent sexist argument for the fascist arguments of behavioral psychology) but in the sense of being a different physical activity — two women in bed together are not the same as a man and woman together or two men. It is different emotionally because it involves two people who have received broadly the same socialization (being both the same gender) and have thus formed their personalities in relation to the same pressures and experiences.

It is socially different because it is oppressed. Oppression enters into straight relationships of course, partly through the legacy of puritanism in its various forms and partly through the oppression within straight relationships by men. But the heterosexual impulse is not of itself condemned (except in extreme instances) and an institutionalized space is allowed for it in marriage. We, on the other hand, have nearly always been condemned even for having gay desires, and no real social legiti-macy (in a wider sense than mere lack of legal constraints) has ever been allowed us. I don't wish to imply that we are different in every way from heterosexuals — in aspects of our lives not directly involving relationships we are, clearly, the same as heterosexuals. Our bodily functions, how we do our work, our intellectual and creative abilities, all these are in no way different from straights . . . except insofar as they involve relationships. The trouble is of course that they do — so much of life is relationships and even where no physical sexual expression is given to them, the sexual reality of our lives necessarily informs them.

What this boils down to in films is that if you are representing sexual and emotional relationships on screen, it does make a difference whether they are gay or straight. One will not do as a metaphor for the other. Nor will either do as general metaphors for human sexuality and relationships. In assessing, for instance, the kind of power struggles and games portrayed in Robert Aldrich's *The Killing of Sister George,* Stanley Donen's *Staircase* (1969), Rainer Werner Fassbinder's *The Bitter Tears of Petra Van Kant* (1972), or William Friedkin's *The Boys in the Band* (1970), one has to decide whether these are the power games going on in gay relationships (formed and practised in a situation of oppression) or whether these are the power games going on in straight relationships (formed and practised in a situation where men oppress women) transposed to ostensibly gay characters in order to give the verdict of ''sick'' and ''neurotic'' to heterosexual hang-ups by ascribing them to homosexual people. The films mentioned seem to me to be lacking in any sense of reality of oppression (the social situation of gayness) and of gay sexuality (the physical activity of gayness), which makes the second interpretation the more likely.

A further reason for accepting this interpretation is that it is a characteristic of some, a minority, gay relationships to imitate straight "marriages." Thus superficially, seen from the outside, gay relationships can be reduced to the forms of conflict of straight ones, while at the same time implying that it is the "tragic" impossibility of gays to actually be married straights that accounts for the conflicts. In this way, such domestic dramas of "gay" life are doubly reassuring for the straight audience — they allow it to view problems of heterosexuality (which psychologically they no doubt need to) without being shown these problems as rooted in the present structure of heterosexual relationships. The ideal of heterosexuality is preserved when we see how its problems work out so tragically for gays. All this is confirmed by the way straight critics, presented with a similar drama involving heterosexuals, *Who's Afraid of Virginia Woolf?* (1966), promptly turned round and asserted, despite Albee's assurances to the contrary, that it was really a disguised homosexual play.

REALISM AND DOMINANT IDEOLOGY

Lingering behind much of the criticism of the representation of gays is the feeling that films about gays are not real, they do not show gay people as they really are.

Realism is one of the trickiest terms in the whole critical vocabulary — yet it is endlessly evoked, often with recourse to synonyms like "convincing," "true-to-life," "plausible" and so on. What this means is that we require films to present us with settings, people or events that as closely as possible resemble day-to-day life, granted a little artistic license. We tend not to recognize how conventional realism in film is, although one only has to look at the realism of earlier periods (British documentary of the 1930s, Italian Neorealism, "Method" acting) to see both how stylized all realisms actually are and how each realist style carries all sorts of cultural and historical connotations with it.

However, the problem with realism is not so much our blindness to the conventionality of the realism of our own times, but the fact that realism is only capable of capturing the surface of life — it cannot "capture" what is going on inside people's heads nor can it capture the social forces that determine the surface of life.

In fact it is very hard for "realism" to do anything but reproduce dominant ideology. That is, in everyday life, objects and appearances have, first, an objective status in the bio-physical world, and second, a range of potential significances for us individually. Dominant in that range is what our culture has taught us to associate with them. But once objects and appearances are filmed, they can only mean to us what they mean in the film. They are signs whose only bio-physical status is celluloid. It then becomes exceedingly difficult for them to mean anything but what they predominantly mean in culture.

Thus, to show gay people "realistically" on the screen means to show them in conventions of the prevailing cinematic realism; which in turn means to reproduce society's prevailing ideas and assumptions about how gays really are. Whatever its intentions (and the intentions of realist filmmakers are seldom anything but generous), a "realist" film about gays is unlikely to challenge the assumptions of most of the audience about what gays are like — for while we as gays may read the everyday surface represented (perhaps quite accurately) according to our subcultural understandings, the rest of the audience is perfectly free to read it according to its dominant cultural understandings.

Realism can, within its conventions, show the look of gay life, but it cannot show how that life feels and what it means to gay people, nor can it show the social pressures that act on gay people and so produce the look of gay life. This I think is neatly shown up by *Victim* (1961), a British film directed by Basil Dearden, which is a mixture of liberal realism and crime thriller. The notion of oppression certainly comes across in the film, but only because of the non-realist elements — that is, because it is a major star (Dirk Bogarde, then a pin-up) who is got at for being gay and because the thriller narrative clearly assigns villainy to the blackmailers and not the gays (this being the sort of thriller in which there is no moral ambiguity about who the goodies and the baddies are). On the other hand, the depiction of gay life is, in the conventions of the time, realistic enough. But the conventions of the time are such that real can only mean the kind of "sickness" view of homosexuality that the film's title would suggest. Thus while it does not reproduce the connotation of gayness as "evil," it does reproduce the connotation of "sickness" that the Wolfenden Report was to reveal as the dominant bourgeois view of gayness.[4]

STEREOTYPES AND IDEOLOGY IN ART

No term is more frequent in gay criticism of the cinema than "stereotype." Certainly we are right to be angry about the succession of pathetic, ridiculous and grotesque figures supposed to be us up there on the screen.

We may define stereotype as a method of one-dimensional characterization — that is, of constructing a total character by the very mention of one dimension of her or his characteristics. Thus to know that a character is lesbian is immediately to know that she is aggressive, frustrated, loud-mouthed, big-boned and perverse. All art, indeed all our thoughts about the world, uses typecasting but when we label some-one a ''grocer'' or ''doctor,'' we usually assume that this does not tell us all we need to know about him (and we usually assume it is a man). Whereas it is assumed by stereotypes such as the dumb blonde, the happy nigger, the bull dyke and the camp queen that we know all we need to.

Thus far we can agree that stereotyping is a Bad Thing. However, behind this notion of stereotypes there lingers another notion which may be equally undesirable. This is the idea of the ''rounded'' character, the type of character construction practised by nineteenth-century novelists and advocated by theorists such as E.M. Forster. This is *not* the ''natu-ral'' way of ''depicting people'' in art, but a particular artistic method for constructing protagonists in a particular narrative tradition. It is a method that has inscribed in it certain of the dominant values of western society — above all, individualism, the belief that an individual is above all important in and for himself, rather than a belief in the impor-tance of the individual for her or his class, community or sisters and brothers. This cardinal precept of bourgeois ideology as against feudal or socialist ideology is built right into the notion of the ''rounded charac-ter,'' who may well feel some pulls of allegiance to groups with whom she or he identifies, but who is ultimately seen as distinct and separate from the group, and in many cases, antagonistic to it. Rounded charac-terization is then far from ideal when you need (as we do) expressions of solidarity, common cause, class consciousness, fraternity and sorority.

What we need is not the replacement of stereotypes by rounded gay characters, though it would I think be wrong to underestimate the *tem-porarily* progressive impact of films that do use rounded character-ization of gay characters; this breaks the rules. It is a surprise to find Peter Finch in John Schlesinger's *Sunday Bloody Sunday* (1971) treated with the same trappings of ''roundness'' as Glenda Jackson. What we need is rather the development of positively valued gay types. This is representation of gay people which, on the one hand, functions against stereotypes, for it does not deny individual differences from the broad category to which the individual belongs. But it also does not function just like ''rounded'' characterizations; it does not diminish our sense of a character's belonging to and acting in solidarity with his or her social group.

What the positions just discussed seem to lack is any concept of the operation of ideology in art. Films are treated as transparent, neutral, a mere medium, and the distorted representation of gayness as a correcta-ble, regrettable fault. As long as the mesh between artistic form and dominant ideology is ignored, no radical critique of gays in films can be accomplished.

Where gayness occurs in films it does so as *part of* dominant ideology. It is not there to express itself, but rather to express something about sexuality in general *as understood by heterosexuals*. Gayness is used to define normality, to suggest the thrill and/or terror of decadence, to embody neurotic sexuality, or to perform various artistic-ideological functions that in the end assert the superiority of heterosexuality. We are wrong to assume that anti-gayness in films is a mere aberration on the part of straight society. How homosexuality is thought and felt by heterosexuals is part and parcel of the way the culture teaches them (and us) to think and feel about their heterosexuality. Anti-gayness is not a discrete ideological system, but part of the overall sexual ideology of our culture.

This ideology is complicated. There are many inflections of the heterosexual norms, and much of the analysis of images of gayness has to take this into account. Gayness in the U.S. thriller tradition called "film noir" — for example, *The Maltese Falcon* (1941), *In A Lonely Place* (1950), *Gilda* (1946), and also arguable later in cases such as *Gunn* (1967) — is part of a web of sexual fear and anxiety (especially in the form of sexually potent women who endanger the hero). Another type of example is *Victim*, which is one of a whole series of British films treating sexual-social issues (such as prostitution, child-molesting, adultery) as "problems" and "sickness." How the gayness is represented derives from the particular inflection of the ideology of the time.

Moreover, and here we can take hope, ideology is contradictory, ambiguous, full of gaps and fissures. Straight culture is attracted as well as repelled by gayness, and films do show the differing pressures of these responses. Gay culture, although itself formed and deformed in the shadow of straight culture, does contain oppositional elements within it. Gayness always at the very least raises the spectre of alternatives to the family, the sex-roles and male dominance. Thus, take an example of an extremely conventional, bourgeois, "well-made" film, *Summer Wishes, Winter Dreams* (1973), a film in which the very briefly shown gay characters are presented as performing ballet grotesques. Not on the face of it a positive assertion of gayness, the film centers on the rifts and cruelties of a heterosexual relationship. At the end of the picture the gay relationship, although not shown, is evoked as a positive, happy one (the fact that it is off-screen suggests how hard it is to find *images* to evoke this). Moreover, the dilemma of the central character (Joanne Woodward) is structured in the film (as the title indicates) through dreams (the nightmare of the ballet-gay) and wishes (sentimental reconciliation of son within the family unit). Her anguish is shown to stem not from realities themselves but from how she thinks about realities. There is thus an undertow to the film which begins to raise questions and intuitions about the whole edifice of marriage, sexual relationships and so on.

It is to such undertows that we should look, for they are the most likely sources of a cinema that undermines heterosexual artistic hegemony from within. In the process these undertows may create a form of artistic language that comprehends all of human sexuality and relationships.

NOTES

[1] See Ed Buscombe, ''Ideas of Authorship,'' in *Screen,* 14: 1973, pp. 75-85.

[2] Gays have been particularly influential in the development of underground cinema; e.g., the work of Kenneth Anger, Constance Beeson, Jack Smith, Gregory Markopoulos.

[3] See Clare Johnston, *Notes on Women's Cinema,* (London: S.E.F.T., 1973).

[4] The Wolfenden report was a government sponsored report on prostitution and homosexuality, which recommended that the latter be made legal between consenting adults over the age of 21 on the grounds that gayness was a relatively harmless and incurable sickness, which moreover could not be successfully policed. It was published in 1957.

CHAPTER 19.

Lesbians and Film

EDITH BECKER, MICHELLE CITRON,
JULIA LESAGE, AND B. RUBY RICH

It sometimes seems to us that lesbianism is the hole in the heart of feminist film criticism. We have been working in this area for a number of years, and while we believe that feminist criticism has developed new theoretical tools for examining cinematic images, structures and themes, nevertheless we see a failure to confront lesbian issues.

It is important, and possible, to begin this work now. The space for such a discussion has been made possible by the evolution of the lesbian movement, both as an autonomous development and in conjunction with feminist, left and gay male struggles. The intellectual and political groundwork has been established, within the lesbian movement, and we can now draw upon this for its application to film. Furthermore, there is now a clear audience and support for such film criticism. The creation of a lesbian film criticism is particularly urgent, given the intensified use of the lesbian as a negative sign in Hollywood movies and the continuing space assigned to lesbians as gratification of male fantasy in pornography and a distressing number of male avant-garde films. Equally important as an impetus for a new criticism is the rise of an independent lesbian cinema, underacknowledged and in need of attention.

Jump Cut has analyzed film practice in our society and its role in reinforcing oppressions based on race, sex or class. Acknowledging connections between the individual psyche and social history, we find it useful to examine film as a cultural institution which excessively promotes as a norm the single option of heterosexuality. The articulation of sexuality is neither natural nor inevitable; it is shaped and determined by a given society within a particular historical moment. (See, for exam-

Lesbians are sharks, vampires, creatures from the deep lagoon, godzillas, hydrogen bombs, inventions of the laboratory, werewolves — all of whom stalk Beverly Hills by night. Christopher Lee, in drag, in the Hammer Films middle-period, is my ideal lesbian.

— Bertha Harris

ple, Weimar Germany or fifth-century Greece for notable examples of difference.) This historically-determined sexuality may be expressed personally between individuals or enforced publicly through institutions. It is always disguised as "natural" to mask its ideological function. What we consider entertainment depends in large part upon our expectations of sexual identity and its depiction in film. Yet, film's role in enforcing heterosexuality has hardly been challenged.

Feminist film criticism has analyzed film texts and film reception to explicate women's place within male culture and to extricate us from that place. Unfortunately, such criticism has too often accepted heterosexuality as its norm. The refusal to deal with a lesbian perspective has warped film criticism as well as the larger political and intellectual context, including discussions of ideology, popular culture and psychoanalysis. A lesbian perspective, however, can connect in new ways our views of culture, fantasy and desire, and women's oppression, clarifying how these replicate a patriarchal power structure and how that, in turn, finds expression on the screen.

The seemingly simple replacement of the subject "woman" with the subject "lesbian" radically redefines feminist film criticism. When the topic is the "image of" the *lesbian* in film or the "function of" the *lesbian* in the text, whole different issues have to be approached. Whole new critical methodologies must be found to deal with these issues.

MAINSTREAM FILM AND THE SUPPRESSION OF POSITIVE IMAGES

Lesbians are nearly invisible in mainstream cinematic history, except as evil or negative-example characters. There is the lesbian as villainess, exemplified in films such as *Windows* (1978). There is the lesbian as vampire, both metaphorically (as in Claude Chabrol's *Les Biches,* 1967, or Roberto Rossellini's *Rome, Open City,* 1944-45) and quite literally, as in the genre of lesbian vampire movies. There is the brutal bull dyke, ranging from the dyke in *Touch of Evil* (1958) who just wants to watch to the dyke in *Farewell My Lovely* (1944) who insists on action. As feminist critics we should pay attention to these negative images because they are not only about lesbianism but, in fact, are about the containment of women's sexuality and independence.

Furthermore, negative stereotypes about lesbians have a lot to teach us about the limitations of any "positive image" approach to the depiction of women in Hollywood film. These limitations come from the fact that positive images, like negative images, suppress contradiction and are thus static. For example, *Julia* (1977) does not develop the complexities of being a writer, or the contradictions of being a political organizer and mother, or the complexities of being lesbians (if in fact they are). We are just asked to admire the female protagonists. Another limitation could be demonstrated by imagining the substitution of lesbians into most of the stories we have on television or in film. For example, if one of Charlie's Angels were a lesbian, this would probably not change the blatant sexism or bourgeois ideology of the show, or its emphasis on individual solutions to social problems.

There are instances in which we could imagine the progressive nature of substitution. For example, the substitution of a lesbian couple for a heterosexual one could in fact substantially alter the narrative structures of film romance. Yet, the economic pressures of marketing and film production guarantee that in a homophobic society, any authentic "positive image" of lesbian romantic love remains too great a risk ever to find direct expression on the screen. *Windows,* for instance, displaces lesbian attraction, turning its expression into violence. Mainstream cinema employs a traditional dichotomy of positive/negative, using allegedly lesbian villainesses to punish those characters who deviate from the norms of domesticity or romantic love. Heterosexuality is the positive, lesbianism the negative.

Ironically, then, the most explicit vision of lesbianism has been left to pornography, where the lesbian loses her menace and becomes a turn-on. Men maintain control over women by creating the fantasy images of women that they need. Pornography "controls" and uses lesbianism by defining it purely as a form of genital sexuality which, in being watched, can thereby be recuperated into male fantasy. As long as lesbianism remains a component of pornography made by and for men, lesbian sexuality will be received by most sectors of the dominant society *as* pornography. Still, pornographic codes are not omnipresent. They cannot be granted so much power that the depiction of sexuality is no longer an option for lesbian filmmakers.

If the love relationship between women is too often a negative image, it would seem logical to look to cinematic portrayals of women's friendships as an alternative. However, female friendship is itself limited in cinema. In the multitude of buddy films, pairs of men get to act out their adventure fantasies. Women's friendships in film, on the other

> Lesbians are women who survive without men financially and emotion-
> ally, representing the ultimate in an independent life style. Lesbians are
> the women who battle day by day to show that women are valid human
> beings, not just appendages of men. . . . Lesbians are the women who are
> penalized for their sexuality more than any other women on earth.
>
> — Sidney Abbott and Barbara Love

hand, bear comparison with the types of sisters in patriarchal literature,
described by Louise Bernikow in *Among Women*. Like those sisters,
women friends are shown as either: trying to get "the man's something" and fighting over who gets it (*All About Eve,* 1950) turning
against each other (*The Women,* 1939) sacrificing self to familial devo-
tion (*Little Women,* 1949) or accepting the Judgment of Paris that splits
women into narrowly defined "I'm This/You're That" sets of roles
(*The Turning Point,* 1977).

In cinema, even women's friendships revolve around men. Just as
the supposed visibility of "woman" and "lesbian" in film has turned
out to be fraudulent, so cinematic friendships between women are
equally illusionary (with the exception of rare token scenes in such films
as *Mildred Pierce,* 1945, or *Coal Miner's Daughter,* 1980). None of
the richness of women's real relations appears.

It is revealing to chart the pairings that are either acceptable or
unacceptable in popular films:

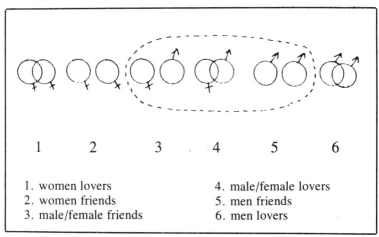

1. women lovers
2. women friends
3. male/female friends
4. male/female lovers
5. men friends
6. men lovers

Both extremes of the spectrum — authentic portrayals of lesbianism or
gay male relations — fall out of bounds for the dominant cinema. In
categories No. 1 and No. 5, there is a discrepancy at work: the ideal-

ization of male friendships and debasement of female friendships. The only honorable categories left to the skewed middle of the chart are predictably male/female friendship, male/male friendship, and male/female coupling. Women don't fare very well in these three categories. Women may appear as a momentary diversion in the buddy films. Women have traditionally been kept in line through family ties and romantic love. In the films that depict male/female friendship, women form an alliance with men that mirrors the power balance in the larger society: in other words, the friendship is a mentor-student model (as in *Norma Rae,* 1979). Or the friendship may simply provide the foreplay for eventual romance (as in *The Electric Horseman,* 1980). Even worse is the male/female friendship that women form at the expense of their friendships with other women, whom the man now replaces (as in *Kramer vs. Kramer,* 1980).

The suppression of categories No. 1 and No. 2 suggests the reality of the very continuum between lesbians and other women that the dominant cinema usually takes pains to deny. Perhaps the real taboo is not sexuality between women, but the affirmation of *any* associations between women that are primary and exclusive of men. Or, perhaps the potential for sexuality between women is itself so strong a threat that it blocks the depiction of even female friendship.

The world of women is banned from film. Female associations could include intellectual relations, work projects or emotional exchanges. Presumably, lesbians deserve visibility in these contexts, but mainstream cinema makes that impossible by separating off the "lesbian" as a being not only defined by, but limited to, her sexuality. Films don't show lesbians working together because that provides no voyeuristic interest for the male viewer. Straight women working together provide just as little interest. Traditionally women are represented in cinema almost exclusively as sexual objects for the use of the male character within the film and/or the man in the audience. Therefore, the depiction of women (whether heterosexual or lesbian) in primary association with each other would be profoundly discomforting and likely to provoke the use of "lesbian" as a derogatory label, because women are acting as self-defined beings, not reacting to men.

Given the absence of any real lesbian "image" on the screen, the lesbian audience over the years has had to make do by identifying with portrayals of strong female characters, adventurous male characters or occasional women's friendships. It's often a case of settling for crumbs. One source of pleasure has been the rare scene of an actress with a cult reputation acting out that rumored sexuality on the screen, such as Marlene Dietrich kissing another woman in *Morocco* (1930).

My only books
Were women's looks.

— Nathalie Barney

THE FILM SUBTEXT, AND GOSSIP

The most important viewing strategy has been to concentrate on the subtext, the "hidden" meaning, of commercial films. The notion of the lesbian subtext depends upon the knowledge, suspicion or hope that some participants in the film (director, actress, screenwriter) were themselves lesbians, and that their perspective can be discerned in the film even though disguised. Subtexting, then, depends for its cues upon gossip.

Gossip provides the official unrecorded history of lesbian participation in film. Actresses and directors have had to hide their identity in order to preserve their careers in a homophobic society. For actresses, the star system has depended upon a vast public's fantasy identification with the glamorous woman; the knowledge that the star was a lesbian would have ended her career. With the advent of the sound-film era and the massive industrialization of film production and distribution, a time when most women directors were drummed out of the field as a financial liability, being openly lesbian was obviously out of the question.

Knowing a director's sexual identity does not necessarily provide a formula for interpreting the work. A film by a lesbian director or writer may or may not advance "positive" lesbian characters; it may have no lesbian content at all. On the other hand, *not* to know details of lesbian participation in film production is a problem in constructing any solid lesbian history. One example is the case of Dorothy Arzner, Hollywood's only woman career-director of the 1920s through the 1940s, whose style of dress and attention to independent woman characters in her films has prompted the search for a lesbian subtext in her work — despite the careful absence of any statements by Arzner herself that could encourage such an undertaking.

In the case of directors whose work isn't specifically feminist, whose lives are strictly closeted, or in the case of lesbian actresses enacting prescribed roles, the burden of proof for a lesbian analysis frequently depends upon the interpretation of style. One example would be the silent film *Salome* (1923), produced by its star Alla Nazimova, whose lesbianism is discussed in Kenneth Anger's book *Hollywood Babylon* and caricatured in Ken Russell's film *Valentino* (1977). *Salome*'s mannered acting, art nouveau costumes and set design, and all-homosexual cast combine to evoke the homosexual aesthetic of the Oscar Wilde, Aubrey Beardsley circle.

The lesbian viewer may also pay attention to the frequence of disjunction between actress and role within a film: that is, an actress with a lesbian reputation may act ''out of character'' and seem to address the audience from the standpoint of her off-screen persona despite her supposed on-screen heterosexuality. A glance, a costume, a gesture, is enough to give the cue.

Gossip feeds into audience expectation and interpretation. Long denigrated in our culture, gossip nevertheless serves a crucial purpose in the survival of subcultural identity within an oppressive society. If oral history is the history of those denied control of the printed record, gossip is the history of those who cannot even speak in their own first-person voice. While gossip transpires at the private level of conversation, subtexting is the route by which dominant cultural products can be used to serve subcultural needs, by annexing a mass product (movies) alien to lesbian identity.

Given the importance of subcultural identification, much lesbian film viewing and criticism depends upon subtexting. Such readings can be valuable and accurate. They can resolve ambiguities otherwise inexplicable in the film text. Or they can construct alternate explications. Lesbian criticism casts a jaundiced eye on self-important heterosexual rituals and in so doing can illuminate the psychosexual structuring of cultural production with the particular clarity of the outsider. However, at other times, subtextual readings can be erroneous. This is a problem, not only for lesbian criticism, but for feminist film criticism in general. For instance, sometimes feminist readings exceed the subtextual and become fantasy-projections, as in one woman's reading of *Star Wars* (1977) as a matriarchal vision. Other times, heterosexual elements of a film are ignored to preserve a lesbian reading, as in one reading of *Little Darlings* (1980) that sees the title characters as little dykes. More serious is the practice of praising films as indictments of the evils awaiting women who engage in heterosexuality, without recognizing to what extent such films actively further the oppression of women. Seeing *Looking For Mr. Goodbar* (1977), for example, as a warning against heterosexual dating games, fails to take seriously the real misogyny and degradation of women central to the film. Subtextual readings are important to the formation of an alternate criticism but, to be convincing, must remember to keep the film in sight.

THE LESBIAN FILMMAKER

Some feminist filmmakers have rejected the rigid sexual roles presented in commercial and documentary films and shown a great flexibility in depicting women's lives, desires and fantasies. The weakened bound-

What is a lesbian? A lesbian is the rage of all women condensed to the point of explosion. She is the woman who, often beginning at an extremely early age, acts in accordance with her inner compulsion to be a more complete and freer human being than her society — perhaps then, but certainly later — cares to allow her. She may not be fully conscious of the political implications of what for her began as personal necessity, but on some level she has not been able to accept the limitations and oppressions laid on her by the most basic role of her society — the female role.

— Radicalesbians

aries of sexual definition in these films mark an advance. For example, French director Nelly Kaplan in her earlier film *A Very Curious Girl* (1967) assigned a lesbian character the same traits as an exploitative man. In her more recent film *Nea* (1976), however, she has a mistreated wife reject her patriarchal husband in favor of a more satisfying lesbian relationship with his sister. The film is fascinating for its attempt to take on the issue of sexuality without hedging, though the sensationalistic aspects of some of the treatment is perhaps questionable.

In the German film *The Second Awakening of Christa Klages* (1978) Margarethe von Trotta traces the revival of a friendship between a woman fugitive and her high-school friend at a time of need. The heroine shifts in the course of the film from hiding out with her male sidekick (who gets killed) to running off to Portugal with her high-school girlfriend in a relationship that is suggested as a lesbian one. Also, Hungarian director Marta Mészáros has consistently made films devoted to the rich friendship between women. Because of her very pessimistic depictions of heterosexual relations and her visual attention to the sensuality of women's bodies, the dynamic between women retains a sexual potential even though such a development is never played out within the films themselves.

Occasionally, in documentary film as well there has been a lessening of censorship regarding the lesbian presence. *We're Alive* (1975) presents women prisoners collectively shaping their own film and offering combined left, lesbian and feminist analyses of their own conditions. The film doesn't separate out the lesbian experience into a separate category. Such fluidity of sexual boundaries is an encouraging sign in feminist filmmaking.

Most feminist films, however, try to challenge male dominance without being self-conscious of their own suppression of lesbianism, or in some cases, homophobia. In *Girl Friends* (1978) the lesbian character is a negative cartoon introduced only to be rejected. Overt homophobia is rare in comparison with the more subtle suppression —

total absence. For example, weren't *any* of the women in the Women's Emergency Brigade documented in *With Babies and Banners* (1978) lesbians? Lesbianism is not a subject of interest to New Day Films, the single largest feminist distributor of documentary films in the United States. Lesbian issues are not addressed in the films, the word does not appear in their catalogue, and only rarely does any woman even appear to be a lesbian in the interviews and portraits that form their film treatments of social issues. It would be foolish to expect heterosexual feminists to produce lesbian films, but if their films are meant to describe the reality of women's experience, they must include lesbians as a part of that reality.

It is to the lesbian filmmaker we must look for consistent lesbian visibility and the political and aesthetic questions such a visibility poses. What is the context of production for lesbian filmmakers? Independent lesbian filmmakers have problems that: (a) all independents have: money, equipment and distribution; (b) all women have: technical deprivation, access, accountability to the demands of a political movement; (c) all lesbians have: self-denial, risk of censorship, retaliation.

Production problems confronting lesbians have both external and internal sources. The risk of economic blacklisting is an ever present one for the lesbian filmmaker, who may lie on a grant application only to find that, once the "real" film is made, she is cut off from funding sources for a future project. Or she may never know, when rejected for money for an accurately described script, whether homophobia was the reason for the lack of funding. Also, existing distribution markets for 16mm independent films can hardly be seen to constitute a receptive environment for lesbian films. Libraries, schools and cable television may be able to absorb broad-based feminist works, but they screen out lesbian work either because of their own homophobia or as a conservative response to their constituency.

External and internal problems cannot be artificially separated. Sometimes, self-censorship occurs as a pragmatic handling of political goals and market realities on the part of a filmmaker. For example, *The Power of Men Is the Patience of Women* (1978) is a German film dramatizing the problem of battered women, the importance of women's shelters and collective alternatives. Director Cristina Perinciola decided to show clearly the double-headed axe (a symbol of lesbian identity) worn by one of the women in the film as a code for lesbian viewers, while at the same time to omit any other reference to lesbianism. This was a deliberate move to ensure the film was televised. It is an interesting solution for maintaining a visibility for the lesbian community given the political urgency of maximum exposure of the issue of wife-beating (particularly through the medium of television, to reach

Is it sapphism which nourishes her intelligence, or is it her intelligence
which makes her a lesbian?

— Jean Royere

women who may in fact not even be able to leave the house). Still, this
is a stop-gap measure and not an ideal solution.

There is a persistent dilemma in lesbians' internalizing the societal
homophobia with which all our lives are saturated. Such an internaliza-
tion may result in conscious or unconscious self-censorship, self-denial
or, in extreme instances, self-hatred. The issue of inhibition is part of
the ongoing struggle in forgoing a lesbian identity, and as such, is part
of an ongoing discussion within the lesbian community.

The lesbian independent filmmaker has not found the worlds of left
political filmmaking or avant-garde film hospitable, regardless of what
her own concerns politically or aesthetically may be. In the "political"
camp, lesbianism has been rated a low "personal" priority on the
political agenda. The left has too often given a clear message that
lesbianism isn't important.

In the "avant-garde" camp, lesbianism isn't treated any better than
in Hollywood or pornography. Werner Nekes's *T(wo) Men*, Steve
Dwoskin's *Chinese Checkers* and Jim Benning's *11 x 14* all use
the depiction of lesbian sexuality (usually a fraudulent one) as the hook
to hold audience interest through their formal experimentations.
Moreover, innovative lesbian films are likely to be marginalized or
discounted within avant-garde film circles because of their charged
content. With "content" still more or less a modernist taboo for avant-
garde filmmakers, the lesbian filmmaker is likely to find her formal
contributions made invisible. Moreover, avant-garde filmmaking
remains one of the last strongholds of the "sensitive artist" tradition
which is by definition male and still mitigates strongly against feminists
and certainly against lesbians.

Because lesbians' films don't fit into the existing distribution networks for independent left or avant-garde films, there is still a large
body of lesbian work that has yet to break out of its local audience into
visible distribution.

TOWARDS A LESBIAN CINEMA

Lesbians, historically bereft of cultural, political and moral contexts,
have especially relied on imaginative literature to dream themselves into
situations of cultural, political and moral power. Twenty years ago,
without Molly Bolt, we were Rhett Butler and Stephen Gordon and the

Count of Monte Christo. It is, of course, much more to the point to be Molly Bolt — or Patience and Sarah or Mrs. Stevens. The trouble with this process (vulgarly referred to as "identifying with") is that while the new lesbian hero is certainly safer for our mental health than Rhett or the Count or Stephen — we do not have to associate power and adventure with the penis any longer; we do not have to call on God to cure us of "inversion" and wear male underwear any longer — and while we see her operating in what some might very loosely call a "cultural" context of tree-hugging, feminist folk/rock, vegetarianism and goddess-worship, her aggressive, strong, even magnificent image is by and large taken on by her beholder still inside the heterosexual/patriarchal definition of moral and political reality. Lesbian literature is not a matter of a woman plus a woman in bed.

— Bertha Harris

At this point, the paucity of lesbian visibility in films has made the presentation of a "positive" lesbian subject a serious priority for lesbian filmmakers. Earlier we talked about the problems in seeking "positive images" of lesbians in Hollywood films: this becomes a very different issue when discussing lesbian filmmakers and movement films. Affirmation has been and remains vital. The most common form this affirming of identity has taken in lesbian filmmaking is the coming-out film. Coming out has been a central ritual of the lesbian movement, and the films by lesbians quantitatively reflect this. Such films offer a public expression of personal experience and are one component of a lesbian culture that shapes, supports and politicizes personal change and self-definition. We must not underestimate the need for films to affirm all aspects of lesbian identity, given the virulent hostility against lesbians in our society. Films are required to reclaim history, offer self-definition and create alternative visions.

The expression of self implicitly includes a struggle against the dominant ideology. An oppressed group, once able to make films, will create positive images both to offer the new self-identity and also to combat the negative stereotypes promulgated by the dominant culture. Therefore, positive images cannot be cut off from the societal pressures that created the original stereotypes or the conditions that maintain them. A positive image of lesbian motherhood is constructed in *In the Best Interests of the Children* (1977), a documentary film made by Liz Stevens and Frances Reid. Such a portrayal of lesbian mothers cannot be cut off from the societal context, that is, the legal battle by lesbian mothers to retain custody of their children. The film was made to serve those custody suits. For this political reason, the filmmakers also chose to film in a traditional documentary mode for maximum credibility, accessibility and persuasiveness with the particular audience (lawyers, juries, social workers) intended for the film. In this sense, the film has

Lesbian: A term understood to mean a woman who relates sexually and
emotionally to other women.

— Barbara Ponse

---

been very successful. It has also provided a boost in morale for many
beleaguered lesbian mothers caught in the same legal traps. On the other
hand, the documentary can be criticized for precisely this positive
approach, that is, for presenting lesbian mothers as perfect, for not
articulating their anger, and for leaving an overly optimistic impression
of the current situation. However, this film should not have to bear the
weight of our entire expectations of what a film about lesbian motherhood might be. Other films can, and should, be made.

One need is for films that deal with variation, complex identities and
contradiction — all outside the scope of the "positive image"
approach. Lesbian films cannot be considered outside the context of the
lesbian community. Within this community, we face daily contradictions (passing as straight at work but being out with friends, public
oppression versus private pleasure, or the seeming contradiction of
multiple political commitments). The recognition and working through
of conflict is a process that is essential to political and personal growth,
and one which our films could be aiding. Unsolved problems, anger,
unpleasant decisions, fights, and other messy material are all dealt with
in our lives and could be portrayed on the screen as well. Barbara
Hammer's film *Double Strength* (1978), for instance, approaches the
question of lesbian relationships, love and romanticism. Jan Oxenberg's
films, in particular, pull humor out of a hatful of contradictions. Susana
Blaustein's self-portrait, *Susana* (1980), wittily visualizes the conflict
between her lesbian lifestyle and traditional Argentine family values
that is precipitated by her sister's visit. We need more films that deal
with the contradictions, details and pleasures of lesbian life.

What about all the aspects of lesbian life that haven't yet made it
into the movies? We have yet to see any film about that venerable
mainstay of lesbian culture, the bars. Despite a network of lesbian and
gay history projects, research has yet to inform lesbian filmmaking: for
example, the slide show "Lesbian Masquerade: Women Who Passed as
Men in Early San Francisco" could provide the basis for a wonderful
film on the phenomenon of "passing women." Again, looking to history, the presence of lesbians in the suffragette movement has yet to be
explored in film. Films are still needed to write lesbians back into
history, to include the lives of lesbians on welfare, lesbians fighting
nationalist struggles, lesbians of color . . . lesbians contributing to struggles both inside and outside the lesbian movement per se. The lesbian
imagination is certainly not limited to the traditionally political. Lesbian

films could explore the interior of a lesbian household or formally study the textures of daily life.

Since lesbians are trying to live lives that reflect new value systems, there is a need for lesbian films that match those value systems both in the range of subject matter and stylistically. Lesbian literature offers an example of new visions, styles, textures and tonalities. Just as lesbian writers have discovered new linguistic structures and narrative styles that both express the lesbian imagination and refute the dominance of patriarchal writing, so must lesbian filmmakers take on this task. A lesbian film style could reveal the interlocking structures in characters' lives and bring a non-oppressive approach to image-making and reception. Fantasy and visionary art are sources of strength, used by lesbians "to dream themselves" into power. Utopianism has both positive and negative connotations, both true: it can be a flight from social change, but can also be a beacon of inspiration. More films need to take up the foundation laid by Monique Wittig, Verena Stefan and Olga Broumas in literature.

For lesbian filmmakers, the tension between creating new forms and maintaining contact with the audience they serve is ever present. Often, contact has been maintained by the use of already acceptable forms. Yet it is important to develop new forms to suit the meaning of the films and not rely solely on existing narrative or documentary styles. Issues, styles and priorities change as more lesbian films come into being. The work is already beginning.

EROTICISM AND PORNOGRAPHY

While lesbian filmmaking is not solely "a matter of a woman plus a woman in bed," nevertheless sexuality cannot and should not be avoided. For the lesbian community, the cinematic depiction of sexuality poses a particular problem. It is important to name this element of lesbianism for what it is, to articulate its nature and to give positive models of lesbian sexuality for younger women coming out. But how can this be reconciled with the objectification of such sexuality in film and the visual arts (from Helmut Newton's high-class-porn photography to advertisements for Twin Sisters scotch)? The visualization of non-voyeuristic, authentic lesbian lovemaking should be attempted. But paradoxically, the continued existence of pornography still clouds the depiction of sexuality.

The representation of women's bodies in art and film has been an issue of concern to feminist critics (see Lucy Lippard on body art in *From the Center*). Due to a history of patriarchal art, to the visual coding of our society and to the presence of a male audience, it some-

The meaning of our love for women is what we have constantly to expand.

— Adrienne Rich

times seems that the attempt for women to reclaim our bodies is doomed. In feminist film such an assessment has often led to a turning away from the depiction of heterosexual lovemaking, because of its inherent power relations and the difficulty in trying to create a new visual iconography to alter those relations.

Lesbian filmmakers are faced with a different situation. The all-woman environment on the screen and in the audience defines sexuality within a lesbian context and therefore should pose no problem to the representation of lesbian lovemaking. It would seem that lesbian filmmakers have no need for puritanism. Even in this context, however, lesbian viewers may still feel themselves made vulnerable by the open sexuality on the screen. French novelist and filmmaker Christiane Rochefort is clear about the reason: "Because we don't want men to look at what we do, I cut the intimate scenes."

The problem is present for the audience as much as for the filmmaker. Feeling so often under siege in society, it is hard to relax in a safehouse. Films showing lesbian lovemaking are vital to the lesbian filmmaker and lesbian community, yet there are always concerns as to what use outside the intended context the film can be put. Aware of how men misappropriate lesbian films, some filmmakers have sought to restrict screenings of films with lesbian lovemaking to all-woman audiences, as in the case of Barbara Hammer's *Dyketactics* (1974). Although unrestrictive of audience, Belgian filmmaker Chantal Akerman tried in her early film *Je, Tu, Il, Elle* (1974) to construct a fresh nonvoyeuristic image of lesbian lovemaking. Yet critics, on the whole, have discussed the film with pornography as their singular reference point, indicating the limitations of the artist's intention. What distinguishes both *Je, Tu, Il, Elle* and *Dyketactics* from other depictions of lesbian lovemaking in film is their visual and editing styles, as well as the presence of the filmmaker as participant in the scene, which conveys an insider's point of view.

Since lesbian sexuality is different from heterosexuality, films about it done from a lesbian perspective rather than an outsider's perspective will have to be different in both form and content. By using visual and musical coding associated with pornography, the lesbian lovemaking scenes in Connie Beeson's *Holding* have been easily co-opted into theatrical marketing for a mass audience. At other times, paradoxically, mass audience films can be appropriated in part by the lesbian audience. The racist soft-core hit *Emmanuelle* (1974) contained scenes of lesbian eroticism that were accepted as satisfying by many lesbian viewers. They could be appropriated, perhaps, because they were suggestively erotic rather than explicitly pornographic: the women were neither naked nor in bed.

While it would be inappropriate to divert our attention here into a lengthy debate on the distinctions between pornography and erotic film, we could mention a few points. The objectification of women and the enactment of male/female power relations are basic to pornography. Furthermore, lesbian depictions within pornography are predicated on standards alien to lesbian sexuality, such as making a fetish of genital sex or displacing emotional involvement. Pornography's exploitative style (of lighting, camera angle and editing) obstructs the possibility of erotic enjoyment. The differences between eroticism and pornography in film can only become clearer as more lesbian filmmakers present sexuality in their work. Nor is the filmmaker's attempt a vain one. The ideal remains of a visual image/style which could rupture even the patriarchal codes by which lesbian sexuality is read. Therefore it is important to keep co-optation from becoming intimidation.

Pornography is the extreme case, yet it points to a widespread phenomenon: the difficulty of defining the terms of lesbian experience when these very terms may mean one thing inside the women's community and something quite different in the gynophobic (woman-hating) society outside. Collective action inside is separatism outside; woman's anger inside is hysteria outside; autonomy inside is man-hating outside. These contradictions cannot be avoided. They emerge whenever a period of struggle is in progress, whenever an oppressed people aggressively assumes the task of self-definition.

THE DEVELOPMENT OF A LESBIAN IDENTITY

The lesbian struggle for self-definition has been in process for a long time in a variety of ways — organizationally, through publications, culturally, in music and poetry, in the bars — and in alliance with a number of other movements, particularly with gay male, left and feminist struggles. In the United States, any history must take into account the founding of the first lesbian organization in the country, the Daughters of Bilitis, in 1955, and its publication, *The Ladder,* published continuously from 1956 to 1972. The official position of the Daughters of Bilitis, brave for its time, stressed education to the general public about homosexuality, self-education, research projects in the social sciences and lobbying for more tolerant legislation. Their emphasis on acceptance is very different from that of the best known lesbian literary tradition, that of Nathalie Barney, Renée Vivien, and their coterie in Paris at the turn of the century. The Paris circle's pride in and celebration of relations and sexual liaisons between women takes no notice of heterosexual society, a luxury which its economic status permitted. These women were able to speak in their own voice early on, due to class status, but it remained to the 1970s to offer equal opportunity.

These very different traditions, of political awareness and cultural pride, were finally brought together with the events leading into and out of the Stonewall Resistance of 1969. At that event, in New York City, gay men and lesbians fought back against police, battling generations of police harassment. The political tradition of that night has been kept alive and furthered by annual Gay Pride Week events each June, with marches in cities all over the country; by organizations, like the Gay Liberation Front, and later the National Gay Task Force, or like the specifically media organization, The National Association of Lesbian and Gay Filmmakers; by actions, like those against the exhibition of *Windows* and the filming and opening of *Cruising* (1980); by national demonstrations, like the Oct. 14, 1979, mass mobilization in Washington in defense of gay rights against the homophobic backlash and increasingly repressive legislation.

Within the left, gays and lesbians have struggled against homophobia, both unconscious and deliberate. While many sectors of the gay and lesbian movement have a non- or anti-leftist perspective, the presence of gays and lesbians in left organizations and national solidarity movements, as well as the participation of gay and lesbian groups in left coalitions, is significant.

The dominant context for the lesbian movement, of course, has been the women's movement, in which lesbian feminists have always been a major presence, from the earliest days of women's liberation to the present. However, that history has been scarred by continual eruptions between lesbians and straight women within the movement, resulting in purges and separate lesbian organizations. Nevertheless, leading in the formulation of feminist theory that critiques patriarchal society and its institutions of power, lesbians have been activists in all spheres of the movement: rape crisis work, battered women's shelters, women's health clinics, reproductive rights struggles, the organizing of women workers, and so on.

We have selected these events above not to provide a thumbnail history, but merely to put into context the discussion of lesbian aesthetics and film history, which cannot be divorced from the political and cultural ferment of its era. The development of a lesbian identity has been especially strong in art, poetry, literature, music and philosophy. This development has occurred both within autonomous lesbian contexts and within the more generalized women's community, though any line of demarcation may be hard to fix.

Women's music offers an outstanding example of how women working together have created not only a pleasurable art form but the entire apparatus necessary to bring that art to its public, the women's community: women composers, musicians, technicians, producers (like the group of women who form Roadworks), recording companies (like Olivia Records) and distribution networks. Women's concerts and coffee-houses have provided a public space within which lesbian audiences can enjoy the creative articulation of a shared culture.

Though cultural, these spaces are also political. Without the journals, galleries, concerts, bars, publishing houses . . . there would be no basis for collective awareness or action, no evidence that things could be otherwise for lesbians in a society of mandatory heterosexuality.

Women have taken possession of the means of production in yet another way through the establishment of a number of publishing houses to ensure a free voice for feminist and lesbian writers. Similarly, lesbian journals have proliferated on both regional and national levels, as have feminist publications in general. On the regional level, the journals play a role in local political struggles, report on issues of interest to lesbians, publish local poetry and graphics, provide a directory for lesbian services, and advertise local businesses and bars. One national publication that follows this format of a news and culture blend is *Off Our Backs,* a magazine that has always maintained a strong political stance.

In 1976-77, four national journals were founded which have contributed to, discussed, and helped shape the renaissance in lesbian culture, theory and politics: *Conditions,* "a magazine of writing by women with an emphasis on writing by lesbians"; *Chrysalis,* "a magazine of woman's culture"; *Heresies,* "a feminist publication on art and politics"; and *Sinister Wisdom,* "a journal of words and pictures for the lesbian imagination in all women." These journals all have a national readership, are handsomely produced, and focus much more on history, philosophical issues, and broad questions of aesthetics and culture than they do upon current events or reporting. These journals are the mechanisms by which a network of feminist thought is spun across the country, establishing a common frame of reference.

The editors of *Heresies, Conditions,* and *Off Our Backs* have opened their publications to the concerns of black and Third World women's experiences. The issues of *Third World Women: the politics of being other (Heresies* 8), *Conditions: 5: the black women's issue,* and *Off Our Backs: ain't I a woman?* (Vol. X, 6) all confront the white feminist/lesbian movements to acknowledge the uniqueness and autonomy of our triply (by race, class and sex) oppressed sisters. In the past, white movement women "have claimed that they could not find any women of color as an excuse for their all-whiteness," write the editors of *Conditions: 5.*

These excuses have dissolved as women "of color" substantiate their continued historical struggles through their diverse modes of artistic expression. If it is only in recent years that the publishers of these national women's journals have made the printing of these women's work a priority, how much longer will those who control the necessary, and more expensive, means for production and distribution of films remain racist, closed to black and Third World women? The relatively few films made by and about these women have yet to reach a mass distribution level. As the *Heresies* 8 collective writes, because black and "Third World women are *other* than the majority and the power-holding class, and . . . have concerns *other* than those of white feminists, white artists and men," their works remain ghettoized and are often only found within their original cultural community.

Naturally, black and latina lesbians are not waiting for the rest of the movement to catch up: there have been black and Third World lesbian conferences in New York and Washington, D.C., in California, and groups such as the Combahee River Collective in Roxbury, Mass., are engaged in ongoing work on the level of theory and practice. Happily, the lesbian and women's community as a whole is participating in the dialogue and not passively forcing Third World and black women to do all the work of education or confrontation.

There will always be differences in the perspectives of lesbians from differing races or class backgrounds. The ideal of a universal sisterhood does not necessitate the suppression of differences. Still, it is only now, with the greater participation of black and Third World lesbians, that we can discuss the degree to which a faulty universalization was previously practised. While lesbians who are not white are less likely to perceive patriarchy as the *primary* enemy, their perspective on class and race oppression can only educate the lesbian movement about political realities.

As the lesbian movement progresses, and as lesbian filmmaking prospers, the kinds of lesbian films we are seeing are bound to change. As there is more of an interchange between filmmakers of all races, lesbian films will be more likely to reflect the connections in our society between homophobia, anti-feminism and the corresponding mechanisms of racism and class oppression. Lesbian films are passionately linked to the lesbian community, both in the sense of political struggle and in the banalities of daily life. It is that immediacy which gives the art its strength and the audience its pleasure. Lesbian filmmaking has begun to develop new editing strategies, tamper with traditional sound/ image relations, and visualize new codes by which women's bodies can be seen. Only such a reassessment of film aesthetics can adequately serve the values of lesbian culture at this time. By moving beyond oppression to liberation, a true lesbian art form and an authentic lesbian aesthetic can emerge.

This is a filmmaking that is not reacting against older, heterosexual images of lesbianism. At the center of the new cinema, there must be a conscious sense of self. In turn, lesbian film theory must begin to dismantle some of the structures of current feminist film theory and film history in order to build a more inclusive foundation. Lesbian criticism can give voice to those things that have long remained silent, and in so doing, point out the extent to which previous feminist film criticism may still be bound into measuring by male or heterosexual standards. A true recognition of lesbianism would seriously challenge the concept of women as inevitable objects of exchange between men, or as fixed in an eternal trap of "sexual difference" based in heterosexuality.

Feminist theory that sees all women on the screen only as the objects of male desire — including, by implication, lesbians — is inadequate. This theoretical framework excludes lesbian experience, and it may in fact diminish the experience of all women.

> I remember a scene. . . . This from a film I want to see. It is a film made by a woman about two women who live together. This is a scene from their daily lives. It is a film about the small daily transformations which women experience, allow, tend to, and which have been invisible in this male culture. In this film, two women touch. In all ways possible they show knowledge of what they have lived through and what they will yet do, and one sees in their movements how they have survived. I am certain that one day this film will exist.
>
> — Susan Griffin

CHAPTER 20.

Comic Critique:
The Films of Jan Oxenberg

MICHELLE CITRON

He: Have you heard the women's movement has no sense of humor?
She: No. How does it go?

Jan Oxenberg makes politically important, humorous films. They are important not only because they are part of a small group of films that describe the lesbian experience in the United States, but also because they have a lot to say about the ideology of film and about feminist filmmakers' expanding search for appropriate film aesthetics.

Oxenberg's films have always been controversial. Depending on the biases of who's doing the judging, they are usually accused of being apolitical, sentimental or technically unrefined. Suffering from the negative criticism levelled at many feminist films, Oxenberg's films are additionally ghettoized by people who cannot relate to the films' lesbian subject matter.

In spite of such criticism, Oxenberg's films have had an enthusiastic reception by lesbian and feminist audiences. The films have been pro- grammed over and over again and have achieved a feminist and lesbian cult reputation. In turn critics have dismissed this phenomenon, saying that lesbian audiences are myopic in their acceptance of these films, misguided by their enthusiasm for the subject matter into ignoring other, and by implication, more important filmic qualities. Frequently feminist films, independently made on very low budgets, are accused by critics of poor technical or "cinematic" quality.

Admittedly, sections of Oxenberg's films do suffer from technical problems arising from the economics of independent filmmaking, which are especially serious for the openly lesbian filmmaker. But technical roughness is rarely a barrier for sympathetic audiences' understanding of the films, although people who want to sidestep the real issues often use this as the excuse to dismiss a film.[1] There are those who find films that critique our heterosexist culture to be too threatening — especially when the films simultaneously take the lesbian experience seriously and validate it. Rather than argue about politics, it is much easier to attack the form.

A less obvious explanation, and one that I'd like to explore further here, is that Oxenberg's films are using a cinematic aesthetic not perceived by most critics.[2] A lot of political analysis in these films, especially in *Comedy in Six Unnatural Acts,* occurs through manipulating the form, and it is lesbians and feminists who have no need to evade the politics of *Comedy*'s formal analysis and jokes and who are receptive to its lessons. Oxenberg's films present, celebrate and validate the lesbian experience. They provide a way of looking at what images do to us as well as at our own attitudes. The films use humor to begin to analyze politically and critique homosexual and heterosexual cultural stereotypes as well as to explore the complex relationship between film and ideology. At the same time they confront the audience with its own prejudices.

SOCIALIZATION AND CHANGE

Home Movie (1972, 12 minutes) intercuts old home-movie images — of a small girl dancing and later playing with a doll and still later performing as a cheerleader at a football game — with footage of a gay rights march and women playing tackle football.

The home-movie images are evocative. The first set of images consists of a small girl (perhaps aged four) dressed "like a doll" and dancing. Her dance is extraordinary. Arms waving frenetically, the child is trying to keep her balance. Then, trying to negotiate a graceful turn, she falls on her ass. It is simultaneously funny and painful to watch. Here is Shirley Temple as performed not by a precocious child star but by a real child. The girl is trying to imitate what she thinks should be cute and feminine, but since she is real, not a male-manufactured icon, she fails at this attempt. Her dance is not graceful or coy. Rather, it's the desperate running around in a circle of a kid who doesn't quite catch on.

The image resonates with our memories of trying to fit in, struggling to be those images of "true femininity" presented in films, magazines and television commercials. This image symbolizes growing up female. On the sound track the woman's voice intones, "I never felt like a girl. They let me be crazy." Few of us could measure up to the ideal, unreal images, always feeling somehow crazy. The image on the screen changes to show a mother holding an infant while the daughter looks on, holding a doll and trying to imitate the mother. Once again, the girl cannot do it right. The mother holds the baby gently and with assurance; the daughter, not quite sure what to do with her doll, holds it upside down by its legs and shakes it. It's an image of basic socialization into the female role: the mother trains her daughter into their own mutual oppression, and the daughter needs to try and please the mother despite having very different feelings and desires. It is an image of imitative behaviour.

The last home-movie image is of the same girl, now a young woman, still trying to fit in and still denying her own reality. Now she is a cheerleader. We see her perform with other young women, while on the soundtrack the same woman years later talks retrospectively of her love for women. She had dated boys while really wanting to be with women. At one point she remarks, ''What if I had held hands with the other cheerleaders? That would have really blown their minds! How would they react? They wouldn't even let us chew gum.'' The audience invariably laughs as they recognize the absurdity of such restrictions on behavior. The film shows that a subversion of the socialization process, though rarely acknowledged, often occurs.

At this point the film starts intercutting the home movies of the cheerleaders with footage of lesbians marching and playing. We see the cheerleaders intercut with shots of women in a gay-rights march, arm in arm and smiling, and with shots of women playing touch football. Tight formations of women all dressed alike are juxtaposed with women running with their hair flying, all wearing different clothes and different hairstyles, with different faces. The second group of women is in the midst of the game, not cheering on the sidelines. There is a sense of women celebrating being strong and free and getting to play.

Football is usually strongly associated with men and serves as an image of male strength and competitiveness. The women in *Home Movie* are subverting the male sports mythology, for in fact this game looks like no male football game I've ever seen. Women run for a pass, catch it, tackle, and land on top of one another hugging and kissing. The game is playful, sexual, non-competitive. The image is one of celebration, especially because it is intercut with the gay-rights march.[3]

A simple content analysis of *Home Movie* rightfully sees the film as analyzing and celebrating being lesbian. Yet the form itself is significant and the title suggestive. Oxenberg uses home movies to underscore the role of the family and school as institutions that perpetuate patriarchal ideology. In the context of this film, home movies, usually a celebratory recording of family life, ironically become a condemnation of the very institutions filmed. Oxenberg celebrates not women's joining family or school, but their release.

Additionally, the 8mm and Super-8 footage depicting the past juxtaposed against the 16mm footage depicting the present suggests Oxenberg's historical approach to the material because the home movies' awkward child is found later playing football and marching in a political demonstration. Freed of false constraints or "false framing," this woman has expanded her life: from mom and dad as "family" to the lesbian movement as "community," from the sideline onto the playing field. The film by its very form suggests: yes, there is socialization and, yes, there is isolation. But there is also potential for change, especially in the context of a social movement.

NAMING AND CLAIMING LESBIANISM

Comedy in Six Unnatural Acts (1975, 26 minutes) continues where *Home Movie* ends, both in analysis and in visual experimentation. It is divided into six separate sections: Wallflower, Role-Playing, Seduction, Non-Monogamy, Child Molester and Stompin' Dyke. Each section critiques pervading myths about lesbian culture. The film works by playing in a comic way on our expectations. It presents icons and behaviors we are accustomed to seeing, seducing us into feeling comfortable about predicting each section's outcome, but then each section ends with a totally different explanation than the traditional one.

An example is "Role-Playing." Shot in soft light with diffusion filters, the sequence shows us a culturally-conventional beautiful woman preparing to go out on a date. Instead of the traditional image of her putting on make-up, we see her dressing "butch": knotting her tie, slapping on cologne, greasing back her hair. This last action is shown in excruciating close-up, the woman's fingers scooping up handfuls of slimy goop. At one point the gel slips out of her fingers onto her nose. The audience laughs and cringes. The image is powerful, resonating with memories of teasing, curling, spraying, plucking and, yes, slicking back hair. The image reinforces our sense of how women twist and contort themselves to fit some cultural notion of beauty and acceptability, whether heterosexual or lesbian. It also suggests male grooming routed through female actions — a strong lesbian stereotype.

The woman puts on her suit jacket, gives herself one last look in the mirror, picks up a bouquet of flowers, and walks off to meet her date. When she rings the doorbell, our expectation is that it will be answered by the "femme" counterpart to this "butch." However, a woman answers dressed in exactly the same way, with suit, tie and slicked-back hair, and she is also holding flowers. The women exchange bouquets, wink at each other, and go off holding hands.

In "Wallflower," we see a high school dance with the inevitable woman on the sidelines pathetically isolated from the dancing couples on the floor. After an excruciatingly long time, her date walks in but stays just off screen. We see the Wallflower turn and look up smiling. As the camera pulls back, we see not a handsome male date but a tall, blonde woman whom the Wallflower adores.

This device, though simple, is much more than just a joke with a visual punchline. It is a set-up. Oxenberg carefully codes sequences in particular ways to ensure a predictable cultural reading of the codes by the audience. For example, in "Role-Playing" she relies on our reading that the woman wearing a suit and tie is a "butch" who, we think, will of course date a "femme" in order for Oxenberg to make her joke. "Wallflower" is much more complex because the codes can be read in a number of different ways. It offers a game of fill-in-the-blanks within the context of the patriarchal ideology of dating. Here, as at the end of each sequence, we realize that we have been led to misread the signs. And these one-line jokes become political precisely because they reveal the cultural construction of the codes themselves.

The sequence leading up to the visual punchline in "Wallflower" is a textbook of teenage, heterosexual game-playing. Men and women dance in bear-hug embraces, the women lost in the physical massiveness of their male partners, the male hands trying to "feel up" their dates, while the women continually push the men's hands away. In the background, visually isolated and looking very uncomfortable, is the Wallflower (a woman without a man is alone). At one point a prospective partner approaches the Wallflower. He gives her the once-over, she sneers at him, and he decides she's not worth it and walks away — to her visible relief. We adjust our reading of the sequence in keeping with our knowledge of the film as a lesbian film (a woman alone is a dyke).

At this point, the record on the turntable skips and the couples turn and look expectingly at the Wallflower, who is obviously supposed to fix it, yet she is too lost in her own world of discomfort to realize what's going on (a dyke alone is pathetic). When the sequence finally ends happily, we have been led through the complexity of our ideological assumptions, the film revealing in each twist and turn yet another level of erroneous assumptions. This woman may be without a man, but her discomfort does not come from loneliness.

These sequences critique not only homophobic assumptions, but heterosexuality itself and the misappropriation of some heterosexual ideology in lesbian culture. These levels have their clearest articulation in "Seduction," where we see two women tentatively approaching each other in the initial stages of romantic acquaintance. They use all the ploys associated with heterosexual courting. There's, "Maybe some day you can come over and see my maps?" along with candlelight, a tipsy violinist and the accidentally spilled glass of wine that gives an excuse for touching. The sequence slips into a satire of lesbian courtship (camping trips and sweetly oversupportive dyke friends helping out a "new" one).

But there is an absurd edge to the women's behavior that is emphasized by the acting: we are not watching real people but actors very obviously playing roles. Beyond the fact that the behavior is "not natural," it also doesn't fit. Despite attempts, lesbians do not fit into the model of romantic love. The film emphasizes this by having the scene played not in a public restaurant as it would be with a heterosexual couple, but in the privacy of someone's living room. The lesbian as an outsider is a theme that runs throughout the film. In "Wallflower" the last shot shows the lesbian couple walking through the parted teenage crowd who throw rice at them. Such a tactic emphasizes once again their "other" status and the impossibility of such a fantasy ending.

Oxenberg is not just criticizing heterosexual romanticism; she is critical of lesbian romanticism as well. In "Non-Monogamy," we see a woman (played by Oxenberg herself) juggling fruits and balls. As the narrator reads from a political tract about the lesbian nation as an army of lovers and about the positive side of non-monogamy, the juggler offers her own critique of that militant platform by increasingly losing control over her balancing act. Oxenberg is saying in this metaphoric act that living within patriarchal culture is difficult and that lesbians should not just imitate heterosexual behavior nor should they try to just do the reverse of the dominant norm. For Oxenberg, lesbians must always be questioning and critical of their actions. The "lesbian nation" is still learning and developing its alternatives.

Except in "Non-Monogamy," the models of romantic love seen in *Comedy* are actions modelled directly on Hollywood movies. This is made explicit when the women first kiss in "Seduction." Suddenly we see a dance production number straight out of the movie musical complete with a montage sequence of women (instead of the heterosexual couple) meeting — with such images as tilted neon signs and women folding laundry together at the laundromat, a chorus line, and the seductress.

Film references are frequent in *Comedy*. In "Role-Playing," the very controlled soft focus, diffuse lighting, and carefully composed close-ups suggest the 1930s glamor style of photography. The undercranked camera, quick cutting, and piano music of another section, "Child Molester," suggests silent film comedies. Oxenberg is clearly acknowledging the power of movies to shape our attitudes and lives.

Comedy is politically important in its concern with naming and claiming lesbianism. In "Role-Playing," Oxenberg chooses to have both women portrayed as butch, not femme (femme is the much more acceptable image of lesbianism in straight society). Role-playing does exist, a mimic of the oppressive heterosexist culture, and to deny its existence is to tell an inaccurate and impoverished history of lesbians. In "Child Molester" Oxenberg has the courage to confront the myth of lesbians' stalking innocent children and to debunk it instead of pretending it doesn't exist. When the child-molester *cum* Girl Scout leader tries to lure two little girls, they just wave at her and walk away together hugging and kissing each other. Oxenberg asks the reactionary question (don't they molest children?) and gives not the liberal answer (these things are not so) but the radical answer (girls love each other).

The film ends with the "Stompin' Dyke" sequence. The sequence consists of the stompin' dyke, strong, powerful, and leather-jacketed, dismounting from her bike in the first shot. She walks tough down the street: a look from her and people swerve out of her way, a bicyclist stares at her and loses his balance and falls. Once again we have the image of the woman as outsider, offering a sense of both isolation and power. She walks down to the beach and disappears down an incline towards the ocean, recalling an image frequently seen in melodrama, where the desolate character walks to a watery suicide (for example, *A Star Is Born* 1937, *Humoresque,* 1946).

But the sequence cuts to a medium shot of the dyke in front of the water; as she steps in, the waters part and she walks through unharmed. This image is crucial. It gives the last, most powerful image in the film to the most extreme lesbian stereotype, the stereotype feared by most women, that of the bull dyke. It is easy to claim the "pretty lesbian" (see in *Playboy* the layouts of beautiful women making love for the titillation of men), but to claim the most feared image is both courageous and politically important. Oxenberg gives the image of most power not to a lesbian whom the women's movement might accept, the chic political lesbian (for example, Rita Mae Brown), but to the bull dyke.

USING HUMOR

The best part of Oxenberg's films is the humor that dominates them, ranging from the quiet snicker of recognition to the vulgar comedy of slapstick. Comedy is a difficult form, and Oxenberg's use of it for political ends is unique in contemporary independent political films. Her films' humor is articulated in many different ways. We are shown the absurdity of stereotypes, which after all are part of our distorted history, as with the Child Molester donning a Girl Scout uniform and trying to lure victims with cookies. We have in *Comedy* the recognition of real lesbian history, even if the actions are no longer appropriate (women do really slick back their hair, a fact no worse than permanents, yet rarely acknowledged with such sympathy). We see a joyous public articulation of lesbian culture (many lesbians' first crushes are on women culturally seen as "mannish" — their gym teachers — for what kind of women would want to play sports anyway?). *Comedy* also has the vulgar humor of broad humor and slapstick, as in the "Seduction" and "Child Molester" sequences. And it provides a laugh that comes from our interpretation of the film's codes and our constant misreading of them.

Oxenberg's films, but especially *Comedy,* are made for lesbian audiences or at least those familiar with lesbian culture. And much of the humor depends on an understanding of that culture. The film plays with stereotypes; it does not make fun of lesbians. At the end of one showing to a primarily heterosexual audience, *Comedy* was attacked for being homophobic. One audience member stated, "I like gay people — why do you make them so awful?" James Wolcott, in his *Village Voice* review of *Comedy* following its eventual showing on WNET, did not find the film funny at all, which meant he completely missed all the political points, for these are made solely through humor. He condemns the film:

> "Child Molester" concerns a lech who dolls herself up in a Girl Scout outfit and haunts playgrounds, lusting after little girls. When she tries to entice a pair of tots with GS cookies, the girls gigglingly kiss each other and scamper off — they don't need the Scout Leader, see, because they're already budding lezzies. (With Oxenberg's sense of humor, America doesn't need the neutron bomb.)[4]

Comedy is so complex in its structure, due to its many levels of critique, analysis and satire, that it does allow for selective perception based on the audience's own experiences and biases. But there is a further division between viewers whose misunderstanding derives from homophobia and those whose misunderstanding arises out of their lack of knowledge and/or experience.

Oxenberg's use of humor, although it elicits different responses from audiences, is not, I think, a limitation of her films. To make a political film for a particular primary audience is one of a number of alternative media strategies. Often, to make a film on lesbianism or homosexuality that is "acceptable" and has a broad appeal is to whitewash or eliminate sexuality itself — which is after all the reason why homosexuality is such a taboo. Oxenberg avoids this. Equally, she avoids the opposite problem and is able to deal with the sexual/political issues involved in a non-voyeuristic way. It is difficult to depict lesbianism in film because film is a medium that historically has used women for the visual pleasure of the male audience.

There is a fine line between "naming the unnamed" and exploiting it. Oxenberg, by dealing with lesbian issues in a humorous cultural/historical way, avoids this pitfall. In her work lesbians are defined by much more than their lovemaking, although she indirectly implies this critical aspect by having the characters prepare for dates, hold hands and kiss. But lesbianism is more broadly political for her, having to do with ideological mechanisms of socialization, male/female gender differentiation, cultural notions of romantic love, and being an outsider. Oxenberg's films deal with all these issues and in an increasingly political and sophisticated way.

NOTES

[1] The most recent case of this is WNET's controversial programming of its 1980 Independent Focus series. *Comedy* was one of the 28 independently made films recommended for programming by a peer review panel. Later it was one of four films refused air time by the station. The station cited poor acting and low technical quality as its reasons. However, in the ensuing protest by the gay community, it became clear that the criterion used was the film's threatening content. Because of the pressure exerted by gay rights groups, the film was later reprogrammed.

[2] For an extraordinary example of this, see James Wolcott's review, "Lesbians Are Lousy Lovers," *Village Voice*, 2 May 1980: "I waited for the apples to come tumbling down — for Oxenberg to acknowledge that lesbians too suffer from spite, envy, jealousy. But no: she really seems to believe that her sisters leap from petal to dewy petal in a daisy chain of sapphic delight. If lesbian life is such a kissy frolic, why did all the women in *Comedy in Six Unnatural Acts* look as if they had just discovered holes in their galoshes?"

[3] This image, though strong, is ambiguous and therefore problematic for me. On the one hand, the women playing football in *Home Movie* are subverting the image. On the other hand, I find the image so culturally laden with male norms that the analysis presented in the film needs to go further. Otherwise the image of women competing in rough sports is open to ambiguous interpretation. I am unsure of its meaning: Women can do anything men can do? Women can move their bodies? Women are like men? But what woman wants to be like a man?

[4] For wonderful reading, I suggest the letters to the editors written in response to this vicious review of *Comedy: Village Voice*, 26 May and 2 June 1980.

PART FIVE

RADICAL THIRD WORLD CINEMA

The Other Francisco, *Director Sergio Giral (Cuba, 1974)*

INTRODUCTION

Letter From Bolivia
I went underground. I learned that the centre where I had been teaching
Super-8 film production had been shut down and that its members were
being persecuted. One of the films I was editing. . . was in that office. I
have not been able to recover it and don't know if I will ever be able to
finish it. . . .

The article you requested for *Jump Cut* on workers' filmmaking in
Bolivia would be meaningless now. All such activity has been brought to
a halt.

Alfonso Gumucio Dagron, to *Jump Cut*, July 1980

"No one in their right mind sets out to make a Third World film,"
states Clyde Taylor in the essay that begins this section. Third World
films start from the specifics of nation, culture, or class, and the artistic
forms vary greatly. Therefore, when reading the essays here, it is
important to keep in mind that the terms Third World and Third World
Cinema are themselves problematic. While they may be useful in some
situations, they are much too general in many others. Taylor emphasizes that large-scale commercial film industries exist in India, Hong
Kong and North Africa; they have their "own unawakened manner. . . devoted to commercial pleasure." But a radical counter-cinema
flourishes as well in many Third World regions, challenging the conventions of the mini-industries and Hollywood.

Teshome Gabriel details the work of Senegal's Ousmane Sembène,
one of the world's leading directors and certainly among the best known
and accomplished African film artists. Sembène's 1974 film *Xala*
shows his unique style based on mastery of western film conventions
plus what Gabriel calls the "African folk narrative tradition." *Xala* is a
major work of the new African cinema.

Film and revolution is another theme running through these essays.
Cuba provides one of the most vivid examples. From the beginning the
political and cultural leadership of the Cuban revolution committed
itself to film as one means of decolonization. Julianne Burton and Tom
Waugh show how this commitment has fostered a strong and wonder-
fully diverse cinema, artistically eclectic and institutionally stable.
Waugh's study of Joris Ivens in Cuba is included for two reasons. First,
the article focuses on the difficulties faced by the Cubans in starting a
counter-cinema from scratch. And second, Waugh shows Ivens as an
example of solidarity with Third World artists. Ivens had experience to

offer, as an artist and a political activist. He was able to communicate that within the Cuban context, encouraging and training native filmmakers to see Cuba with new eyes.

Julia Lesage's "For Our Urgent Use" brings us right into one of the crucial political struggles of the 1980s — the role of the United States in Central America. Lesage deals with films beyond the pale of commercial exhibition, but films nonetheless used extensively by thousands of smaller audiences to understand life and the liberation movements in Central America. She argues that these films demand closer attention because they can teach us a great deal about film form and cultural difference. In order to use films such as *Time of Daring* from El Salvador, we in North America need to develop a cross-cultural understanding. To do otherwise runs not only the risk of racism but also the loss of pleasures very different from our own: pleasures that a Latin American film culture can offer.

CHAPTER 21.

Third World Cinema:
One Struggle, Many Fronts

CLYDE TAYLOR

> For us, a revolutionary people in a revolutionary process, the value of cultural and artistic creations is determined by their usefulness for the people, by what they contribute to man, by what they contribute to the liberation and happiness of man.
>
> Our standards are political. There cannot be aesthetic value without human content or in opposition to man, justice, welfare, liberation, and the happiness of man.
>
> — Fidel Castro

Is there such a thing as a Third World film? The evolutionary reality of Third World cinema is sometimes the victim of the conspiracy to overwhelm us with lies, drown-outs and cover stories. As Fernando Solanas and Octavio Getino put it:

> Imperialism and capitalism, whether in the consumer society or in the neocolonized country, veil everything behind a screen of images and appearances. *The image of reality* is more important than reality itself. It is a world peopled with fantasies and phantoms in which what is hideous is clothed in beauty, while beauty is disguised as the hideous.[1]

Suppose that every time you heard the word "music," the habits and memories of a thousand occasions forced you to think "disco"; that in the 24 hours of your daily life, disco was all your ears could find, except for a few non-disco selections tolerated in a corner of the music dial in one isolated hour when most people sleep. With predictable ingenuity, your mind might be forced to unfold your little disco ditch into a universe, complete with all the possibilities of human musical creativity, as far as you're concerned, including your preference for South Milwaukee disco over the dozens of Texas varieties and endless other choices, from historical romance disco, soap-opera disco, evangelist disco to creature-feature disco, to computer-tape disco to gasoline-war disco, and on and on, stretching to the limits of your wide, musical horizons.

This may sound fantastic, but something like it has been done to us with visual entertainment, with films. And we begin to understand what Third World films might be when we understand the political history that brought us to this place where "film" means "movie," and why it has only the most obscure, neglected space reserved for the cinematic expression of Third World people.

From a global perspective, the political history of the cinema mirrors the political history of the modern world, the central episode of which is a simple story of misemployment and destruction by certain classes in the West of the rest of us, and the continuing fight to change that history for a better one. The films we call Third World form an anti-propaganda movement for a mental reality free of the self-serving symbolism of the monopolist political machine. The intent of the culture industry has been to concoct an artificial mental landscape harmonious with its needs, to depersonalize its audience into zombies of its economy and addicts of its industrial culture, and to trash, trivialize and erase the natural human cultures that supply its victims. The awakened films of Third World people form the decisive challenge to this symbolic enslavement because they have been the absolute target of all three of these propaganda objectives.

MISPORTRAYAL AND THE MAKING
OF THIRD WORLD FILM

From the beginning, western commercial cinema has treated symbolic representatives of Third World people with genocidal contempt. Around 1900, several films shot on lawns in England and the United States claimed to be actual newsreels of China's Boxer Rebellion. They fabricated lurid, fake scenes — in which the Chinese were really Englishmen or Americans — such as the beheading of a Boxer or the swarming of a missionary's home and family by a Chinese "horde." A few years later, we were given *A Kiss in the Dark,* in which a white masher makes attempts to kiss a young woman sitting in a lower window: she puts her hands over his eyes and substitutes "a fat Negro Mammy," who kisses him enthusiastically.

From such beginnings, people of color have been imprisoned in world-current images as coolies, "savage" Africans, easy-bedding

Polynesian maidens, sleepy Indians slouching outside of saloons, treacherous Fu Manchus, wily Japs, faithful Gunga Dins and Uncle Toms, vivacious Chiquitas, grinning banditos, slaphappy Sambos, a succession of tagalong, begging boys, or legions of faceless, falling targets for the nick-o'-time cavalry, riding to the rescue with the same message across China, the North African desert or the western plains: flatter us with your subservience, or die. This legacy of misportrayal of the world's majority as invisible, incomprehensible or inconsequential becomes a witness to the insanity of western racism, once the cameras fall into the hands of their former victims and films finally appear where these cartoons and comic shadows assume vital coherence, guided by their own intelligence.

The concept of a Third World cinema arises slowly, relatively. For a while longer, there may be some revelation in the manifestation of non-European faces in human contexts on the screen. But a film is obviously not Third World merely because it was made in Africa, Asia or Latin America by indigenous people. The mini-film industries of Hong Kong, India, Egypt and North Africa, Manila and Mexico are as devoted to commercial pleasure, in their own unawakened manner, as any disco flick. Third World films reflect a necessary awareness of dilemmas too specific in their historic and political dimensions to be merely "human." Obviously, that awareness in the minds of many is replaced by disco variations, and for the same reasons, many even doubt the ideas of the Third World itself.

No one in their right mind sets out to make a Third World film. The origin of the best of them is, first, concern with a particular national issue, a certain class or culture. The films themselves, therefore, reflect a diversity of history and circumstance too great for us to speak of unifying artistic criteria. There are the "living poster," operatic epics of the Chinese Republic. There is the *Cinema Novo* of Brazil, with its mocking, popular symbolism (and, for my taste, a too-easy liaison between leering eroticism and residual racism). There is the post-independence African film movement, so varied as to be still in search of its essential Africanness. There are the recent masterpieces of sophisticated Cuban film art, made possible, perhaps, by the advanced appreciation of its Cuban audiences. The relative validity of individual and national styles is demonstrated by observing the specific successes of two films on similar themes, like *O Povo Organizado* (The People Organized, 1977), on Mozambique after the revolution and *Angola, Spear of the Nation* (1977), on that country's post-independence.

THE ALTERNATIVE TO DISCO MOVIELAND

The look and style of Third World cinema is often anti-disco, anti-commercial and pro-reality. Therefore, it is common to find in these films techniques designed to puncture the slick, closed facade of Hollywood's classical style of cinematography. There is the use of non-actors; of less expensive, more naturalistic hand-held cameras; the employment of open frame shots into which characters may wander from the top of the frame, so to speak, or of foreground intervention, where a passerby walks between camera and subject, to suggest the unrehearsed unpredictability of the documentary; the repetition of shots, the alternation between color and black and white and other devices meant to interrupt the hypnotic rhythm of the film and thereby demand the viewer's conscious participation; and the more honest, less seductive use of music. The search for dismanipulative techniques has produced, to be sure, its inevitable body of clichés. But neither the chosen strategy nor its occasional overuse reflect an inclusive appreciation of the rehumanizing possibilities of international film craft.

It is in theme and ideological direction that we find Third World cinema's crucial identifications. Given the commitment to the context of the daily life of uninvented people and the relentlessness of Euro-capitalist intervention, you can, not surprisingly, find certain recurring concerns: high unemployment in slums where former subsistence farmers were dumped, after being replaced by commercial crops; absentee or heartless landlordism; migrant workers recruited, abused and abandoned; genocidal "health" policies administered to the system's "surplus" labor; small, arrogant elites, investing their luxurious loot elsewhere; the readers and writers cannibalizing the talkers; the erosion and cancellation of ancient, traditional lifeways; hunger; and the effort to reverse these injustices.

A visual narrative nevertheless becomes Third World after the fact of its production, in its acceptance by its reflected community, or by people who see their condition mirrored in it, despite differences of geography or political condition. And clandestine or banned films sometimes become Third World in their adoption by world public opinion. Films become Third World, in short, by their function, once made, "by their usefulness for the people," as Fidel Castro said, "by what they contribute to man, by what they contribute to the liberation and happiness of man."

Yet even though the Third World is a mental state for which no one holds an official passport, it would be wrong to emphasize Third World cinema's local and national preoccupations at the expense of its resolute internationalism. The making of *O Povo Organizado* in Mozambique by Bob Van Lierop, an African American, or of *Sambizanga* (1972), about Angola, by Guadaloupian Sara Maldoror, or the Ethiopian Haile Gerima's *Bush Mama* (1975), set in Los Angeles, or Gillo Pontecorvo's *The Battle of Algiers* (1965), or the several Latin American and African films created by Cubans, or the many Third World films made by Europeans and white Americans — all suggest the cross-fertilization of an embryonic transnational Third World cinema movement. Young Third World filmmakers now exploit the inspiration of earlier Third World cinema successes while their elders were fortunate to find models only or mainly in Italian Neorealism. These international enrichments, unparalleled in other media, help to illustrate the priority of Third World cinema as the effective medium for the public transmission of information about the rest of us.

The internationalism of this deadliest alternative to disco movieland is more than a reflex of communications mobility, it is also, again, an accurate mirroring of the political history of people now moving across borders and breaking down past isolation in search of a just world order. The dissipation of Third World isolation will be no small accomplishment, considering the past development of cultural images in the western-controlled entertainment market-place. "Peking saw its first films in January 1902," a program of scenes including "a beautiful woman turning her head to us and smiling, women dancing like butterflies, a Negro eating watermelon, a bicycle race, a horse scaling a wall and climbing a roof."[2]

For decades, we have seen each other only through the eyes of those who had strictly barnyard uses for us. In the films of Third World cinema, on the other hand, we finally recognize each other as we are, as we struggle in our many sectors the one great struggle.

NOTES

[1]Fernando Solanas and Octavio Getino, "Towards a Third World Cinema," in Bill Nichols, ed., *Movies and Methods* (Berkeley: Univ. of California Press, 1976).

[2]Jay Leyda, *Dianying (Electric Shadows): An Account of Films and the Film Audience in China,* (Boston: MIT Press, 1972).

CHAPTER 22.

Xala: A Cinema of Wax and Gold

TESHOME H. GABRIEL

Ousmane Sembène of Senegal possesses the vision of a committed cineaste of social change. All his films, self-critical ones, offer constructs to interpret the cultural jumble that covers Africa. In the Sembènian universe, film depicts not simply individuals bereft of context, caught between the traditional and the modern or the foreign and domestic, but shows the collision of two mutually exclusive symbol-systems, which serve their own set of icons and are equally arbitrary and mutually worthless to each other.

Whereas in *Emitai* (1971) and *Ceddo* (1977), two historical films set in rural Africa, Sembène deals with Africans' isolation in a colonial environment, in *Borom Sarret* (1963), *Tauw* (1970), *Black Girl* (1966) and *Mandabi* (1969) he treats individuals' alienation as they live between two cultures in contemporary Africa.[1] In *Xala* (1974 — pronounced "halla") Sembène portrays a man seemingly successful in both worlds and both systems. Here, unlike in the other films, the African has at last gained access to and mastered both value systems, but his very stance leaves him vulnerable.

The film centers on El Hadji Abdou Kader Beye (El Hadji is a title meaning "pilgrim" and in Islam it refers to one who has been to Mecca and has come back holy) as the prototype of the emerging African bourgeoisie, who destroy the continent, politically and economically, in the name of "African Socialism" and "Progress." To Sembène this new class of nouveau riche in Africa presents a much more sinister force than the openly exploitative European colonialists. Whereas the colonialists could be readily identified by race, language, dress, custom and manner of worship, the new enemy insidiously shares all the Africans' outward aspects and cultural attributes and has assumed his inimical role through a conscious political choice.

As the film opens, we note the transfer of power taking place in an unnamed African country. To "spice-up" the independence celebration El Hadji Abdou Kader Beye, a board member in a "Chamber of Commerce," announces his third marriage, to the 19-year-old N'Goné, the same age as his daughter Rama. Unfortunately, the weight of El Hadji's 50 years and his psychological make-up prevent him from consummating the marriage. El Hadji believes himself hexed — someone, an enemy, has put the spell of "xala," impotence, upon him. He suspects his other two wives and even a colleague. His increasing anxiety and desperation as he seeks to break the spell of xala set the film's pace, as El Hadji goes from one marabout (a Moslem hermit or saint) to another, from wife to wife, searching for the cause and cure of his lost virility. His wallet grows lighter as he must pay for each visitation. He becomes so obsessed with regaining his potency that he neglects his work as a member of the "Chamber of Commerce" and quite literally becomes impotent not only in the bedroom, but also in the boardroom.

Xala is on one level a comedy. El Hadji's desire to regain his "manhood" (as he defines it) is presented in an extremely humorous way. The film illustrates a simple moral tale of a man who loses everything as a result of living beyond his age and means. On another level, however, the film offers a poignant satire about Africa's neocolonial leaders.

"WAX AND GOLD" AS A METHOD

The film language of *Xala* can be constructed on the model of an African poetic form called "sem-enna-worq," which literally means "wax and gold."[2] The term refers to the "lost wax" process in which a goldsmith creates a wax form, casts a clay mold around it, then drains out the wax and pours in molten gold to form the valued object. Applied to poetics, the concept acknowledges two levels of interpretation, distinct in theory and representation. Such poetic form aims to attain maximum ideas with minimum words. "Wax" refers to the most obvious and superficial meaning, whereas the "gold" embedded in the art work offers the "true" meaning, which may be inaccessible unless one understands the nuances of folk culture.

In the novel *Xala,* the structural key that explains the story's surface political meaning links a sexual metaphor with a sociological message.[3] In the film *Xala,* to unearth the "gold" we must go beyond the manifest content and beyond the sexual metaphor. To restore the "gold" in its purity in *Xala* means, therefore, to perform an autopsy to remove the "wax," the comedy format, in order to gain access to the text's ideology.

How does Sembène, the filmmaker, help us discover the ideological underpinnings which lie mute within the comedic form? What arrays of cultural codes and filmic modes does he employ to mark the film's immanent meaning? His search for African cinema, I believe, comes in his use of these two modes of discourse: cultural fabric and film style.

CULTURAL CODES

Many symbols in *Xala* expose the manipulators of the new social order: the westernized Africans who like chameleons are ready to change their appearance to protect their selfish interests. At the film's beginning the board members in the "Chamber of Commerce" (euphemism for government) wear native dress as they acknowledge their assumption of political/economic power. They then change into well-cut, European, three-piece suits once they reach the board room's sanctity. Similarly, the secretary of El Hadji's warehouse wears a traditional African dress while outside in the streets, but once in the office she takes off this outer layer to reveal a European dress underneath.

El Hadji's two initial wives represent the duality that has become Africa. The first wife, Adja Awa Astou (Adja refers to a female pilgrim), is a woman with dignity and wears the traditional African dress. She understands the institution of polygamy, which she knows in her wisdom and womanhood she cannot change. She accepts the traditional role of service to her husband without undue concern for money and success. The second wife, Oumi N'Doye, never talks to El Hadji except about sex and money. She, unlike Awa, who always speaks Wolof, almost always addresses El Hadji and her children in French. She likes western dress and to appear sexy. She stands as a symbolic figure of neocolonial destruction.

The choice of language as spoken throughout the film is symbolic in the way it is used. The use of French in *Xala* clearly sets those acculturated to European ways apart from the masses who speak Wolof and are seen as the preservers of indigenous culture. El Hadji speaks French throughout, to the disgust of his progressive daughter Rama:

> El Hadji: (angrily) Rama, why do you answer in Wolof when I speak to you in French?
> Rama: (in Wolof) Father, have a good day.[1]

Acting as her father's conscience, questioning his motives and behavior but not intimidated by him, Rama also represents the omnipresent and omniscient voice behind the film. As the hope of liberated Africa, all progressive statements in the film are associated with her.

> El Hadji: (angrily) Who are "dirty dogs," Rama?
> Rama: Men!

El Hadji: Why are they "dirty dogs"?!
Rama: Every polygamous man is a liar!
El Hadji: (astounded but firmly) Say that again?!
Rama: Every polygamous man is a liar.

In the special meeting of the board called to determine the advisability of retaining El Hadji in the administration, El Hadji is summoned to answer for misuse of funds and for writing bad checks. Here, however, he uses the same words of his daughter Rama against his adversaries. Furthermore, his request to speak in Wolof rather than French indicates a reversal in his moral character:

Board Member: El Hadji, the colonial period is finished. We govern the country. You collaborate with the government, Big Mouth!
El Hadji: President, I will speak in Wolof.
Board Member: President, point of order! In French, old boy. The official language is French.
President: Calm down, act civilized. El Hadji, you may speak, but in French. Even the insults in the purest tradition of Francophonic.
El Hadji: Each one of us is a "dirty dog." I repeat, "dirty dogs," probably worse than I. We are crabs in a single basket. We have all given bad checks.

The entire spectrum of symbols used in the film reminds us of Africa-in-its-otherness flirting with Africa-rooted-in-its-own. All the cited cultural codes serve as open symbols whose meaning is quite literal: Africa stripped of her cultural identity. The film also explicitly criticizes those who command political and economic power for their myopic vision of independence and for their confused mixing of their class interests with those of African liberation.

THE CLASS CODE

Throughout the film there is a game of opposition between the nouveau riche and the people — those who speak French and those who do not — those assimilated by the system and those who are its rejects. These two groups share a common heritage and a form of interdependency. Their paths, however, differ in one crucial area: wealth.

Sembène wastes no time in making a dialectical logic of the two classes' intersection. A band of crippled beggars makes us uneasy, but as we follow the lives of the affluent, it is the bourgeoisie's class nature that dominates.[5] The beggars are often seen but, except for the theme music that comments on their situation, they are not heard, so they remind us only mutely of harsh realities in urban Africa.

The film's use of mass beggars offers a real picture of urban Africa. Sembène depicts the less fortunate as victims of the bourgeoisie who deprive them of basic needs and view them with utter contempt. The beggars do not have a way to redress wrongs done to them. In their despair, therefore, after El Hadji has been stripped of his wealth and his second and third wives have deserted him, the beggars confront him in Awa's villa. (Since Awa represents traditional Africa, El Hadji's return to her symbolizes the exile's complete return to his roots.) Seated like a tribal jury, this band tells El Hadji that they alone can cure his impotence.

El Hadji: (as he emerges from his bedroom in pyjamas) What is this, "robbery"?!

Gogul, the blind man: Robbery, no, "Vengeance!!" Our story goes back a long time ago, before your first marriage with this lady. What I have become is your fault. You appropriated our inheritance. You falsified our names and we were expropriated. I was thrown in prison. I am of the Beye family. Now I will get my revenge. I arranged your xala.

If you want to be a man, undress nude in front of everyone. We will spit on you.

Again, it is the concern for self which motivates El Hadji to submit himself to this debasement and revenge by the beggars, whom he had once called "human rubbish." The symbolic class implications are enormous.

Sembène does not use stereotypes, such as depicting the exploiter as ridiculously evil and the exploited as simply heroic. In *Xala* we feel empathy for both El Hadji and the beggars. As Sembène warns the emerging bourgeoisie not to lose sight of its own trauma and inevitable fall from power, the filmmaker clearly shows a difference between human nature and the corrupting influence of imposed systems and cultures on Africa.

"Xala," in fact, indicates a "temporary sexual impotence"; temporary suggests that the bourgeois era will end one day. It also implies that the new bourgeoisie when re-educated and having undergone proletarianization will become active and valuable cadres when the dominated class seizes power. Just as the oppressed offer a cure for El Hadji's xala, therefore, so too they do for Africa.

What has given most viewers of *Xala* an uncertain feeling of the film's ending is the ritual of spitting on El Hadji. The scene challenges spectators to forget their viewing habits, to fight conventional codes and to attend to an experience, a new code. The spitting seems like a vomiting of bile: a symbolic social act. Its treatment in film language makes it a powerful "trope" of cinematic rhetoric to connote the bourgeoisie's expression of anger against that class. Furthermore, the spitting on El Hadji helps reincorporate him into the people's fold. In other words, the ritual becomes a folk method of purgation which makes El Hadji a literal incarnation of all members of the class or group that spit on him and consequently reintegrates him into folk society.

FILMIC CODES AND THE CULTURAL CURTAIN

If we accept the notion that artistic choice also connotes ideological choice, we must begin to investigate the ideological weight carried by a film's formal elements. Spectator involvement in *Xala* does not come, I contend, from the plot and the story structure alone but also from the execution of some basic cinematic elements such as editing, composition, camera positioning and movement.

Sembène acts effectively in *Xala* in his editing strategy and composition within the frame. An excellent instance of his editing comes in the sequence of the wedding reception, an event documenting the foibles of the emerging bourgeoisie. Two men, a minister and a deputy, meet at a doorway:

Deputy: Mr. Minister, after you.
Minister: No, Mr. Deputy, after you.
Deputy: No, Minister, you are the government representative.
Minister: But you represent the people.
Deputy: I will wait.
Minister and Deputy: Let us wait.

They remain erect by the door. In the next shot we see the bride's mother and aunt cutting up the meat, followed by a shot of the wedding cake where everyone is waiting for a share. Here are two government officials splitting the nation into halves by claiming they represent either "the people" or "the government." They gut Africa as if it were a piece of meat where people assemble to get their share.

As for composition, there are two examples in the film that are indeed remarkable. One is at the wedding reception. We see the bride's mother and aunt, Ya Binta, coming towards the camera to greet El Hadji's first and second wives who enter the frame from the right side. The camera lingers on this shot while we listen to them exchange greetings. We notice their dress — all have African dresses except El Hadji's second wife, Oumi. But the dress worn by the bride's aunt reveals much about the film's nature and complexity. She wears a most colorful dress that appears, at first sight, authentically African; however, it is spotted with white figures that resemble Queen Elizabeth of England.

The composition of images takes greater meaning in a scene in El Hadji's warehouse office, where Rama, seated in front of a map of Africa, talks to her father. (Note the double entendre in the dialogue.

According to folk habit, xala is usually attributed to the first wife's jealousy so that in private and public quarters Awa will be blamed for it.)

> El Hadji: Rama, my child, sit down: How is school?
> Rama: I do my best. And the activities?
> El Hadji: Ok, ok. Everything all right at home?
> Rama: Yes.
> El Hadji: Did your mother send you?
> Rama: No, I came on my own. I am old enough to understand certain things.
> El Hadji: (suspecting that she might be referring to his xala) Understand what?!
> Rama: Mother is suffering.
> El Hadji: Is she sick?
> Rama: Physically, no. I remind you, father, that mother is your first wife.
> El Hadji: I know, my daughter. I will come by. Tell her so.
> Rama: No, she doesn't know I have come.

Before Rama stands up to walk out of the frame Sembène makes us once again take note of the map of Africa behind her. We notice too that the color of the map reflects the exact same colors of Rama's traditional boubou, native costume — blue, purple, green and yellow — and it is not divided into boundaries and states. It denotes pan-Africanism.

> El Hadji: My child, you don't need anything? (He searches his wallet)
> Rama: Just my mother's happiness. (She then walks out of the frame as the camera lingers on the map.)

What Sembène is saying to us is quite direct and no longer inaccessible. On one level, Rama shows concern for her mother — it occupies a place of meaning in the dialogue. On another level, when we consider the African map which occupies the same screen space as Rama, her concern becomes not only her maternal mother but "Mother Africa." This notion carries an extended meaning when we observe the shot of El Hadji — to his side we see a huge colonial map of Africa. The "wax" and "gold" are posited jointly by a single instance of composition. Two realities fight to command the frame, but finally the "gold" meaning leaps out and breaks the boundaries of the screen.

Low and high angle shots, common connotative devices in filmmaking, abound in *Xala*. Their use in the film has visual and ideological meaning. For instance, as the film is introduced to us, in a quick visual montage and a voice-over narration on "African Socialism," we see the colonial representatives leave, taking their miniature statues and busts of white figures with them. Immediately following, the Africans in the new government enter a huge building — they are shot from a low angle, a shot that connotes power. The next time we see them, shot from a high angle, which diminishes the people depicted, they are opening briefcases full of money handed to them by the whites we saw leaving just a short while back.

In the high-angle shot of the board room we see the members of the Chamber seated around what appears to be a pool table. The color is green, the color of the money that their business meeting will generate. The six men seated around the table seem to represent the six pool table pockets. In the meeting room, a white advisor stands in the background, like an overseer as in the colonial era, still visible and still calling the shots. The composition makes us realize that any change in power is merely illusory and only cosmetic.

Gorgul, the blind man, the leader of the beggars, does not have many lines to speak (he does not speak until a few minutes before the film ends), but has visual importance. All through the film when the beggars are shown, we see the blind man singled out, shot mostly from a low angle, giving him an appearance of some kind of power and a sense of majesty. When the film's point of view coincides with that of the other beggars, however, we see him shot at eye-level.

So long as there exists a "cultural curtain" falling between peoples and nations, knowing how films articulate space and time becomes crucial to understanding films coming from a geographical and cultural distance. African films (or other Third World films, for that matter) when shown outside of their cultural context tend to lose their message. Therefore, the degree to which films transcend the "cultural curtain" becomes critical to any discussion of film's effectiveness.[6] These matters often depend on the issue of film's spatial-temporal significations.

In *Xala*, there is one continuous scene which calls attention to itself. It is a scene where Modu, El Hadji's chauffeur, opens a bottle of imported mineral water (El Hadji's favorite drink), empties it into the Mercedes's radiator, discards the empty bottle, and closes the hood. Screen time here is identical to the actual time it would take in real life. Any U.S. film student might be tempted to shorten the scene without any loss in "meaning." But the issue is not what the film lacks but what it possesses. We must interpret the scene as it is coded. We need to remember that of all the characters in *Xala*, Modu is the only person engaged in any kind of labor. Sembène, a man understanding Marx and Lenin, does not want the scene's implication to go unnoticed. The scene, therefore, forces time to become space and space to become time to emphasize these elements and the comedy inherent in the character's labor.

Another instance of Sembène's use of time and space occurs in the last few scenes, when El Hadji submits to the beggars who spit on him. First, the camera pans (a shot that maintains integrity of the space) around the proud figure of El Hadji standing half-naked, the spittle covering his shoulders and chest. The camera then registers a medium shot of his son and daughter standing by watching their father's humiliation, and lingers on an intimate image of Awa in tears. Then time is stuck, frozen — the image of El Hadji is caught as in a freeze frame. And we too must stop for a moment to ponder the meaning of this man and his suffering. Since we cannot rely on El Hadji to "stay put" in the predicted space offered by the changing world of the screen, we are denied any easy identification with his fate. We skip to a different period — the time of the Independence celebration. Time has played a cruel trick on El Hadji and the class he represents. We watch and reconstruct a picture of Africa that allows us to be analytical and objective and demands of us that we take sides.

Xala is not simply another film made by an African and which treats African themes and elements. It does not rely on the concepts and propositions of conventional cinema, be it U.S., Russian or European. *Xala* uniquely takes African folk-narrative tradition and translates it fully into filmic form.

Cinema does not have to tell a story only one way. It does not have to perpetuate the status quo. The meaningful road to African cinema lies in a cinema that draws from the wealth of its cultural and aesthetic traditions. *Xala* marks and signals a turning point in the development of African cinema in that folk-narrative tradition and cinema acquire a measure of peaceful coexistence. This requires the establishment of a new cinematic code, one which will evolve its own system governed by its own set of rules and criteria of excellence. This brief study has attempted to critically appraise the code-in-formation and the direction of a new cinema — a cinema of wax and gold.

NOTES

[1] Ousmane Sembène has directed nine films including *Xala. The Songhai Empire,* made as a thesis film under Donskoi and Guerassimov in the Soviet Union, has never been distributed. *Borom Sarret* (1963) is a 19-minute short with no dialogue but a voice-over commentary which documents a day in the life of a horse-cart driver. *Niaye* (1964), another short, treats the subject of incest, suicide and murder with a voice-over narration of an African riot. *Black Girl* is a story of a young African woman who cannot speak French but is taken to France as a maid. *Mandabi,* a feature film, tells the tale of a simple old man and the ironies of life in modern Dakar, Senegal. Ibrahima Dieng, the lead character, is a person broken; the modern system has outstripped the cultural values that nurtured him. *Tauw*, a 20-minute film, presents a young man who cannot find employment in Senegal's dominant neocolonialist system and depicts the hopelessness and modern bureaucratic maze in Senegal. *Emitai*

shows the courageous resistance of the Dialo women against the French in the closing days of the Second World War. _Ceddo_ treats the subject of Muslim imperialism. "Ceddo," meaning "outsiders," represents Africans who resisted wholesale conversion to Islam.

[2] "Sem-enna-worq" is a favorite form of poetry in Ethiopia. The concept, however, exists in most African languages. For its unique uses and meaning, see Donald Levine, _Wax and Gold: Tradition and Innovation in Ethiopia_ (Chicago: University of Chicago Press, 1965).

[3] Sembène, Ousmane, _Xala_ (Westport, Conn.: Lawrence Hill & Co, 1976). _Xala,_ the novel, differs significantly from the film version. The book explores interpersonal relationships and individual inner states more fully. For instance, in the novel El Hadji's negative side comes from his own nature and attitudes towards others, whereas the film captures his negative side mostly by a contrast established between his lifestyle and that of the beggars. The film omits many family relationships; for instance, Awa's father is present as a Christian character in the novel, and Rama has a fiancé, Pathe, a psychiatrist with whom Rama discusses her father's xala. Dimensions of Oumi's, Awa's and Rama's personal and family lives are altogether left out in the film version.

[4] Most of the dialogue in this study is taken from the film itself.

[5] Although I have referred to beggars continuously, Sembène shows a peasant among them (not in the novel) representing the destitute rural workers. When a skillful pickpocket, Thierry (the man who replaces El Hadji as a board member), steals the money his villagers gave him to buy food, ashamed to return to the village, he joins the beggar band in the city. Sembène includes a peasant in an urban setting so that the national issue will not be forgotten.

[6] If a spectator's initial introduction to Sembène's filmic work is, for instance either _Emitai_ or _Ceddo,_ both employing a collective heroism and shot in social space, one might conclude that Sembène does not understand the value of intimate shots. However, in an earlier film, _Mandabi,_ shot with individual space and much camera intimacy, Sembène has shown mastery of close-up shots. In fact, anyone who has seen the film is sure to remember the face, the feet and even the nostril of the lead character, Ibrahima Dieng. The details remain in our visual memory. In each of the above cases one thing is certain — Sembène's search for an African cinema is evident. In each instance, style modifies subject-matter.

CHAPTER 23.

Film and Revolution in Cuba: The First 25 Years

JULIANNE BURTON

In the initial moments of Tomás Gutiérrez Alea's *La Muerte de un Burocrata* (The Death of a Bureaucrat, 1966) there is an audacious and brilliantly comic sequence. The deceased worker around whose disinterred remains the plot will revolve is seen in semi-animated flashback at his workplace. An "exemplary" proletarian artist, he has reduced art to a science, having devised a machine that produces busts of Cuban national poet and patriot José Marti with the monotonous regularity of cogs emerging from a press. In a moment of carelessness, the worker falls prey to his own invention. The last bust to emerge is his own; he has been martyred to his misguided concept of art.

The sequence imaginatively conveys the Cuban film industry's rejection of mechanical concepts mechanically imposed on the creative process. In 1973, to their surprise, U.S. audiences discovered the delightful unpredictability that characterized many Cuban films of the 1960s and 1970s with the theatrical release of *Memories of Underdevelopment* (Tomás Gutiérrez Alea, 1968). Disarmed by its complexity and inventiveness, by its sophisticated wit and sympathetic portrayal of its bourgeois protagonist, U.S. critics greeted the film with ringing praise. *The New York Times* listed it among the year's 10 best films. The National Society of Film Critics offered its director a special award, though the State Department's refusal to grant him a visa prevented him from attending the ceremony. However regrettable, such a response was not unexpected given how the Treasury Department had shut down the First New York Festival of Cuban Cinema the previous year, confiscating all prints on the second day of the week-long program and eventually driving American Documentary Films, co-sponsors of the festival, into bankruptcy.[1]

For a quarter century the United States has sought to isolate Cuba from the rest of the world by imposing an economic and cultural blockade on the island. During this period, Cuban cinema and the related arts of music and poster design have continued to break through the cultural blockade to assert the creative energy of this struggling socialist society.

CINEMA AND CULTURAL PRIORITIES

The leaders of the guerrilla struggle were quick to perceive the artistic and educational supremacy of the film medium. In early 1959, soon after Fidel Castro became head of the new revolutionary government, he ranked cinema and television, in that order, as the most important forms of artistic expression. A decade later, the First National Congress on Education and Culture pointed to radio, television, the cinema and the press as "powerful instruments of ideological education, molders of the collective consciousness whose use and development must not be left to improvisation or spontaneity." The congress singled out film as "the art *par excellence* in our century."

Histories of postrevolutionary Cuban cinema customarily begin by observing that the decree founding the Cuban Institute of Cinematographic Art and Industry (ICAIC) on March 24, 1959, was the first cultural act of the revolutionary government, coming less than three months after the overthrow of dictator Fulgencio Batista. In fact, another revolutionary film organization preceded ICAIC. Cine Rebelde, part of the Rebel Army's National Board of Culture, was founded as soon as the rebels took power. After producing two documentary shorts, Tomás Gutiérrez Alea's *Esta Tierra Nuestra* (This is our Land) and Julio García Espinosa's *La Vivienda* (Housing), Cine Rebelde became part of the newly founded film institute. Alfredo Guevara, founding Director of ICAIC, insists that film was in fact the second priority of the new government, preceding but subordinate in importance and in impact to the national literacy campaign of 1960-61.

PREREVOLUTIONARY HISTORY

Cubans frequently stress the absence of a cinematic tradition in pre-revolutionary Cuba, as Castro did in his Report to the First Party Congress (1975) when he commended the achievements of "a new art form, without a history or a tradition in our country." Leading filmmaker and theorist Julio García Espinosa concurs regarding the dearth of constructive models but emphasizes the potential impact of what was in fact a powerful negative heritage.

Cuban film historians emphasize the parallel historical development of the film medium, the U.S. drive towards extraterritorial expansion, and the history of Cuba as a nation. Cubans were exposed to the moving image as early as citizens of any country on the continent when the first Lumière films made their debut there in 1897. By 1898, Cuban audiences were already being treated to the cinema as a vehicle for historical falsification imposed upon them by their neighbors to the north. *Fighting With Our Boys in Cuba, Raising Old Glory Over Moro Caste, The Battle of San Juan Hill* and the like alternated authentic footage with blatant simulations filmed not in Cuba but in the United States. Their purpose was less to relay an accurate picture of the Cuban War for Independence from Spain than to rouse patriotic Yankee sentiment in favor of U.S. intervention in that war.

In the early years of the U.S. movie industry, independents fleeing the watchful and monopolizing eye of Edison's Motion Picture Patents Company took refuge on Cuban shores before eventually setting up shop in southern California. Sporadic attempts to establish a national Cuban film industry capable of competing with entrenched foreign concerns seemed doomed to perennial failure and were virtually abandoned after the advent of sound. Film production, distribution and exhibition in Cuba became the province of U.S. and Mexican companies. From the 1930s through the 1950s, Cuba's major cinematic role was to furnish exotic sets, sultry sex queens and a tropical beat for Hollywood and Mexican productions. Cuba offered an audience as well. In proportion to its population, the Cuban movie market was the most lucrative in Latin America. A population of less than seven million people produced the astonishing number of one and a half million movie-goers per week, despite the fact that large segments of the rural population had never seen a single film.

Escapist tropical musicals, melodramas and detective flicks characterized national film production during the 20 years preceding Batista's overthrow. The 8,000 workers in the industry were primarily employed in the production of advertising shorts for theaters and television, newsreels for local consumption, and technical or scientific films for specialized audiences. One other specialty of the prerevolutionary film industry deserves mention: Cuba had more than its share of enterprising pornographers.[2]

During the 1950s, most serious film activity was centered in film societies, in particular the Nuestro Tiempo (Our Times) and Visión groups. In 1954, two members of the former, Julio García Espinosa and Tomás Gutiérrez Alea, fresh from two years of film study at the Centro Sperimentale in Rome, collaborated with several other Cubans on a short dramatic feature in the style of the Italian Neorealists, called *El*

Megano (The Charcoal Worker). This denunciation of the hardships of charcoal production on the island's southern coast was confiscated by Batista. Though its style and formulation now seem embarrassingly naive, the film still enjoys the special distinction of being the only recognized antecedent of postrevolutionary cinema. All who collaborated on it have gone on to become leading figures in ICAIC: screenwriter Alfredo Guevara was head of the Film Institute from its founding until 1982; production assistant Jorge Fraga, now a director in his own right, has also served as head of film production since 1978; cameraman Jorge Haydú is a leading cinematographer; Gutiérrez Alea is ICAIC's foremost director, and Julio García Espinosa — filmmaker, script consultant, theoretician — was appointed to succeed Guevara as head of ICAIC in 1982.

Despite the remarkable size of the national film audience, the most reliable estimates conclude that the Cuban film industry produced no more than 150 features in its six decades of prerevolutionary history. Aside from newsreels, noncommercial documentaries were virtually unheard of. In the succeeding 24 years, ICAIC produced 112 full-length films (feature and documentary), some 900 documentary shorts — educational, scientific and technical as well as animated and fictional films — and more than 1,300 weekly newsreels.[3]

EMPHASIZING DOCUMENTARY

As these production statistics demonstrate, ICAIC has given priority to documentary over fictional subjects. Both economic and ideological factors motivate this preference. The economic motivations are obvious: when funds and equipment are limited, professional actors, elaborate scripts, costuming and studio sets can be regarded as nonessentials. In a society that subscribes to the principles of Marxism-Leninism, it is believed fitting that creative activity be based on the confrontation with material reality.

The impulse to document the euphoria of the rebel victory and popular response to the resulting social transformations brought aspiring filmmakers out into the streets. What had previously been an impossible dream — making serious cinema in Cuba — was now an immediate possibility for scores of young cinemaphiles. This attempt to record the first convulsive moments of revolutionary victory had a profound effect on artists who had previously conceived of filmmaking as above all a vehicle for personal expression. In their documentary apprenticeship, Cuban filmmakers came face to face with unimagined aspects of national life. Their newfound growth in awareness and social sensitivity was largely responsible for the intense dialectic between historical circumstance and individual response that informs fictional as well as documentary production in postrevolutionary Cuban cinema.

The newsreels, produced under the direction of Santiago Alvarez and aimed not just at Cuban audiences but towards all of Latin America, are exceptional examples of the genre. Alvarez explains that his concern:

> has not been to make each news item independent of the others, but to connect them in such a way that they pass before the spectator as a unified whole, according to a single discursive line. This accounts for the deliberate structuration which we use to achieve this thematic unity. For this reason, many classify our newsreels as genuine and autonomous documentaries.[4]

Initially restricted by the shortage of funds, material and resources, Alvarez was one of many Cuban filmmakers to turn practical handicaps into expressive assets. Obliged to draw from existing film archives and such ''second-hand'' sources as news photos and television footage, he developed a methodology that circumvented the need for on-the-spot footage, and elevated the film-collage to a high level of political and artistic quality.

The innovative display of secondary footage, rhythmic editing with dramatic variations in pace, graphically innovative titles and eclectic musical selections (in preference to any spoken narration), superimposition and other experimental montage techniques characterize his early films. Material and political circumstances encouraged Alvarez, like his spiritual ancestor Dziga Vertov, to create the essence of his art on the editing table. As circumstances changed and more resources were put at his disposal, he shifted from black and white to color and began making longer films in which primary footage predominates. More recent films are characterized by more traditional cinematography, longer takes, less experimental editing and the frequent use of voice-over narration.

In general, we can loosely divide Cuban documentary production into five thematic categories. Films that deal with *domestic politics* promote governmental policies and encourage popular participation and mass mobilization. *Historical* films chart various aspects of the formation of national identity through the five centuries of the island's recorded history. Documentaries of a *cultural* nature may be either national or international in their focus. Films that take *international relations* for their theme might focus on Cuba's role in international affairs, analyze the developed sector or express solidarity with other Third World nations. Finally, *didactic* documentaries, highly technical or scientific in nature, are generally produced by specific agencies rather than ICAIC.

PROJECT AND PROCESS

Two central themes run through all of Cuban cinema, fictional and documentary production alike: history and underdevelopment. Cubans interpret each of these terms in a broad and fluid way. Underdevelopment is the economic and technological heritage of colonial dependency, which has its more stubborn manifestations in individual and collective psychology, ideology and culture. History is a complex of formative influences, which elucidates the present and informs the future.

Both themes have had an impact on the form as well as the content of revolutionary Cuban cinema. The dialectical tension between practical limitations and artistic aspirations has encouraged innovation and spontaneity. The filming of *Memories of Underdevelopment,* for example, became itself a "memory of underdevelopment" as Gutiérrez Alea describes it:

> At each step we felt the touch of underdevelopment. It limited us. . . . It conditioned the language with which we expressed ourselves. . . . I have to say that this is the film in which I have felt most free in spite of the everpresent limitations imposed by underdevelopment. Perhaps I felt free precisely because of those limitations.[5]

After a visit to the island in 1975, Francis Ford Coppola attempted to compare the situation of Cuban filmmakers with their U.S. counterparts. Having perceived the kind of creative freedom that comes from overcoming practical constraints, Coppola observed, "We don't have the advantage of their disadvantages."[6]

At an early stage in the development of ICAIC, founder Alfredo Guevara expressed the organization's determination to lay bare the form and technique of the filmmaker's craft and formulated the purpose of the Cuban film project: "to demystify cinema for the entire population; to work, in a way, against our own power; to reveal all the tricks, all the resources of language; to dismantle all the mechanisms of cinematic hypnosis."[7] In part, this determination grows out of the conviction that all forms of artistic expression carry an ideological dimension. If this ideological bias is veiled in the vast majority of art works produced in capitalist societies, Cuban filmmakers reason, it should be made explicit in the artistic production of a revolutionary socialist regime. Thus the eclecticism of Cuban film style is in part the result of the effort to appropriate forms of cinematic expression from the developed capitalist sector in order to dismantle them and expose their inner workings. Cubans call this operation "decolonization" and consider it the first priority of their film effort.

The fact that the transformation of film content in Cuba has most often been accompanied by the will to make the form manifest produces a process-oriented rather than a product-oriented cinema, whether in the documentary or the fictional mode. Fiction films in particular have often experimented with more open forms in order to stimulate the critical participation of the viewer.

Cuban filmmakers have used many formal devices in their attempt to convert the audience from passive consumer into active participant. The Bazinian realism of the first postrevolutionary feature, Tomás Gutiérrez Alea's *Historias de la Revolución* (Stories from the Revolution, 1960), soon gave way to more self-reflexive forms, exploring the paradoxical Brechtian contention that dislocation and distancing, rather than unbroken identification, increase the conscious and critical participation of the spectator. Formal self-consciousness, initially apparent in the allusions to leading world filmmakers in the early feature *The Death of a Bureaucrat* (1966) and in García Espinosa's picaresque farce *The Adventures of Juan Quin Quin* (1967), has subsequently found expression in multiple self-reflexive devices. García Espinosa's feature-length documentary *Third World, Third World War* (1970) incorporates the actual filmmaking process into the finished picture, as do the subsequent feature-length documentary *Bay of Pigs* (Manuel Herrera, 1972) and the historical biography *Mella* (Enrique Pineda Barnet, 1975).

Established film genres are often parodied and subverted: the Hollywood war movie in *Bay of Pigs*; the ahistorical Latin melodrama in *The Other Francisco* (Sergio Giral, 1974). Octavio Cortazar's poignant account of one mountain community's first exposure to moving pictures — *For the First Time* (1967) — is an early example of the film-within-a-film device. *With the Cuban Women* (1974), by the same director, opens with startling disjunction between aural and visual information.

Films such as *Memories of Underdevelopment, Lucia* (1968), and *The Other Francisco* are characterized by a marked shift between lyrical and naturalistic visual styles. Experimentation with film stock, laboratory techniques, lighting and camera lenses accounts for the visual expressionism of Manuel Octavio Gómez's *The First Charge of the Machete* (1969), Part I of Humberto Solás's *Lucia,* and the same director's first color film, *Simparele* (1964), as well as many of the Alvarez documentaries. Other self-reflexive devices include the experimentation with musical and nonmusical sound and the print medium, which also characterizes Alvarez's work and that of several other directors, and, finally, the dramatization of the documentary form through the appropriation of narrative techniques traditionally associated with fictional filmmaking. This devise is used in shorts such as Alejandro Saderman's *Hombres de Mal Tiempo* (Men from Mal Tiempo, 1968), Oscar

Valdés's _Muerte y Vida en el Morillo_ (Death and Life in El Morrillo, 1971) and Miguel Torre's _Historia de una Infamia_ (History of an Infamy, 1983). The reverse of this operation informs _Memories of Underdevelopment, The Other Francisco, Bay of Pigs, One Way or Another_ (1974/1977), and Gutiérrez Alea's feature, _Hasta Cierto Punto_ (Up to a Certain Point, 1983).

But formal self-reflexiveness is not a _sine qua non_ of Cuban film production. As Jorge Fraga, head of artistic production at ICAIC, puts it: "We are not in favor of firing merely for the pleasure of hearing the shot. We shoot in order to hit the target." Many recent films seem to have subordinated issues of formal candor to other considerations and other goals. Gutiérrez Alea's _The Last Supper_ (1977) and Pastor Vega's _Portrait of Teresa_ (1979) are but two examples of recent films that opt for classical over modernist form. The power of Hollywood's "transparent" style continues to fascinate the Cubans, whose goal is to use that capacity to galvanize an audience for less ideologically veiled and alienating ends. In a society that purports to derive its vitality from a constant process of re-examination and renewal, even apparently conventional strategies can be used in innovative ways, and what was once innovative can become constrictive.

ICAIC's leadership stresses each film's potential for "communicability" as the crucial determinant of its worth, but continues to recognize multiple strategies for achieving this end. In Julio García Espinosa's words, the greatest responsibility of Cuban filmmakers is to create a kind of cinema "where the human factor, imagination and talent are more important than technical considerations; where artistic conception is completely in tune with actual existing resources."[8]

However impressive the quantity and quality of film production in a country which had no national film industry before 1959, this is but one aspect of a comprehensive national film program whose primary goals are universal film literacy and universal access to the medium. Consistent with the priority placed on human development over technical acquisition in the production sector, scarce financial resources channeled into exhibition in the early years were concentrated on providing the largest number of uninitiated viewers with access to film. Faced with the dire shortage of movie theaters in rural areas, and the financial and temporal obstacles to constructing the number needed, the Cubans devised the famous "mobile cinemas." Trucks, mule teams, even small boats, all fitted out with projection equipment and stocked with an eclectic repertoire of film titles, were sent to the most remote sections of the island. In more densely populated regions throughout the island, topical film "cycles" are continually presented at theatres. This program, run by the Cinemateca de Cuba, a division of ICAIC, provides films for 100,000 spectators per week — presumably a world's record for an institution of its kind.[9] Two national television programs provide ongoing education in film history, language and technique.[10]

Though the prevalence of praxis (filmmaking and active organizational work) over theoretical deliberation in written form has been characteristic of the Film Institute to date, ICAIC's contribution to film theory has been far from negligible. Alfredo Guevara, founder and director of ICAIC, has continually given ideological direction and theoretical orientation through speeches and essays. His leadership has been a guiding force not only within Cuba but throughout Latin America for politically-committed filmmakers, who have been invited to Havana to use ICAIC's facilities or to participate in the international festivals of the New Latin American Cinema held annually since 1979.

Efforts to define in writing the nature and role of film in a revolutionary society began in 1960 with the first issues of the Cuban film magazine *Cine Cubana,* and related deliberations continue to appear in its pages. The first theoretical formulation to generate broad impact outside the island was Julio García Espinosa's "For an Imperfect Cinema" (1970). García Espinosa has subsequently written several other essays that attempt to build a bridge between practice and theory. In 1979 these were collected under the title *Una imagen recorre el mundo* (Havana: Letras Cubanas). Tomás Gutiérrez Alea has also carried out parallel pursuits. His *Dialectica del espectador* (Havana: Cuadernos de la Revista Union, 1982) was named one of the 10 best books of the year.[11]

THE EVOLUTION OF ICAIC: A CHRONOLOGY

The initial period of ICAIC's history, from 1959 to 1960, was characterized by explosive optimism and a great sense of release, by the jubilant return of many exiled artists, the influx of foreign talent and the artistic debut of many young and untried nationals. Enthusiastic organizational activity included the founding of ICAIC and the nationalization of all film-related holdings in foreign hands. The attitude of the government and the population at large was one of uncritical enthusiasm for artistic and intellectual activity of all sorts. Among the artists themselves, united-front politics predominated. The first film efforts were generally celebrative works in an epic or journalistic style and focused on the trajectory and triumph of the insurrection and on the corruption and injustice of the former regime.

In a second period, 1960 to 1969, the concept of revolutionary art and of the revolutionary artist became gradually more defined through a series of debates and polemics as well as the lived experience of the revolution. Ideological maturation and intensified class conflict began to curb the "anything goes" atmosphere in the artistic sector. The concept of art as praxis and of the artist as militant participant rather than detached observer began to dominate. The broad and initially uncritical assimilation of foreign models, the virtually unlimited hospitality to visiting artists and intellectuals, and the attentive quest for their approval gave way to a more critical stance and to the growing influence of artistic inspiration from national sources and other Third World countries — particularly other Latin American nations — in preference to the developed sector.

At the beginning of this period, the prevalence of visiting foreign filmmakers at ICAIC and the organization's involvement in a number of co-productions with various countries contributed to a rather superficial and exoticized interpretation of Cuban culture. The celebration of "One Hundred Years of Struggle" in 1968 to commemorate the fight for national autonomy that had begun a century before sparked a much richer and more penetrating analysis of national history and identity. The pervasive influence of Italian Neorealism in the early 1960s and the fascination with the French New Wave in mid-decade had, by the end of this period given way to broad-based stylistic experimentation and characteristically Cuban eclecticism. By 1964, the Cuban documentary was beginning to gain international attention through the work of Santiago Alvarez. Fictional production came into its own four years later with the release of *Memories of Underdevelopment* and *Lucia*. This period also saw signs of diminishing tolerance for a liberal interpretation of artistic freedom and responsibility. For numerous reasons, the process of defining the role of art in a revolutionary socialist society met with more difficulties in the realm of letters, with its centuries-long tradition of isolated individual production, than in the film sector or the other more co-operative and social arts. The tensions between individual ambition and the needs of the collectivity were played out between the years 1967 and 1971 in the life and career of one particular poet, Heberto Padilla, who became an international *cause célèbre* upon his imprisonment in 1971.[12]

The failure of the projected ten-million-ton sugar harvest in 1970 brought about a critical reappraisal of policies and priorities in all sectors of society, beginning with Castro himself and including ICAIC and other cultural agencies. The period between 1970 and 1974 saw an increased emphasis on mass participation and the search for more indigenous cultural forms. Elitism and manifestations of artistic privilege were rejected in favor of an attempt to define and produce a genuine people's culture. At ICAIC there was a consequent decline — by no means absolute — in formal experimentation, which had reached a peak

of virtuosity in the late 1960s. The emphasis on documentary production extended during these years to the realm of feature-length films,
where for the first time nonfictional subjects outnumbered fictional
ones.

The year 1975, which saw the first National Congress of the Cuban
Communist Party, marked the inception of a period of sweeping reorganization within ICAIC, a process that may or may not have culminated
with the naming in 1983 of Julio García Espinosa to succeed Alfredo
Guevara as head of the Institute. In 1976, the process of "institutionalization of the Revolution," which began in 1970, reached the cultural
sector.[13] The formation of a national Ministry of Culture, which incorporated ICAIC under Guevara's continuing direction as one of its five
vice-ministers, marked the symbolic loss of the privileged autonomy the
Institute had enjoyed since its founding. Lest the motivations for the
economic reorganization and redefinition of ICAIC appear to have come
largely from outside the agency, it is important to note that these directives coincided with internal concerns to lower costs and increase productivity, concerns that date from the beginning of the decade.

Alfredo Guevara has stated that the greatest innovations of the
Cuban film industry have been in the social relations of the labor process, and other leaders within ICAIC have seconded this claim. The
Cubans have tried to balance the needs of the collectivity with those of
personal creative expression through their commitment to workers' control and the collective evaluation of each other's work, as well as
through the high degree of initiative granted to the director. *Con-
sciencia* (socio-political awareness and sense of responsibility) and *sub-
jectividad* (personal artistic judgment) are regarded as the dual components of the creative process.

ARTISTIC PRACTICE AND MASS SOCIETY

As Julio García Espinosa and a number of others have pointed out,
though nationalization gave Cubans ownership of the movie theaters in
the early 1960s, they have still not been able to claim full ownership of
the screens. Of the 130 to 140 feature films annually premiered in Cuba
to supply the 510 theaters on the island, only about 3 per cent are
national products; the vast majority are imported from abroad. The
potential demand of Cuban audiences for Cuban features far exceeds
current ICAIC prodiction levels. The institution of positive and negative
material incentives to increase efficiency and productivity is one strategy to make greater use of existing resources. International coproduc-
tions are another. Whether or not one views these methods as construc-

tive and consistent with ICAIC's ideology and goals, they do not seem fully proportionate to the dimensions of the problem.

Despite the ideological importance conferred upon the documentary, fictional filmmaking continues to be regarded as the highest expression of the cinematic vocation, at least as much by the members of ICAIC as by the filmgoing public. With a single exception (Humberto Solás) all of ICAIC's filmmakers started as documentarists. The opportunity to make feature-length fiction films is a "promotion" earned through a long process of "documentary apprenticeship." Rather than increasing over time, the number of documentarists who "graduate" to fiction has declined.

Between 1974 and 1976, as a response to the need to inject "new blood" into the institution, ICAIC took on a score of university graduates (the vast majority of them women) for training as *analistas,* using them as apprentices in all sectors of the production process from script research to assistant direction. These aspiring filmmakers face an additional hurdle, the jump from assistant or apprentice to documentarist. Here, too, the process of ascent seems deplorably slow.

North American visitors to ICAIC continue to question the dearth of women directors and the limited number of blacks. Sara Gómez, who belonged to both the above categories, died in 1974 of acute asthma on the verge of completing her first feature, *One Way or Another*. Sergio Giral, the only black feature director, made his third feature (*Maluala*) in 1979. Among the documentarists, there is one black (Rigoberto López) and three women (Marisol Trujillo, Belkis Vega and Rebeca Chávez).

In response to this criticism, the Cubans reply that they reject any notion of quotas as inherently discriminatory, and that they have had only 25 years to try to reverse the centuries-old legacies of discrimination. Mayra Vilaris, assistant director, stated in a recent interview, "I would feel personally offended if I were told to start working on a film as the director because we need more women directors."[14] Her position is representative of many women at ICAIC. In a 1977 interview, Sergio Giral stated, "Not even I, as a black man, can conceive of a 'black' filmmaker or a 'black' film. . . . We have to retain the concept of race as an historical, social category."[15] Their primary identification, these Cuban cineastes declare, is as Cubans, not as women, or blacks, or Chinese; and it is as Cubans that they feel they can best work together to create a society that, in Jorge Fraga's words, "permits everyone the possibility to develop fully."[16]

As an island, Cuba has always been aware of how much a vigorous national culture depends upon the quantity and quality of visits to and visitors from abroad and what baggage they bring ashore. Under Minister of Culture, Armando Hart, Cuban artists and intellectuals have enjoyed increased opportunities for foreign travel, but even more important to the people and the project of ICAIC has been the influx since 1979 of filmmakers and critics from all over the world to attend the International Festival of the New Latin American Cinema held annually under its auspices. This remarkable forum for cultural exchange and discussion also testifies to the support and leadership role that ICAIC continues to play in the evolution and development of oppositional cinema in Latin America. In order to increase the worldwide diffusion of Latin American films, the Latin American Film Market (MECLA) was launched at the Second International Festival in 1980. The Fifth International Festival (December 1983) expanded its exhibition scope northward to include more than a decade of U.S. independent filmmaking in a program called "The Other Face: Independent Films in the United States."

Cuban poet and patriot José Marti said that the only way to do away with the need for soldiers is to become one. Leary of professional critics, Cuban filmmakers decided early on to assume the critic's task in *Cine Cubano* themselves rather than cede it to specialists. Some 25 years later, ICAIC has only two full-time critics: Carlos Galiano, who also writes reviews for the national daily *Granma,* and hosts a weekly TV show called "History of the Cinema," and Enrique Colina, whose prime-time program "Twenty-four Frames a Second" has been one of the most popular in Cuba for over a decade. If the televised film history and criticism are remarkably sophisticated, their print counterpart is deplorably limited — both a legacy and a confirmation of the general view of the critical act as arbitrary, intrusive and superfluous. As García Espinosa wrote in 1970, "Imperfect cinema rejects whatever services criticism has to offer and considers the function of mediators and intermediaries anachronistic."[17]

Largely as a result of such attitudes, *Cine Cubana* has not kept pace with the explosion of theoretical and methodological inquiry in the field of film studies over the past two decades. It remains primarily a promotional publication, and as such is of limited use to serious students of Cuban cinema. Fortunately, critical discussion, ideological debates and theoretical deliberations continue to be encouraged within the ranks of ICAIC (in the weekly *cine debates* attended by artistic and technical personnel as well as staff) and through the individual writings of a number of filmmakers, screenwriters and *analistas*. Increased exposure to critical and theoretical currents from abroad promises to stimulate further development in the fields of film theory, criticism and scholarship, as does the refreshingly down-to-earth theoretical bent of ICAIC's new director.

García Espinosa's assumption of the directorship of ICAIC was greeted with general approval and optimism. More than for his experience as a filmmaker or theorist, this founding member of ICAIC is valued for his ability to unleash the creative energies of others. He has served as adviser on scores of Cuban films and a list of his screenplay collaborations contain some of ICAIC's most outstanding and experimental films: Humberto Solás's *Lucia,* Manuel Octavio Gómez's *First Charge of the Machete,* and the feature-length documentaries *Bay of Pigs* (Manuel Herrera), *Viva la República!* (Pastor Vega) and *The Battle of Chile* (Patricio Guzmán).

Throughout his career, García Espinosa has been concerned with reconciling artistic practice and mass society. His goal has been to displace elitist cultural forms in favor of genuinely popular ones created with the participation of broad sectors of society. His longstanding interest in problems of genre stems from his perception of both the mass appeal and transformative potential of conventional narrative formulae. In a recent interview he recalled:

> Through the experience of filming *The Adventures of Juan Quin Quin* (1967), it became clear to me for the first time that it is in fact impossible to question a given reality without questioning the particular genre you select or inherit to depict that reality. Normally the artist's critique of the genre is done dependently, and only the results of the process are shared with the viewer. The challenge I faced was to discover how this critical process itself, rather than simply the results of that process, could be integrated into the film.[18]

In an earlier essay, he maintained:

> Until now, we have viewed the cinema as a means of reflecting reality, without realizing that cinema in itself is a reality, with its own history, conventions, and traditions. Cinema can only be constructed on the ashes of what already exists. Moreover, to make a new cinema is, in fact, to reveal the process of destruction of the one that came before. . . . We have to make a spectacle out of the destruction of the spectacle. This process cannot be individual. . . . What is needed is to perform this process jointly with the viewer.[19]

García Espinosa envisions a Tarzan film in which the hero takes part in contemporary political conflicts, marries an African woman, and is assimilated into African culture. He believes that the musical is a "natural" genre for Cuba, and his own *Son o No Son* (an untranslatable pun on Hamlet's "to be or not to be" and the Cuban musical form, *son*), which obtained a belated and limited release in 1980, is a delightfully comic imitation of the genre, both subversive and self-critical without ceasing to be enormously entertaining. Manuel Octavio Gómez's *Patakin,* billed as "the first Cuban musical," premiered at the 1983 Festival to mixed reviews and testifies to García Espinosa's continued encouragement of such efforts. His previous experience with documentary suggests that this area, site of so much extraordinary creativity over the last decade, will not be neglected.

Beyond the production sector, García Espinosa would like to see differentiated viewing environments (workplace-associated or workplace-disassociated, depending upon the nature of the films screened) and a future time when Cuba will have the technological resources to make filmmaking a genuinely mass activity: "Short of this, we have only made it halfway as filmmakers." He believes that as the electronic media invade the home and make conventional movie theaters obsolete, people will seek out cultural products that offer a more direct, less vicarious interaction, and that this *reto de masividad* (challenge of mass society), the greatest challenge facing cultural workers today, must not be ceded to purely commercial interests. As he wrote in 1970, in the closing lines of his famous essay "For an Imperfect Cinema" whose ideas still reverberate through ICAIC, "The future lies with folk art but then there will be no need to call it that [since there will be no need to connote the limits of popular creativity]: Art will not disappear into nothingness, it will disappear into everything."[20]

NOTES

[1] See Gary Crowdus, "The Spring 1972 Cuban Film Festival Bust," *Film Society Review* (March/April/May 1972): 23-26.

[2] Regarding this last point, see Peter Brook, "The Cuban Enterprise," *Sight and Sound* 30 (Spring 1961): 78-79. The principal source for prerevolutionary film history is Arturo Agramonte, *Cronologia del cine cubano* (Havana: Ediciones ICAIC, 1966); see also Julio Matas, "Theater and Cinematography," in Carmelo Mesa-Lago, ed., *Revolutionary Change in Cuba* (Pittsburgh: Univ. of Pittsburgh Press, 1971), pp. 436-442.

[3] My own updating of original figures from *Granma Weekly Review,* January 1977, based on *Filmografia del cine cubano, 1959-1981,* and Supplement: January 1982-November 1983 (Havana: Producción ICAIC 1982, 1983).

[4] "Santiago Alvarez habla de su cine," *Hablemos de cine* 54 (Lima, July-August 1970): 30.

[5] Tomás Gutiérrez Alea, *"Memorias del subdesarrollo:* Notas de trabajo," *Cine cubano* 45/46 (Havana 1968): 24-25.

[6] Francis Ford Coppola, "Robert Scheer Interviews Francis Ford Coppola on Cuba, Castro, Communism and the Mafia," *City of San Francisco* (December 2, 1975): 22.

[7] Cited in Marjorie Rosen, "The Great Cuban Fiasco," *Saturday Review* (June 17, 1972): 53.

[8] Julio García Espinosa, "Cinco preguntas a ICAIC," *Cine al dia* 12 (Caracas, March 1971): 22.

[9] See José Manuel Pardo, "El Cine-móvil ICAIC," *Cine Cubano* 73/74/75 (Havana, 1971): 93-104.

[10] On the most successful of these programs, see Jorge Silva, "Film Criticism in Cuba: An Interview with Enrique Colina," *Jump Cut* 22 (May 1980): 32-33.

[11] See *Jump Cut* 29 and 30: 1984 and 1985 for Julia Lesage's translation of this text under the title "The Viewer's Dialectic."

[12] For full documentation of this famous case, see Lourdes Casal, *El caso Padilla: Literatura y revolucíon en cuba: Documentos* (Miami: Nueva Atlántida, 1971).

[13] See Nelson P. Valdés, "Revolution and Institutionalization in Cuba," *Cuban Studies/Estudios Cubanos* 6 (January 1976): 1-37.

[14] Susan Fanshel, "Three Women in ICAIC: An Interview with Gloria Argüelles, Mayra Vilaris, and Marisol Trujillo," in *A Decade of Cuban Documentary Film: 1972-1982* (New York: Young Filmmakers Foundation, 1982), p. 10.

[15] Julianne Burton and Gary Crowdus, "Cuban Cinema and the Afro-Cuban Heritage: An Interview with Sergio Giral," *The Black Scholar* 8 (Summer 1977): 65.

[16] Fanshel, "The Cuban Film Institute: Past and Present: An Interview with Jorge Fraga," in Fanshel, *A Decade,* p. 13.

[17] Julio García Espinosa, "For an Imperfect Cinema," trans. Julianne Burton, in Michael Chanan, ed., *Twenty-Five Years of the New Latin American Cinema* (London: British Film Institute and Channel Four Books, 1983), p. 32.

[18] Julianne Burton, "Theory and Practice of Film and Popular Culture in Cuba: A Conversation with Julio García Espinosa," *Quarterly Review of Film Studies* (Fall 1982): 345.

[19] Julio García Espinosa, "Carta a la revista chilena *Primer Plano,*" *Una imagen recorre el mundo* (Havana: Letras Cubanas, 1979), pp. 26-27.

[20] García Espinosa in Chanan, *Twenty-Five Years,* p. 33.

CHAPTER 24.

In Solidarity: Joris Ivens and the Birth of Cuban Cinema

TOM WAUGH

> This young nation needs a brand new cinema . . . and it needs it quickly.
> The cinema for a free people isn't a carnival sideshow. The screen is for
> laughing and crying . . . the screen is for singing the sufferings of the
> past, the struggles of yesterday, and the hopes of today. The Cuban
> cinema is born . . . young filmmakers, young cinema, young nation. . . .
> In Cuba everyone is young.[1]

In the fall of 1960, Joris Ivens made a teaching-filmmaking visit to
Cuba and attached this voice-over impression of the new Cuban cinema
to one of the two short films — *Carnet de Viaje (Travel Notebook)* and
Pueblo Armado (A People in Arms) — that resulted. When Ivens came
to Cuba, he had already been filming revolutionary struggles for over 30
years. He had begun within the workers' newsreel movement in his
native Holland during the late 1920s and had since worked on virtually
every continent.

His most famous film had been *The Spanish Earth* (1937), a document of the Spanish Civil War, but he had also filmed the combat
against fascism in China, the United States and Canada and against
imperialism in Indonesia. He had also paused regularly along the way to
film the peaceful struggles of socialist construction — in the Soviet
Union (1932), in Eastern Europe (1946-56), and in China (1958).

The two Cuban films extended both of these currents of his career:
Travel Notebook surveyed the accomplishments of the Revolution at
the end of its second year, and *A People in Arms* focused on its defense
against continuing external threats.

The purpose of this article is not to make a claim for Ivens as a
major formative influence on the Cuban cinema. By the fall of 1960, the

Cuban cinema had already built up its own distinctive momentum under the vigorous leadership of the Institute of Cinematographic Art and Industry (ICAIC) and Alfredo Guevara, and of such already established directors as Tomás Gutiérrez Alea and Julio Garcí Espinosa. My intent is simply to shed some light on the two lines of film history intersecting at the point of Ivens's Cuban work — to fill in a little known chapter in the career of the dean of all socialist filmmakers and to suggest at the same time some elements of the exhilarating creative struggle taken up by Cuban documentarists in the early days of the revolution.

THE MILITANT, THE POET, AND THE TRAVELLER

Although *Travel Notebook* and *A People in Arms* are very much the product of their Cuban context, it is helpful first of all to locate them as "Ivens films," as personal works fully consistent with the evolution Ivens had been undergoing since his move to Paris from East Berlin in 1957. During the prolific decade that followed this move, Ivens worked primarily within the "lyrical essay" mode, both in Europe and the Third World. The films from this period are mostly short, poetic works, full of humor and warmth, sentimentality and whimsy. But there is also the ever-present base of political analysis beneath the surface of the lyricism, articulated with varying degrees of explicitness.

Le Mistral (1965), for example, Ivens's essay on the landscapes and winds of Provence, just happens to explore shantytowns of North African immigrant workers and to record how difficult it is to carry water by hand to the workers' homes. *A Valparaíso* (1963) uses its engaging confrontation with the hilly topography of this Chilean port city as an entry point for an essay on historical and political topography.

The new personal tone of such films suggested an abrupt turnabout from the cold, official quality of some of the less inspired work of the Eastern Bloc period, a period in which Ivens had been moving further and further from the cinema and was nearly absorbed into the film-industry bureaucracy of the German Democratic Republic. Western critics were quick to acclaim the return of the 60-year-old filmmaker to the "art" of his youth after his distraction by "Ideas" and "Politics" for decades. But Ivens repudiated this response with great vehemence, maintaining that the militant and the poet had always both been present in his work and that in effect the two were inseparable.

Between his last East Berlin film of 1956 and his Indochina series of the late 1960s, Ivens made films in China, Cuba, Mali and (twice) Chile. He also saw one Brazilian project aborted by the 1964 coup while another in Venezuela never got off the ground. His European work took him to Italy and France, where he examined underdevelopment in Sicily and Provence, and finally, in 1965, to the homeland from which he had been exiled 30 years before, to make a "come-home-all-is-forgiven" commissioned film on the port of Rotterdam.

EIGHT FILMMAKERS, TWO CAMERAS, ONE JEEP

Joris Ivens was in the new African republic of Mali when an invitation reached him in early 1960 from Alfredo Guevara, head of the recently formed ICAIC. Ivens took the next few months to finish his ongoing project, *Demain à Nanguila* (*Tomorrow at Nanguila,* 1960), a survey of the economic and personal challenges of African independence, boy-meets-irrigation-dam variety, and then headed for Havana.

On the evening of his arrival, the entire staff of ICAIC, already 300 strong, turned out for the lecture he had been asked to make. Not untypically, the lecture was turned into a dialogue by the Cubans' impatience to get to know their mythical visitor. The third day, the arrangements for Ivens's filmmaking tour with a group of young ICAIC filmmakers were finalized and they set off in a jeep on the tour of the island — a trip recounted in *Travel Notebook.*

Along with Ivens were two camerapersons, two assistant operators, two assistant directors, a business manager, and two portable 35mm cameras. This crew included Jorge Herrera, who became one of ICAIC's leading camerapersons and well known abroad for having shot Humberto Solás's *Cantata de Chile* (1973-76) and Manuel Octavio Gómez's *The First Charge of the Machete* (1969); Jorge Fraga, who went on to become a leading documentarist (*The New School*, 1973); José Massip, who also went on to direct documentaries, including some prize-winning ones about dance; Ramon Suerez, an operator who had directed a few shorts under the old regime and was to shoot all of Tomás Gutiérrez Alea's features through *Memories of Underdevelopment* (1968) before finally emigrating; and Alberto Roldán, an assistant director who also wound up directing documentaries. The excursion was co-ordinated by Saul Yelin, ICAIC's Head of International Relations until his much-lamented death in 1977. The filming was to be silent since Cuba's only sound system at that time was being used in a major feature project already underway. A general outline had been drawn up for *Travel Notebook*, but there was plenty of room for improvisation.

For the second project, on the People's Militia, the group waited until they reached the mountainous Escambray region where they were able to follow a mopping-up offensive against bands of U.S.-armed counter-revolutionaries.

After six weeks of filming (during the peak of the rainy season), the crew returned to Havana and Ivens to Paris, the rushes under his arm, leaving Fraga and the others to finish some shooting for both films. The material was processed in Paris — a technically delicate matter as Ivens said in a letter back to Yelin — but only two of the shots were out of focus.[2]

Other letters back to Havana requested additional material as the editing progressed, criticized with a firm professorial tone footage that was too abstract, undefined or lacking in variety and dynamism, and enthusiastically praised the rest. When the Cubans apologized for delays in returning the required shots because of an "imminent invasion," Ivens gently reminded them of the crucial propaganda function envisioned for the two films, which were to inform "hundreds of millions" of spectators of Cuba's strength.

The French censors swooped down the moment Ivens tried to release the films that same year, demanding and getting the excision of all unfriendly references to the United States (of which there were a fair share). The films eventually reached a substantial public in French political and cine-club circles in this censored form and among the domestic Cuban public in their undiluted Spanish versions.

Today, Ivens's two Cuban films are seldom revived except in connection with Ivens retrospectives (including Ivens's eightieth birthday celebration in Amsterdam in November 1978). They deserve wider exposure. Not only are they fascinating documents on the early days of the Cuban revolution; they also offer stirring models of the kind of Third World film activism that Ivens almost singlehandedly pioneered a whole generation before anyone else on the western left, an activism that lends solidarity and resources to local initiatives without imposing external models of any kind.

All of the thematic preoccupations of the Cuban cinema in its early years, when ICAIC production was overwhelmingly dominated by the documentary mode, emerge in *Travel Notebook* and *A People in Arms*. A memorable sequence in the latter film, for example, demonstrates the top-priority job of promoting the national literacy campaign: an illiterate recruit is learning to write, a close-up catching his rough peasant's hand firmly guided by the hand of his teacher. The early emphasis on housing and co-operatives is also reflected in one of *Notebook*'s better sequences, an intense before-and-after treatment of a fishing village transformed by the introduction of a co-operative. The same film also echoes the early interest of Cuban documentarists in experimental forms of popular democracy.

Ivens's two films in general express the concomitant feelings of extreme urgency and euphoria which were prevalent in the filmmaking community in the early years. Cuban filmmakers felt very much involved in a race against the inevitable Bay of Pigs (it happened the following year). They saw their films as essential to the survival of the revolution and exulted in this new conception of the role of the filmmaker in Cuban society. *A People in Arms* contains angry denunciations of American interference in Latin America, including footage of sugar fields set ablaze by incendiary rockets and close-ups of American labels on captured weapons (shots almost identical to those in *Spanish Earth* 20 years earlier, which had denounced the Nazi arms in use in Spain).

In this context, Ivens has recently revealed that he was more involved in the defense of the revolution than had previously been thought. In addition to the work he undertook with the young documentarists, Ivens spent some weeks giving emergency instruction in combat cinematography within the Cuban army.

TRAVEL NOTEBOOK

Of Ivens's two Cuban films, *Travel Notebook* is the one that follows most closely the travelogue pattern that appealed so much to his French contemporaries. Literally tracking Ivens's progress around the country on his tour, the film first shows each stage of the trip on a map sketched in front of the camera. Each new location is used as the pretext for the exploration of yet another aspect of the revolution: education, culture, health care, defense, agriculture, industry and political organization. Perhaps just as important for the non-Cuban public, each stopover also provides glimpses of the quality of life in the abstract, the atmosphere both of normalcy and of preparedness: that Cubans are happy and healthy, hard at work and still fond of baseball, that children are playing everywhere.

At each stopover, it is an exploration of the physical environment, usually an architectural one, which leads directly into the specific aspect of the revolution to be highlighted. Panning shots of the skyline of Havana, for example, lead into an analysis of the country's branch-plant economy before the revolution and then to a dynamic visual depiction of the act of nationalization itself. The posters and banners of the demonstrators are seen covering up the signs of the U.S. corporations; the procession of coffins announces the demise of each corporation. Ivens intercuts all of this with shots taken from vehicles moving through streets filled with life and energy. The viewer gets the impression of a busy, healthy society repossessing its own environment. A similar procedure occurs in the Trinidad segment: a survey of the town's colonial architecture leads to a recognition of the importance of the Cuban artistic heritage and how it must be preserved in a "positive" way.

The sequences dealing with the marsh region of Zapata and with the fishing co-operative at Manzanilla are perhaps the most successful in tying the physical landscape to the political landscape. In both cases, the visuals clearly and simply pursue the basic before-and-after logic of the film. In the Zapata sequence, the camera first moves about the marshes absorbing the landscape and noting the penurious traditional industries of the region, finally moving in on a new sight, a file of workers harvesting the rice for which "there had to be a revolution to plant, yet which was so simple." There are also some concise but evocative glimpses of the local lumber industry with the late-afternoon light in a mill casting a romantic tinge on workers gathered about the saw.

The sequence concludes with the waterborne camera gliding up and down the new canals to demonstrate the metamorphosis of a landscape in the wake of revolution. Ivens has always found this theme, with its potential for great panoramas of earth-moving equipment and cranes, irresistible. In the final shot, the camera eases out into open water past a tourist city being built on a platform above the marsh, another new industry in view. The newly dredged canals reminded Ivens of his native Holland; this reflection added to the commentary is one of his frequent personal touches, which tend to give the whole film the authenticity of an eye-witness account.

Ivens's cross section of the new Cuban society also includes some glimpses of the Cuban cinema, which add considerably to its interest for film historians. The new Chaplin cine-club which Castro had pointed out to him at the beginning of his visit enters the film as a symbol of the rebirth of the national cinema. Ivens used footage of the conversion of an old movie palace into the club in the introduction and epilogue of the film. He added the detail that it had originally been built for the mistress of a government official under Batista and addressed a dedication to Chaplin himself, "who used to sing so often of liberty and justice in your films, that it is good to find your name linked to Cuba, to images of hope and joy."

The Manzanilla sequence has a similar rhythm. First some fine sunny footage at close range shows the village fishermen unloading their catch. Then Ivens exposes the squalor of their customary living conditions. Naked children roam about through a cluster of fly-ridden huts, apparently on equal terms with the local pigs, and passively drink the milk offered to them in front of the camera. Such scenes — once the picturesque staples of photo albums, the commentary suggests sardonically — are now becoming bad memories. The remark has the effect of deflating the "exotic" reading inevitably imposed on the scene by a western public's stereotypes of "straw huts and naked children under a tropical sky.'' Ivens later recalled how he had urged the crew in this scene to avoid the neutral sentimental eye of observation and to ''attack reality.''

A sudden close-up of a bulldozer blade abruptly interrupts the scene at this point and shatters the stereotype to usher in a sequence boasting of the new construction transforming the village, another architectural metamorphosis which provides an index of the revolution's accomplishments. The camera now confronts rows of gleaming prefabricated houses and wanders through their interiors. Topping it all off is a final romantic vista of a new settlement rising up by the sea. For Ivens, the old chronicler of revolutions, social change must be visualized in material terms, as changes in people's everyday lives, their work, and their living conditions.

Other reflections on the ''brand new cinema'' going about its job are scattered throughout the film. After repeating the slogans ''Yankee go home,'' and then ''Nylon go home,'' the commentary adds a new one, ''Western go home.'' At another point, there is a sequence showing Ivens among ICAIC students in an editing room where he is demonstrating some kind of animation technique. Live-action views of firefighters in burning canefields are followed by animated depictions of them based on children's paintings. The commentary explains that the cinema is born in the simple job of recounting just such struggles. It adds that the cinema must show how the revolution was not a spontaneous accident, but that it ''comes from way back, from decades of struggles,'' at which point the camera moves through the editing-room group (including Gutiérrez Alea and Jorge Fraga) onto a Moviola screen where archive footage of those struggles then appears. There are pre-revolutionary demonstrations, guerrilla groups in 1958 with guitars as well as guns, a shot of Castro and Che relaxing around a campfire and then one of them leading a liberation procession on horseback. Later on in the film, we see the director Oscar Torres shooting a film about peasant uprisings in the 1930s (*Realengo 18)* on location in the colonial city of Trinidad, and the commentary reminds us again that the Cuban cinema must remember and retell this history.

From time to time other landscapes as well conjure up memories of Cuba's revolutionary past. The streets of Santiago de Cuba reveal traces of past struggles — a plaque, for example, which points out the spot where a revolutionary hero, Frank Pais, ''the soul of the underground struggle,'' was assassinated. The Havana section of the film includes a funeral sequence in which six million flowers, one for every Cuban, are sent out to sea in memory of Camilo Cienfuegos, another revolutionary leader, recently dead. It is a passage which communicates in simple but compelling terms the intense collective emotions Ivens witnessed and participated in on this occasion.

It is clear from this brief description of *Travel Notebook* that Ivens had quickly assimilated all of the concerns of the new Cuban cinema and had incorporated them into this work. As one of Ivens's students recalled later, Ivens came to Cuba not so much to make *his* films but to be of service to Cubans making *theirs*.[3] Rather than the subjective impressions of a tourist, *Travel Notebook* is a summation of Cubans' images of themselves in 1960; an open, passionate tribute to the revolution, not an ''objective'' evaluation. This historical resonance and ideological commitment, together with the personal Ivens touches and inflections throughout, give the film a continuing relevance, despite the occasional evidence of hasty shooting, of the obvious shortage of stock, or of inexperienced camera handling. In fact, these latter aspects of the film increase its impact and vitality insofar as they evoke the learning situation going on behind the camera during every take.

A PEOPLE IN ARMS

A People in Arms has for its subject popular preparations for national defense and thus contains a much more concentrated dramatic and topical focus than its companion film. The urgency of the subject comes across clearly in the film, giving it a stronger emotional force. The film was designed to inform western audiences of the Cuban people's mobilization and of their unanimous determination to defend their revolution. In the domestic market, it was intended to reinforce this determination and aid in recruitment for the volunteer militia, like a number of ICAIC documentaries on related subjects, such as Gutiérrez Alea's *Muerte al Invasor* (Death to the Invader, 1961), a 1961 Bay of Pigs reportage. Ivens's particular slant in his film was the genuinely popular character of the Cuban mobilization, the fact that the Cuban masses themselves and not just a professional army were participating fully in it. The film commentary constantly hammers home this message:

> With 500 million dollars, a fleet, and rockets you can buy a government, but you can't snuff out the will of the people. To retake these oil refineries, you'd need six million mercenaries, one for each Cuban.
>
> Only a government that fully answers the aspirations of a people can distribute arms to it. . . . Every factory becomes a fortress, every furrow a trench.

The recurring images of the film are just that — views of whole crowds of men and women being issued guns or rushing out of a workplace for militia exercises.

Because of this populist inspiration and because the film crew followed a single brigade over an extended period, the film has a more intimate feel than *Notebook*. A number of individuals acquire a concise but vivid identity in short close-up confrontations with the camera. The brigade itself apparently grew accustomed to Ivens and the crew and began to relax in front of the camera: there are some fine informal scenes of soldiers lunching, clowning with each other, grouped under plastic tarpaulins in the pouring rain, or boisterously strumming their guns like guitars on the back of a truck. Ivens's relationship with the militia also meant that he was easily able to reconstruct the lengthy combat sequences with the men, filming jungle skirmishes and pursuits that are quite effective within the terms of the semi-dramatized classical documentary form that he still used at this point.

To emphasize the grass-roots bases of the Cuban mobilization, Ivens begins the film in a remote mountain village, watching the local men drilling for the first time. The scene is affectionately comic with its inclusion of the confusion and errors of these peasants who have never had to march together before. They are obviously embarrassed by their children running alongside, imitating them and making fun. From this point, the structure of the film is climactic, the militia appearing more and more disciplined and formidable as the film progresses through various early phases of the training, notably the literacy program. The film then follows the seasoned brigade in its pursuit of counter-revolutionaries in the last part of the film.

The final note is one of confidence, even defiance, a strong "up" ending being a requirement of the agitprop filmmaking mastered by Ivens decades earlier. The initial perspective of the single village steadily expands through views of mass militia drills in large urban and industrial settings until an entire nation, editorially synthesized, seems on the march.

The film is more than a conglomeration of marching columns, however. Everywhere there are indications of the new life which is to be defended. Aside from the pointed reference to the literacy campaign, there are also hints of changing sex roles, of advances in agriculture and health care, low-key scenes of soldiers fraternizing with peasants, and once again continually recurring views of children at play. There are also pauses in the sprightly pace of the film for a particularly lyrical perspective of some landscape or other, a waterbird taking off from a jungle river or mountain mists filtering through waving trees. Every sequence projects the insistence that life goes on in the midst of crisis, as it had in *Spanish Earth* and would in *The Seventeenth Parallel*, and that it is beautiful.

The commentary for *A People in Arms* leaves a somewhat more overbearing impression than *Notebook* does, perhaps because the visuals in the militia film are tighter and need a verbal counterpoint less. Some of the mannerisms of the late classical documentary soundtrack seem unnecessarily distracting in *A People in Arms*: dramatized voice-over dialogue, for instance, to liven up a few silently filmed group scenes, ironic musical phrases (an off-key Marine hymn when the counter-revolutionaries are captured), and the somewhat excessive use of "action" music and percussion during the semi-dramatized combat scenes.

The commentary itself is less personal than the other film's reflective counterpoint. In short, too often the soundtrack appears to be trying to compensate for the lack of sync recording rather than making a virtue of necessity like the other film and the best pre-verité travelogues. But this is the only major aspect of the film to have aged badly. Otherwise, it stands well among Ivens's records of the courage of peoples under siege.

IVENS AND CINÉMA VÉRITÉ

One of the most interesting aspects of *A People in Arms* is the light it sheds on the problem posed for Ivens and the Third World as a whole by the ascendancy of cinéma-vérité during the early 1960s. On the surface, this film has more of a verité orientation than *Travel Notebook*, not only because of its greater intimacy with its subjects and the spontaneity this implies but also because of the greater flexibility and mobility of its camera handling.

Despite the awkwardness of the 35mm format, the severe limitation of silent shooting, and a low shooting ratio, Ivens and his Cuban crew were clearly responding to the potential of vérité improvisation in the film — in the encounters with the colorful "bit-part" characters scattered throughout, as well as with the soldiers, and in the pursuit scenes with their opportunities for experimentation with hand-held and walking movements. In these latter scenes, there are a number of walking shots of considerable agility through the jungle undergrowth, and frequent use of swish pans both expressively and as editing devices. In *Notebook* as well, there is a sequence where the camera literally takes part in a folk dance, moving rhythmically through a double column of dancers.

José Massip later remembered shooting a scene which puts the crew's growing awareness of vérité into relief.[4] Massip recalled the exhausted men in the patrol resting around in a farmyard, some asleep, others drinking water or lounging around. An old peasant wandered up carrying bundles of squawking chickens at each end of a long pole resting over his shoulder. This opportunity for a colorful scene was unexpected and unnoticed by the ICAIC men until they suddenly saw inspiration light up in Ivens's eyes. Ivens got them quickly to move the camera spontaneously in medium and close range about the old man and his indignant load as he chatted with the patrol. The scene is short but works well, with its dynamic energy and the internal contrast between the resting soldiers, the frantic birds and the man's vivid and natural gestures. The students thus saw their usual inclination towards careful planning and setting up challenged by this openness to spur-of-the-moment inspiration.

For the most part, however, it must be said that the vérité sensibility does not dominate the film. Most of it shows the careful precision of a director who is watching the footage meter very carefully (though both films must have looked much more like the real, raw thing to contemporary audiences). In fact, the factor of economy alone may be responsible for cautious use of vérité in the western sense by both Ivens and most Third-World filmmakers throughout the 1960s. They simply couldn't afford the large shooting ratios that western directors in TV and in state-subsidized bodies like the National Film Board of Canada took for granted.

The most typical shots in unstructured situations in *A People in Arms* involve careful setups in which subjects pass the camera in close-up one by one on a jungle path. Tripod shots are a staple of the film, as are the long motorized tracks from jeeps and boats (and even a helicopter), which Ivens found at this point in his career to be not only an inexpensive but expressive alternative to tripod setups but also more reliable than hand-held improvisation.

There is another consideration as well in Ivens' continuing reliance on classical shooting techniques during the sixties, an instinctive distrust of the more flamboyant uses of verité then becoming common. This distrust arises partly from what had always been Ivens' instinctive formal conservatism, his preference for the fully understood language of a given period over innovative effects which might have startled his public or drawn attention away from his subject itself. A second obvious factor was that Ivens had not shot in a country where his native language is spoken since 1933; the European variant of verité, the *cinéma-direct*, required the director's spontaneous linguistic participation in the event being filmed rather than simply a visual observation of it.* Ivens' partnership in the late sixties with Marceline Loridan, a trained soundperson, would help him overcome this particular handicap.

* Not to be confused with the U.S.-style *Direct Cinema*, which emphasized complete non-intervention on the part of the filmmakers (ed).

Throughout the mid-sixties, however, Ivens expressed specifically ideological reservations about verité which are worth considering. For one thing, verité quickly became associated with the auteurist cinema of individualist personal expression, clearly a second priority for the Third World, and for the same reasons for European radical filmmaking as well. Ivens also felt that verité encouraged filmmakers to avoid taking a political stand. "In verité," he said, "people often talk too much and the director not enough." It furthermore didn't require young directors to think during the shoot and sometimes even afterwards. "If you know how to swim," Ivens told an interviewer on another occasion, "it's better to swim towards something rather than to flounder about." As late as 1965, he would insist that only a commentary re-establishes the fully responsible, personal intervention of the director, the author, or the commentator, the stand taken by the film. Verité posed the danger of staying on the surface of the truth, of "caressing reality instead of penetrating it."[5]

LESSONS WITH JORIS

By late 1960, Cubans were already feeling the effects of an embargo that was cultural as well as economic. This is one reason, no doubt, that ICAIC so eagerly welcomed the procession of foreign filmmakers who came to Cuba in the early years to witness and to film the achievements of the revolution. The foreigners' contributions to the Cuban cinema varied widely.

One filmmaker referred to Ivens's role as that of a "technical advisor" rather than a "theoretician" and that his influence was less as the maker of films to be imitated than as a filmmaker whose "conduct . . . in the face of today's reality" was an inspiration.[6] The impression Ivens made seems to have been out of all proportion to the briefness of his two visits.[7]

Undoubtedly it was the period in the jeep with the seven young filmmakers which was most responsible for this impression, each sequence turning out to be a valuable lesson. One sequence which had considerable pedagogical impact was a filmed conversation of two militiamen guarding a bridge. Quite by accident, the crew had come across the pair, an old peasant animatedly telling stories to his partner, a much younger man. The final version of *A People in Arms* retains only a few shots from the incident, a jeep-borne track coming up to the bridge, panning as the camera discovers and picks out the two guards, and then close-up explorations of their faces as they talk. For all the brevity of the scene, the effect is one of concentrated energy. At the time of the shoot, the crew was struck not only by Ivens's instinctual recognition of a good scene and of "natural actors" but also of the way in which he was able to make the two subjects feel comfortable and trustful with regard to the camera. Aside from absorbing the mechanics of shooting such a scene — the avoidance of a close-up lens and the provision of good covering material — the students watched how Ivens picked out the expressive and typical details of the men's gestures and appearances. His additional secret for bringing out the "natural actors" in such subjects was his authentic respect for them, his involvement with them as human beings rather than as subjects.

The ICAIC filmmakers drew another lesson from the shooting of the village drilling sequence, where the new recruits are training for the first time. The camera enters a small neighboring house at a given moment where the wife of one of the participants is laundering, and for a few moments the drilling is seen from her point of view, framed by her doorway and verandah. As her husband takes his shirt to go to join the drill, Ivens decided to involve the woman more completely in the scene by the simple twist of having her hand him the shirt as he was leaving. The gesture is eliminated from the final version as far as I can see, but the crew were impressed with the importance of involving all elements in a given scene in dynamic interaction to enhance its dramatic value.

This is not to say that Ivens's two Cuban films do not perceive more radical changes in women's roles than what is implied by this anecdote. Although the village recruits and the jungle patrol do not involve women, the scenes depicting industrial and urban militia organization have women participating fully and the issue is emphasized on the soundtrack in a voice-over "conversation" between two male militiamen: "You know that the women in my village have organized a brigade? My wife with a gun? I'd sure like to see that." The narrator concludes, "All the same at 30 years of age, it's hard to begin . . . but a people in revolution learn very quickly."

Ivens's decision to involve the woman in the drilling sequence has another implication. His perpetual readiness to intervene and recreate reality through the use of semi-documentary dramatization is not very easily digested by contemporary spectators nurtured on the non-intervention orthodoxy of vérité. The controversy between pro-interventionists and those who argue that the filmmaker must record reality from the outside only is not a recent one in relation to Ivens's career. He defended his right to restage reality for the first time with the Vertov camp in the USSR in 1932 when he reconstructed a scene for his film, *Song of Heroes,* on blast-furnace construction in the Urals. The scene in question was a night-time shock-brigade procession, torchlit, that could not be filmed at its original occurrence. Ivens continued to insist on this right to reconstruct even during the period of the orthodoxy of vérité, maintaining that the classical documentarist's use of mise-en-scène was in no way outmoded by the new flexibility of camera technology. One of his Cuban students even praised the way Ivens reconstructs events, when necessary, in "the simplest way that most resembles life."[8]

Ivens provided another insight for his crew on *Travel Notebook* when it came to filming the archetypal Cuban activity, sugar-cane cutting. Ivens convinced the ICAIC group to get involved themselves in the action of cutting cane so that they would understand directly and subjectively all aspects of this action, the totality of the physical components of the job, including the resistance offered by the cane. Ivens urged them to discover "the true secret of the rhythm of the mechanical action of cutting cane, the moment at which this rhythm can be interrupted by another action, drying one's sweat, taking a drink of water, resting." Ivens had evidently never forgotten the Soviet workers in the early 1930s who had praised his Dutch film of Zuiderzee dike construction because of its scrupulous adherence to shot angles, camera placements and editing rhythms that authentically reflected the physical requirements of the work and the point of view of the workers themselves.

The final essence of what Ivens reinforced in his Cuban co-workers' minds during his visits was that the immediate, urgent task of filming the revolution was more important than the development of individual techniques or styles or a foreknowledge of the classical principles of film aesthetics. He encouraged them to rely on their own instinctual feelings about a task, to trust in their own innate human sympathies and interactions with their fellow Cubans in a dialectical relationship with their own clearly defined ideological aims. Perhaps thinking of his decade in the moribund East German film industry of the pre-thaw period, Ivens's advice was to avoid becoming "bureaucrats of the camera" and to "let life into the studios."

This accumulation of immediate, urgent material, this filming directly and quickly of all that was happening, he said, was the major means of achieving a national cinema.[9] Ivens was uncannily perceptive in pinpointing in this way the formula by which the Cubans were already building one of the most dynamic of all contemporary national cinemas.

NOTES

[1] This and all other quotations from the commentaries of *Carnet de Viaje* and *Pueblo Armado* are my translations from the French. I have consulted the copies of these two films in the archives of the Nederlands Filmmuseum, Amsterdam, and La Cinemathèque québécoise, Montreal, for the purposes of this article.

[2] This and other quotations from and paraphrases of the correspondence between Ivens and his Cuban associates are taken with thanks from the Joris Ivens Archive, Nederlands Filmmuseum, Amsterdam.

[3] José Massip's recollections of his work with Ivens were included in the special Ivens issue of *Cine Cubano* 1 (Havana, 1960): 24-28. Translation of this and other material from *Cine Cubano* by Ross Higgins and myself.

[4] *Ibid.*

[5] Ivens's major pronouncements on cinéma-vérité, as referred to in this discussion, are: interview on *Le Ciel, La Terre* (*Image et son,* Paris, 1965) translated and reprinted in Joris Ivens, *The Camera and I* (New York, 1968), p. 257; plus three interviews I have translated from the French for the purposes of citations and paraphrases in this article — *Jeune Cinema* 15 (Paris, May 1966), *France Nouvelle* 1035 (Paris, April 18, 1965), and *Lettres françaises* 970 (Paris, March 27, 1963).

[6] Fausto Canel, interviewed by Ameria and Gerard Gozlan (January 1963), reprinted in Robert Grelier, *Joris Ivens* (Paris, 1965), pp. 128-29. My translation.

[7] "Mesa Redonda Sobre Joris Ivens," *Cine Cubano* 2 : 18-40. An interesting discussion by a panel of Cuban filmmakers testifying to Ivens's influence on the Cuban cinema.

[8] *Ibid.*

[9] *Ibid.*

CHAPTER 25.

For Our Urgent Use: Films on Central America

JULIA LESAGE

When someone goes to see a left-oriented film, slideshow or videotape about Nicaragua or El Salvador, that act represents a judgment and a decision. The judgment is that the mass media are not offering enough information or only filtered and distorted information about Central America. The decision is that we need to do things to keep ourselves better informed. Much of the organizing being done around support for revolution in El Salvador and Nicaragua begins from this generally felt public need, as people turn away from establishment media to other sources to find more complete analyses of Central American politics.

In the Vietnam era, a flourishing alternate left and feminist press and radio as well as film were important vehicles for providing information around Southeast Asia. Film and slide-show presentations offered occasions to bring people together for militant action. In the 1980s alternative film and video seem to play an even more important role in organizing work, since there are considerably more films and tapes available now on Central American than there were in the earlier period about Vietnam.[1]

Many such films and tapes are made with an eye to getting on U.S. television stations. However, although films such as *El Salvador: Another Vietnam* (1981) and *Americas in Transition* (1982) have a great deal of cinematic polish and present their points effectively and clearly, their format is conventional and digestible. Films like those made in a television documentary style are characterized by an essay-like argumentative structure and often use maps, charts, authorities, lists and captioned portraits. North American and European viewers find this organization comfortably familiar, with its interviews, voice-overs, authoritative narrator, and comparison contrast editing.

Nevertheless, the format itself is ideological and hides certain things. For example, it often reduces to generalities the voices of Latin American revolutionary organizers and peasant fighters; rarely do they speak the analysis that shapes the work. Furthermore, the form assumes images are self-explanatory, and so we do not get to learn from those images how *different* Latin American culture is from our own; that is, the uniqueness of the social organization of the culture from which those images emanate. If we can assume that we "know" the connotations of an image, let us say, of a child with a rifle, just as soon as we see it; if that is the way the film or tape uses that image — flatly, as self-explanatory — then we are not taught what that image means to the people among whom the child lives.

Like television news, these films and tapes also do not demonstrate the structural nature of capitalism and imperialism. Beyond providing the shiver of viewing tortured and mutilated bodies, this kind of media does not challenge viewers sufficiently when it asks them only to struggle against direct U.S. governmental intervention abroad. CIA ties with the AFL-CIO, for example, and the willing collaboration of the AFL-CIO in undermining labor unions, communist analyses, and organizing in the Third World: these are the kind of structural contradictions inherent in U.S. capitalism that the television documentary does not explore. We need media that demonstrate how and why we should ally ourselves with the liberation forces themselves. If a film or tape takes this on as a goal, it will not likely get on U.S. television.

In a sense, movement organizers can justify wanting visual media made in a familiar format — so as not to "confuse" the audience, to make memorable points, and so on. But the ideological restrictions of that format are rarely challenged by those who use the work. This poses a dilemma not only for organizers but also for media makers, who need to question at what point they would create an aesthetic break and make audiences confront new forms. It is a crucial issue, for without stylistic innovation the filmmakers may not be able to express politically what they understand the solidarity movement needs.

CROSS-CULTURAL UNDERSTANDING AND THE IMAGES OF REVOLUTION

The films and tapes commonly judged most effective as organizing tools are those made primarily for North American or European audiences by artists familiar with these countries' media conventions, especially their television conventions. Media made by Latin Americans on the revolutionary struggle often elicit a different and even unsympathetic response from anglo audiences than from latino ones. Certain connotative details and rhythms of presenting material cinematically or on video seem to make more sense to audiences in a Spanish-speaking environment than in an English-speaking one. For example, what a North American film audience may interpret as an image connoting "poverty" may signify "a farm family's daily life" in its country of origin.

In general, elements in Latin American films that most distress U.S. viewers are those that seem to connote "militarism" or "left rhetoric." In *El Salvador: El Pueblo Vencerá (El Salvador: The People Will Win,* 1980*)*, made by Puerto Rican filmmaker Diego de la Texera and the nascent Film Institute of Revolutionary El Salvador, we see many images of young people with rifles and red face-masks — images criticized here as glorifying militarism. As *Jump Cut* reviewer Michael Chanan noted, these images of taking up arms and active military participation in the guerrilla movements are presented with eyes of love by Latin American militant filmmakers and are images that connote "the people's will." Yet understanding the emotion invested in such images is often difficult for U.S. left and feminist viewers to comprehend.[2]

In fact, images of people who have suffered oppression but are now bearing arms have a liberating function in Central America. They serve as images of empowerment for people who have not previously had social, political or cultural power. The examples of Nicaragua and Cuba serve a similar function, presenting images of countries that successfully fought wars of liberation and proceeded after that to effect social and economic revolution. And within Cuba and Nicaragua themselves images of guns and martyrdom still have an emotional force. Political and cultural leaders are not seen just as politicians or functionaries; they are revered as those who made the revolution.

Ordinary people in Cuba and Nicaragua understand the U.S. government's intent to destroy their social gains. When I was in Nicaragua in November 1981, one woman explained her version of "military imagery": "When your tanks come rolling in, I want to meet them with a gun, not without one. Whoever conquers us will find only a cemetery, because we all will have died defending what our loved ones have already paid for with their lives." In Nicaragua, the call to the citizenry to participate in the popular militia evokes a sense of both national and personal pride, especially among women, because they make up over half of the Nicaraguan popular militia.

Genocide, usually paid for by U.S. military assistance, already exists in Central America. For poor people in El Salvador and Guatemala, massacre by government troops and government-paid paramilitary organizations is too commonplace a reality, one only alluded to and not fully described in our "news." For the exploited, public images of armed resistance to genocide provide a form of empowerment, psychologically and socially. Such images, deriving from the work of armed revolutionary organizations whose members live among the peasantry, help poor people believe that it is not necessary or "natural" to live under an exploitative regime. Such images are part of the building of an alternative, revolutionary culture, which teaches people to understand how they can take power over their own lives.

In his key essay, "Concerning Violence," Frantz Fanon contrasts international capitalism's institutionalized violence with Third World armed struggles to seize state power.[3] What Fanon explains is how only the act of bearing arms adequately expresses the submerged anger of the oppressed; at the moment of revolution, it is the principal cure for the colonized mind. How do oppressed people come to understand that large-scale social change is possible? How do they come to *will* it? For many Central American peasants, these are recent possibilities, ones developed by the revolutionary culture as it enters their lives.

In the film *El Salvador: El Pueblo Vencerá,* a small boy speaks a militant eulogy over his murdered father's grave. Then he formally joins the guerrilla forces. Some U.S. viewers have interpreted this sequence as "staged" or "rhetorical." In fact, revolutionary culture, as a way of teaching about social structures and processes of change, is the first twentieth-century intellectual vehicle that many Central American workers and peasants, traditionally kept isolated and illiterate, have been exposed to. This is the source of the language the boy in the film uses. Revolutionary culture teaches people a mode of collective social participation. It is an empowering culture; its aim is literally empowerment. Guerrilla fighters in the zones they now control in El Salvador have created a space where people do not have to live in ignorance and constant fear; and from this point on, revolutionary consciousness grows exponentially with the people's "decision to win" (the title of another Salvadoran-made film about life in a controlled zone in 1981).[4] Fanon described this phenomenon: "It is at the moment that he [the "native"] realizes his humanity that he begins to sharpen the weapons with which he will secure his victory."[5]

In Nicaragua I met with a women's group that was being formally addressed by Comandante Leticia Herrera. When she entered the room, I understood the force of her presence there as both a national heroine and as the embodiment of a "new woman." Another woman's example similarly affected the group: a Salvadoran participant's strident call for support caused all the women there to identify with her situation; she intuited that identification as she cried out, "Our mothers see their children killed; our children see their mothers killed; we fight your battle." As Margaret Randall described this kind of feminist unity in her book *Sandino's Daughters,* the Nicaraguan women who took up arms are revered because they fought and suffered rape and torture — and saw their loved ones tortured — to secure the immense social gains other women now have; these women also represent a whole new model of socially, politically and physically active womanhood that stands in dramatic contrast to the usual roles for women available in Latin America.[6]

In colonized countries or those with a dependent capitalist economy, peasant women work brutally hard and are imprisoned spiritually by poverty, illiteracy, and machismo; middle-class women often stay isolated in the home, removed from social participation, and face ill health because of a lack of physical culture for women and girls even in the schools. The social image of women participating in the development of the Nicaraguan Revolution provides a new icon of "contemporary women"; this image, often of women in arms, has a connotative impact that speaks to women in other Third World countries in a way that such an image has not yet done in the United States. The film by Victoria Schultz, *Women in Arms* (1980), offers a significant exception as it captures a sense of the exuberance that Nicaraguan women feel in their new roles. Integral to the new roles is the co-partnership in national defense.

The U.S. military-industrial complex has consistently supported the institutionalized violence that is structurally inherent in colonialism. The United States has engaged its military forces in Central America innumerable times over the last century to shore up U.S. economic and military domination of that area: to do that we have created alliances with the oppressive national bourgeoisie of each country, such as the coffee oligarchy of El Salvador or the Somoza family in Nicaragua. Central American history always tells the same story: how the U.S. government manipulates other countries' national politics and co-operates militarily with genocidal governments.

At this point in their own history, many U.S. citizens mistrust the pronouncements of political leaders. They are aware of how politicians present a line to the mass media, and they feel a sentiment of isolationism and an unwillingness to send U.S. youth abroad to die in an unjust cause. Nevertheless, U.S. viewers who look at images of Latin American peasants in arms and see in them the same iconic significance as images of U.S. soldiers bearing arms or images, tiredly reiterated, against a supposed "communist military threat" should learn to distinguish between people's common reaction to such images here and the common interpretation of those images in the Third World. Fanon presents this distinction:

> Castro, sitting in military uniform in the United Nations Organization, does not scandalize the underdeveloped countries. What Castro demonstrates is the consciousness he has of the continuing existence of the rule of violence. . . . Strengthened by the unconditional support of the socialist countries, the colonized peoples fling themselves with whatever arms they have against the impregnable citadel of colonialism. . . . The violence of the native is only hopeless if we compare it in the abstract to the military machine of the oppressor. On the other hand, if we situate that violence in the dynamics of the international situation, we see at once that it constitutes a terrible menace for the oppressor. . . . Capitalism realizes that its military strategy has everything to lose by the outbreak of nationalist wars.[7]

I am asking for a cross-cultural understanding of what bearing arms means in people's lives. It is a crucial issue for both political organizers and people working in contemporary media to deal with. Commercial media, North American and European governments manipulate precisely these images and distort them flagrantly to denigrate feminism, gays and the left. Too often lying headlines scream at us: supposed "feminists" attempted to kill President Ford; "rioting" prisoners in Attica were assumed to have "brutally slaughtered" guards; "Palestinian" becomes paired with the word "terrorist"; social gains for workers in Libya become erased under the labels attached to Colonel Qaddafi. The all-inclusive epithet "terrorism" applies to what the media depict as the acts of crazy, often disenfranchised individuals or isolated groups, whose behavior then takes up disproportionate media space. In this way, newspapers and television inhibit viewers from looking beyond those images of "disorder" and "insanity" (presumably emanating from a socially irresponsible left) to learn what bearing arms might mean for an oppressed people when armed struggle is a key element in the national movement organized to achieve their liberation.

Television images of the military have a different relation to the public in a country like Nicaragua, where national defense depends on the large popular militia. Citizens learn to bear arms, as they did in North Vietnam. When the people do the soldiering, many ordinary citizens see what is going on militarily, enough to understand the farce of U.S. media pronouncements about Cuban or Soviet control of their armed forces. If we interpret media images of bearing arms as "militarist" we react justifiably against our government's huge economic investment in building a nuclear arsenal and intervening in other countries' affairs. But this is also a culture-bound reaction on our part. In the case of media dealing with Third World revolutionary movements, viewers must learn to go beyond their initial reaction to look at images of military participation in a more complex way, so as to interpret more accurately the social realities these images are intended to convey.

Organizing around issues of U.S. imperialism should be a way of uniting anglo and latino cultures *within* the United States, and the burden of extending oneself to understand the other culture falls on the white left.[8] The need to understand Latin American culture on its own terms often gets bypassed, even within anti-imperialist organizing — and that has to be acknowledged as a form of racism. To make or use films and tapes which speak to audiences only in "mainstream" ways is to deny the existence and validity of a Latin American voice right here in our own culture. For non-latinos to do anti-imperialist work around El Salvador but not to promote an understanding of the cultural structures and forms of expression of Latin American life is a contradiction that must be surpassed.

SEXISM, SEXUAL POLITICS AND POLITICAL ISSUES

At the same time, militant cinema coming from Central America must be criticized for its sexism — both overt and implied. The visual media emerging from the revolutionary forces seem to lag behind the actual participation of women in those revolutions; in both Nicaragua and El Salvador, women hold key positions in the structure of the revolutionary command. Sometimes in the films listed here, female or gay sexuality is used as an icon for "bourgeois decadence."

This is the case with both Peter Lilienthal's *The Uprising* (West Germany, 1980) and *El Salvador: El Pueblo Vencerá* (1981). The latter film has the camera tilt slowly up from a bourgeois woman's shoes to linger on her hips, clothed in tight blue jeans. To equate rich decadence with openly expressed female sexuality and the female body is an old filmic convention but one that the filmmakers should have known better to avoid. Furthermore, this woman does not look much different from a large portion of working-class women in North America, where jeans are worn by the entire range of classes. Understandably, the case could be made that in Latin America, U.S.-style jeans are worn by the bourgeoisie and those who want to imitate that lifestyle, as opposed to the vast majority of the population — so in the film, this image provides an example of cross-cultural code-switching. However, the use of a U.S. jazz track and the way the camera moves up the woman's body indicate that "female sexuality" is the supposed pointer to the evils of the wealthy class's mores.

If filmmakers want to avoid this iconographic trap, they could easily make the same point by contrasting the lives of rich and poor women. In that way, women's images would represent women's realities, and the image of female sexuality would not be used to represent (an almost always derogatory) something else. If my sexuality so easily becomes a male artist's metaphor, it means he cannot see what it means to me — with all its contradictions and on my terms.[9]

Films and tapes made about Central America that are to be used for support work in the United States, Canada and Europe must deal with issues of sexual politics sensitively, both through themes treated and in cinematic style. Otherwise the filmmakers will lose the constituency they wish to recruit. Thus, if organizers are going to use *The Uprising* effectively with an audience that has an understanding of sexual politics, program notes or a spoken introduction should be used to denounce the way the director attaches homosexual traits to the abusive villain, an army captain who seeks to maintain control over the young male protagonist, his communications technician, both emotionally and through military force. The old cinematic tactic of representing decadence through images of ''sexual derangement'' characteristically abuses women and gays, and the relatively advanced development of the women's and gay movements means these issues cannot be ignored.

Beyond that, the women's and gay movements in these countries have made a contribution to left culture as a whole in delineating how issues of sexual politics interact with all other political issues. If militant Latin American filmmakers do not deal in detail with women's participation in the revolution, implicit cinematic sexism once again erases women from history and relegates us to visual icons, static representative images — as mother, girl, decadent or even armed militant.

Feminists have developed a profound cultural analysis, part of which explains how the visual media manipulate, and depend on, the image of women. Feminists also understand how history has been written and filmed either to include, or more likely to exclude, women's specific experience of a given place and time. Over and over again, Third World feminists tell us that their struggle cannot be considered apart from struggles against imperialism, from their own national liberation struggles, from communist revolution.[10] The militant filmmakers from Latin America, mostly male, who want their films to elicit international support, must listen to these revolutionary feminist voices from within their own struggles, and include them more fully in the films.

AUDIENCES FOR CENTRAL AMERICAN MEDIA

Significantly, much of the Central American solidarity work in various media has been directed by women, and deals with themes of interest to such audiences as women's studies classes. Helena Solberg-Ladd, of Brazilian origin, made the documentary *From the Ashes: Nicaragua Today* (1981) with a great cultural sensitivity and focusing on the life of one family. Other women directors have focused on church women in Central America (*Roses in December,* 1982, *Seeds of Liberty,* 1981). Videotapes made by Jackie Reiter and Wolf Tirado, independent producers living in Managua, focus both on Nicaraguan women (*Women in Nicaragua,* 1982) and on U.S. healthcare worker Mary Ellsberg, working on Nicaragua's Atlantic coast (*Nicaragua: The Other Invasion,* 1984). Similarly, U.S. videomaker Dee Dee Halleck filmed U.S. citizens living and working in Nicaragua and opposed to U.S. intervention (*Waiting for the Invasion,* 1984). Other films by Canadian and European women are also available abroad. Any women's media event being organized today could well have a section on women activist filmmakers documenting Central America.

Another target audience would be church groups. Most films on El Salvador have long segments about the martyred Archbishop Pedro Romero and the role of the church in the revolution. The videotape *These Same Hands* (Neil Reichline, 1980) shows Nicaraguan life through its music and poetry, focusing on Ernesto Cardenal, the poet and priest who is Nicaragua's Minister of Culture. *Roses in December* relates the story of Jean Donovan, one of four U.S. religious women murdered in El Salvador. Jackie Reiter and Wolf Tirado, along with Jan Kees de Rooy, have made a number of films and tapes from inside Nicaragua on the role of the Catholic church there. The most significant of them is a tape depicting the Pope's visit (*The Pope: Pilgrim of Peace?,* 1983) and the conflicting forces within the Catholic church there.

An older film that has a special use with church groups is *Paraiso* (*Paradise,* 1976), made by the Maryknoll Order in Nicaragua well before the revolution. The principal figure is Maryknoll priest Miguel D'Escoto, now Nicaragua's Secretary of State. The roots of D'Escoto's revolutionary philosophy were seen in the way he then directed a new housing project, to be constructed with the social development of its members in mind. The film shows D'Escoto trying to convince one of the construction workers and that man's family to move into the new project. Although the rent was very low, they feared they might not be able to pay it if one of them got sick, so they refused to move, because then to have to move out would have meant an insufferable shame. The film provides a vivid contrast to *From the Ashes,* which focuses on the life of a similar family in 1980. The contrast the two films reveal about the families' living conditions, social integration, political consciousness and degree of pessimism or optimism indicates the kinds of changes the Nicaraguan revolution has effected in ordinary people's lives, and especially in their outlook and confidence.

Such sectoral targeting of audience — mass-communications students, speakers of Spanish, women's studies groups, church groups, medical groups — represents both an organizing strategy and a media-making strategy. It may be that the omnibus film, which tries to explain history, life today in that country, U.S. foreign policy, the role of the church, rural and urban life, revolutionary strategy, and so on, has itself become a predictable genre in solidarity media. More specific works that give both the detail and evocative connotations of daily life and "small" events also have their place and may even have more emotional force. A close look at craft and labor organizing might speak more effectively to the working class. Skeptical audiences in the United States and Canada mistrust "rhetoric" or views of life abroad that leave out the contradictions and complexities for the sake of offering an "overall view." Enough solidarity work is being produced now that we have space and a great need for variety in the themes explored and styles used.

Furthermore, audio-visual material does not stand by itself as a teaching device but takes its place within a larger program for educating and motivating viewers. The person or group presenting a film should determine what values it puts forth and what is needed to supplement it to give a more complete understanding of revolutionary situations and the U.S. response to them. Frankly discussing a film's limitations before showing it can serve to diffuse routine criticism and let the audience's attention dwell on the strengths the film possesses. Organizers of film showings will want to think about how to introduce Latin American-made films to make them more accessible to anglo audiences, perhaps by talking about unique aspects of Latin culture. Similarly, a Latin American audience in the United States or Canada may be more accustomed to a highly motivated and emotionally charged presentation, and the U.S. or European-made documentaries may seem dry or emotionally sterile.

How to surround the film presentation — with speakers, songs or poetry readings — becomes an organizational and pedagogic decision that shapes how the film will be received. Furthermore, since both the solidarity movement in North America and the revolutions in El Salvador and Nicaragua are developing within the context of an ongoing and ever more interactive process, we will need different educational tools and different strategies for this solidarity work. These films and my discussion of them may be historically located at the very beginning of our work.

NOTES

[1] In his book, *Documentary: A History of the Non-Fiction Film* (New York: Oxford University Press, 1974), Erik Barnouw details how U.S. television networks actively collaborated with the government to present a sanitized view of what was happening in Vietnam. Many films about Vietnam were available from abroad, but the U.S. networks bought only fragments of footage from such films, a policy also followed later with films made by Latin Americans.

[2] See Alfonso Gumucio, "Cine y Revolucion en Nicaragua," *Plural* (Mexico City), January-February, 1982); Peter Steven, *"El Salvador: Revolution or Death," Jump Cut* 26 (1981). Also in that issue of *Jump Cut*, Michael Chanan, "El Salvador: The People Will Win," and Margaret Henry, *"El Salvador: Portrait of a Liberated Zone,"* dir. Michael Chanan and Peter Chapell, 1981). In photojournalism, see *Nicaragua* by Susan Meiselas (New York: Pantheon, 1981) and *El Salvador — Work of 30 Photographers,* edited by Susan Meiselas, Harry Mattison, Fae Rubenstein; text by Carolyn Forché (New York: Writers and Readers Publishing Cooperative, 1983).

[3] Frantz Fanon, "Concerning Violence," *The Wretched of the Earth,* trans. Constance Farrington (New York: Grove Press, 1968).

[4] Lucio Lleras, Daniel Solis, *Jump Cut,* 29 (1984).

[5] Fanon, "Concerning Violence," p. 43.

[6] Margaret Randall, *Sandino's Daughters,* ed. Lynda Yanz (Vancouver: New Star Books, 1981).

[7] Fanon, "Concerning Violence," pp. 78-79.

[8] For understanding the social role of the artist in Latin America, see Jean Franco, *The Modern Culture of Latin America: Society and the Artist* (Baltimore: Penguin, 1970).

[9] Variations of this sexist kind of metaphor include the following: the rape of nations or of the forest, etc.; mother earth; the whore of Babylon; prostituting one's abilities; a bastardized language or culture.

[10] Consider Cuban director Sara Gómez's feature-length *One Way or Another.* See my article on the film in the context of the Marxist concept of dialectics, *Jump Cut* 19 (December 1978). See also an interview with Cuban women directors in Susan Fanshel's *A Decade of Cuban Documentary Film: 1972-1982* (New York: Young Filmmakers Foundation, 4 Rivington St., New York, N.Y. 10002, 1982).

Appendix: Most Widely Used Films on Central America

LATIN AMERICA — GENERAL

1. *Americas in Transition.* Obie Benz. U.S. foreign policy in Latin America (1981 / U.S.A. / 30 min. / Icarus, DEC, IDERA).*
2. *Central America in Crisis.* Yvan Patrie and Alter-Cine. History, culture and politics (1983 / Quebec / 13 parts, each 30 min. / DEC).

EL SALVADOR

3. *El Salvador: Revolution or Death.* Frank Diamond. History, politics, U.S. foreign policy (1980 / Netherlands / 48 min. / Cinema Guild, DEC, IDERA).
4. *La Zona Intertidal (The Strand).* Collectivo "Vago." Personal experience of present-day El Salvador (1980 / El Salvador / 15 min. / Commission on Human Rights in El Salvador).
5. *El Salvador: The People Will Win.* Diego de la Texera and The Film Institute of Revolutionary El Salvador. History, politics, culture (1981 / El Salvador / 90 min. / Commusal, DEC, IDERA).
6. *El Salvador: Another Vietnam.* Glen Silber and Tete Vasconcellos. History, politics, U.S. foreign policy (1981 / U.S.A. / 60 min. / Icarus, DEC).
7. *Roses in December.* Ana Carrigan. The murder of four U.S. religious women (1981 / U.S.A. / 60 min. / First Run).
8. *El Salvador: Decision to Win.* Radio Venceremos System. Life in the control zones of the FMLN (1982 / El Salvador / 60 min. / Icarus, DEC, IDERA).
9. *Letter from Morázan.* Radio Venceremos System. Life in the control zones of the FMLN (1983 / El Salvador / 60 min. / Icarus, DEC).
10. *Seeds of Hope.* Radio Venceremos System. The church in El Salvador (1983 / El Salvador / 30 min. / Icarus, DEC).

* Distributors' addresses are at the end of the filmography.

11. *Time of Daring*. Radio Venceremos System. Civil war in the country and the city (1984 / El Salvador / 40 min. / Icarus, DEC).
12. *Guazapa*. Don North. A journalist's report on life for the guerrillas in Guazapa province (1984 / El Salvador / U.S.A. / 37 min. / Northstar, DEC).
13. *In The Name of Democracy*. Film Institute of Revolutionary El Salvador and Commusal. Elections in El Salvador (1984 / El Salvador / 30 min. / Commusal, DEC).
14. *Road to Liberty*. Film Institute of Revolutionary El Salvador. Life in the control zones of the FMLN (1984 / El Salvador / 60 min. / Fred Baker Films, Commusal).

NICARAGUA: THE FIGHTING 1978-1984

15. *Free Homeland or Death*. Antonio Yglesias and Victor Vega. The year before the triumph (1978 / Costa Rica / 75 min. / Cinema Guild).
16. *Nicaragua: September 78*. Frank Diamond. The last months before the triumph (1978 / Netherlands / 41 min. / Cinema Guild, DEC).
17. *Scenes From the Revolution*. John Chapman. The triumph and the first 100 days (1980 / U.S.A. / 30 min. / Cinema Guild).
18. *The Uprising*. Peter Lilienthal. Drama based on the revolution (1980 / Nicaragua / West Germany / 96 min. / Kino, DEC).
19. *Alsino and the Condor*. Miguel Littin. Fiction based on the revolution (1982 / Nicaragua / 90 min. / Almi).
20. *Target Nicaragua*. Sol Landau and Haskell Wexler. Attacks from the Contras and the CIA (1982 / U.S.A. / 40 min. / New Time, DEC).
21. *Report From the Front*. Pam Yates and Tom Sigel. Attacks from the Contras and the CIA (1983 / U.S.A. / 30 min. / Skylight, IDERA).

NICARAGUA: DAILY LIFE 1976-1984

22. *Paraiso (Paradise)*. Maryknoll Order. Life before the revolution (1976 / Nicaragua / Modern).
23. *After The Earthquake*. Lourdes Portillo. Experimental drama on Nicaraguans in the U.S. (1979 / U.S.A. / 23 min. / Lourdes Portillo).

24. *INCINE Newsreels*. INCINE (Nicaraguan Film Institute). Health, literacy, agrarian reform (1980-82 / Nicaragua / 15 min. each / DEC, Communica).
25. *Women in Arms*. Victoria Schultz. All aspects of women's lives (1980 / U.S.A. / 60 min. / Hudson River, DEC).
26. *Banana Company*. Ramiro Lacayo. Banana production before and after the revolution (1981 / Nicaragua / 15 min. / Icarus).
27. *Thank God and the Revolution*. Jackie Reiter and Wolf Tirado and Tercer Cine. Church and society (1981 / Nicaragua / 50 min. / Icarus, DEC).
28. *From The Ashes*. Helena Solberg-Ladd. Daily life, women, literacy (1981 / U.S.A. / 60 min. / Cinema Guild, DEC, IDERA).
29. *Los Hijos de Sandino (Children of Sandino)*. Kimberley Safford and Fred Barney Taylor. Popular culture (1982 / U.S.A. / 42 min. / Third World Newsreel, DEC).
30. *Dawn of the People*. Jay Craven and Doreen Kraft. Literacy crusade (1983 / U.S.A. / 30 min. / Icarus, DEC).
31. *Waiting for the Invasion*. Dee Dee Halleck. U.S citizens in Nicaragua (1983 / U.S.A. / 40 min. / Halleck).
32. *Dream of Sandino*. Leuten Rojas. Production and defense (1983 / Canada / 60 min. / DEC).
33. *Women in Nicaragua: The Second Revolution*. Jackie Reiter and Wolf Tirado. Daily life and the revolution (1983 / Nicaragua / 30 min. / Women Make Movies, DEC).
34. *The Other Invasion*. Jackie Reiter and Wolf Tirado and Alter Cine. Health care (1984 / Nicaragua, Quebec / 30 min. / Committee on Health, DEC).
35. *Manzana Por Manzana*. John Greyson, Eric Shultz, Mary Anne Yanulis. Community organizing in the city of Esteli (1984 / U.S.A. / 40 min. / Icarus, DEC).

GUATEMALA

36. *My Country Occupied*. Third World Newsreel. A woman joins the guerrillas (1971 / U.S.A. / 30 min. / Third World Newsreel, DEC).
37. *When the Mountains Tremble*. Tom Sigel and Pam Yates. Rigoberta Menchú tells the story of her history (1983 / U.S.A. / 75 min. / First Run, DEC, IDERA).

DISTRIBUTORS

Almi Libra Cinema 5 Films, 1585 Broadway, New York, N.Y. 10036.

Cinema Guild, 211 East 43rd St., New York, N.Y. 10017.

Commission on Human Rights in El Salvador, 3411 W. Diversey, Chicago, Il. 60647.

Committee on Health Rights in Central America, Box 1405, Berkeley, Ca. 94704.

Commusal, 2936 W. 8th St., Suite 304, Los Angeles, Ca. 90005.

DEC Films, 229 College St., Toronto, Ont. M5T 1R4.

Dee Dee Halleck, 165 W. 91st St. 14F, New York, N.Y. 10024.

First Run Features, Box 686, New York, N.Y. 10276.

Hudson River Productions, Box 515, Franklin Lakes, N.J. 07417.

Icarus Films, 200 Park Ave. S., New York, N.Y. 10016.

IDERA Films, 2425 Cypress St., Vancouver, B.C.

Kino International, 250 W. 57th St., Rm. 314, New York, N.Y. 10019.

Modern Talking Picture Service, 5000 Park St. N., St. Petersburg, Fl. 33709.

Northstar Productions, 3003 0 St. N.W., #1, Washington, D.C. 20007.

New Time Films, 74 Varrick St., New York, N.Y. 10014.

Lourdes Portillo, 989 Esmeralda St., San Francisco, Ca. 94110.

Skylight Pictures, 330 W. 42nd St., New York, N.Y. 10036.

Third World Newsreel, 160 5th Ave., Rm. 911, New York, N.Y. 10010.

Women Make Movies, 19 W. 21st St., New York, N.Y. 10010.

A Readers' Guide to Film and Politics

This short bibliography is for readers who wish to learn more about the history of cinema and some of the ways in which cinema has been approached politically. I have emphasized books that provide a good overview of issues, especially works of film history.

The bibliography should be useful to two groups of readers: those who have a political analysis of society and wish to know more about the specifics of cinema, and those who know the cinema but wish to develop a political understanding of how the cinema functions in our society.

1. GENERAL INTRODUCTIONS

Bordwell, David and Thompson, Kristin. *Film Art*. Reading, Mass.: Addison-Wesley, 1979.
Monaco, James. *How to Read a Film*. New York: Oxford, 1977.

2. HOLLYWOOD

Balio, Tino, ed. *The American Film Industry*. Madison: University of Wisconsin Press, 1976.
Monaco, James. *The American Film Now*. New York: Oxford, 1979.
Stanley, Robert. *The Celluloid Empire*. New York: Hastings House, 1978.
Talbot, David and Zheutlin, Barbara. *Creative Differences*. Boston: South End Press, 1978.

3. DOCUMENTARY: GENERAL

Barnouw, Eric. *Documentary*. New York: Oxford, 1974.
Jacobs, Lewis. *The Documentary Tradition*. New York: Norton, 1979.
Rosenthal, Alan. *The Documentary Conscience*. Berkeley: University of California Press, 1980.
Waugh, Thomas. *Show Us Life*. Metuchen, N.J.: Scarecrow Press, 1984.

4. THEORY: THE CLASSICS

Andrew, J. Dudley. *The Major Film Theories*. New York: Oxford, 1976.

Bazin, André. *What is Cinema I and II*. Berkeley, U. of Cal. 1976, 1971.

Eagleton, Terry. *Marxism and Literary Criticism*. London: Methuen, 1976.

Eisenstein, Sergei. *Film Form and Film Sense*. New York: Harcourt, Brace, 1949, 1942.

5. THEORY: CONTEMPORARY

Barth, Roland. *Mythologies*. London: Jonathan Cape, 1972.

Berger, John. *The Ways of Seeing*. London: BBC and Penguin, 1972.

Fiske, John and Hartley, John. *Reading Television*. London: Methuen, 1978.

Kaplan, E. Ann. *Women and Film*. New York and London: Methuen, 1983.

MacBean, James Roy. *Film and Revolution*. Bloomington, University of Indiana Press, 1975.

Mattelart, Armand. *Multinational Corporations and the Control of Culture*. Sussex: Harvester, 1979.

Nichols, Bill. *Movies and Methods*. Berkeley: University of California Press, 1976.

Wollen, Peter. *Signs and Meaning in the Cinema*. London: Secker and Warburg, 1974.

6. CRITICISM AND HISTORY

Alexander, William. *Film on the Left*. Princeton: Princeton University Press, 1981.

Bogle, Donald. *Toms, Coons, Mulattoes, Mammies and Bucks*. New York: Viking, 1973.

Burton, Julianne. *The New Latin American Cinema*. New York: Smyrna, 1983.

Dyer, Richard. *Gays and Film*. London: British Film Institute, 1977.

Dyer, Richard. *Stars*. London: British Film Institute, 1979.

Gabriel, Teshome H. *Third Cinema in the Third World*. UMI Research Press, 1982.

García Espinosa, Julio. "For an Imperfect Cinema." *Jump Cut* No. 20, May 1979.

Haskell, Molly. *From Reverence to Rape*. New York: Penguin, 1974.
Verronneau, Pierre. *Self Portraits: Essays on the Canadian and Quebec Cinemas*. Ottawa: Canadian Film Institute, 1980.

Contributors

Linda Artel, a former teacher, programs children's films and does development work for the Pacific Film Archive, University of California, Berkeley. She has also taught women and film courses at Bay Area community colleges and is the author of *Women and Work: A Guide to Non-Print Media.*

Serafina Bathrick is an assistant professor at Hunter College. She has written about the *Mary Tyler Moore Show* (British Film Institute, forthcoming) and is writing a book on representations of women in U.S. mass culture.

Edith Becker is a writer and filmmaker living in New York. She is currently editing a movie called *After All Is Said and Done.*

Julianne Burton, compiler of *The New Latin American Cinema: An Annotated Bibliography* (the third edition is forthcoming in 1986) teaches Latin American literature and film at the University of California at Santa Cruz.

Russell Campbell is a lecturer in film at Victoria University of Wellington, New Zealand, author of *Cinema Strikes Back* (Ann Arbor, UMI Press, 1983).

Michelle Citron is a filmmaker (*Daughter Rite,* 1978, *What You Take for Granted . . . ,* 1983) and associate professor in the Department of Radio-Television-Film, Northwestern University, Evanston, Illinois.

Richard Dyer teaches film at Warwick University, England. He is the author of *Stars* (British Film Institute, 1979), *Heavenly Bodies* (forthcoming), and editor of *Gays and Film* (BFI, 1977). He organized the gay film season at the National Film Theatre, London, 1977.

Charles Eckert (1927-1976), at the time of his death, was working on a book about Hollywood in the 1930s. "Marked Window" appeared in *Quarterly Review of Film Studies.* He taught at the University of Indiana, Bloomington.

Patricia Erens is editor of the *Journal of Film and Video.* Her most recent book *The Jew in American Cinema* was published by Indiana University Press in January, 1985.

Teshome H. Gabriel is an associate professor in the Department of Theater Arts and the assistant director of the African Studies Center at the University of California, Los Angeles. He is the author of *Third Cinema in the Third World: The Aesthetics of Liberation* (UMI Research Press, Ann Arbor, Michigan, 1982).

Linda Gordon is a professor of History at the University of Wisconsin in Madison. She is the author of a history of the birth control movement (*Woman's Body, Woman's Right,* Viking/Penguin, 1976) and numerous other works on women's history and feminism.

Sara Halprin (formerly Barbara Halpern Martineau) is a filmmaker, writer and teacher who works in collaboration with friends to create a new world. *Tales of Tomorrow, Heroes* and *Keltie's Beard: A Woman's Story* are recent films; in progress is *For a Woman in El Salvador, Speaking*.

John Hess is a *Jump Cut* co-founder and co-editor, and a "temporary" lecturer in film at San Francisco State University. As an active trade unionist he is working to increase solidarity with Central America in the labor movement.

Chuck Kleinhans, a *Jump Cut* co-founder and co-editor, was active in the underground press and anti-war movement in the 1960s and 1970s. He teaches photography and filmmaking at Northwestern University, with a special interest in the consumer technologies, Super 8 and video. He is finishing a book on avant-garde film.

Julia Lesage, a *Jump Cut* co-editor, has been writing on women and film, and Latin America for many years. She has taught film and women's studies at the University of Rochester and San Francisco State, and is currently editing a series of video-tapes from material she shot in Nicaragua.

Sherry Millner's work includes a film about corporate crime, *Crime Around the Collar,* a tape on the social contradictions of pregnancy, *Womb with a View,* and a tape about a two-year-old's perception of U.S. intervention in Central America. She teaches film and video at Antioch University in Ohio.

B. Ruby Rich works at the New York State Council on the Arts. She has written for many years on Hollywood, women and film, and the avant-garde, in publications that include *American Film, The Village Voice, Heresies,* and the *Chicago Reader*.

Dan Rubey teaches part-time at the University of Montana and writes film and art criticism for *Jump Cut, Artweek, High Performance* and Montana newspapers.

Ellen Seiter is a writer and filmmaker teaching film and television at the University of Oregon, in Eugene. She is writing a book on women and melodrama.

Clyde Taylor is founder of the African Film Society and associate professor, English Department, Tufts University. He is presently compiling an anthology of critical essays on Third World cinema.

Tom Waugh is the editor of *Show Us Life — Toward a History and Aesthetics of the Committed Documentary* (Scarecrow Press, 1984) and a contributor to the *Body Politic* as well as *Jump Cut*. He teaches film studies at Concordia University in Montreal.

Diane Waldman is an assistant professor in the Department of Mass Communications, University of Denver. She has published articles on film and mass culture in *New German Critique, Wide Angle,* and *Cinema Journal.*

Susan Wengraf is the co-author of *Positive Images: Non-Sexist Films for Young People.*

Claire Whitaker (formerly Judy) has recently changed her first name, for good but obscure and esoteric reasons. She asks patience from friends and associates. Claire is an independent filmmaker working in Chicago.

Index